Wir wollen Sicherheitsmaßstäbe setzen in einer noch jungen Offshore Industrie.

We want to set a safety benchmark in a still young offshore industry.

Nous voulons établir un standard de sécurité dans une industrie de l'éolien offshore, encore jeune.

Jean Huby   Wolfgang J. Wilms   Fred Koch

Michael Munder-Oschimek   Jens-Karkov Jakobsen

ALPHA VENTUS
Unternehmen Offshore Operation offshore

DANKSAGUNG ACKNOWLEDGEMENT

Der Herausgeber dankt dem Bundesumweltministerium und den beteiligten Firmen AREVA Multibrid, DOTI, REpower und transpower, ohne deren personelle und finanzielle Unterstützung das umfangreiche Buchprojekt nicht zustande gekommen wäre.

The editor would like to thank the Federal Ministry for Environment, as well as the members of the Editorial Board from AREVA Multibrid, DOTI, REpower and transpower. Without their commitment this publication would not have been possible.

IMPRESSUM IMPRINT

alpha ventus Unternehmen Offshore
Operation offshore

Herausgeber Editor Stiftung Offshore-Windenergie, www.offshore-stiftung.de

Verlag Publishers BVA Bielefelder Verlag GmbH & Co. KG
www.bva-bielefeld.de

ISBN 978-3-87073-479-4

3. Auflage 2011 3rd edition 2011

Projektmanagement Project management Dierk Jensen, Andreas Wagner

Autoren Authors Dierk Jensen, Dr. Detlef Koenemann

Bildredaktion Photo editors Dierk Jensen, Andreas Wagner

Fotografen Photographers Detlev Gehring, Mathias Ibeler, Jan Oelker

Redaktionsbeirat Editorial Board
Cornelia Junge, Caroline Stubenvoll, Jörgen Thiele,
Andreas Wagner, Lutz Wiese, Heike Winkler

Buchgestaltung Graphics and typesetting
zimmermann und spiegel grafik_raum_konzept

Titelfoto Cover
Matthias Ibeler

Übersetzung Translations Paul Addison, Thomas Schickling (IRTS)

Lektorat deutsche Texte Editing of German texts Bettina von Bülow

Korrektorat deutsche Texte Proofreading of German texts Heidrun Uta Ehrhardt

Editing englische Texte Editing of English texts Jim Blake, World2World

Druck Print Druck-Center Drake + Huber GmbH, Bad Oeynhausen

Copyright Stiftung Offshore-Windenergie, BVA Bielefelder Verlag GmbH & Co. KG

Printed in Germany

INHALT CONTENTS

6	**Ein Gemeinschaftswerk** Vorwort von Jörg Kuhbier **A joint project** Preface by Jörg Kuhbier
9	**Hoch über dem Meer** Aufbau M5000 **High above the sea** Installation of an M5000
13	Tripod – starkes Dreibein Strong tripod
30	Interview mit Félix Debierre (AREVA Multibrid) Interview with Félix Debierre (AREVA Multibrid)
37	**Von der Vision bis zur Wirklichkeit** **From vision to reality**
60	Interview mit Dr. Knud Rehfeldt (Stiftung Offshore-Windenergie) Interview with Dr. Knud Rehfeldt (German Offshore Wind Energy Foundation)
67	**Energieversorger steigen ins Offshore-Geschäft ein** **Power companies enter the offshore business**
72	Respekt vor den Gefahren auf See Respecting the dangers of the high seas
89	**Forschung und Messtechnik** **Research and metrology**
103	**Arbeit an Land – Technik auf See** **Work on land for technology at sea**
	Offshore-Windenergie schafft neue Arbeit an der Küste Offshore wind energy creating new jobs in coastal regions
	Der lange Weg des Stroms vom Meer zum Festland Offshore power on a long haul from sea to mainland
112	Kabel durch Watt und Insel A cable through mudflats and an island
131	**Packendes Finale zwischen Herbststürmen** Aufbau 5M **Exciting finish between autumn storms** Installation of an 5M
141	Jacket – große Durchlässigkeit Jacket – light yet strong
154	Interview mit Matthias Schubert (REpower Systems AG) Interview with Matthias Schubert (REpower Systems AG)
165	**Die Zukunft hat bereits begonnen** **The future has already begun**
173	**Anhang Appendix**
174	Übersichtskarte Cartographic overview
176	Chronologie Chronology
180	Glossar Glossary
184	Fotonachweis Photo Credits

Ein Gemeinschaftswerk A joint project

JÖRG KUHBIER VORSTAND DER STIFTUNG OFFSHORE WINDENERGIE
BOARD OF DIRECTORS STIFTUNG OFFSHORE WINDENERGIE

Große Ideen scheitern oftmals im ersten Anlauf. So leitete vor 30 Jahren der „Growian" (Große Windenergieanlage) mit drei Megawatt Leistung nicht die Erfolgsstory der Windenergie ein. Das Projekt bewies – was es vielleicht auch beweisen sollte – dass es mit den damaligen Konzepten und Materialien nicht gehen würde.

Etwa zehn Jahre später, beflügelt durch das erste Gesetz zur Förderung der erneuerbaren Energien (Stromeinspeisungsgesetz) im Jahr 1991, startete die Windenergie an Land durch. Ihre später rasant verlaufende Entwicklung versetzte alle Welt in Staunen, besonders diejenigen, die regenerative Energieerzeugung als eine Domäne von Weltverbesserern und unter Umständen liebenswerten Spinnern angesehen hatten.

Wiederum fast 20 Jahre später ist nun mit alpha ventus der endgültige Durchbruch auf hoher See gelungen. Dabei ist die Offshore-Windenergie nicht die lineare Fortsetzung von Onshore, sondern eine eigenständige, hoch komplizierte technische Entwicklung mit besonderen Rahmenbedingungen. Sie hat ganz andere Herausforderungen zu meistern als die Windenergie an Land.

Gleichzeitig schließen Offshore-Windparks mit ihrer Leistung und ihrer Verfügbarkeit zu konventionellen Kraftwerken auf. Das gilt auch für die aufzubringenden Investitionen. Daher wird Windenergie auf dem Meer eine wichtige Rolle im Energiemix der Zukunft spielen, fossile Brennstoffe ersetzen und einen bedeutsamen Beitrag zum Klimaschutz beisteuern. Damit sind auch Konflikte programmiert, mit denen die Offshore-Windenergiebranche aber seit Langem umzugehen versteht.

alpha ventus ist der erfolgreiche Aufbruch in eine neue Ära. Das Testfeld läutet den Beginn eines vielversprechenden Offshore-Windenergie-Zeitalters in Deutschland ein. Schon bald werden weitere Parks in der deutschen Nord- und Ostsee folgen. Wie immer bei solchen Entwicklungen hat der Erfolg viele Väter. Besonders hervorzuheben sind die Anlagenhersteller REpower und AREVA Multibrid, die schon zu einem sehr frühen Zeitpunkt an die Off-

It seems that the first attempts at any great idea often end in failure. That's what happened thirty years ago when the three megawatt 'Growian' (an abbreviation of the German: Große Windenergieanlage – Large Wind Energy Turbine) failed to mark the beginnings of the wind-energy success story. The project proved that it wouldn't work with the concepts and materials of the time – which is quite possibly what it was also meant to prove.

Some ten years later and encouraged by the first law passed to promote renewable energies in Germany – the Electricity Feed-in Act of 1991 – wind energy picked up speed onshore. Its later development moved extremely quickly and astonished everyone, especially those who regarded renewable energy as the domain of 'dreamers of a better world' or even endearing madmen.

Almost another 20 years later we have seen a further clear breakthrough on the high seas with alpha ventus. And offshore wind energy is not just the logical continuation of onshore generation but an independent, highly complex technical development with its own special set of circumstances: completely different challenges have to be mastered compared to harvesting wind energy on land.

At the same time, offshore wind farms are catching up with conventional power stations in terms of performance and output availability. This also applies to the investments required. For these reasons, in the gradual replacement of fossil fuels, wind energy at sea will play an important role in the energy mix of the future and will make a key contribution to climate protection. However, this means that conflicts are inevitable; in fact, the offshore wind energy sector has had to cope with these for a while now.

alpha ventus is the successful start of a new era and this test field represents the bright dawn for the offshore wind-energy age in Germany. It will not be long before further wind farms follow in the North and Baltic Seas off the German coast. As always with such developments, the success has numerous founding fathers. Deserving of a special mention here are the turbine manufacturers

shore-Idee geglaubt und Anlagen der 5-Megawatt-Klasse entwickelt haben, die speziell für den Einsatz auf dem Meer geeignet sind. Des Weiteren ist das Bundesumweltministerium zu nennen, das als unermüdlicher Motor das Projekt alpha ventus immer wieder vom drohenden Abgrund zurückgeholt hat. Zu loben ist auch das Bundesamt für Seeschifffahrt und Hydrographie (BSH), das als Genehmigungsbehörde kreatives Handeln bewies. Schließlich darf die mittelständische Firma Prokon Nord Energiesysteme nicht unerwähnt bleiben: Sie hat mit hohem persönlichen und finanziellen Einsatz die Genehmigung des Offshore-Windparks alpha ventus und seiner Kabelanbindung frühzeitig vorangebracht.

Dieses Buch berichtet über die vielen Schritte, die getan werden mussten, bis die erste Offshore-Windenergieanlage in Deutschland tatsächlich Strom produzieren konnte. Es erzählt von den großen Anstrengungen der einzelnen Akteure, die sich miteinander abstimmen mussten und die am Ende mit Erfolg belohnt wurden. Darüber hinaus zeigt dieser Band die vielfältigen Probleme, die es zu lösen galt. Außerdem schildern die Autoren herausragende Ingenieurleistungen und Fehleinschätzungen; sie erzählen von Euphorien und Enttäuschungen und dem großen Engagement ganz vieler Beteiligter.

Vor allem aber dokumentiert der vorliegende Band, dass es sich bei alpha ventus um ein Gemeinschaftswerk handelt, an dem Politik, Verwaltung, Hersteller und Zulieferer, Logistikunternehmen, Planer, die transpower stromübertragungs gmbh als Netzbetreiber und die Deutsche Offshore-Testfeld und Infrastrukturgesellschaft mbH & Co. KG (DOTI) mit den beteiligten Unternehmen EWE, E.ON und Vattenfall als Investoren und Betreiber sowie die Stiftung Offshore Windenergie konstruktiv zusammengewirkt haben. Der Verdienst jedes Einzelnen tritt hinter diesem Gemeinschaftserfolg zurück.

REpower and AREVA Multibrid, who placed their belief early on in the offshore concept and developed turbines in the 5-megawatt class especially suitable for operation at sea. Furthermore, the German Federal Environment Ministry, as a never-tiring engine of the alpha ventus project, repeatedly pulled things back from the brink of failure. The German Federal Maritime and Hydrographic Agency (BSH) has also earned itself a great deal of praise, and as the licensing authority has demonstrated a great deal of creativity. Last but by no means least, Prokon Nord Energiesysteme dedicated enormous human resources and financial effort into getting the alpha ventus offshore wind farm licensed and was behind the push for its eventual cable connection to the power grid.

This book describes the many steps that had to be taken before the first offshore wind farm in Germany really did start generating electricity. It tells the story of the titanic efforts made by the individual protagonists who needed to work closely with each other and who were finally rewarded with the success they deserved. Furthermore, this book discusses the multitude of problems that had to be overcome. The authors detail the outstanding engineering work, describe the errors of judgement, bring the disappointments and euphoria alive – and reflect the unwavering commitment of the many dedicated individuals involved.

Above all, this book documents the fact that alpha ventus was a collective exercise of unprecedented proportions in the European renewable energy sector. In this huge undertaking, the Deutsche Offshore-Testfeld und Infrastrukturgesellschaft mbH & Co. KG (DOTI) with its member companies EWE, E.ON and Vattenfall, as well as the Offshore Wind Energy Foundation and grid operator transpower stromübertragungs GmbH, joined forces with political decision-makers, administrators, developers, manufacturers, suppliers, logistics companies and investors to make alpha ventus a success. And the achievements of every individual are what made this collective success possible.

Hoch über dem Meer
High above the sea

Warten. Warten. Und noch mal Warten. Die Kaffeemaschine in der Kantine der Hubinsel JB 114 kann gar nicht so viel Kaffee ausspucken wie die ausharrende Mannschaft trinkt. Stunden vergehen, bis die Plattform, beladen mit Turmsegment, Maschinenhaus und Rotor der M5000, die anvisierte Höhe von luftigen 40 Metern über der Nordsee erreicht hat. Vor dem Heben haben die PS-starken Schlepper Banckert und Smit Barracuda vier Anker in mehreren Hundert Metern Entfernung ausgebracht. Anschließend hat Kapitän Martijn Tersteeg per Satellitennavigation seine eiserne Insel im Zusammenspiel mit den vier Ankerwinden fast punktgenau zum Bestimmungsplatz direkt neben den aus der Nordsee herauslugenden Turmsegmenten, auf denen das Kürzel AV 7 zu lesen ist, bugsiert. Nachdem die Position mit nur wenigen Zentimetern Abweichung eingenommen worden ist, bedient er die Hydraulik, die die mächtigen Stützpfeiler an den vier Ecken der Hubinsel ins Wasser hinabsinken lassen. Als die mächtigen Stelzen den hier sandigen Meeresboden 30 Meter unter der Wasseroberfläche erreicht haben, beginnt der Hubvorgang – das „Jacken" wie die englisch sprechende Welt der Meere das Heben beschreibt. Unter metallischem Dröhnen hieven die hydraulischen Pumpen das mit der Fracht zusammen weit mehr als 1.000 Tonnen schwere stählerne Ungetüm Stück für Stück in die Höhe. Bestenfalls einen halben Meter pro Minute. Dumpfe Schläge der Wellen gegen die Rumpfunterseite signalisieren der Crew, dass sich die Barge unmittelbar über der Wasseroberfläche befindet. Dieser Moment ist der kritischste des gesamten Jack-ups: Schlagen die Wellen zu hoch, kann es im Extremfall vorkommen, dass sie den Rumpf kurz anheben und zu schweren Schäden an den Stützpfeilern führen. Schlimmstenfalls kentert die Barge. Die JB 114 ist so konstruiert, dass sie eine maximale Wellenhöhe von zwei Metern meistert.

Das Meer zeigt sich an diesem Tag von der freundlichen Seite. Es ist warm, sonnig und es weht schwacher Wind, der sanft über die Nordsee streicht. Nur wenige Schaumkronen auf den Wellen signalisieren jedem an Bord, dass es noch heute mit der Montage der fünften, 5-Megawatt großen Offshore-Anlage des Herstellers AREVA Multibrid aus Bremerhaven im Testfeld von alpha ventus wahrscheinlich losgehen wird.

Während sich im Osten die vierte, einige Tage vorher aufgestellte Turbine schon probeweise dreht, neigt sich die Abendsonne im Westen gen Horizont. Dann wird es, endlich, gegen sieben Uhr abends, ernst. Der Chef der Multibrid-Mannschaft, Projektleiter Michael Klingele, trommelt sein Team zur Lagebesprechung in die Kantine zusammen. Unspektakulär erklärt er, wie und was in den nächsten Stunden passieren soll. Gespannten Blickes folgen die für den Job von den Spezialfirmen Reetec aus Bremen und Global Energy Services (GES) aus

Waiting. Waiting. And more waiting. The coffee machine in the canteen of the jack-up barge JB 114 just can't keep up with the coffee consumption of the team who are there, waiting. Hours pass before the platform, loaded with the tower segment, nacelle and rotor of the M5000, has reached the planned height of 40 metres above the North Sea. Before the lift could be started, the powerful tugs 'Banckert' and 'Smit Barracuda' took out the four anchors to a distance of several hundred metres. Then Captain Martijn Tersteeg manoeuvred his iron platform and the four anchor winches to their destination using satellite navigation with almost perfect accuracy. The aim is to locate it directly next to the tower segment, already protruding above the surface of the sea, bearing the name of 'AV 7' in huge letters. After getting into position with only a few centimetres 'leeway' he operates the hydraulic system that lowers the support pillars on the four corners of the jack-up barge into the water. The sandy seabed here is about 30 metres below the surface of the North Sea. Once the powerful stilts have reached the bottom the lifting process begins. The working language at sea is English and even the Germans call this "jacken". To the sound of creaking metal the hydraulic pumps heave the steel monster, which together with the freight weighs more than 1,000 tonnes, piece by piece into the air. The best that can be managed is half a metre a minute. The dull sound of waves beating against the underside of the body signals to the crew that the barge is now coming out of the water. This is the most critical moment of the whole jack-up process: if the waves are too high, in extreme cases it may happen that they briefly lift the platform body, which can then become damaged when thumped back down on the support posts. In the worst case the barge may capsize. However, there is no danger of that today, as barge JB 114 has been designed to master a maximum wave height of two metres. It was commissioned to be built in Singapore by the Dutch owner Jack-up-Barges B.V..

The sea is showing its friendly side today. It's warm and sunny, with a light wind gently blowing over the North Sea. There are a few white crests on the waves, a sign for everyone on board that the assembly of the fifth 5-megawatt offshore wind turbine from the manufacturer AREVA Multibrid in Bremerhaven can probably be started today in the test field alpha ventus.

Meanwhile to the east, the fourth turbine, installed a few days previously, is now revolving in a test run. As the evening sun moves slowly towards the horizon, at around seven in the evening things start getting serious. Project Manager Michael Klingele, head of the Multibrid team, calls his staff together in the canteen for a briefing. Calmly and factually he explains what is to happen and how it is to be done in the coming hours. The mechanical fitters and crane operators listen

Warten: Monteur Thorsten Janschker und die Inbetriebnehmer Niels Brand und Lutz Grohe (v.l.n.r.) warten in der Kantine der Jack-up Barge JB 114 auf ihren nächsten Einsatz. Fitter Thorsten Janschker and start-up engineers Niels Brand and Lutz Grohe (from left to right) are waiting in the JB 114 jack-up barge's canteen for their next assignment.

Hamburg und Kronschnabel aus Bremerhaven geheuerten Monteure und Kranfahrer seinen Instruktionen. Die anstehenden Arbeiten werden zugeteilt: wer auf der JB 114 bleibt, wer die Laschen des Turmsegments löst und wer zur Montage auf die Anlage kommt. Es bedarf nur weniger Worte und die junge Crew im Durchschnittsalter von 30 Jahren weiß genau, was zu tun ist. Erst das Turmsegment S 1 rüberheben, dann festschrauben und später, gegen Mitternacht, das Maschinenhaus von den Halterungen lösen, an den Kranhaken hängen, in die Höhe bringen und bis in die frühen Morgenstunden auf den Turmkranz setzen und fest montieren. Letztlich ist dies „Business as usual", verfügt doch jeder der Monteure über viele Erfahrungen mit der Montage von Windenergieanlagen – an Land. Am Ende der knappen Besprechung geht Klingele noch auf eine Besonderheit ein. „Wir müssen das Maschinenhaus in diesem Fall noch etwas drehen (yawen), weil dies bei der Produktion an Land versäumt wurde", sagt der 38-Jährige.

Dann geht's los. Die Bedingungen sind gut, der Wind hat sich noch mehr gelegt, bewegt sich mit unter acht Metern pro Sekunde. Vier Monteure werden vom Kran auf den Turmstumpf gehoben. Danach schwenkt der Kran zurück, legt den Korb ab und nähert sich mit dem Haken vorsichtig über eine Traverse, an der das exakt 104 Tonnen

attentively to his instructions. They are employed by the specialist companies Reetec from Bremen, Global Energy Services (GES) from Hamburg and Kronschnabel from Bremerhaven. The upcoming work is allocated: the team is told who stays on the barge JB 114, who releases the straps on the tower segment and who goes onto the turbine for the assembly. Only a few words are required before the young team, with an average age of 30, knows exactly what to do. First, lift over tower segment S1, then bolt it tight; later, at about midnight, release the nacelle from its fastenings, hang it on the crane hooks, raise it to the required height and then, working into the early hours of the morning, place it on the tower flange of the segment and fasten it tight. After all, this is 'routine stuff'; each of the technicians has had years of experience in assembling wind turbines – even if only on land. At the end of the short meeting, Klingele mentions a specific matter: "In this case we have to slightly turn (yaw) the nacelle, as they forgot to do this when assembling it on land", explains the 38-year-old.

Then they're off. The conditions are good: the wind has dropped even further, now having a speed of less than eight metres a second. The crane takes four technicians in a lifting basket to the already assembled stump of the tower. Then it swivels back, puts the basket on the ground and subsequently places its hook carefully over a beam to

Rund zwölf Stunden benötigen zwei Schlepper, um die mit Bauteilen der M5000 beladene JB 114 von Eemshaven ins Baufeld von alpha ventus zu ziehen. JB 114 loaded with M5000 components. Towing it from Eemshaven to the alpha ventus installation site takes two tugs about twelve hours.

schwere Turmrohr befestigt ist. Nachdem die Monteure die Trossen an den Haken gehängt haben, wird das 32 Meter lange und fünf Meter dicke Segment behutsam mit dem Kran hochgehoben und vorsichtig auf das aus dem Meer ragende Teilstück abgesenkt. Alles geht zügig, routiniert voran, nach kurzer Zeit brummen die ersten Hydraulik-Schrauber auf. Am Haken hängend wird die losgelöste Traverse mit dem Deckel des Turmsegments dann wieder auf die JB 114 zurückgeholt.

Eigentlich würde der auf der Plattform stehende Kran jetzt ruhen, bis zum Hub des etwa 300 Tonnen schweren Maschinenhauses. Doch da sich jetzt unerwarteter Weise ein Schlauchboot der Hubinsel nähert, das die für Inbetriebnahme der bereits stehenden Anlagen beauftragten Elektromaschinenbauer Lutz Groche und den Mechatroniker Nils Brand zum in Sichtweite liegenden Versorgungsschiff Petr Kottsov übersetzen soll, wird der Mannkorb wieder aktiviert. Das Duo von Multibrid wird zwei Wochen im Testfeld verbringen und die Offshore-Anlagen ans Netz bringen. Mit kleinen Booten werden sie frühmorgens ihre schwimmende Nacht- und Versorgungsstätte auf der Petr Kottsov, einem altgedienten, eistauglichen russischen Expeditionsschiff, verlassen und abends dorthin wieder zurückkehren. Den ganzen Tag hat das Monteur-Team auf der JB 114 auf diesen Moment gewartet. Aber

which the next 104-tonne tower-tube segment is fastened. After the mechanical fitters have hung the cables onto the hook, the 32-metre-long and five-metre-wide segment is cautiously lifted by the crane and slowly lowered onto the section already protruding out of the sea. It all goes routinely, and after a short while the hydraulic bolt tensioners are buzzing away. Still hanging on the hook, the beam is returned with the cover of the tower segment back to the JB 114.

Normally the crane standing on the platform would remain still until it needed to lift the approximately 300-tonne nacelle. However, this time a rubber dinghy approaches the jack-up barge unexpectedly; it has come to take two men, electromechanical engineer Lutz Groche and mechatronician Nils Brand, to the supply ship 'Petr Kottsov'. Their job is to commission already-assembled turbines. The long-serving Russian expedition ship, suitable for icy conditions, is now within view of the barge. Time to use the man-basket. The two from Multibrid are to spend a fortnight in the test field and connect the offshore turbines to the grid. They will leave their floating hostel, the 'Petr Kottsov', early each morning in small boats and return in the evening. The team has been waiting on the JB 114 the whole day for this moment; however, they have not been able to transfer until the waves let up and this hasn't been until late in the evening, when it's already getting dark.

Projektmanager Michael Klingele im Testfeld alpha ventus.
Project manager Michael Klingele in the alpha ventus test field.

der erst jetzt nachlassende Wellengang lässt den Transfer spät abends, es dämmert schon, zu. Gelassen werfen sie ihre vollgepackten Taschen, Equipment für den Aufenthalt im Testfeld alpha ventus, in den Korb. „Tschüß, macht's gut, bis dann", rufen ihnen die Kollegen hinterher, als sie 40 Meter über dem Wasser langsam nach unten gesenkt werden.

Während Michael Klingele federführend auf der Anlage das Verschrauben des Turmsegments leitet, dirigiert Frank Mettbach, für den Aufbau der sechs Multibrid-Anlagen geheuerter Offshore Construction Manager, die Vorbereitungen für das Hochhieven des Maschinenhauses, das auf der Mitte der 50 Meter langen und 32 Meter breiten JB 114 festgezurrt thront. Der frühere Offizier und Kampftaucher bei der Bundeswehr ist so etwas wie der uneingeschränkte Herr an Deck. Er bestimmt das Timing, er bestimmt, was wie zu tun ist. Dabei wird jeder Handgriff von Peter Valland, dem vom Investoren-Konsortium DOTI beauftragten Bauaufseher, mit Argusaugen verfolgt. Er würde sofort intervenieren, wenn er beobachtet, dass die Sicherheitsbestimmungen nicht eingehalten würden.

Es ist Mitternacht. Die Sterne funkeln am Himmel. Die Befeuerungslichter von zwei der bereits errichteten vier Multibrid-Anlagen leuchten rot in die Dunkelheit hinein. Ebenso strahlen die Forschungsstation

They casually throw their fully-packed bags and other equipment for their stay in the alpha ventus test field into the basket and call back to their colleagues, "All the best, see you later!" as they are slowly lowe-red from 40 metres over the sea.

While Michael Klingele is overseeing the bolting-on of the tower segment, Frank Mettbach, who has been hired as Offshore Construction Manager to set up the Multibrid turbines, makes the preparations for heaving up the nacelle, which is sitting lashed down in the middle of the 50-metre-long and 32-metre-wide JB 114. The former German Federal Army officer and combat diver is something like a 'lord on deck'. He decides what is done and when it is done. And every move is watched with eagle eyes by Peter Valland, the Construction Supervisor employed by the consortium of investors EWE, E.ON and Vattenfall (DOTI). He has to intervene should safety regulations not be respected.

It is a clear, starry midnight. The navigation lights on two of the four already-assembled Multibrid turbines light up the dark. Next to them there are the artificial lights shining into the night from the research platform FINO 1, the guard vessel 'Otto Treplin', there to keep an eye on the test field during the complete construction work period, the two anchored tugs 'Banckert' and 'Smit Barracuda' as well as from the 'Petr Kottsov'. The powerful on-board lights of the jack-up barge 'Buzzard',

STARKES DREIBEIN

Das Besondere liegt oft im Verborgenen. So auch im Testfeld von alpha ventus. Die mächtigen Windturbinen oberhalb des Meeresspiegels sind zwar weithin sichtbar, doch liegt eine der größten technischen Herausforderungen beim Bau der Offshore-Anlagen unter der Wasserlinie: die Gründungskonstruktion.

Wegen der großen Wassertiefe ist als Fundament für die AREVA Multibrid-Windturbine zum ersten Mal eine so genannte Tripod-Konstruktion zum Einsatz gekommen. Ein Tripod ist vereinfacht gesagt ein stählernes Dreibein, das im Meeresgrund verankert steht und der darauf montierten Anlage ein stabiles Fundament gegen Sturm, Strömung und Wellen bietet. Gebaut und zusammengeschweißt wurde es auf der Aker Kværner Werft im norwegischen Verdal, 50 Kilometer nordöstlich von Trondheim; anschließend wurden je drei Stück auf einer flachen Barge quer durch die Nordsee nach Wilhelmshaven transportiert. Dann brachte ein Schwimmkran die sechs Tripods für die sechs AREVA Multibrid-Anlagen im Frühjahr 2009 einzeln zum Bauplatz.

Jeder Tripod ist so hoch wie ein zehnstöckiges Hochhaus. Stattliche 45 Meter misst das Dreibein. Er ist ein wahres Schwergewicht: 667 Tonnen bringt er auf die Waage. Damit der Tripod im Meeresboden festen Halt findet, ist an jedem Fußpunkt ein senkrechtes Rohr (Pile sleeve) angeschweißt, das sich nach oben hin erweitert. Von einem Arbeitsschiff aus werden in diese Rohrhülsen 30 Meter lange und 100 Tonnen schwere Gründungspfähle „eingefädelt" und anschließend in den Meeresboden gerammt. Der Aufbau eines Tripods dauert bei guten äußeren Bedingungen zwei bis drei Tage. Weil aber das Installations-Team zwischendurch immer wieder auf gutes Wetter warten musste, dehnte sich der Zeitraum für die gesamten Gründungsarbeiten deutlich aus. Am Ende waren 40 Tage dafür erforderlich, und zwar vom 23. April bis zum 1. Juni.

Welche gewaltigen Dimensionen ein Tripod tatsächlich hat, erschließt sich dem Betrachter eigentlich nur an Land, am Besten in der Werft, wo er gebaut wird: eine mächtige und klobige Konstruktion. Wer genauer auf die Form achtet, dem fällt auf, dass sich der Tripod den statischen Anforderungen entsprechend aus konisch zulaufenden Rohren zusammensetzt. Die drei Beine verjüngen sich zum Fußende hin; das gilt auch für die drei Streben an der Basis des Tripods.

STRONG TRIPOD

When something is mostly hidden from view it's often hard to recognize what makes it special. This is also the case at the alpha ventus test field, where the powerful wind turbines can be seen towering above sea level from a long way off. However, one of the greatest technical challenges in setting up these offshore turbines is under the waterline: the foundation construction.

Because the water is so deep, a so-called tripod construction has been used for the first time for the foundations of the AREVA Multibrid wind turbines. Put simply, a tripod is a standing, three-legged construction made of steel and anchored to the seabed, providing the turbine assembled onto it with a stable foundation against storms, currents and waves. They were built and welded together at the Aker Kværner shipyard in Verdal in Norway, 50 kilometres to the north of Trondheim; subsequently three of them at a time were loaded onto a flat barge and transported right across the North Sea to Wilhelmshaven. From there, a floating crane took the six tripods for the six AREVA Multibrid turbines one at a time to the construction site in spring 2009.

Each of these tripods is as high as a ten-storey building, with the three-legged construction measuring a proud 45 metres. And they really are heavyweights, weighing in at 667 tonnes. So that the tripod has a firm hold on the seabed there is a vertical pipe (pile sleeve) welded onto each foot which protrudes upwards. The 30-metre long, 100-tonne foundation piles are 'thread' through these tubular pipes from a work-ship and then driven into the seabed. Setting up a tripod takes two to three days when the conditions are good. However, as the installation team frequently has to wait for good weather, the period for the complete foundation work can be much longer. It ended up taking 40 days, from April 23rd until June 1st.

The observer can only comprehend what huge dimensions a tripod really has when it is on land, at best in the shipyard where it is being built. It's a powerful and bulky construction. If you take a close look at the shape you'll notice that it's made of conically-shaped tubes, enabling it to fulfil the statics requirements. The three legs taper off towards the foot end, as do the three connecting pieces at the base of the tripod.

FINO 1, das Guard-Schiff Otto Treplin, das während der ganzen Bauarbeiten das Testfeld überwacht, die beiden ankernden Schlepper Banckert und Smit Barracuda sowie die Petr Kottsov künstliches Licht in die Nacht hinein. Auch die großen Bordlampen von der Rammstation Buzzard, die die Gründungsarbeiten für die sechs REpower-Anlagen rund um die Uhr vornehmen, setzen grelle Leuchtpunkte; von Weitem setzen vorbeiziehende Tanker und Frachter weiteres Licht. Kein Zweifel, es ist viel los in und um die schwimmenden Baustelle alpha ventus – weit draußen auf hoher See, unmittelbar nördlich des 54. Breitengrades, der genau durch die Umspannstation des Windparks verläuft. Obwohl 45 Kilometer vor der Küste der ostfriesischen Insel Borkum gelegen, wird hier noch ein Tidenhub von etwa anderthalb Meter gemessen.

Der Mond hängt malerisch im Nachthimmel. Steigende Anspannung ist den Gesichtern der Beteiligten abzulesen. Der Wind hat leicht zugenommen. Das Turmsegment ist nun fertig verankert, jetzt muss das Maschinenhaus unverzüglich darauf montiert werden. Nur mit der Last des Maschinenhauses bekommt der Turm die nötige Stabilität. Professionell entfernt das Team die Laschen. Alles geht ziemlich schnell, schon hängt die Turbine am beeindruckenden Schäkel, der einen Bolzen hat, der nur mit einem 100er Spezialschraubenschlüssel zu bändigen wäre. Beim Anheben des Herzstücks der Windenergieanlage stöhnt der Motor des Krans auf und krächzt. Langsam streckt sich der Kranausleger in die Höhe, dreht sich dabei bedächtig um 180 Grad und zieht die hängende Fracht direkt über das offene Segment. Jetzt kommt die heikle Phase, wo der Kranfahrer – ohne Sichtkontakt, aber im ständigen Funkkontakt zu Michael Klingele und dem Montage-Team – das Maschinenhaus passgenau auf die Bolzen absetzen muss. Drei, zwei, eins, null ... und das wuchtige Ding ist sicher gelandet. Die Mimik von allen Beteiligten entspannt sich. Während sich das Bordteam nach ein paar Aufräumarbeiten in die Koje legen kann, hat das Team oben im Turm noch die ganze Nacht vor sich, gilt es doch das Maschinenhaus zu yawen und alles fachgerecht miteinander zu verschrauben und verkabeln.

Nach fünf Uhr morgens, es wird langsam wieder hell, ist alles vollbracht: Müde, aber zufrieden setzt der Kran Michael Kingele und sein Team im Mannkorb auf die JB 114 über. „Das war Rekordzeit. Wir werden immer besser", freut sich Klingele nach Schichtende. Ab in die Federn.

Während das Montage-Team sich im Schlaf wiegt, ist die Besatzung der in einer Werft in Singapur gebauten JB 114 des Eigentümers Jack-up-Barges B.V. aus den Niederlanden wieder in Aktion. Denn für das Hochziehen des auf der Plattform liegenden Rotorsterns, von dem ein Flügel weit über die Reling hinausragt, muss die Hubinsel weiter weg von der Windenergieanlage gerückt werden. Es sind zwar nur rund zehn Meter, aber diese fehlen dem Kran beim Ausschwenken. Deshalb muss die stählerne Insel wieder abgesetzt, die Stützpfeiler vom Nordseegrund hochgehoben werden, um schließlich, verrückt um ein paar Meter, die nächste Position einzunehmen: Dafür heißt es in den nächsten Stunden wieder Pfeiler hochfahren, sich mit Hilfe der Ankerwinden neu positionieren, wieder absetzen und sich schließlich wieder aus dem Wasser zu drücken. Als die JB 114 schon die Marke 25 Meter über den Meeresspiegel erreicht hat, trudelt die Nachtschicht noch ziemlich verschlafen in die Kantine zum Mittagessen ein. Gemurmel. Inzwischen ist das Wetter draußen umgeschlagen. Der Himmel ist grau und der Wind weht in Nabenhöhe weit über acht Meter pro Sekunde. Bei den Bedingungen lässt sich der Rotor nicht

that is conducting the foundation work for the six REpower turbines around the clock, are also shining brightly. There are flickering lights of tankers and freighters passing in the distance. There is no doubt that there's a lot going on in and around the floating construction site alpha ventus – out here on the high seas, directly to the north of the 54° latitude parallel, which at this location runs right through the transformer station of the wind farm. Although 45 kilometres off the coast of the East Frisian island of Borkum there is still a tidal range of about one and a half metres.

The moon is picturesque in the night sky. You can clearly feel the excitement increasing amongst all those involved on site. The wind has risen slightly: the tower segment has now been fastened and the nacelle has to be fitted to it without delay, because only when the tower has the weight of the nacelle holding it down will it have the necessary stability. The team removes the straps with their professional ease. It all goes fairly quickly and very soon the nacelle is hanging on the impressive shackle, which has a bolt so large that a special 100 mm spanner is required. The crane's engine moans and groans while lifting the heart of the wind turbine. The jib slowly moves outwards, turns 180° seemingly in slow motion and lifts the hanging freight directly over the open tower-segment. This is where it gets tricky, where the crane operator – without having a direct view, but in permanent radio contact with Michael Klingele and the assembly team – has to set the nacelle exactly onto the bolts. Three, two, one, zero ... the huge object has landed safely. The relief is written on everyone's face. After a bit of clearing up the on-board team can go and lay down in their berths – but the team up there in the tower has the whole night ahead of them, as the technicians have to yaw the nacelle and bolt everything together and cable it all up properly.

It's now five in the morning, slowly getting light, and everything is finished. Tired but contented, the crane takes Klingele and his team in the basket over to the JB 114. "That was done in record time! We're getting better and better at this", comments Klingele happily at the end of this shift and moves off to bed.

While the assembly team are lying in their bunks, the crew of the JB 114 are back in action. In order to lift the rotor, still lying on the platform and whose one blade is protruding a long way over the railing, the jack-up barge has to be moved. It may only require around ten metres – but the crane does not have this reach when it swings out. The supporting pillars of the steel island have, therefore, to be lifted from the North Sea bed only to take up the next position a few metres away. Hours are required to lift the supporting legs, to reposition using the anchor windlasses and then push the platform again out of the water. Just as the JB 114 reaches the 25-metre point over sea level the night shift trundles into the canteen, still somewhat bleary-eyed, for their lunch. There are mumblings: in the meantime the weather has turned, the sky is leaden-grey and there is a wind at the hub height of over eight metres a second. In these conditions the rotor cannot be lifted. Nevertheless, the crane operator starts up the engines at around 2 pm and gets the hook into position.

Then the waiting starts all over again. Klingele has hydrographer Alexander Labrenz, who is up there on the bridge working out all positional and weather data with his equipment, inform him of the wind speed at regular intervals. In the meantime anyone watching carefully will see a beautiful scene: a pied oystercatcher is sitting on the tip of the 56 metre long rotor blade protruding out over board and is holding his orange beak silently into the west wind. "Doesn't look that good

An Deck der Jack-up Barge JB 114 werden die letzten Vorbereitungen zum Ziehen des Rotorsterns getroffen. Last preparations before the rotor star is hoisted.

ziehen. Trotzdem wirft der Kranfahrer gegen 14 Uhr den Motor an und bringt den Haken schon mal in Position.

Dann beginnt das Warten von Neuem. Klingele lässt sich vom Hydrographen Alexander Labrenz, der oben auf der Brücke an seinen Geräten sämtliche Positions- und Wetterdaten bearbeitet, in kurzen Intervallen die Windgeschwindigkeiten durchgeben. Derweil bietet sich dem aufmerksamen Beobachter ein schönes stilles Bild: Ein Austernfischer sitzt seelenruhig auf der Spitze des über Bord ragenden 56 Meter langen Rotorflügels und hält seinen orange Schnabel stumm in den Westwind. „Sieht nicht richtig gut aus", sagt indessen Labrenz und schaut auf seine Bildschirme. „Aber vielleicht legt sich der Wind noch mal am Abend. Dann bekommen wir noch mal ein kleines Zeitfenster für die Rotoren."

Gegen sieben Uhr abends kommt Klingele nach oben auf die Brücke. Er fragt Labrenz, was vom Wettergeschehen tatsächlich zu erwarten ist. „Wir sind derzeit bei 7,9 Metern pro Sekunde", heißt die Antwort. „Zuviel", entgegnet ihm der Chef der Montage-Mission seufzend. Und fügt hinzu: „Wenn die Wetterwerte im Abstand von 20 Minuten dreimal nacheinander unter sieben Metern liegen, dann fangen wir an." Unterdessen sind die letzten Vorkehrungen fürs Hieven des Rotorsterns vollbracht worden. Zig Taue und Seile sind ausgelegt worden.

Alle Männer sind in voller Montur und einsatzbereit; doch gibt's immer noch kein Okay, dafür steht vor der wahrscheinlich kommenden Nachtschicht warmes Essen in der Kantine bereit: Der belgische Koch hat Lamm, Bohnen und Reis zubereitet. Alternativ dazu gibt es Sauerbraten im Angebot. Passt irgendwie zum Warten.

Dann, gegen zehn Uhr abends, es ist schon fast dunkel, geben Klingele und Mettbach plötzlich das Zeichen zum Start. Ruck, zuck sind alle Beteiligten an ihren Positionen, ein Team wird aufs Maschinenhaus gehoben, die anderen ziehen und hantieren an diversen Seilen, während der große Kran den Rotor hochzieht und der kleine Kran einen Flügel an den Haken nimmt, ihn hochfährt und dadurch den ganzen Rotor von der Waagerechten in die Vertikale bringt. Sehr viel Feingefühl ist gefragt, um nirgendwo gegenzustoßen und nach ein paar Minuten hängt der Rotor mit drei Metern Abstand an der Steuerbordseite der JB 114. Alles gut. Doch dann beginnt ein kleines Drama. Die zwei Kantenschoner, die am unteren Teil des Rotorblattes die Last beim Transport aufnehmen, haben sich an der Außenhaut des über dem Meer hängenden Flügels festgesogen. „Ein Scheißding", fluchen die Männer. Sie versuchen, den etwa drei mal zwei Meter großen Schoner abzutrennen. Improvisieren ist jetzt gefragt. Mit Haken, Seilen und vereinten Kräften. Es wird gezogen und geschüttelt, doch der Kantenschoner aus Polyester will einfach nicht weichen. Alles vergeblich. Es gilt, die Nerven trotzdem zu behalten, obwohl die Zeit davonrennt, ist doch das Zeitfenster relativ klein … Grimmige Blicke irren, es wird geflucht. Erst die Idee, eine Kette zu nehmen, die man an Bord fixiert und durch einen Haken mit dem Schoner verbindet und zugleich den Rotor vorsichtig mit dem Kran anhebt, bringt die Lösung des Problems. Das Ding fliegt in die dunkle Tiefe. Nun ist das Kantenstück gegenüber dran. Tatsächlich lässt es sich relativ leicht lösen, sinkt dann aber unkontrolliert weg und verletzt ganz leicht die Außenhaut. Ärgerlich, aber Gott sei Dank nur ein Kratzer, der sich beheben lässt.

Anspannung pur. Der Wind hat zugenommen und das prognostizierte Zeitfenster ist mit der Aktion fast verplempert worden. Mettbach will aber nicht abbrechen. „Los, los, los", herrscht er sein Team an. Die Monteure springen, ziehen an vielen Seilen, der Kran wummert, zieht den Rotor hoch, schwenkt ihn hinterm Heck um die JB 114 herum und befördert ihn Stück für Stück in die dunkle Nacht nach oben. Auf der Backbordseite wird das empfindliche Objekt schließlich vis-à-vis zum Maschinenhaus in Position gebracht. Es ist jetzt kurz nach zwei Uhr, der Wind hat in der Zwischenzeit zugenommen. Jetzt muss der richtige Moment abgepasst werden, um den Rotor an das Maschinenhaus anzudocken. Die Männer an Bord verfolgen gebannt, den Kopf im Nacken nach oben blickend, das nur noch schemenhaft zu erkennende Geschehen oben an der Gondel. Dann kommt die erlösende Nachricht per Funk: „Das Ding steckt." Entspannung macht sich breit. Die Mission ist erfolgreich beendet worden. Die fünfte Anlage steht, muss nur noch verschraubt werden und kann in den nachfolgenden Tagen in Betrieb genommen werden. Zur Belohnung gibt's noch einen Kaffee und manche nehmen noch ein Nachtmahl, hat doch der Koch bei Rockabilly-Musik überbackene Chicorée und Stampfkartoffeln zubereitet. Nach dem Essen geht die Nachtschicht weiter. Aufräumen ist angesagt: Die Männer zurren Laschen, rollen Seile auf und verstauen Ketten. Gegen sieben Uhr morgens ist der Rotor komplett montiert und das Montageteam um Michael Klingele kehrt geschlaucht, aber zufrieden von der Gondel über den Mannkorb an Bord zurück.

at all", says Labrenz looking at his monitor. "But maybe the wind will drop this evening. Then we'll have a small window for the rotor." It is about seven in the evening when Klingele comes up to the bridge. He asks Labrenz what can be expected from the weather. "We're currently at 7.9 metres a second", is the answer. "Too fast", sighs the head of the assembly mission, and adds: "Once the wind figures are less than seven metres in three successive measurements taken at intervals of 20 minutes – then we'll start." Meanwhile, the final preparations for lifting the rotor have been completed. Numerous ropes and cables have been laid out, all the men are in full gear and ready to go… but the go-ahead has still not been given. At least there is a hot meal ready for the night shift waiting for them in the canteen. The Belgian cook has made lamb, beans and rice. And as an alternative there's a hearty Sauerbraten.

At about ten in the evening, it is almost pitch-black when Klingele and Mettbach suddenly give the signal to get going. Everyone gets into position quickly: a team is lifted onto the nacelle, the others pull and move various ropes and cables about, while the large crane lifts up the rotor and the small crane hooks up and lifts one of the blades, thus moving the whole rotor from a horizontal into a vertical position. The crane operators have to demonstrate all their considerable skill so they don't hit anything. After a few minutes the rotor is hanging at a distance of three metres on the starboard side of the JB 114. All well and good. However, all of a sudden a small drama unfolds: the two edge protectors that take the load at the lower part of the rotor blade during transport have sucked themselves tightly onto the outer casing of the blade hanging over the sea. "Devil's own job to get 'em off", curse the men. They attempt to remove a three-metre-long protector – in vain. It's time for improvisation: using hooks, ropes and all their combined strength they pull and shake, but the polyester edge-protectors is stuck fast. Time is running out, but everyone has to keep their nerve. The time-window is tight and getter tighter by the minute … it's frowns all round, and curses in seven different languages can be heard clearly above the gusting wind. It is not until someone has the idea of fastening a chain on board, connecting it to the rotor protector using hooks and at the same time carefully lifting the rotor with the crane that a possible solution to the problem comes into view. And it works! The protector positively flies off and sinks into the inky depths. Now it's time for the opposite edge. It can be removed easily, dropping away in an uncontrolled manner but slightly damaging the outer skin. Annoying – but thankfully it's only a scratch that can be swiftly repaired.

But the tension remains high. The wind has increased and the predicted time window has almost been exhausted with this operation. However, Mettbach does not want to cancel everything and barks "Go, go, go!" at his team. The technicians jump into action and fix cables: the crane boom swings away, pulls up the rotor, swivels it around the stern of the JB 114 and moves it bit by bit upwards into the dark night. On the port side the delicate huge object is finally positioned face-to-face with the nacelle. By this time it is almost two in the morning and the wind has picked up considerably. Now they have to choose the right moment to dock the rotor onto the nacelle. The men on board are watching spellbound, heads thrown back, seeing only the outline of what is going on up there at the nacelle. The news is radioed down: "It's in!" Mission successfully completed and the relief is palpable. The fifth turbine is up, now all they have to do is bolt it together and it can be commissioned in the coming days. As a reward there is another coffee. Some enjoy another nighttime meal: to the sound of rockabilly

Komplett: Der Rotor sitzt an der Maschine.
Mission completed: turbine with rotor.

Während das Team in den verdienten Schlaf fällt, macht die Mannschaft der Jack-Up Barge, so der englische Begriff für die Hubinsel, augenblicklich die Rückkehr zum niederländischen Hafen Eemshaven klar. Eine Prozedur, die wieder wie gewohnt einige Stunden in Anspruch nimmt. Gilt es doch auch nach dem erfolgreichen Aufbau keine Zeit zu verlieren. Denn jede Minute zählt und kostet. Da kommt bei einer Montagezeit von April bis August eine stattliche Summe zusammen. Hinzu kommen noch die Posten für den Einsatz der zwei beteiligten Schlepper, ohne die die Hubinsel nicht manövrierfähig ist und die für ihre Zugarbeiten reichlich Treibstoff schlucken. Obendrein muss die Bordcrew und das Montageteam laufend versorgt werden, ohne Vollverpflegung würde die Stimmung wohl schnell unterzuckern. Der Kapitän der JB 114 drückt auf der Kommandobrücke manche Schalter und Knöpfe und die Hubinsel wird heruntergefahren.

Danach heben die Schlepper die Anker und ziehen das stählerne Viereck wieder gen Küste. Vor dem Bug zieht einer der Schlepper mit einem dicken Stahlseil, hinter dem Heck stabilisiert der zweite. Langsam verschwinden die fünf Anlagen am Horizont. Die Seeschifffahrtslinie, auf der wie Perlenketten Container und Frachtschiffe ihren Kurs halten und einen grau-gelben Schleier hinterlassen, wird gequert. Noch

music the beaming cook serves up piles of grilled chicory and steaming mashed potatoes. After the meal the night shift continues. Time to tidy up, and the men tie down straps, roll up cables and stow heavy chains. At about seven in the morning the rotor has been completely fitted and the assembly team organised by Michael Klingele return in the basket back on board from the nacelle, tired but happy.

While the team are enjoying their well-earned sleep, the crew of the jack-up barge gets ready to return without delay to the Dutch port of Eemshaven. A procedure that takes, as usual, a few hours. But every minute counts, as time is money. In an assembly period stretching from April to August it all adds up. On top of this are the costs for the two tugs involved, which burn up a considerable amount of fuel while doing the tugging but without which the platform would simply not be manoeuvrable. Moreover, the on-board crew and assembly team have to be catered for around the clock – without the 'full board' arrangement, the atmosphere would quickly go downhill. The captain of the JB 114 presses the knobs and buttons on the command bridge and the jack-up barge is slowly but surely lowered.

Then the tugs weigh anchor and start pulling the flat, square steel monolith back towards the coast. One tug pulls with a thick steel cable from the bow, while to the stern the second tug stabilises it. The five

Geschafft: Aufräumen auf dem Deck der JB 114.
Finished: tidying up the JB 114 deck.

ein paar Stunden weiter und die ersten Umrisse der ost- und westfriesischen Küste tauchen auf. Im Westen sind die Konturen der Insel Rottumeroog und Sandbänke schemenhaft zu erkennen. Dann geht es mit sicherem Abstand gemächlich vorbei an der Uferpromenade von Borkum, wo sich die Urlauber am Strand sonnen und einige Mutige den Sprung in die Nordsee wagen. An der niederländischen Küste erscheint der Windpark Eemsmond, einer der größten Onshore-Windparks Europas. Schließlich bugsiert die Banckert die JB 114 in die Hafeneinfahrt von Eemshaven.

Dieser Industriehafen entstand in den siebziger Jahren auf dem Reißbrett auf der westlichen Seite der Ems in einem neu eingedeichten Polder. Er ist wahrlich nichts für Romantiker, sondern einfach nur nüchtern, aber dafür äußerst funktional: Breite Kaiflächen gewähren ein problemloses Be- und Endladen der Windenergieanlagen-Riesen. Große rechteckig angelegte Hafenbecken bieten Platz fürs Manövrieren, wie für den Schubverband Mega-Motti, der Rotoren, Gondeln und Turmsegmente von Stade und Bremerhaven hierher transportiert. Die entscheidenden Vorzüge von Eemshaven als Ausgangspunkt sind jedoch die Nähe zum Baufeld und dass der Hafen keine Schleuse hat. Es ist schon Abend, als die Hubinsel am Kai anlegt und ihre Stahlrohre

turbines disappear slowly over the horizon. The nautical caravan crosses the busy shipping lane, dotted with container and freight ships like a chain of pearls against a grey-yellow haze. After only a few hours the first outlines of the East and West Frisian coast can be seen. To the west, the silhouette of the West Frisian island Rottumeroog and a few sandbanks are just about visible. Keeping a safe distance, the procession slowly passes the waterfront of Borkum, where the holidaymakers are sunning themselves on the beach and a few hardy souls have even dared to plunge into the North Sea. The wind farm Eemsmond appears on the Dutch coast, one of the largest onshore wind farms in Europe. On its east side the 'Banckert' finally manoeuvres the JB 114 into the port entrance of Eemshaven.

This industrial port was planned in the 1970s and constructed on the west bank of the River Ems within a newly raised dyke. The port is nothing at all for romantics – down-to-earth, but extremely functional: wide quayside areas enable problem-free loading and unloading of the giant wind turbines. Large, rectangular inner harbour basins provide space for manoeuvring and for the transport-combine Mega-Motti, which brings the rotors, nacelles and tower segments from Stade and Bremerhaven to here. However, the decisive benefits of Eemshaven as

Thomas Piasta, Sebastian Degner und Robert Nuglisch (v.l.n.r.) nach erfolgreicher Montage der ersten Turbine im Windpark. Thomas Piasta, Sebastian Degner and Robert Nuglisch (from left to right) after setting up the first turbine in the wind farm.

in den Hafengrund hineindrückt. An der Hafenkante liegt bereits die sechste und letzte Anlage von AREVA Multibrid für alpha ventus bereit.

Am nächsten Morgen beginnt die Verladung. Nach einer Mütze Schlaf und getaner Arbeit zeigt sich Michael Klingele zuversichtlich. Das Projekt steht kurz vor dem Abschluss, die Pioniertat ist trotz aller Widerstände erfolgreich bewältigt worden. Dafür hat AREVA Multibrid viel Lehrgeld zahlen müssen. Dazu gehören auch die Erfahrungen aus dem extrem stürmischen August 2008, als man mit einem kleineren Ponton, beladen mit drei Tripods, schon in Richtung Testfeld aufgebrochen war und dann kurz vor dem Erreichen der Bestimmungsorte wieder umkehren musste, weil der Schwimmkran nicht die technischen Anforderungen, die der Versicherer stellte, erfüllen konnte. Bitter. Wenngleich es dafür von den Medien und auch innerhalb der Windenergieszene reichlich Spott prasselte, haben doch die Pioniere aus den Fehlern zügig gelernt. Das Entwicklungsteam um Klingele ließ sich nicht beirren und hat stattdessen über den Winter 2008/009 eine neue Strategie mit größerer Gerätschaft für den Aufbau geschmiedet. Dabei lief auch im Jahr 2009 nicht alles nach Wunsch. So hat beispielsweise das Ausrichten der Tripods mit einer so genann-

starting point are its geographical proximity to the alpha ventus field, and the fact that this port has no canal locks and can therefore be used non-stop.

It's already evening when the jack-up barge finally docks and pushes its steel pipes into the bottom of the harbour for mooring stability. On the quayside the sixth and last turbine from AREVA Multibrid is already waiting to be shipped out to alpha ventus.

The loading-up starts the next morning. After catching a bit of sleep and finishing the work, Michael Klingele seems confident. The project is close to completion and the pioneering work has been successfully mastered in spite of all kinds of obstacles. However, AREVA Multibrid has had to learn the hard way. This also includes the experience gathered in the extremely stormy August of 2008, when the team set off with a smaller pontoon loaded with three tripods towards the test field, only having to turn back shortly before reaching the destination because the floating crane did not fulfil the technical requirements that were laid down by the insurer – a bitter setback. Even if they were ridiculed by the media and also by their own colleagues within the wind-energy sector, these pioneers quickly learned from such mistakes. The engineering team around Klingele remained steadfastly goal-focused

ten Ausgleichsvorrichtung, dem so genannten Levelling Tool nicht geklappt. Nach der zweiten Gründung haben die Verantwortlichen dann kurzerhand ohne Levelling-Tools gearbeitet, was sich fortan als die genau richtige Entscheidung herausstellen sollte. Das Versenken, Rammen und Rütteln der Gründungskonstruktionen, entwickelt über Jahre von der im Jahre 2001 gegründeten Firma Offshore Wind Technologie (OWT) wurde immer schneller bewältigt. Gelernt hat die Mannschaft aber nicht nur auf dem Meer im Testfeld. Der Lernprozess begann schon Jahre vorher. Er begann eigentlich schon beim Errichten des ersten Prototyps der M5000 im Dezember 2004 hinterm Deich nördlich von Bremerhaven. Seitdem hat das Entwicklungsteam um Klingele unzählige Trockenübungen absolviert, um sich bestmöglich für alle Eventualitäten auf dem Meer zu präparieren. Mit allen Rückschlägen und Fortschritten, die so ein mutiges Projekt mit sich bringt.

„Ich glaube tiefen Herzens an die Offshore-Technik", sagt Michael Klingele während der Rückkehr an Land. Nach fünf installierten Anlagen macht er keinen Hehl daraus, dass er zu Beginn der Bauarbeiten im Testfeld, trotz aller Trainings und Vorkehrungen, zur Hälfte nicht wusste, ob es tatsächlich klappen würde. Es gab in Wassertiefen von 30 Metern einfach ganz viele Unbekannte, bei denen die Beteiligten nicht auf Erfahrungswerte von irgendjemand hätten zurückgreifen können. Hat doch niemand auf der ganzen Welt vorher in so einer Entfernung von der Küste und Wassertiefen von 30 Metern Turbinen aufgestellt. Bis auf REpower – mit den Windparks Beatrice und Thornton Bank – hatte niemand auf der Welt vorher in so einer großen Entfernung von der Küste, in Wassertiefen von 30 Metern und mehr, Turbinen aufgestellt. Für den studierten Wirtschaftsingenieur endet mit der Fertigstellung der sechs Anlagen im Testfeld alpha ventus eine aufregende Prototypenphase, die mit seinem Einstieg bei Multibrid im Jahr 2007 begann. Der frühere Firmenchef Ingo de Buhr begeisterte ihn für die Idee, Offshore-Anlagen zu bauen, und warb ihn vom Wettbewerber, Suzlon Energy ab, für die er einige Jahre in Indien unterwegs war. „Wir haben immer auf ein geschlossenes, relativ leichtes System gesetzt. Alles ist kompakt konstruiert. Es sollte keinen aufgelösten Triebstrang geben, der Generator wird als ein Gussteil gefertigt. Und wir haben uns frühzeitig für ein einstufiges Getriebe entschieden", begeistert sich Klingele am technischen Konzept der Fünf-Megawatt-Offshoreanlage. Wenn die Fertigungsabläufe in den nächsten Jahren professionalisiert sind, die Anlagen in Serie gebaut werden und die Aufstellungstechnik – Stichworte wie horizontale Einzelblattmontage auf Höhe der Nabe fallen – sich weiterentwickelt hat, dann besteht für Klingele kein Zweifel, dass Offshore eine große ökonomische Zukunft vor sich hat. Im Übrigen erwartet er, dass sogar Turbinen mit einer Leistung von acht Megawatt kommen werden. Und außerdem: „Wir stören hier draußen niemand und wir gewinnen grüne Energie im großen Stil. Was will man mehr?"

Mit großem Erfolg, wie spätestens am 12. August klar wurde, als der erste deutsche Offshore-Windstrom von der Anlage AV 9 aus der Ausschließlichen Wirtschaftszone (AWZ) an Land floss. Und zwar exakt um 21.15 Uhr. Für die Mitarbeiter von AREVA Multibrid und für DOTI war dies, nach jahrelangen Bemühungen, eine große Genugtuung und für die deutsche Energiebranche sicherlich der Einstieg in eine neue Ära.

and created a new strategy in the winter of 2008/09 with larger equipment. But then again, the year 2009 did not always go as hoped. For example, the alignment of the tripods using a certain compensating device, the so-called 'levelling tool' did not work correctly. After completing the second foundation, the on-site technicians had to start work without the levelling tools, which turned out to be just the right decision. The team was then able to carry out the plunging, ramming and shakedown procedures of the foundation, as painstakingly developed by Offshore Wind Technologie (OWT) founded in 2001, with greater and greater ease. However, the team had not only gone through these learning processes on the open sea in the test field: the learning curve had begun years before, as soon as they began setting up the first prototype of the M5000 in December 2004 behind the embankments to the north of Bremerhaven. Since then Klingele's engineering team has practiced in numerous dry test-runs so as to be as well prepared as possible for any eventualities at sea, with all the setbacks and successes that such a courageouous project involves.

"I firmly believe in the offshore technology", says Michael Klingele during the return to shore. Having installed five turbines he does not even try to hide the fact that, at the start of the construction work in the test field, in spite of all the practice and provisions he did not know for sure whether it would all really work. There were just too many unknowns in waters that were 30 metres deep; there was no past experience that those involved could fall back on. Except for REpower – with the wind farms Beatrice and Thornton Bank – no one in the world had previously set up turbines so far away from the coast in such a depth of water. For the trained industrial engineer, completing the installation of the six turbines in the alpha ventus test field will end an exciting prototype phase that started when he joined Multibrid in 2007. The former boss there, Ingo de Buhr, got him interested in the idea of constructing offshore turbines and enticed him away from the competitor Suzlon Energy, for whom he had been working for some years in India. "We always placed our bets on a capsulated and lightweight system. Everything is designed to be compact. There should be no separate drive train and the generator and rotor bearing were shrunk down into the nacelle so as to save space. Moreover, we made the decision early on for a single-stage gearbox", enthuses Klingele about the technical concept of the Multibrid M5000. Once the manufacturing and assembly processes become increasingly standardized in the coming years, the turbines will go into serial production – Klingele uses buzzwords here such as "horizontal single-blade assembly at hub height." The installation techniques will also be developed further. He has no doubts that offshore wind power has a great economic future and is already looking forward to turbines with an output of eight megawatts. "What's more," he smiles, "we're not disturbing anyone out there and are establishing green power generation on a large scale. What more can anyone ask?!"

That's why the 12th of August 2009 was a very special date for Klingele and his team: late that evening at 9.15 pm, the first kilowatt-hours of offshore wind power flowed from a Multibrid M5000 in the German Exclusive Economic Zone (EEZ) onto land. For the employees of AREVA Multibrid and for DOTI this was, after years of hard work, tremendously satisfying – and the start into a bright new era for the German energy sector.

Das Turmsegment wird von der Hubinsel hochgehoben und anschließend montiert.
The tower section is hoisted from the jack-up barge and then mounted.

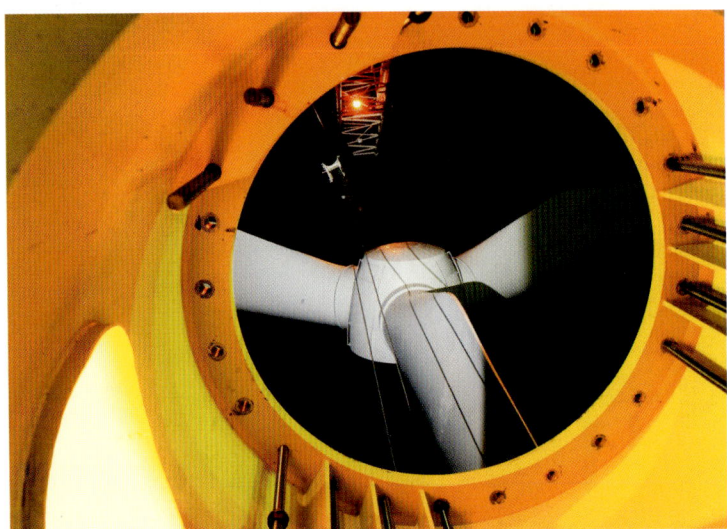

Ohne Menschen geht es nicht. Mit vereinten Kräften wird das Seil am Kranhaken angeschlagen. Die Arbeiten gehen Hand in Hand, jeder Einzelne muss sich auf das Team verlassen können. Manpower is still required. Together, workers tie the rope to which the rotor star will eventually be attached, to the crane hook. Work goes hand in hand, so each member must be able to rely on the team.

Herausforderungen annehmen Facing challenges

FÉLIX DEBIERRE SPRECHER DER GESCHÄFTSFÜHRUNG AREVA MULTIBRID GMBH
AREVA MULTIBRID EXECUTIVE MANAGEMENT SPOKESMAN

Félix Debierre

Félix Debierre ist seit Ende 2007 Sprecher der Geschäftsführung von AREVA Multibrid und für AREVAs Windaktivitäten zuständig. Er studierte in Berlin und Paris. An der Ecole Polytechnique und Ecole des Ponts-et-Chaussées schloss er sein Studium zum Hochbau- und Tiefbauingenieur mit Diplom und einem Master of International Economics ab. Seine berufliche Karriere begann im französischen Finanzministerium und im Bankensektor, in dem er in Paris, in den USA und Japan arbeitete. Über den Kabelkonzern Nexans kam er in die Industrie. Als Geschäftsführer in China brachte er ein Lichtwellenkabel Joint Venture auf den Weg und war später weltweit für einen Konzernbereich verantwortlich. Seit 2004 ist Félix Debierre für den Energiekonzern AREVA tätig.

Félix Debierre has been CEO of AREVA Multibrid since 2007 and in charge of AREVA wind activities. He studied in Berlin and Paris, and graduated as Engineer from the Ecole Polytechnique and the Ecole des Ponts-et-Chaussees (Civil engineer), as well as with a Master of International Economics. He has spent his initial career as a civil servant at the French Treasury and in the banking sector, where he has worked in Paris, the USA and Japan. He joined the industrial world for the Nexans cable group, a.o. to set up an optical fiber cable joint venture in China and later as world-wide business line manager. He has been with AREVA since 2004.

alpha ventus war für AREVA Multibrid der erste große Test für das raue Offshore-Geschäft. Ihnen muss doch ein Stein vom Herzen gefallen sein, als die sechs Anlagen Ihres Unternehmens im Spätsommer 2009 erfolgreich errichtet waren, oder?

Die Umsetzung des Projekts alpha ventus hat unsere Erwartungen übertroffen. Die Einsatzfähigkeit der M5000 im Offshore-Betrieb ist nun bestätigt. Das ist für uns das wichtigste Ergebnis. Daneben standen die Sicherheitsaspekte im Mittelpunkt unserer Aufmerksamkeit. Ich denke, wir können besonders stolz auf unseren hohen Sicherheitsstandard sein. Die schnelle, professionelle und unfallfreie Installation der sechs Anlagen sowie erste Leistungsnachweise des Service-Teams sind für unsere zukünftigen Kunden ein gutes Fundament und beweisen die Vielfältigkeit des Offshore-Portfolios des AREVA-Konzerns.

Welche Bedeutung hat das Projekt alpha ventus für die Weiterentwicklung Ihres Unternehmens?

alpha ventus ist der Startschuss für eine Reihe von Offshore-Parks, die aus den Fünf-Megawatt-Windenergieanlagen des Typs M5000 bestehen werden. Wir erweitern unsere Produktionskapazitäten: Nach dem alpha-ventus-Testfeld werden die zukünftigen kommerziellen Offshore-Projekte jeweils bis zu 80 Windenergieanlagen umfassen. Unser

alpha ventus was the first big test of the rough offshore business for AREVA Multibrid. It must have been a huge relief for you when the six turbines from your company were successfully installed in the late summer of 2009.

The outcome of the alpha ventus project has exceeded our expectations. The suitability of the M5000 for offshore operations has now been proven, and that is the most important thing for us. Throughout, our primary focus was on the safety aspects, and I think we can be very proud of our high safety standard. The fast, professional, accident-free installation of the six turbines, plus the initial performance reports of our service team, are a good foundation for future business and demonstrate the versatility of the AREVA offshore portfolio.

What is the significance of the alpha ventus project for the future development of your company?

alpha ventus is the kickoff for a series of offshore wind farms that will use our 5-megawatt M5000 wind turbines. We're expanding our production capacity, because the com-mercial offshore farms that are set to follow the alpha ventus test field will use up to 80 turbines each. alpha ventus has given us the certainty that we are on the right path with our ongoing growth.

Now that the turbines have been operating in the North Sea for a few months, can you say anything as to the technical performance of the Multibrid M5000?

The six M5000 generated almost 30 million kilowatt-hours from their commissioning in the

Die Nabe der M5000 wird in der Produktionshalle von AREVA Multibrid in Bremerhaven gefertigt. The M5000 hub is assembled in the AREVA Multibrid production hall in Bremerhaven.

Unternehmen hat durch alpha ventus die Gewissheit erhalten, mit dem beständigen Wachstum auf dem richtigen Weg zu sein.

Können Sie nach den ersten Betriebsmonaten auf der Nordsee schon Aussagen zum technischen Verhalten der Multibrid M5000 treffen?

Die sechs M5000 generierten von der Inbetriebnahme im Herbst bis Dezember 2009 bereits nahezu 30 Millionen Kilowattstunden. Allein in der zweiten Novemberhälfte 2009 erzeugten die sechs Anlagen im Volllastbetrieb über zehn Millionen Kilowattstunden, und das bei einer Verfügbarkeit von 99 Prozent. Diese überraschend positiven Ergebnisse schon im Probebetrieb haben unsere Erwartungen deutlich übertroffen.

Was erhoffen Sie sich von der wissenschaftlichen Begleitforschung im Rahmen des RAVE-Programms, die in den nächsten Jahren im Testfeld alpha ventus unternommen wird?

Wir erhoffen uns technisch innovative Lösungen, wir setzen darauf, dass einheitliche

autumn until December 2009. During the second half of November alone, they operated at full capacity and generated over ten million kilowatt hours, with an availability of 99 percent. These surprisingly positive results during test operations have significantly exceeded our expectations.

What benefits do you anticipate from the scientific research in the RAVE programme that is planned for the alpha ventus test field in the coming years?

We're hoping for technical innovations, and we're looking to the programme to result in uniform standards and progress on the logistical as well as environmental questions surrounding offshore wind energy.

Unlike the manufacturer REpower, for the alpha ventus project you delivered your turbines as 'turn-key'. What exactly does that mean?

AREVA Multibrid supplied and installed the foundations and then set up the turbines on-site. We delivered them to the customer 'turn-key', in the literal sense of the word – that is, absolutely ready to go into operation. To do this we had to do much more than just manufacture the turbines. We had to build up the necessary infrastructure of suppliers, and also get a handle on the logistical elements of the project. We took care of delivering the components, weighing many tonnes each, and installing them with special construction ships, anchoring the tripod foundation structures and erecting the six M5000 units. All in all it was a big challenge, which I am happy to say we were able to master.

Does your company intend to stick to the turn-key strategy? Or will you also act just as a manufacturer in some instances?

AREVA Multibrid intends to offer potential offshore wind farm operators a multifaceted solution portfolio. In order to reinforce and extend our position on the world market, we need to provide the flexibility our customers demand. Our primary focus is on manufacturing and providing maintenance for the M5000.

Standards erarbeitet und Fortschritte in den logistischen wie auch umweltbezogenen Fragestellungen im Offshore-Windenergiebereich unternommen werden.

Sie haben im Projekt alpha ventus im Gegensatz zum Hersteller REpower die Turbinen „schlüsselfertig" geliefert. Was heißt das eigentlich?

AREVA Multibrid hat die Gründungsstrukturen geliefert und installiert und danach die Windenergieanlagen offshore errichtet. Wir haben sie dem Auftraggeber im wörtlichen Sinne schlüsselfertig übergeben. Dazu mussten wir nicht nur die Herstellung bewerkstelligen und die notwendige Infrastruktur an Zulieferunternehmen aufbauen, sondern auch die logistische Dimension des Projekts in den Griff bekommen. Wir haben die Auslieferung der tonnenschweren Komponenten, die Installation mit Errichterschiffen und die Verankerung der Tripod-Gründungsstrukturen sowie das Errichten der sechs M5000 übernommen. Alles in allem eine große Herausforderung, die wir aber sehr gut bewältigt haben.

Will das Unternehmen an der Strategie „schlüsselfertiger" Lieferungen festhalten? Oder werden Sie im Einzelfall auch nur als Hersteller von Offshore-Windenergieanlagen agieren?

AREVA Multibrid will potenziellen Offshore-Windpark-Betreibern ein vielfältiges Lösungs-Portfolio anbieten. Um unsere Position auf dem Weltmarkt zu festigen und auszubauen, müssen wir die Flexibilität mitbringen, die unsere Kunden erwarten. Unser Schwerpunkt liegt in erster Linie auf der Herstellung und Wartung der M5000. Darüber hinaus passen wir die M5000 an die jeweiligen Standorte und technischen Erfordernisse der zukünftigen Offshore-Parkbetreiber an.

Sind in der nahen Zukunft noch technische Veränderungen an der Turbine der M5000 zu erwarten?

Die technische Weiterentwicklung der M5000 wird im Unternehmen parallel zur Serienfertigung laufen. Die unterschiedlichen Standorte der Windparks erfordern jeweils spezifische Anpassungen, zudem werden konkrete Kundenwünsche in die technische Ausführung unseres Hightech-Produkts einfließen. Wenn Sie sich

We also adapt the M5000 to the specific sites and technical requirements of future offshore wind farm operators.

Can we expect technical modifications to the M5000 turbines in the near future?

Technical development of the M5000 will proceed in parallel with series production at our company. Different wind-farm sites require different modifications, and we will also incorporate specific customer wishes into their versions of our high-tech product. If you're referring to the rated output of the turbine that currently generates five megawatts, then we first need to define "near future."

Where do you see the most difficult technical challenges in offshore wind energy? Is there room for improvement?

The greatest technical challenge is the maximisation of the energy output of our offshore turbines. The M5000 is already at a very high level of development, but together with our customers we are working towards further improvements in the installation and operation of our systems and will continue to do so over the entire lifetime of a given wind farm.

Do you share the opinion that offshore wind energy will be a success story similar to that of onshore wind energy during the past 20 years?

Yes, the signs point to offshore wind energy becoming every bit as much a success story in the future as wind energy on land is today. The greater energy yield from high-capacity turbines plus the considerably stronger and steadier winds at sea, in combination with ongoing cost reductions, will ensure high demand.

Assuming your assessment is correct, where will the offshore market develop most rapidly in the next decade?

We're keeping an eye on the different European markets, and see great potential in the UK and Germany. We also expect strong market development in North America and China.

What types of turbines do you plan to launch in the coming years? In addition to series production of the 5-megawatt class, will we see even larger turbines from AREVA Multibrid?

Over the short term, we are prioritising the optimisation of the technical possibilities of the M5000 and the expansion of our production capacity. Series production for orders in hand, and further research and development, are naturally proceeding in parallel through the support of our parent company. The 5-megawatt class looks very promising, with the onshore results and the energy these

157 m Kölner Dom Cologne Cathedral
148 m Blattspitze Blade tip
147 m Cheops Pyramide Cheops Pyramid

116 m Rotordurchmesser Rotor diameter

Helikopter-Plattform Helicopter platform
Gondel Nacelle
Nabe Hub (90 m)
85 m Sacré-Cœur, Paris Sacré-Cœur, Paris

Turm Tower

Anleger Boat landing
Hochwasser High tide
Niedrigwasser Low tide

Tripod Tripod

WEA AREVA Multibrid M5000
Stand 04/2009
[nicht maßstabsgetreu]

M5000 AREVA Multibrid WEC
Status 04/2009
[not to scale]

−28 m

TECHNISCHE DATEN AREVA MULTIBRID M5000
TECHNICAL DATA AREVA MULTIBRID M5000

Gesamthöhe ab Meeresgrund **Overall height above seabed**	178 m
Nennleistung **Rated capacity**	5 MW
Drehzahl **Speed**	5,9 bis 14,8 U/min **5.9 to 14.8 rpm**
Einschaltwindgeschwindigkeit **Cut-in wind speed**	3,5 m/s (Windstärke 3) **3,5 m/s (wind force 3)**
Nennwindgeschwindigkeit **Rated wind speed**	12,5 m/s (Windstärke 6) **12,5 m/s (wind force 6)**
Ausschaltwindgeschwindigkeit **Cut-out wind speed**	25 m/s (Windstärke 10) **25 m/s (wind force 10)**
Blattspitzengeschwindigkeit **Blade tip speed**	90 m/s (324 km/h)
Gondelmasse mit Rotor und Nabe **Nacelle mass with rotor and hub**	357,8 t
Stahlmasse (Gründung, Turm, Gondel) **Steel mass (foundation, tower, nacelle)**	1.390 t
Stahlmasse der Gründung allein **Steel mass of foundation alone**	667 t

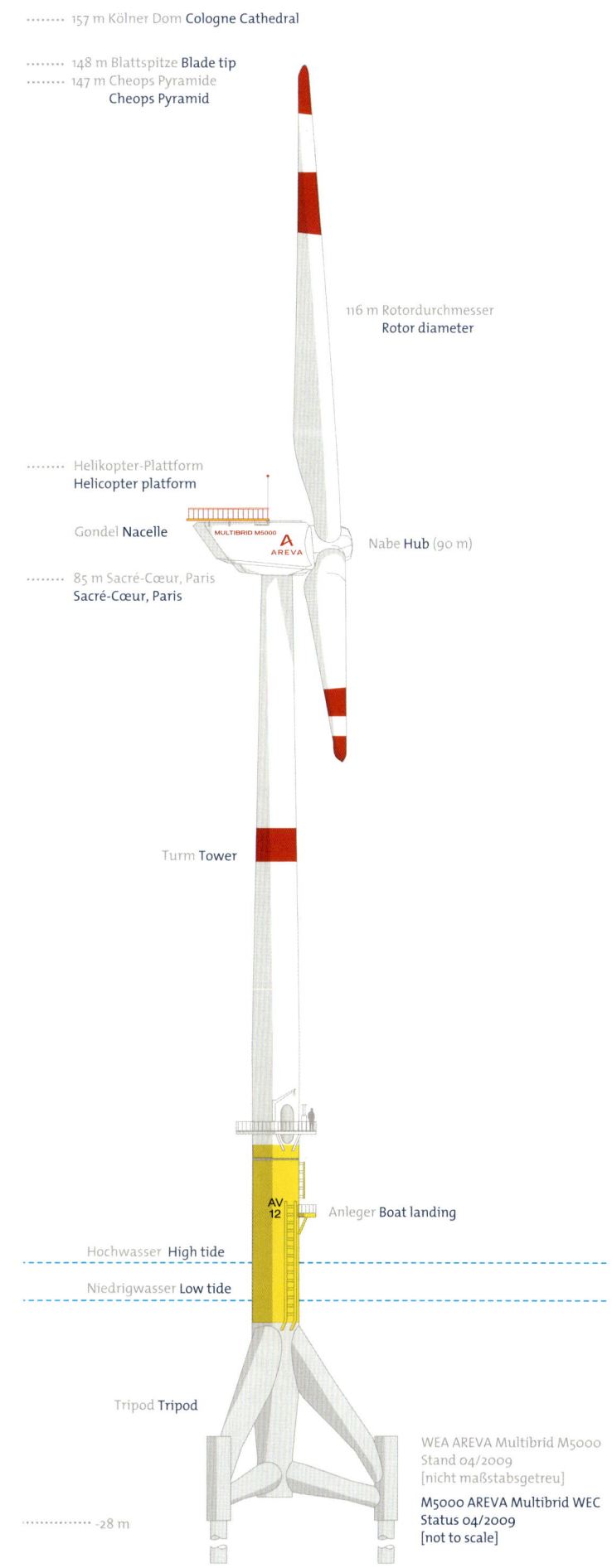

Herausforderungen annehmen Facing challenges

auf die Nennleistung der bisher fünf Megawatt generierenden Anlage beziehen, dann sollte man erst einmal „nahe Zukunft" definieren.

Worin sehen Sie zukünftig im Bereich der Offshore-Windenergie die schwierigsten technischen Herausforderungen? Gibt es noch Potenziale zur Optimierung?

Die größte technische Herausforderung ist sicherlich die Maximierung des Energieertrags unserer Offshore-Anlage. Die M5000 ist bereits auf einem sehr hohen Stand der technischen Optimierung. Dennoch streben wir gemeinsam mit unseren Kunden weitere Optimierungen im Prozess der Errichtung und während des Betriebs über die gesamte Lebensdauer der Windparks an.

Sind Sie auch der Überzeugung, dass die Offshore-Windenergie eine ähnliche Erfolgsstory wird, wie es die Windenergie in den letzten 20 Jahren an Land war?

Ja, die Zeichen weisen darauf hin, dass die Offshore-Windenergie – wie heute die Windenergie an Land – in Zukunft eine Erfolgsstory werden könnte. Der hohe Energiegewinn der leistungsstarken Anlagen wird durch die Kombination mit dem wesentlich stärkeren und stetigeren Wind auf See und einer fortschreitenden Kostenminimierung eine hohe Nachfrage garantieren.

Vorausgesetzt, Ihre Einschätzung stimmt, wo wird sich in den nächsten zehn Jahren der Offshore-Markt am dynamischsten entwickeln?

Wir beobachten die verschiedenen Märkte in Europa und sehen große Potenziale in Großbritannien und Deutschland. Weitere starke Marktentwicklungen werden in Nordamerika und in China erwartet.

Mit welchen Anlagentypen wollen Sie in den nächsten Jahren ins Geschehen eingreifen? Wird es neben der Serienproduktion der 5-MW-Klasse noch größere Anlagen aus der Produktion von AREVA Multibrid geben?

In einer kurzfristigen Perspektive geben wir der Optimierung der technischen Möglichkeiten der M5000 und dem Ausbau der Fertigungskapazitäten den Vorrang. Die Serienproduktion für die beauftragten Windenergieanlagen und die weitere Forschung und Entwicklung laufen selbstverständlich durch die Unterstützung des Mutterkonzerns parallel. Die 5-MW-Klasse sieht heute mit den Ergebnissen onshore und der bereits generierten Energie auf der Nordsee vielversprechend aus, und eine höhere Megawatt-Klasse wird dem Parkbetreiber dieselben Vorteile gewährleisten müssen.

... also wird aus der Multibrid M5000 schon bald eine M6000 werden?

Unsere Überlegungen gehen in verschiedene Richtungen und richten sich in erster Linie nach den Wünschen unserer Kunden. Sicherlich ist die Vergrößerung der Nennleistung ein Aspekt, aber größere Rotordurchmesser und Anpassungen an entsprechende Windstandorte werden ebenfalls bearbeitet.

Welche ökonomischen Vorteile haben denn Hersteller und Betreiber bei einem Megawatt zusätzlich pro Turbine?

Diese Frage ist nur standortspezifisch zu beantworten, der Mehrertrag kann aber jährlich bis zu mehreren Hunderttausend Euro pro Anlage betragen.

Haben Sie eine Vorstellung davon, wie viele Offshore-Anlagen von AREVA Multibrid bis 2020 im Meer stehen werden?

Abhängig von der Entwicklung der internationalen Marktnachfrage gehen wir von 500 bis 1000 installierten Offshore-Anlagen aus.

AREVA ist ein großer Konzern mit vielen Tochterunternehmen. Das Engagement im Bereich der Windenergie ist noch relativ neu. Mit welcher Motivation hat das Unternehmen Multibrid erworben und damit den Einstieg in die Windenergie unternommen?

Die Geschäftseinheit AREVA Renewables wurde 2006 gegründet. 2007 kaufte der Konzern 51 Prozent der Multibrid GmbH, um bis 2011 die 100 Prozent zu erreichen. Unsere Vision ist es, CO_2-freie Lösungen für die weltweite Energiewirtschaft anzubieten. Das erklärt den Aufbau des „Erneuerbaren Energie-Geschäftsbereichs". So kam auch der Einstieg in die Windenergie zustande. Wir haben 2009 unser Engagement im Bereich der Windenergie durch den Zukauf von 100 Prozent des Rotorblattherstellers PNR mit Sitz in Stade weiter bekräftigt.

Welchen Stellenwert wird die Offshore-Windenergie in Zukunft für die Konzernmutter spielen?

Seit 2009 ist die Offshore-Windenergie ein wesentlicher Bestandteil der Konzernstrategie. Die Geschäftseinheit AREVA Renewables deckt Wind, Solar, Biomasse und die Entwicklung von Speichermedien für Wasserstoff ab. Wobei auf dem Geschäftsfeld „Offshore-Wind" derzeit die höchsten Erwartungen für wirtschaftliches Wachstum liegen. Die Verbindung von hochqualifizierter deutscher Ingenieursarbeit und der Finanzkraft eines weltweit agierenden Energiekonzerns bietet die besten Erfolgsaussichten für einen hohen internationalen Marktanteil in naher Zukunft.

turbines are already generating in the North Sea. A higher power-output class will have to offer farm operators the same innovative advantages.

... so will the Multibrid M5000 soon become an M6000?

Our thinking is following several different channels, and is aligned first and foremost with the desires of our customers. Increased rated capacity is certainly one aspect, but larger rotor diameters and modifications for specific wind sites are also on our list.

What financial benefits do manufacturers and operators get from another megawatt per turbine?

This question can only be answered on a site-per-site basis. But the additional output can add up to several hundred thousand euros earned per turbine per year.

Do you have an idea how many AREVA Multibrid offshore turbines will be standing in the sea by 2020?

We project 500 to 1,000 installed offshore turbines, depending on how international demand develops.

AREVA is a large group with many subsidiary companies. Its wind energy activities are relatively new. What motivated AREVA to acquire Multibrid and thereby enter the wind-energy market?

The AREVA Renewables Division was founded in 2006. In 2007 the group bought 51 percent of Multibrid GmbH, and will have acquired 100 percent by 2011. Our vision is to offer CO_2-free solutions to the worldwide energy market. That is the motivation behind our establishment of the Renewables Division, and that's why we got into wind energy. In 2009 we further strengthened our commitment to wind energy with the purchase of 100 percent of the rotor-blade manufacturer PNR in Stade, Germany.

What role will offshore wind energy play for the parent company in the future?

Offshore wind energy has been a key element in our group's strategy since 2009. The AREVA Renewables Division covers wind, solar, biomass and the development of hydrogen storage media. Our expectations for business growth are highest in the offshore wind field. The combination of highly qualified German engineering and the financial power of a worldwide energy group offer excellent prospects for a high international market share in the near future.

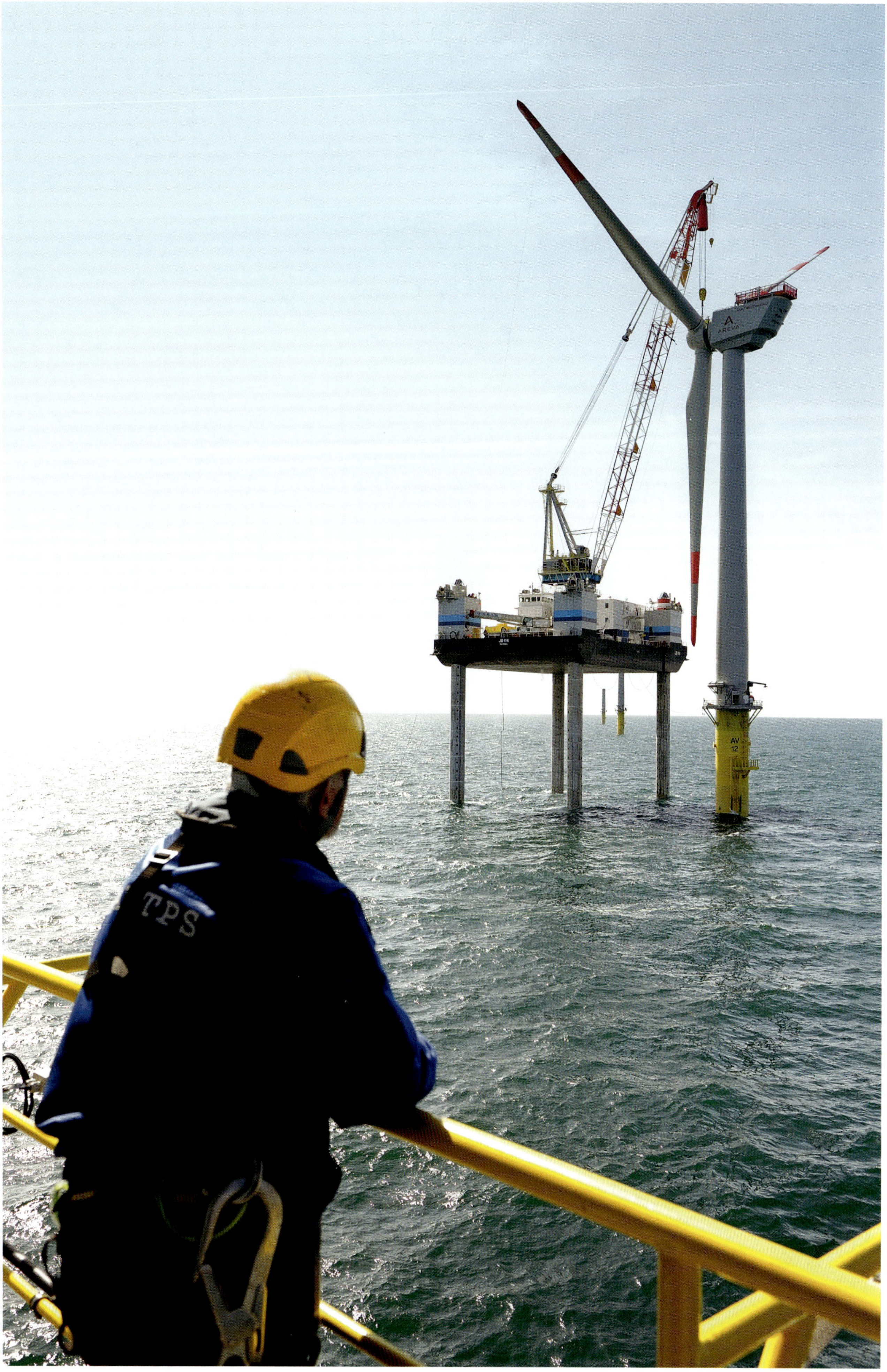
AREVA
AV
12
TPS

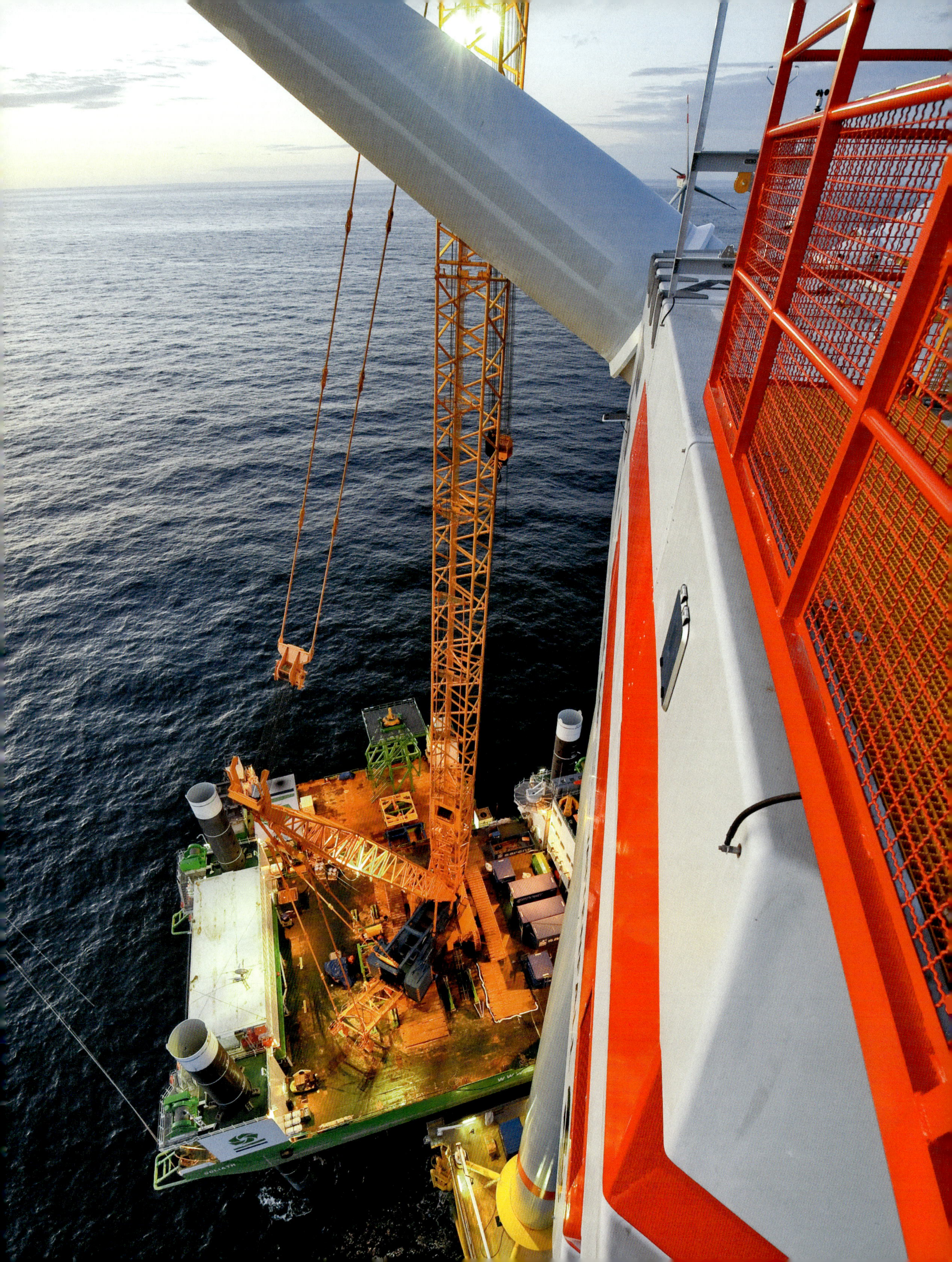

Von der Vision zur Wirklichkeit
From vision to reality

Ideen zur Nutzung von Windenergie auf dem Meer gibt es schon lange. Manche waren kurios. Wie die von Günter Wagner etwa, der 1982 auf einen Kutter einen 25 Meter langen Arbeitsflügel und einen kürzeren, rechtwinklig angebauten Stabilisierungsflügel montieren ließ. Mit dieser Konstruktion, die auf eine Leistung von 250 Kilowatt kommen sollte, wollte der findige Berliner Geschäftsmann auf der Nordsee Strom erzeugen. Allerdings kam er über das Experimentierstadium nie hinaus, obwohl er überall vollmundig erzählte, diesen Typ in einer Größe von 100 Megawatt bauen zu wollen.

Andere Ideen dagegen waren technisch fundierter. Sie kamen zumindest äußerlich den heutigen Offshore-Anlagen schon erstaunlich nah. Bemerkenswerte Dokumente findet man im Archiv von Erich Hau, der als Flugzeugbauingenieur bei der MAN Neue Technologien Anfang der achtziger Jahre für die Aerodynamik der Großen Windenergieanlage GROWIAN verantwortlich war. So ist eine farbige Zeichnung aus den Endsiebzigern zu finden, die einen Zweiflügler auf einem von zwei Streben abgestiften Turm im schäumenden Meer abbildet. Am Horizont der stimmungsvollen Zeichnung sind schemenhaft weitere Offshore-Riesen zu erkennen. Auf einer anderen handgezeichneten Abbildung aus etwa dieser Zeit mit der Überschrift „Windenergie für Helgoland" steht ein Dreiflügler im Wasser – wenn auch nur unmittelbar an der Kaimauer.

Doch das ist alles nur Vorgeschichte. Konkreter in Sachen Offshore-Windenergie wird es erst in der zweiten Hälfte der neunziger Jahre. Zu diesem Zeitpunkt hatte sich die Windenergie-Branche an Land nach einer zähen und widerstandsreichen Pionierphase bereits zu einer erfolgreichen Industrie entwickelt, die von der Energiebranche zunehmend ernst genommen wurde. Zudem war die erste rot-grüne Bundesregierung seit 1998 im Amt. Sie arbeitete emsig am Erneuerbaren-Energien-Gesetz (EEG), das schließlich im Jahr 2000 in Kraft trat und das seit 1991 geltende Stromeinspeisungsgesetz ersetzte. Mit dem EEG erhielt die Stromerzeugung aus Wind, Sonne, Wasser und Biomasse den energiepolitischen Rahmen, der den erneuerbaren Energien auf allen Ebenen einen nachhaltigen Durchbruch bescherte. Im Übrigen wurde im EEG zum ersten Mal überhaupt der Tarif für Strom aus Offshore-Windenergie definiert.

Dieses positive Umfeld inspirierte Ende der neunziger Jahre verschiedene Ingenieure, Projektierer und Hersteller zu ersten kühnen Offshore-Plänen in Nord- und Ostsee. Auf der Messe HusumWind in der nordfriesischen Kreisstadt standen im September 1999 diverse Offshore-Aktivitäten im Mittelpunkt von Gesprächen. Schweden und Engländer machten mit küstennahen Offshore-Windparks gerade erste Erfahrungen und auch in den Niederlanden gab es Offshore-Pläne. Doch vor allem kamen aus dem Mutterland der Windenergie, Däne-

The notion of generating wind power at sea has been around for quite a while. Some ideas have been strange. Like those of Günter Wagner who, in 1982, installed a 25-metre-long working blade with a shorter stabilization blade attached at a right-angle. Using this construction, intended to achieve a rated capacity of 250 kilowatts, the smart Berlin businessman proposed generating electricity on the North Sea. However, he never got past the experimental stage, although he told everyone brashly that he intended to build this construction with a rated power of 100 megawatts.

Other ideas, on the other hand, were technologically sounder. At least at first glance they were astonishingly similar to today's offshore turbines. There are remarkable documents to be found in Erich Hau's archives, an aircraft construction engineer at MAN Neue Technologien who at the beginning of the 'eighties was responsible for the aerodynamics of the large-scale GROWIAN wind turbine. You will find a coloured blueprint dating from the end of the 'seventies showing a two-bladed rotor on a tower braced with two stays on a foaming sea. The outlines of further offshore giants are to be seen on the horizon in this atmospheric illustration. In another hand-drawn illustration from around this time, with the title 'Wind Energy for Helgoland', there is a three-blader standing in the water – even if it is directly next to the quay wall.

But that's all history. Offshore wind energy only really took shape in the second half of the 'nineties. At this time, the wind-energy sector on land had already taken off. However, it had had to battle through a tough pioneering phase and a great deal of resistance to become an increasingly successful industry that was taken more and more seriously by the energy sector. Moreover, the first Social Democratic Party/ Green Party coalition government took power in 1998. They worked painstakingly on the Renewable Energy Act, which finally came into effect in 2000 and replaced the Electricity Act that had been in force since 1991. The new law provided electricity generation from wind, sun, water and biomass with the energy-political framework that was required to give renewable energies a lasting breakthrough on all levels. Moreover, the Renewable Energy Act defined a tariff for electricity from offshore wind energy for the first time.

This positive environment inspired various engineers, wind-energy developers and manufacturers at the end of the 'nineties to suggest initial and ambitious offshore plans in the North and Baltic Seas. In September 1999, various offshore activities became the focal point of discussions at the wind-energy trade fair 'HusumWind' in the North Friesian town of Husum. The Swedes and British were beginning to gather their first experience with offshore wind farms near the coast and there were also offshore plans in the Netherlands. Moreover, an important

mark, wichtige Impulse. Die Dänen hatten nämlich schon 1991 den allerersten Offshore-Windpark (Vindeby) mit einer installierten Leistung von fünf Megawatt in der Ostsee errichtet, 1995 folgte im Kattegatt mit Tunø Knob das zweite Offshore-Projekt mit ebenfalls fünf Megawatt Leistung. Und weitere, größere Vorhaben befanden sich zur gleichen Zeit im fortgeschrittenen Stadium: Das ästhetisch überzeugende Projekt Middelgrunden mit 20 Windenergieanlagen und insgesamt 40 Megawatt Leistung unmittelbar vor Kopenhagen sowie Horns Rev mit geplanten 160 Megawatt in der Nordsee. Das Staunen war groß, die Skepsis manchmal noch größer. Trotzdem setzte sich das Thema Offshore Stück für Stück in den Köpfen der Branche fest.

Aller Anfang in Ostfriesland

Wer den Ursprüngen von alpha ventus auf der Spur ist, landet zuerst in Leer. In der ostfriesischen Stadt begann nämlich all das, was rund zehn Jahre später tatsächlich verwirklicht werden sollte. Ingo de Buhr, studierter Elektroingenieur und begeisterter Entrepreneur in Sachen erneuerbare Energien, hatte 1997 in seiner Geburtsstadt das Unternehmen Prokon Nord Energiesysteme GmbH mit drei Mitarbeitern gegründet. Mit diversen Windenergieprojekten machte es sich schnell einen Namen. Die Firma zählt heute über 400 Mitarbeiter. Zielstrebig und ausdauernd gelang es de Buhr, einen Windpark nach dem anderen an Land zu realisieren. Sicherlich hätten sich viele Projektentwickler mit diesem erfolgreichen Geschäft zufriedengegeben, nicht aber Ingo de Buhr. Der Sohn eines Kapitäns wollte weiter hinaus. Er gehört zu den Menschen, die ständig neue Herausforderungen suchen, ja brauchen. Was lag da näher, als auf See einen eigenen Offshore-Windpark zu planen?

Dabei fingen Ingo de Buhr und seine Mitstreiter beim absoluten Nullpunkt an. Sie konnten noch nicht einmal auf öffentlich zugängliches Kartenmaterial für die Nord- und Ostsee, das detaillierte Daten zu Meeresgrund, Wassertiefe, Strömung, Tidehub, Schifffahrtswegen und Windverhältnissen geliefert hätte, zurückgreifen. Deshalb musste Prokon Nord beim Bundesamt für Seeschifffahrt und Hydrographie (BSH) eigens einen Antrag auf Genehmigung für Kopien von Seekarten stellen. Um einen besseren Eindruck von der Materie zu bekommen, fuhren die deutschen Offshore-Vordenker aus Leer zum schwedischen Offshore-Windpark Utgrunden im Sund zwischen Kalmar und der Insel Öland, den die amerikanische Enron Wind, die später zu GE Wind Energy umfirmierte, errichtete und einige Jahre später an den Energiekonzern Vattenfall abgab. Schließlich, nach vielen Besuchen, Konsultationen und dem akribischen Studium der Seekarten, fiel die Wahl von de Buhr und seinen Mitstreitern auf einen Meeresabschnitt, der mehr oder weniger direkt vor der ostfriesischen Haustür liegt. Der geplante Windpark sollte nördlich der Insel Borkum, zwischen den beiden Hauptrouten der internationalen Seehandelsschifffahrt, der nördlichen German Bight Western Approach und der südlichen Terschelling-German Bight, liegen. Anders als an Land konnten die Offshore-Windenergie-Pioniere für dieses Gebiet auf keine exakten Winddaten zurückgreifen. Es lagen beim BSH nur Windmessungen von Feuerschiffen unmittelbar über der Wasseroberfläche vor, die Windexperten dann auf entsprechende Höhen hochrechneten. Mit ihren optimistischen Prognosen für den Standort vor Borkum lagen sie ziemlich richtig, wie die späteren, ab 2003 beginnenden Windmessungen auf der Forschungsplattform FINO 1 ergaben. Auf dem dortigen Windmast ist in 100 Metern Höhe am Rande des heutigen Testfeldes von

stimulus was provided particularly from the motherland of wind energy – Denmark. The Danes had already set up the very first offshore wind farm in the Baltic Sea (Vindeby) in 1991 with a rated power of five megawatts; Tunø Knob (Kattegatt), the second offshore project, followed in 1995, likewise with a rated capacity of five megawatts. And at the same time, other larger projects were in their advanced stages: the aesthetically pleasing project, Middelgrunden, with its 20 wind turbines and a total of 40 megawatts directly off Copenhagen as well as Horns Rev with a planned capacity of 160 megawatts in the North Sea. There was great astonishment in the air, sometimes even greater scepticism. Nevertheless, the subject of 'offshore' was becoming firmly engrained into the minds of the sector.

It all began in East Friesland

If you are searching for the origins of alpha ventus you will first find yourself in Leer. It all began in this East Friesian town – everything that was to actually become reality ten years later. In 1997, Ingo de Buhr, electrical engineer and enthusiastic entrepreneur in all matters involving renewable energies, founded the company Prokon Nord Energiesysteme GmbH in his birthplace, with three employees. It quickly made a name for itself with various wind energy projects. The company now has over 400 employees. His determination and persistence enabled de Buhr to develop one wind farm after the other on land. Others would have been satisfied with this successful business, but not de Buhr: the son of a ship's captain wanted to go further. He's one of those people who is constantly looking for new challenges. In fact he probably needs them. What could have been more obvious than to start developing his own offshore wind farm at sea?

To do so, Ingo de Buhr and his employees had to start from scratch. There weren't even publicly available maps of the North and Baltic Seas to fall back on, which would have provided detailed information on the seabed conditions, water depths, currents, mean tidal ranges, shipping routes and wind conditions. Therefore, Prokon Nord had to make a special application to the German Federal Maritime and Hydrographic Agency (BSH) for permission to make copies of the nautical maps. In order to gain a better and more practical understanding of the subject matter, these German offshore pioneers travelled from Leer to the Swedish offshore wind farm Utgrunden between Kalmar and the island Oland. The project was built by the German subsidiary of Enron Wind, later acquired by General Electric. Some years later the wind farm was handed over to the energy company Vattenfall. Then, after numerous visits, consultations and extensive analysis of the nautical maps, de Buhr and his fellow pioneers finally chose a section of the sea that was, in fact, more or less directly in front of their East Friesian front door. The planned wind farm was to be set up to the north of the island of Borkum, between two busy international maritime shipping routes: to the north, the German Bight Western Approach and to the south, Terschelling-German Bight. In contrast to onshore developments, these offshore wind energy pathfinders had no exact, useable data on the real wind conditions in this area. The BSH merely had wind measurements available from lightships measured directly above the water surface, which the wind experts then had to extrapolate to the respective heights. However, they were fairly accurate with their optimistic predictions for the site off Borkum, as was found later on the research platform FINO 1, which started measuring the winds in 2003. The wind measurement-mast registered an average

alpha ventus eine Windgeschwindigkeit von durchschnittlich etwas mehr als zehn Metern pro Sekunde registriert worden. Zum Vergleich: Gute Standorte am küstennahen Festland kommen auf rund sieben Meter pro Sekunde.

„Wir waren die ersten, die ein solches Projekt außerhalb der Zwölf-Seemeilen-Zone planten", sagt der Mittvierziger de Buhr und zieht dabei tief an einer Zigarette. „Wir haben uns die gesamte Küstenlandschaft und das Wattenmeer angeguckt und kamen zum Ergebnis, dass jede Planung südlich der Verkehrstrennungsgebiete nicht wirklich machbar ist."

Es bleibt zwar sein Geheimnis, wann genau er sich für den Standort mit dem selbstkreierten Namen „Borkum West" 45 Kilometer vor Borkum entschieden hat. Doch muss es auf jeden Fall vor Ende September 1999 gewesen sein, weil er in diesem Monat zum ersten Mal das Hamburger Bundesamt für Seeschifffahrt und Hydrographie (BSH) aufsuchte. Er legte seine erste grobe Projektskizze dem Juristen Christian Dahlke vor. Der heutige Leiter des Referats M5 „Ordnung des Meeres" war kurz vorher von der Wasser- und Schifffahrtsdirektion Süd in Würzburg zur Hamburger BSH gewechselt. Dahlke hatte die Leitung eines Referats beim BSH übernommen, das sich mit juristischen Fragen und seerechtlichen Angelegenheiten in der so genannten deutschen Ausschließlichen Wirtschaftszone (AWZ) beschäftigte. Dabei ist die AWZ völkerrechtlich erst seit dem Inkrafttreten des UN-Seerechtübereinkommens im Jahr 1995 ein international anerkanntes Meeresgebiet, über dessen wirtschaftliche Nutzung die jeweiligen Anrainerstaaten und eben auch Deutschland seither bestimmen können. Die AWZ erstreckt sich von der Zwölf-Seemeilen-Zone bis 200 Seemeilen aufs Meer. Die AWZ ist historisch betrachtet eine expansive Fortführung maritimer Einflusssphären: Im frühen 20. Jahrhundert gab es die Drei-Seemeilen-Zone; das war die Distanz, die eine Kanonenkugel fliegen konnte. 1982 wurde die Zwölf-Seemeilen-Zone in das internationale Seerechtsübereinkommen aufgenommen. Als vorläufigen Schlusspunkt der zivilisatorischen Expansion auf dem Meer ist nun die AWZ mit 200 Seemeilen Ausdehnung in den Seekarten eingezeichnet. Dieses Seegebiet gehört zwar nicht zum hoheitlichen Staatsgebiet, doch verfügt der jeweilige Küstenstaat über eine ganze Reihe souveräner Nutzungsrechte: traditionell für die Fischerei und für den Bergbau sowie für die Öl- und Gasnutzung und seit Kurzem eben auch für die Stromgewinnung aus Windenergie. Die Bundesrepublik erklärte ihre AWZ in Nord- und Ostsee am 1. Januar 1995: 28.600 Quadratkilometer in der Nordsee und 4.500 Quadratkilometer in der Ostsee. Wohl nur die wenigsten ahnten zur Jahrtausendwende, dass die anfänglich übersichtliche, blau-monochrome Seekarte der AWZ innerhalb von nur 15 Jahren mit inzwischen weit über 30 geplanten Offshore-Windenergie-Projekten komplexe, ja fast expressionistisch anmutende Strukturen annehmen würde.

Wahrscheinlich auch Dahlke nicht. Doch kaum war sein Büro mit Blick auf die Elbe vollständig eingerichtet und die Gasleitung Europipe II von Norwegen quer durch die Nordsee in juristischer Hinsicht abgeschlossen, da brach mit immer neuen Anträgen für Offshore-Windenergieprojekte eine wahre Flut über seinen Arbeitstisch ein. Auf diesen Ansturm war die Behörde einfach nicht vorbereitet.

Eifrig geplant wurde nicht nur in der Nordsee, sondern auch in der Ostsee. An erster Stelle sind die Projekte Baltic I und Kriegers Flak zu nennen. Schon 1997 befasste sich eine interministerielle Arbeitsgruppe der mecklenburgischen Landesregierung mit Voruntersuchungen für Baltic I, dessen Standort sich innerhalb der Zwölf-Seemeilen-Zone

wind speed of just over ten metres per second at a height of 100 metres on the edge of what is today the alpha ventus test field. As a comparison, good coastal locations on the German mainland only get around seven metres per second.

"We were the first to plan such a project outside the 12-nautical-mile zone" says the mid-forty year-old de Buhr drawing deeply on his cigarette. "We had looked at the whole coastal landscape and the Wadden Sea region and came to the conclusion that any plans south of the Traffic Separation Zone were not feasible."

It remains his personal secret when exactly they decided on the location and the name they gave it of 'Borkum West', 45 kilometres off Borkum. However, this must have been before the end of September 1999, because it was in this month that he went for the first time to the Hamburg Federal Maritime and Hydrographic Agency (BSH) where he presented his draft project plans to lawyer Christian Dahlke, Head of Unit 'M5 – Management of the Oceans. At the time he had just moved from the 'Water and Shipping Directorate, South' in Würzburg to the BSH. Dahlke had become head of a unit that handles legal questions and maritime law matters within the German Exclusive Economic Zone (EEZ).

The EEZ only became an internationally-recognized nautical area under international law when the UN Convention on the Law of the Sea came into force in 1995. This has since enabled the respective countries bordering it, including Germany, to determine its economic exploitation. The EEZ stretches from the 12-nautical-mile zone to 200 nautical miles out at sea. Seen from a historical perspective, the EEZ is a huge extension of maritime spheres of influence. In the early 20th century there was the 3-nautical-mile zone, which corresponded to the range of a cannon ball. In 1982 the 12-nautical-mile zone was included under the Convention on the Law of the Sea. The end, for now, of civilization's spread onto the seas is the inclusion of the EEZ into the sea charts, with its range of over 200 nautical miles. This maritime area may not be a part of the sovereign state; however, the respective coastal country has numerous rights to its exploitation, traditionally for fishing and mining as well as for oil and gas exploration. Most recently, this has come to include the generation of electricity from wind power. The Federal Republic of Germany declared its EEZ in the North and Baltic Sea on 1st January, 1995: 28,600 square kilometres of the North Sea and 4,500 square kilometres of the Baltic Sea. Only a few, however, could have imagined at the turn of the century that what was initially a plain blue nautical chart of the EEZ would now, within only 15 years, display more than 30 planned offshore wind energy projects in a complex arrangement with an almost expressionist feel.

Dahlke probably didn't either. Nevertheless, he had only just finished setting up his office with a view over the River Elbe, and the gas pipeline Europipe II from Norway across the North Sea had just been legally finalized, when more and more applications for offshore wind energy projects started flooding onto his desk. The Agency was just not prepared for this rush.

There were busy plans not only for the North Sea, but also for the Baltic. Deserving of first mention here are the projects Baltic I and Kriegers Flak. As early as 1997, an inter-ministerial Working group of the German Federal State government of Mecklenburg-Western Pomerania was working on preliminary studies for the Baltic I site, which is located within the 12-nautical-mile zone to the north of the Fischland-Darß-Zingst peninsula. This project is a prime example of how long-

Der Prototyp der REpower 5M wird im Industriegebiet von Brunsbüttel aufgebaut und geht im November 2004 ans Netz.
The 5M REpower prototype was installed in the Brunsbüttel industrial zone and went online in November 2004.

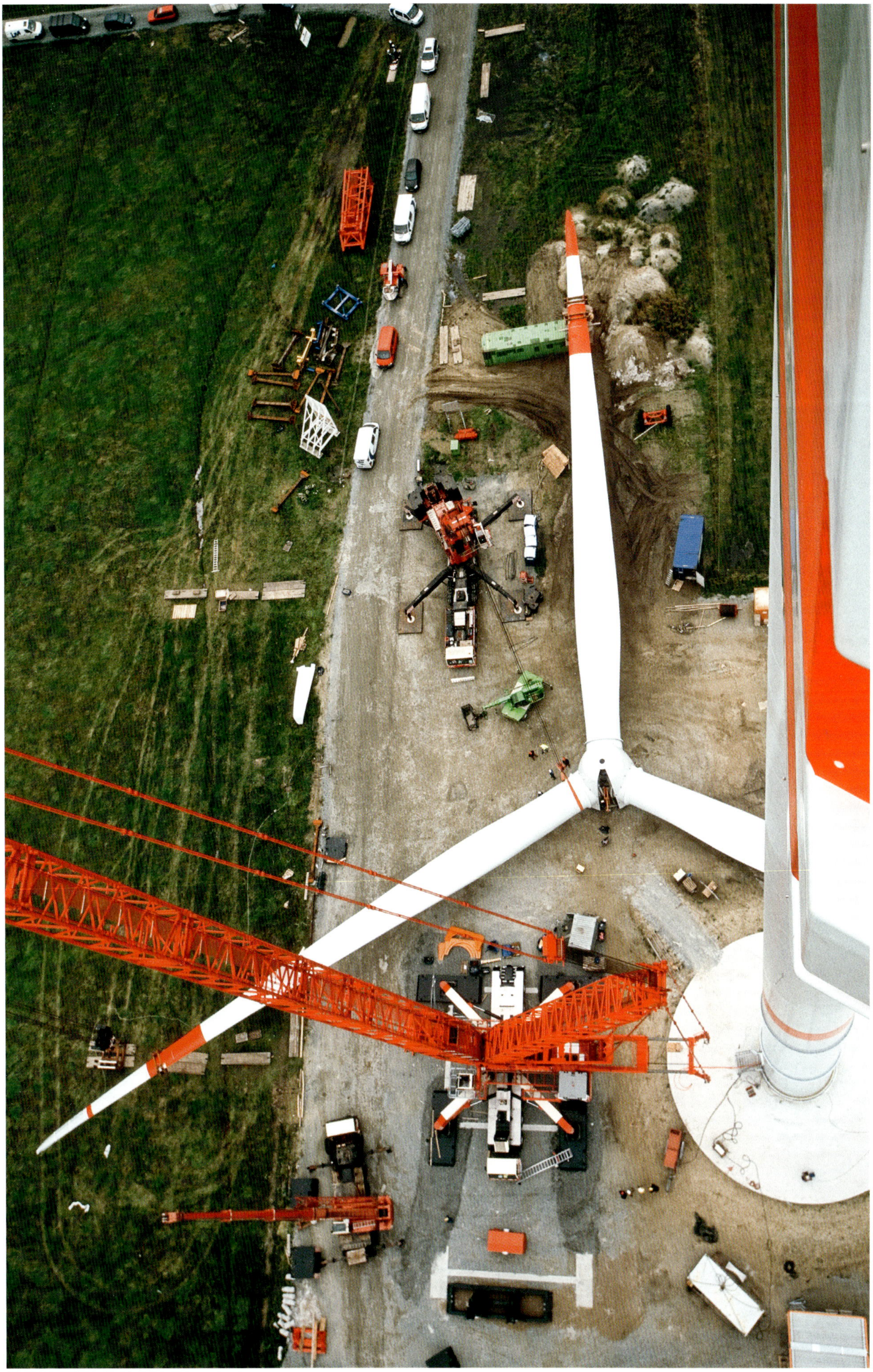

nördlich der Halbinsel Fischland-Darß-Zingst befindet. Wie langwierig und vielschichtig sich ein Genehmigungsprozess für einen küstennahen Offshore-Windpark gestalteten konnte, zeigte sich exemplarisch an diesem Projekt. Es bedurfte umfangreicher Umweltverträglichkeitsuntersuchungen, eines Raumordnungsverfahrens des Landes Mecklenburg-Vorpommern und eines Verfahrens nach dem Bundesimmissionsschutzgesetz (BImSchG). Und so dauerte es fast ein Jahrzehnt, bis im März 2006 alle Genehmigungen auf dem Tisch lagen. Etwas schneller kam der Projektantrag für Kriegers Flak über die Ziellinie: Im April 2005 erteilte die BSH der damaligen Antragstellerin, der Offshore Ostsee Wind AG (OOW AG) in Börgerende, für das in der AWZ der Ostsee geplante Projekt die Genehmigungen für den Windpark und die Kabeltrasse.

Neue Nutzungsansprüche auf dem Meer

Der Verwaltungsjurist Dahlke sah sich also sowohl in der Nord- wie auch in der Ostsee einem vehement artikulierten Nutzungsbegehren in der AWZ gegenüber. Doch konnte er auf keinerlei Erfahrungen innerhalb seiner Behörde zurückgreifen. Es gab keine ausgetretenen Rechtspfade, geschweige denn einen (AWZ)-Raumordnungsplan und schon gar keine anwendbaren Maßstäbe für ein Genehmigungsverfahren in diesem Raum. Windernte auf hoher See war schlicht Neuland. Denn die rechtlichen Belange und Pflichten, die innerhalb der Zwölf-Seemeilen-Zone gelten, sind für die AWZ ohne Relevanz. So waren zwar die Grenzen der AWZ völkerrechtlich anerkannt und verbindlich, aber innerhalb dieser Grenzen war die AWZ gegen Ende der neunziger Jahre ein mehr oder weniger rechtsfreier Raum. Einfach aus dem Grund, so Dahlke, weil bis dahin niemand an diesen Raum oberhalb des Meeresbodens „exklusive, ortsfeste" Nutzungsansprüche gestellt hatte. Und wo keine „ortsfeste" Nutzung, da gibt es auch keine Verteidigung anderer Interessen, wie die der Fischerei, der Seeschifffahrt, des Militärs, des Flugverkehrs und, ganz wichtig, des Naturschutzes, der sich vor allem um den Bestand der Seevögel und Schweinswale sorgt.

Genau mit dieser ortsfesten Nutzung, und zwar mit Windenergieanlagen, sah sich Dahlke nun ab Spätsommer 1999 konfrontiert. Doch statt auszuweichen oder aufzuschieben, fackelte er nicht lange und formulierte die ersten Grundsätze eines zukünftigen Genehmigungsprozesses. „Er hat schnell reagiert", lobt auch Ingo de Buhr das Wirken des unkonventionell und pragmatisch handelnden BSH-Beamten, der sich in seiner Behörde anfänglich fast im Alleingang um diese Fragen kümmerte. So hat Dahlke dem unregulierten Raum auf hoher See Schritt für Schritt eine inhaltliche Struktur verpasst. Allerdings bedauert er im Rückblick, dass wegen des steten Zeit- und Handlungsdruckes nie ein rechtlich abgesichertes, den Rechtsfrieden stiftendes System aus einem Guss entwickelt und konstituiert wurde. Dieses Manko trifft insbesondere für alle Netzanbindungsfragen: Kabeltrassen, Netzkorridore und Netzknoten zu. „Es ist einfach misslich, dass die Genehmigung von Windpark und Windparkanschluss nicht in einem Verfahren gebündelt ist." Zudem gab es nie einen AWZ-„Masterplan", der die Nutzungsansprüche Einzelner mit denen gemeinschaftlicher Interessen geregelt hätte. Daher will Dahlke im Nachhinein auch nicht klüger sein als damals. „Es wäre nicht sonderlich clever gewesen, eine Infrastruktur zu entwickeln, ohne zu wissen, wo eigentlich die Planer ihre Projekte hinsetzen wollen und was eigentlich an Land mit dem Stromnetz passiert."

winded and multi-faceted a licencing process for an offshore wind farm close to the German coastline can be. It required comprehensive environmental analysis, a spatial planning process from the state of Mecklenburg-Western Pomerania and a Federal Emissions Control Ordinance investigation. It took therefore almost a decade until all the licences were granted in March 2006. The project application for Kriegers Flak, situated in the EEZ, crossed the finishing line somewhat more quickly: in April 2005 the BSH granted the applicant, the Offshore Ostsee Wind AG (OOW AG) from Börgerende, a licence for their planned project within the EEZ in the Baltic Sea, approving the wind farm and the cable route.

New exploitation claims at sea

Since the late 1990s, the public service lawyer Dahlke was increasingly confronted with massive applications to exploit the EEZ, both in the North Sea and also the Baltic Sea. However, at the time there was no experience at all in Germany with such requests within his authority for him to fall back on. There was no well-trodden legal pathway, let alone an (EEZ) spatial planning strategy, and no usable precedents for a licencing process at all in this area. Harvesting wind energy on the high seas was simply virgin territory. The legal requirements and obligations that are valid within the twelve-nautical-mile zone had no relevance for the EEZ. This meant that the borders of the EEZ had been legally recognized and were binding under international law, but as Dahlke puts it, at the end of the 'nineties within these borders the EEZ was more or less without legal jurisdiction because up until then no-one had made 'exclusive' claims to any definite area above the seabed. And where there is no utilization of any specific area, there is no defence either of other interests such as fishing, shipping, military, aviation – and crucially here, nature conservation, which in particular should protect sea birds and harbour porpoises.

It was precisely this exploitation of specific locations, namely with offshore wind turbines, with which Dahlke was confronted starting in late summer 1999. Nevertheless, instead of dodging the issue or putting it off, he did not waste a minute and worded the first basic principles for a future licencing process. "He reacted quickly", is Ingo de Buhr's praise for the unconventional and pragmatic action of the BSH civil servant who initially handled these questions almost on his own within his Agency. In this way, Dahlke created a sound regulatory framework for these open sea areas step by step, which until then had not been regulated. However, in retrospect he regrets that due to a permanent lack of time and the pressure to act, he never developed and put into place a legally sound, coherent juridical framework in one go. This shortcoming particularly affects all matters involving the grid connection – cable routes, transmission line corridors and grid nodes. "It's simply an awkward fact that the licence for a wind farm and the wind-farm grid connection have not been bundled together into a single procedure." Moreover, there has never been an "EEZ master plan" that regulates individual companies' claims to exploitation in accordance with the common interest. That's why Dahlke does not pretend to be any wiser now than before. "It would not have been particularly clever to develop an infrastructure without knowing where the developers intended to locate their projects and what was going to happen with the electricity grid on land."

It's a different matter nowadays. "The grid operators, transpower and Vattenfall, should now draw up a master plan with the support of the

Heute sieht das anders aus. „Die Netzbetreiber transpower und Vattenfall müssen nun, unterstützt von der Bundesnetzagentur, einen Masterplan erstellen", fordert Dahlke. Unabhängig von dieser noch offenen Frage zum Netzausbau ist die im Herbst 2009 in Kraft getretene Raumordnung für die AWZ ein Meilenstein für eine „nachhaltige Raumentwicklung, um die sozialen und wirtschaftlichen Ansprüche an den Raum mit seinen ökologischen Funktionen endlich auch systematisch in Einklang zu bringen".

Unterdessen hält das Nutzungsbegehren auf den Meeresraum offenbar ungebrochen an. Es klingt unglaublich und ist doch wahr: „In vielen Gebieten der AWZ ist es richtig eng geworden, da feilschen wir um 50 oder 100 Meter von virtuellen Windmühlenstandorten des 21. oder 22. Windparks, die hoffentlich noch in der nächsten Dekade oder in der übernächsten entstehen", räumt Dahlke ein. Auf eine erteilte Offshore-Genehmigung kommen vier neue Projektanträge. „Das ist die Höchststrafe", feixt Dahlke und stellt aber im gleichen Atemzug nüchtern klar: „Das Meer bleibt das Meer, die Offshore-Nutzung ist keine Verlängerung der Landnutzung. Auf dem Meer haben deshalb auch Operationen, die nicht maritim sind, nichts zu suchen. Schnellrestaurants gehören nicht aufs Meer. Im Prinzip ist das Meer sowieso ein Raum, wo der Mensch nur Gast ist. Wenn er da etwas einräumt, soll er es auch ausräumen."

Der Chef der BSH-Genehmigungsverfahren nimmt den Naturschutz sehr ernst. „Wir haben bereits im Jahr 2002 ein Standarduntersuchungskonzept für die Umweltverträglichkeitsstudien vorgelegt. Das hat die ökologische Debatte über den Einfluss von Windenergieanlagen im Rahmen des Genehmigungsprozesses versachlicht und viele Diskussionen verkürzt", freut sich Dahlke. Um die komplexe Materie zu verstehen, hat er sich im Laufe der Jahre in viele naturschutzfachliche Themen hineingearbeitet, beispielsweise in die Ornithologie. „Das ist phantastisch, was die Vögel können", begeistert sich der Jurist über die Welt der Zweiflügler und hält aus dem Stegreif ein Referat über deren Brut- und Flugeigenschaften.

Er erinnert sich noch gut an die ersten Antragskonferenzen in den Jahren 2001 bis 2003, als das Thema Meeresumwelt zu nimmer endenden Diskussionen führte. „Da wurden Redeschlachten geführt, die sich von morgens bis in den späten Abend zogen", blickt der Jurist zurück. Dass die Genehmigungsverfahren in der AWZ, deren Fläche seit September 2005 zu rund einem Drittel unter Naturschutz steht, nicht nur Alibi-Veranstaltungen sind, bewies das BSH mit der Ablehnung zweier Projekte in der Ostsee. Sie scheiterten, weil ornithologische Fachgutachten ermittelten, dass an den Projektstandorten „Adlergrund" und „Pommersche Bucht" sowohl Trauer-, Samt- als auch Eiderenten in ihren von der Flora-Fauna-Habitat (FFH)-Richtlinie geschützten Beständen bedroht gewesen wären, da sie sensitiv mit der Folge von Habitatsverlust auf die Errichtung von Windparks hätten reagieren können.

So wurde Dahlke schnell der Herr des Offshore-Verfahrens, das er improvisierend und Stück für Stück erschloss: juristisch, inhaltlich und vor allem verfahrenstechnisch. „Wir haben ein vollkommen neues Antragsverfahren entwickelt", unterstreicht der BSH-Mann, dessen Abteilung inzwischen stetig gewachsen ist. Nicht selten musste Dahlke öffentliche Angriffe ertragen. Bevor das erste Genehmigungsverfahren abgeschlossen war, hatte er sich bereits kursierender Vorwürfe zu erwehren, die ihm persönlich unterstellten, er würde einer flächendeckenden Industrialisierung der Meere zustimmen. Kritik kam vor allem von den Naturschutzverbänden. Und dies, obwohl Dahlke in

Federal Network Agency", Dahlke insists. Notwithstanding this unresolved matter of developing the offshore grid and extending it onshore, the spatial plan that came into effect for the German EEZ in the autumn of 2009 was a milestone on the way to a "sustainable spatial development, in order to finally – and also systematically – accommodate all socio-economic claims to the area with the ecological functions".

And the applications to exploit this area at sea apparently never cease. It may sound incredible but it is true: "It's getting quite crowded in some areas of the EEZ… we end up bartering about 50 or 100 metres of virtual space for wind turbines in the 21st or 22nd wind farm, which will hopefully get built in the next decade – or the one after next", admits Dahlke. For every offshore licence granted he receives four new project applications. "That's the high price you have to pay", he jokes and in the same breath clarifies soberly: "The sea will remain the sea. Offshore exploitation is not simply the extension of exploitation on land. Therefore, there should be no operations at sea that are not maritime ones. There's no room for fast-food restaurants or the like on the open sea. Basically, the sea is a place where human beings are only guests anyway. If we put anything there then we also have to clean it up."

The head of the BSH licencing procedures takes nature conservation very seriously. "As early as 2002 we presented a standard procedure for environmental studies. This gave the ecological debate on the impact of wind turbines a sound and factual base within the framework of the licencing process and thus cut short many of the discussions", Dahlke is pleased to say. In order to understand the complex subject matter he has learned a lot over the years about many of the nature protection issues, for example ornithology. "It's fantastic, what birds can do", enthuses the lawyer about the world of these two-winged creatures and gives an impromptu talk on breeding and flying patterns.

He can still remember well the first application conferences in the years 2001 to 2003, when the subject of the marine environment led to never-ending discussions. The lawyer looks back and says: "They ended up in a war of words that lasted from the morning until late in the evening". The fact that the licencing procedures for the EEZ, around a third of which has been a nature reserve since September 2005, were not just for 'show' was proven when the BSH rejected two projects in the Baltic Sea. They failed because ornithological studies ascertained that the project locations 'Adlergrund' and 'Pommersche Bucht' would have threatened stocks of black scoters, velvet scoters and eider ducks, all protected by the EU Birds and Habitats Directive. The birds would have reacted sensitively to the construction of the wind farms, the consequence of which could have been the loss of their habitat.

Dahlke quickly became 'lord' of the offshore licencing procedures which he established, initially improvising and then developed further, step by step – in legal, content and in particular procedural terms. "We developed a completely new application process", emphasizes the BSH man. Nevertheless, it was not uncommon for Dahlke to be the subject of public attacks: even before the first application process had even been completed he had had to fend off criticism, in particular from nature conservation organizations, suggesting that he would personally approve a complete industrialization of the sea. The attacks came although Dahlke had insisted on a specific environmental impact assessment within the licencing processes, which would provide the best possible proof of whether an offshore wind farm is really environmentally safe at the site where it is planned.

Im Dezember 2004 ging der erste
Prototyp der Multibrid M5000 ans Netz.
Die zweite Maschine dieses Typs
wurde zwei Jahre später in Bremerhaven auf einem Tripod errichtet.
In December 2004 the first prototype
of the M5000 was connected to
the grid. Two years later the second
machine of this type was installed
on a tripod near Bremerhaven.

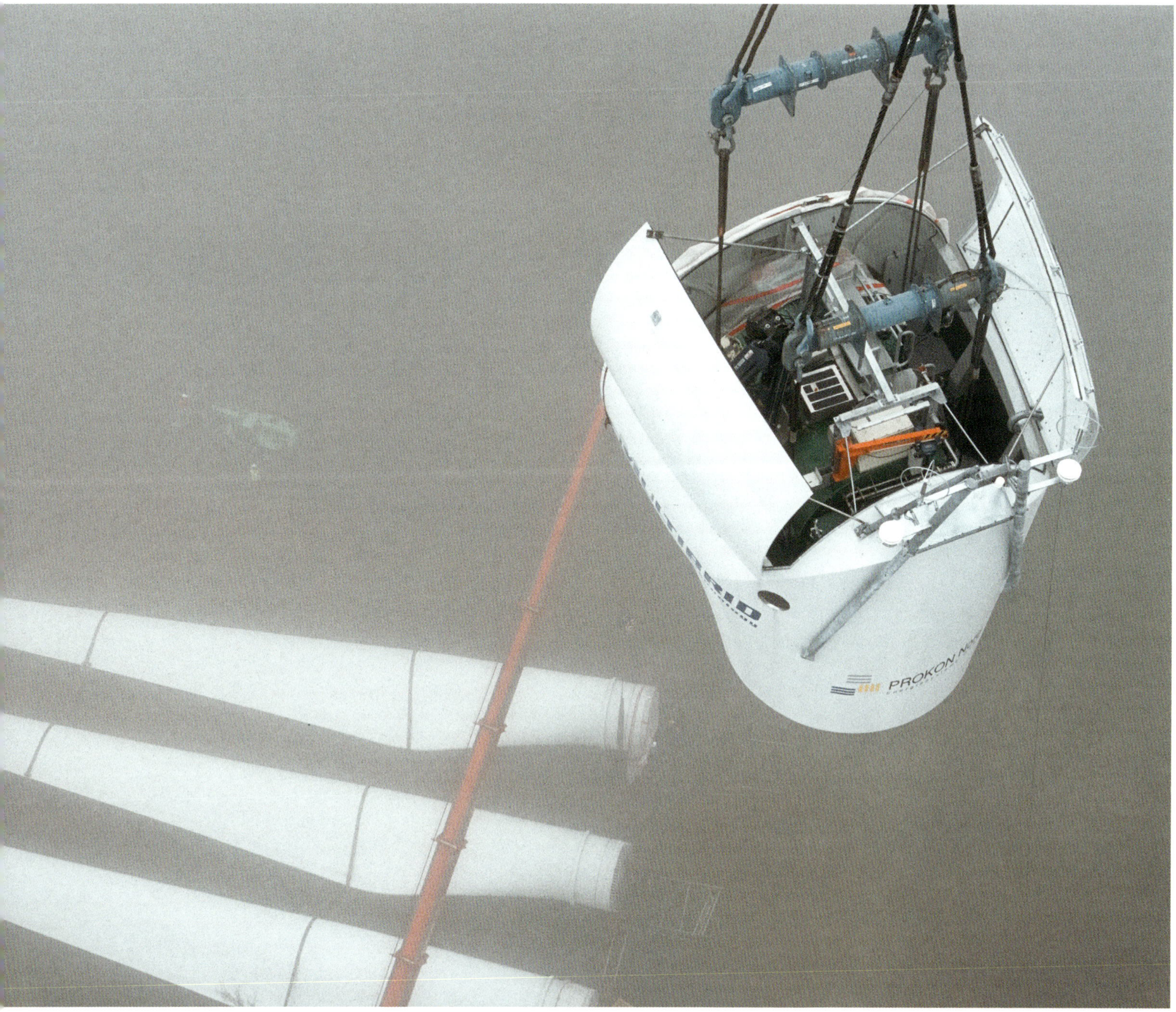
PROKON
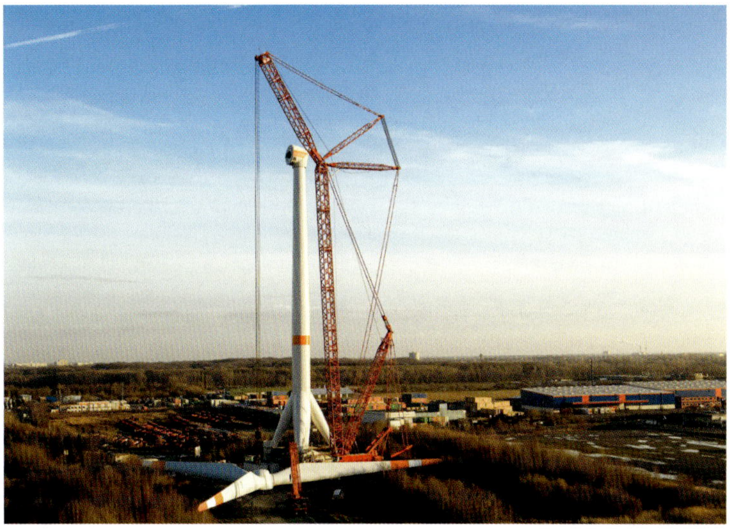
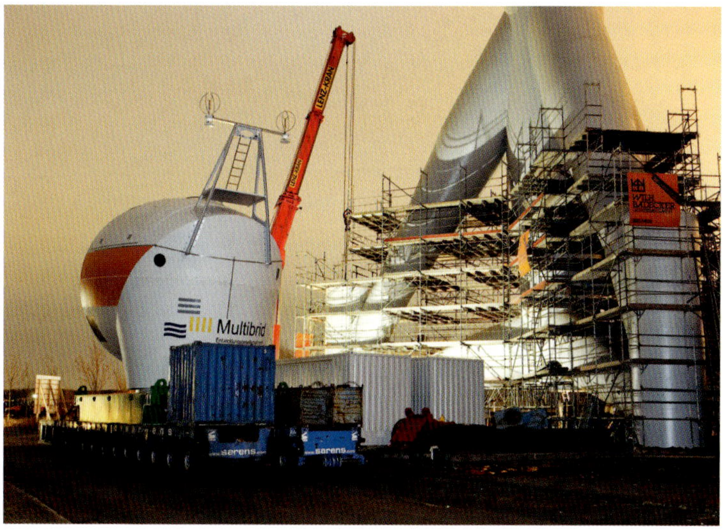
Multibrid

seinem Verfahren eine dezidierte Umweltverträglichkeitsprüfung einforderte, die bestmöglich nachweist, ob Offshore-Windparks an ihren geplanten Standorten tatsächlich verträglich sind oder eben nicht. Während Dahlke in Hamburg in Papieren wühlte, die Seeanlagenverordnung studierte und überarbeitete und Raumplanungsakten hin und her wälzte, erledigte Ingo de Buhr in Leer seine Hausaufgaben. Er machte vor, was später all die anderen Projekt-Büros nach ihm auch taten. Er gab ein Windgutachten beim Deutschen Windenergie-Institut (DEWI GmbH) in Auftrag, beauftragte den Germanischen Lloyd mit einer Schifffahrtsrisiko-Analyse und führte kontroverse Gespräche mit Fischereiverbänden. Parallel dazu unternahm sein Prokon-Nord-Kollege, der Biologe Freerk Nanninga, aufwändige Zählungen von Meeressäugern und Vögeln; zudem untersuchte das Alfred-Wegener-Institut die Fischwelt und die Lebewesen, die auf und im sandigen Meeresgrund (Benthos-Habitat) des zwölf Quadratkilometer großen Projektgebietes von Borkum West leben. Nebenher kümmerte sich Prokon Nord bei den zuständigen Stellen des Landes Niedersachsen um die zwingend erforderliche Kabeltrasse ans Festland. Während die Netzanbindung noch ungeklärt war, erteilte das BSH den Pionieren von Prokon Nord nach der Antragskonferenz, weiteren Gesprächsterminen und eingehenden Prüfungen der vorgelegten Dokumente im Herbst 2001, an einem in anderer Hinsicht geschichtsträchtigen Tag, dem 9. November – als erstem Projekt überhaupt –, eine Baugenehmigung für einen Offshore-Windpark: Borkum West.

Kurz darauf, im Januar 2002, kam Rückenwind aus Berlin. Die rot-grüne Bundesregierung veröffentlichte ihr später mehrfach bestätigtes und grundsätzlich noch heute gültiges Strategiepapier „Zur Windenergienutzung auf See". Unter der Überschrift „Zielsetzung" war zu lesen, dass „unter den gegenwärtigen Bedingungen auf den aus heutiger Sicht voraussichtlich verfügbaren Flächen in der Startphase (erste Baustufen von Windparks) bis 2006 insgesamt mindestens 500 Megawatt und mittelfristig, bis 2010, 2.000 bis 3.000 Megawatt Leistung zur Windenergienutzung auf See erreicht werden. Langfristig, das heißt bis 2025 bzw. 2030, sind bei Erreichen der Wirtschaftlichkeit etwa 20.000 bis 25.000 Megawatt installierter Leistung möglich (Küstenmeer und AWZ). Dazu ist erforderlich, dass Investoren von Offshore-Windparks und die Stromwirtschaft die Voraussetzungen für den Transport von offshore erzeugtem Strom in der Größenordnung schaffen (ausreichende Seekabel-Kapazitäten, Anbindung an das Festlandnetz, gegebenenfalls Netzkapazitäten an Land)."

Es kam anders als gedacht. Ganz anders. Eigentlich wollten die Ostfriesen von Prokon Nord schon 2003 mit dem Aufbau der Offshore-Anlagen beginnen. Doch obwohl Ingo de Buhr am 30. April 2002 von der Bezirksregierung Weser-Ems eine positive landesplanerische Feststellung für die Kabeltrasse erhielt, regte sich zunächst großer Widerstand an der Küste. Die Inselgemeinde Borkum und einige Fischer legten Klage gegen die Baugenehmigung der BSH ein. Später wurde diese mangels Klagebefugnis allerdings vom Verwaltungsgericht abgewiesen.

Auch auf den anderen Ebenen ging es nur zäh voran. Erst im Januar 2004 wurde dem Antrag auf Befreiung vom Bauverbot für die Kabeltrasse im niedersächsischen Wattenmeer stattgegeben. Gleichzeitig liefen die naturschutzfachlichen Begleituntersuchungen in diesem sensiblen Naturraum. Schließlich erhielt Prokon Nord im November des gleichen Jahres die Genehmigung, im Wattenmeer ein Kabel verlegen zu dürfen.

Es war ein Genehmigungsmarathon, der viel Zeit und sehr viel Geld kostete. Ähnlich ging es anderen Offshore-Projekten, die zwischen-

While Dahlke was fighting with the paperwork in Hamburg, studying and reworking the German Marine Facilities Ordinance and opening and closing the maritime spatial planning files, Ingo de Buhr was doing his homework in Leer. He started doing what all other project developers were also doing after him. He commissioned an Offshore Wind Resource Assessment from the German Wind Energy Institute (DEWI), commissioned Hamburg-based Germanischer Lloyd with a Shipping Risk Analysis and had numerous in-depth discussions with fishermen and their associations. At the same time his Prokon Nord colleague, biologist Freerk Nanninga, conducted numerous counts of sea mammals and birds. Moreover, the Alfred-Wegener-Institut investigated the situation of the fish and other beings living on and in the sandy seabed (benthos habitat) of the twelve-square-kilometre project area of Borkum West. As well as this, Prokon Nord worked with the respective authorities of the German Federal State of Lower Saxony, who had to arrange for the urgently necessary cable route to the mainland. In the autumn of 2001 the grid connection issue was still unresolved. Nevertheless, following the conclusion of the Application Conference in which an in-depth examination of the documents had been presented, on the historic day of 9th November (also for other reasons) the BSH finally granted the pioneers from Prokon Nord construction approval for the first-ever project of all: Borkum West.

Shortly after this, in January 2002 they benefited from a tailwind from Berlin. The Social Democrats – Green Party coalition government officially adopted an offshore strategy paper 'On the use of wind energy at sea', which was later confirmed and received widespread approval by subsequent governments. Essentially it is still valid today. Under the chapter heading of title 'Objectives' it states that: "under the current conditions and in the areas that will be presumably available in the initial phase (for the initial construction stage), from today's perspective a total of at least 500 megawatts of installed capacity can be achieved from wind energy exploitation at sea by 2006, and in the medium-term, 2,000 to 3,000 megawatts by 2010. In the long term this will mean that, by 2025 or 2030, when economical feasibility has been achieved, about 20,000 to 25,000 megawatts of installed capacity will be possible (coastal waters and EEZ). To do this, it is necessary that investors in offshore wind farms and the electricity industry create the preconditions for the transport of such amounts of offshore-generated electricity (sufficient sea cable capacities, connection to the mainland grid, if necessary creation of additional grid capacities on land)".

But things did not turn out at all as expected. In fact, the East Friesians at Prokon Nord wanted to start assembling the offshore turbines in 2003. However, although Ingo de Buhr received a positive State Planning Declaration for the cable route to the coast from the Weser-Ems regional government on 30th April 2002, there was initially a great amount of opposition on the coast. The island community of Borkum and some fishermen filed a complaint against the building approval issued by the BSH. This was, however, later rejected by an administrative tribunal due to insubstantiality.

It was also hard going in other ways. It wasn't until January 2004 that the application to lift the construction ban in Lower Saxony's Wadden Sea region was approved, thus opening up the desired cable route. At the same time there were accompanying nature-conservation analyses of this sensitive area. Prokon Nord finally received the licence in November of the same year to lay a cable across the Wadden Sea.

It had been a marathon of consultation and consent and had taken a lot of time and cost a lot of money. It was a similar situation for other

zeitlich beim BSH ihre Anträge gestellt hatten. Viele waren beflügelt von der Aussicht auf große Projekte, die an Land nicht zu realisieren waren. Eine durch den Verband Deutscher Maschinen- und Anlagenbau (VDMA) in Auftrag gegebene Studie prognostizierte im Bereich Offshore-Windenergie Investitionen von knapp 50 Milliarden Euro. „Viele mittelständische Projektierer sind losgestiefelt und haben geglaubt, Parks mit 80 und mehr Anlagen selber betreiben zu können", analysiert Norbert Giese, heutiger Direktor der Business Unit Offshore der REpower Systems AG, die damalige wirtschaftliche Machbarkeit der geplanten Projekte. „Dabei entspricht ein Offshore-Windenergiepark mit 80 Anlagen ungefähr dem Investitionsvolumen eines 800 Megawatt großen Kohlekraftwerks. Diese Tatsache ist unterschätzt worden, genauso wie das Projektmanagement auf See." Das Projektvolumen hat nämlich weitreichende Konsequenzen für die Finanzierung. Nicht ohne Grund haben viele mittelständische Projektfirmen später entweder große strategische Partner mit ins Boot geholt oder sogar ihre Offshore-Pläne an die Großen im Energiegeschäft veräußert. Für Giese, der lange Zeit den Vorsitz der Windkraftanlagenhersteller im VDMA Fachverband Power Systems innehatte, ist ganz klar: „Offshore ist keine Verlängerung der Onshore-Aktivitäten. Es ist eine eigenständige erneuerbare Energieform." Insofern steht die Windenergie-Branche vor einem Paradigmenwechsel. Waren es in den Anfangszeiten vor allem die privaten, dezentralen Betreiber von Windenergieanlagen, die die Szene beherrschten, drängen jetzt große Konzerne, unter anderen auch die klassischen Energieversorger, in die Offshore-Windenergie. Dieser neuen Situation müsse sich auch der Bundesverband WindEnergie (BWE) öffnen, so Giese weiter. Diese Erkenntnis brauche aber Zeit, sie durchdringe erst langsam die Windenergie-Branche.

Das Offshore-Thema stellte und stellt aber nicht nur Planer, Projektierer, Betreiber und Verbände vor vollkommen neuen Aufgaben, sondern auch die Hersteller von Offshore-Turbinen. Wie schwierig sich der Start in diese neue Phase gerade für die Hersteller darstellte, zeigte sich insbesondere in den Jahren 2003 bis 2005. Die Herstellerfirmen Enercon, REpower und Multibrid hatten unter großen Anstrengungen ihre ersten 5 Megawatt-Prototypen an den Start gebracht. Doch wo waren potente Auftragnehmer? Wo waren die Partner in der maritimen Wirtschaft, die die Offshore-Windenergie als ein neues Betätigungsfeld erachteten und entsprechende Logistik für den Aufbau auf dem Meer entwickelt hatten und bereitstellen konnten? Darüber hinaus blieb eine Kardinalfrage unbeantwortet: Welche Offshore-Projekte waren überhaupt in greifbarer Nähe, sodass eine ökonomisch vernünftige Planung und Finanzierung für den Bau von neuen Produktionsstraßen und eine auftragsbezogene Fertigung von Multimegawatt-Anlagen möglich gewesen wäre? Während sich in jenen Jahren in Dänemark, den Niederlanden, Schweden und England schon erste Märkte entwickelten, blieb die deutsche Offshore-Szene auf halber Strecke stecken. Ihr fehlten einfach kleine, überschaubare Einstiegsprojekte. Stattdessen plagten sich die Akteure mit endlosen Diskursen über die fehlenden Netzanbindungen und deren potenzielle Finanzierung. Sie diskutierten mit Naturschützern und Tourismus-Managern über den Trassenbau durch das Wattenmeer. Sie stritten mit Experten aus Schifffahrt und Militär über mögliche Kollisionsrisiken für Tanker, Frachter und U-Boote. Und sie blitzten mit ihren Anliegen nicht selten bei Banken und Versicherungen ab, weil diese das Risiko, mit der Windenergie offshore zu gehen, offenbar höher einschätzten, als in Hedgefonds oder auf den Bahamas zu investieren. Zudem gab es

offshore project developments that had, in the meantime, submitted their applications to the BSH. Many had been inspired by the prospects of very large projects that could not have been implemented on land. A study commissioned by the German Engineering Association (VDMA) predicted investments in the offshore wind energy sector of about 50 billion euros. "Numerous SME (small and medium-sized enterprise) project developers had rushed in, believing that they could operate farms themselves with 80 and more turbines", reflects Norbert Giese, today Director of REpower Systems AG's Offshore business unit, on the economic feasibility of the planned projects of the time. "However, an offshore wind farm with 80 turbines corresponds approximately to the volume of investment required for an 800-megawatt coal-fired power station. This fact was underestimated, likewise the challenge of project management at sea. "The size of the projects has far-reaching consequences for financing; there is a reason why many SME developers either got large strategic partners on board, or went with their offshore plans to the big players in the energy sector. If you ask Giese, long-time Chairman of the wind-turbine manufacturer section of VDMA, the reasons are clear: "Offshore is not just an extension of onshore activities. It is a new form of renewable energy of its own." The wind-energy sector was thus faced with a paradigm shift. While in the early stages in particular, small, private and decentralized owners and operators of wind turbines had dominated the scene, it was now the large corporations which were pushing their way into the offshore wind-energy sector, including the classic energy providers. The German Wind Energy Association (BWE) had to adapt to this new situation, continues Giese. However, this took time and the wind-energy sector only slowly realized this.

Offshore wind power placed and still places new demands, not only on the developers, project managers, operators and associations, but also on the manufacturers and suppliers of offshore turbines. It can be seen how difficult the start into this phase was, especially for the manufacturers, by looking in particular at the years 2003 to 2005. The wind turbine manufacturers Enercon, REpower and Multibrid had started to make concerted efforts to get their first 5-megawatt prototypes installed. However, where were the influential customers? And where were the partners in the maritime industry who regarded offshore wind energy as a new business opportunity, having developed and made available the respective logistics for wind-power installations at sea? Moreover, the key question remained unanswered. Which offshore projects at all were close to realisation: those that would allow for economically-viable planning and financing of the new production lines – or those that would result in firm orders for multi-megawatt turbines?

While during this period the first markets had developed in Denmark, the Netherlands, Sweden and England, the German offshore scene had got stuck half-way. There was a clear lack of small, well-defined projects to enter the market. Instead the offshore developers were plagued with endless discussions about the lack of grid connections and their potential financing. They had been discussing the laying of a cable through the Wadden Sea with nature conservationists and tourism managers. They had argued with the experts from the shipping industry and the Navy about possible collision risks for tankers, freighters and submarines. And they had quite frequently and repeatedly been turned away by banks and insurance companies with their plans. Apparently, the financial sector regarded the risk of offshore wind energy as greater than investing in hedge funds on the Bahamas. To make matters worse, at the time the EEG feed-in tariff for electricity

Foto links: Nichts für Menschen mit Höhenangst: Ein Crewmitglied verlässt die Hubinsel JB 114 mit dem „Mannkorb".
Photo left: Not ideal for people with vertigo: a crew member leaves the jack-up barge with the cherry picker.

Jörgen Thiele (li.) forderte auf der 4. Maritimen Konferenz ein deutsches Windenergie-Testfeld. Christian Dahlke (re.) entwickelte das Genehmigungsverfahren für Offshore-Windenergieanlagen.
At the 4th Maritime Conference, Jörgen Thiele (left) called for a German wind energy test field. Christian Dahlke (right) developed an approval procedure for offshore wind farms.

seinerzeit noch keine höheren EEG-Vergütungssätze für Strom aus Offshore-Windenergie und auch das spätere Infrastruktur-Planungsbeschleunigungsgesetz stand noch nicht zur Debatte. Zudem stiegen die Preise für Stahl, Kupfer und andere Rohstoffe stetig höher. Die Situation war vertrackt und die Politik zauderte.

In den Mühlen der Politik

Kanzler Schröder erwähnte in seiner Auftaktrede zur Vierten Maritimen Konferenz in Bremen Ende Januar 2005 die Offshore-Windenergie nicht mit einem Wort. Den etwa 50 Zuhörern aus den Reihen der Windenergie fiel sprichwörtlich die Kinnlade herunter. War das ein Affront gegen die Offshore-Windenergie oder einfach nur ein Versäumnis? Die Windenergie-Akteure hielten trotz der Ignoranz des Kanzlers ihren erstmals im Rahmen dieser Konferenz stattfindenden Workshop „Offshore Windenergie" ab, für den sich im Vorfeld vor allem Ministerialrat Fritz Lücke aus dem schleswig-holsteinischen Wirtschaftsministerium und die Gesellschaft für Meerestechnik (GMT) mit ihrem Vorsitzenden Dr.-Ing. Joachim Schwarz eingesetzt hatten. Das Impulsreferat für den Workshop hielt Jörgen Thiele, Geschäftsführer der Schweriner Maschinenbau GmbH. Als Schlusspunkt forderte Thiele ein deutsches Windenergie-Testfeld im Tiefwasser und fand

from offshore wind energy was not much higher than that for onshore wind, and the subsequent Infrastructure Planning Acceleration Act was not yet on the agenda. Moreover, the prices for steel, copper and other raw materials were rising continually. The situation had gone off track and the politicians were dithering.

The wheel of politics grind slowly

German Chancellor Gerhard Schröder did not mention offshore wind once during his opening speech at the 4th National Maritime Conference in Bremen in late January 2005. The chins of some 50 delegates from the wind-energy sector dropped. Was this an affront to offshore wind energy – or simply an oversight? In spite of this 'faux pas' by the Chancellor, the offshore wind energy community held a separate workshop for the first time on 'Offshore Wind Energy' at the Maritime Conference. In particular, Fritz Lücke, a civil servant from the Schleswig-Holstein Ministry of Economics and Dr.-Ing. Joachim Schwarz, Director of the German Association for Marine Technology (GMT), had put in a lot of effort beforehand to get the workshop going. The keynote speech for the workshop was given by Jörgen Thiele, MD of the Schwerin Maschinenbau (machine toolmaker) company. At the end of his speech Thiele called for a German wind-energy test field in deep waters and received unanimous agreement in the subsequent discussion from the participants of the workshop.

In order to get the results from the small working group effectively represented in the large final meeting organized for that afternoon, Udo Paschedag, Unit Head at the Federal Ministry for the Environment with responsibility for hydropower, wind energy and grid integration of renewable energies, and Jens Eckhoff, Bremen State Senator for Construction, Environment and Transport and host of the event, got together in a back room of the Bremen Congress Centre. In order to rescue what they could they drafted the most important demands of the offshore wind-energy sector. The Bremen Senator wrote down in keywords the essential requirements: 1. Offshore test field; 2. Easier financing; 3. Simplified licencing procedures; 4. Grid connection and extension and 5. Research and development.

These notes provided the mental framework for the rhetorical counterattack, which Jens Eckhoff then delivered in front of the large audience of around 800 representatives from shipyards, shipping companies and port operators. "I was very clear in what I said", remembers Eckhoff. He unflinchingly criticized the Chancellor for not treating offshore seriously. "It is, however, a central task for the Federal Government to coordinate offshore developments", demanded Eckhoff. "That's why a situation just cannot be accepted where German wind-

damit unter den Teilnehmern des Workshops in der anschließenden Diskussion einhelligen Zuspruch.

Um die Ergebnisse des kleinen Arbeitskreises wirkungsvoll in die am Nachmittag angesetzte große Abschlussrunde hineinzutragen, zogen sich Udo Paschedag, Ministerialrat im Bundesumweltministerium und zuständig für das Referat Wasserkraft, Windenergie und Netzintegration der erneuerbaren Energien, und Jens Eckhoff, Bremer Senator für Bau, Umwelt und Verkehr sowie Gastgeber der Veranstaltung, konspirativ in ein Hinterzimmer des Bremer Kongresszentrums zurück. Um zu retten, was noch zu retten war, fassten sie die wichtigsten Forderungen der Offshore-Windenergie-Entrepreneure zusammen. Jens Eckhoff schrieb die Kernforderungen stichwortartig auf: 1. Offshore-Testfeld, 2. erleichterte Finanzierung, 3. vereinfachtes Genehmigungsverfahren, 4. Ausbau des Hochspannungsnetzes und 5. Forschung und Entwicklung.

Die Notizen lieferten das gedankliche Gerüst für die verbale Konterattacke, zu der Jens Eckhoff vor dem großen Podium, rund 800 Vertretern der Werften, Reedereien und Hafenunternehmen, ausholte. „Ich bin sehr deutlich geworden", erinnert sich Eckhoff. Unerschrocken kritisierte er den Kanzler dafür, dass er sich des Themas Offshore nicht annähme. „Es ist aber eine zentrale Aufgabe der deutschen Bundesregierung, die Offshore-Entwicklung zu koordinieren", forderte Eckhoff, „daher geht es nicht an, dass deutsche Windenergieanlagenhersteller in der deutschen AWZ nicht zeigen dürfen, was sie können." Mit Nachdruck unterstrich der Bremer Senator die Bedeutung, die die Offshore-Windenergie für Deutschland im Allgemeinen und für die Energieversorgung im Besonderen haben wird. Das Statement des Bremers saß. Der Maritime Koordinator des Bundeskanzlers, Georg Wilhelm Adamowitsch, fühlte sich offenbar auf den Schlips getreten. Spontan reagierte er auf die Kritik und eilte zum Mikrofon. „Wieso beschwert sich die Windenergiebranche?", fragte er brüsk in die Runde. Er bügelte die vom CDU-Landespolitiker vorgetragenen Forderungen rundum ab und verwies auf die vermeintlichen Versäumnisse seitens der Windenergieindustrie.

Das war Ende Januar 2005. Die Zeit drängte. Obwohl die ersten Genehmigungen für die Errichtung von Offshore-Windparks in der AWZ schon in der zweiten Jahreshälfte 2001 vom BSH erteilt worden waren, traten die Projekte auf der Stelle. Es wurde zwar umtriebig geplant, doch tauchten ständig neue Fragen auf, auf die es von Seiten der Politik und Verwaltung keine dezidierten Antworten gab. Sollte die wenige Jahre zuvor heiß entfachte Offshore-Euphorie tatsächlich verglühen, bevor überhaupt ein einziger Windpark in deutschen Gewässern installiert worden war? Enttäuschung machte sich vor allem unter den mittelständischen Planern breit, weil sie befürchteten, dass ihre Projekte in der Entwicklungsschleife steckenbleiben würden.

Die deutschen Protagonisten der Offshore-Windenergie sahen ihre Felle wegschwimmen. Es rumorte in der Branche. Die Banken und Versicherer wollten nicht, die Hersteller konnten nicht, die Netzbetreiber waren noch nicht soweit und die Kosten eilten aufgrund gestiegener Rohstoffpreise davon. Der Bundesverband WindEnergie (BWE) warb für mehr Unterstützung. Und hinter den Kulissen intervenierte das 2001 gegründete Offshore Forum Windenergie mit seinem geschäftsführenden Vorstand Jörg Kuhbier in zäher Kleinarbeit bei den politischen Entscheidungsträgern. Der ehemalige Hamburger Umweltsenator erkannte wohl als einer der Ersten, dass Offshore-Windenergie, wie er betont, „industrielle Stromgewinnung ist" und dies eine Liga sei, die nicht alleine von mittelständischen Firmen der erneuerbaren Energien zu meistern ist. „Ohne das Engagement der gro-

turbine manufacturers are not able to demonstrate in the German EEZ what they can really do." The Senator from Bremen insistently emphasized the importance offshore wind energy will have for Germany in general and for energy supplies in particular. The statement of the Bremen senator touched a nerve. The Chancellor's Coordinator of Maritime Policy, Georg Wilhelm Adamowitsch, obviously felt that his toes had been trodden on. He reacted spontaneously to the criticism and rushed to a microphone. "What is the wind-energy sector complaining about?" he asked around abruptly. He completely dismissed the demands made by the CDU state politician and pointed out supposed shortcomings of the wind-energy industry.

That was the end of January 2005. Time was running out. Although the first licences for offshore wind farms in the EEZ had already been granted by the BSH in the second half of 2001, the projects were stuck. Developers may have been busily making plans; however new issues kept cropping up for which politics and administrators had no definite solutions. Was the offshore euphoria that had been ignited only a few years before going to end up in a puff of smoke before a single wind farm had been installed in German waters? Disappointment was spreading, especially amongst the SME offshore developers as they feared that their projects would get stuck in the development phase – if they went anywhere at all.

The German offshore wind-energy stakeholders saw their chances dwindling. There were rumours going around in the business. The banks and insurance companies did not want to play along; the turbine manufacturers just couldn't; the grid operators were not ready and costs were soaring due to increasing raw material prices. The German Wind Energy Association [BWE] was rallying for more support. And behind the scenes the Offshore Wind Energy Forum, founded in 2001, and its Member of the Executive Board Jörg Kuhbier were having painstaking discussions with political decision-makers. The former Hamburg Senator for the Environment was the first to recognize that offshore wind energy, as he emphasizes it, is "industrial electricity generation". This was an area that could not be mastered by SMEs from the renewable energy sector alone. "Without commitment from the large energy companies it's not going to work", Kuhbier was convinced. During his time as Senator he was also Chairman of the Supervisory Board of the Hamburg municipal electricity utility (HEW), later taken over by Vattenfall. "I am thoroughly familiar with large energy producers' structures and the way they think", he says. "They are not as flexible as the smaller companies and they need to know what the long-term targets are going to look like."

However, it was not the long-term that the burgeoning offshore sector was looking at in the spring of 2005. After a few years of waiting they needed short-term perspectives. "If we had continued to hang around at the time, then we probably would not have any offshore wind energy by 2020 in Germany", is Udo Paschedag's retrospective assessment of that period, a time when everyone was desperately looking for solutions.

In the meantime, the confrontation regarding offshore wind energy was coming to a head within the federal ministries in Berlin. Even if the SDP / Green federal government coalition had come up with ambitious ideas of setting up 10,000 megawatts of power as their offshore strategic target, the ideas on how this could be implemented were almost diametrically opposite in the Economics Ministry and the Environment Ministry. Simply the fact that Adamowitsch had previously categorically rejected the Federal Ministry for the Environment,

ßen Energiekonzerne wird es nicht funktionieren", wusste Kuhbier, der aus seiner Zeit als Hamburger Umweltsenator zugleich auch Aufsichtsratsvorsitzender der Hamburgischen Electricitäts-Werke (HEW) war, die später von Vattenfall übernommen wurden. „Ich kenne die Strukturen und die Denkweise der großen Energieerzeuger ganz gut", sagt er, „die sind nicht so beweglich wie die kleinen Unternehmen und brauchen langfristige Vorgaben." Langfristigkeit war aber im Frühjahr 2005 nicht eben das, was die junge Offshore-Branche brauchte. Nach einigen Jahren des Wartens waren kurzfristig neue Perspektiven gefordert. „Wenn wir damals weiter abgewartet hätten, dann hätten wir wahrscheinlich noch bis 2020 keine Offshore-Windenergie in Deutschland", beurteilt Udo Paschedag rückblickend die damalige Situation, als alle händeringend nach Lösungen suchten.

Derweil spitzte sich die Konfrontation um das Thema Offshore-Windenergie innerhalb der Berliner Bundesministerien zu. Wenngleich die Offshore-Strategie der rot-grünen Bundesregierung mit ambitionierten Aufstellungszahlen von 10.000 Megawatt im Raum standen, liefen die Auffassungen, wie diese denn zu realisieren seien, zwischen Wirtschaftsministerium und Umweltministerium nahezu diametral gegeneinander. Allein die Tatsache, dass Adamowitsch es im Vorfeld kategorisch abgelehnt hatte, dass sich das Bundesumweltministerium mit eigenen Vertretern beim ersten Workshop für Offshore-Windenergie auf der Vierten Maritimen Konferenz beteiligt, zeigt dies deutlich.

Nach der denkwürdigen Bremer Veranstaltung stand das Telefon von Udo Paschedag in seinem Büro im Berliner Umweltministerium nicht mehr still. Alle fragten sich, wie es weitergehen solle. Unter den Herstellern traute sich keiner, nach vorne zu preschen. „Das Wirtschaftsministerium interessierte sich nicht für Offshore. Jeder Schritt verlief unheimlich zäh", so der Ministerialrat. „Wir haben von unserer Seite immer wieder versucht, das Thema Offshore-Windenergie auf die politische Agenda zu heben, aber letztlich vergeblich."

Es brauchte in der ersten Hälfte des Jahres 2005 dringend einen „Eisbrecher", wie Paschedag sagt. Alle Hersteller hatten auf dem Workshop in Bremen bekundet, dass sie ein Testfeld wünschten. Sogar Aloys Wobben, Gründer und Chef des deutschen Branchenführers Enercon, begrüßte das Projekt. „Das ist genau das, was wir jetzt brauchen", soll er gesagt haben. Doch trotz aller Zustimmung stellte sich die entscheidende Frage: Wer soll es machen? Zumindest Paschedag war vollkommen klar, dass nur eine konzertierte Aktion weiterhelfen würde. Es musste ein Konstrukt geschaffen werden, bei dem das Risiko auf mehrere Schultern gerecht verteilt werden konnte. Banken, Versicherer, Hersteller, Zulieferer, Energieversorger, Netzbetreiber und nicht zuletzt die Projektfirmen sollten gemeinsam das gewünschte Testfeld auf den Weg bringen. Was tun? Plötzlich kam ihm die Idee einer Stiftung in den Sinn. „In den USA wird für alles Mögliche eine Stiftung ins Leben gerufen, wieso nicht auch für die Offshore-Industrie", ging Paschedag durch den Kopf.

Hamburger Ideenschmiede: Einigkeit in kleiner Runde

Das Kaminfeuer soll geflackert haben. Im hanseatisch-gediegenen Café des noblen Hyatt-Hotels in der Hamburger Innenstadt traf sich an einem grau-ungemütlichen Tag im Februar 2005 zum ersten Mal ein illustrer Kreis von Mitstreitern, die Paschedag zusammengetrommelt hatte. Alle Anwesenden befürworteten seine Idee spontan und wollten diese aktiv unterstützen: Dr. Martin Skiba vom Hersteller REpower, Andreas Düser von Enercon, Jörgen Thiele vom Turmhersteller KGW

Nature Conservation and Nuclear Safety being represented with its own staff during the first workshop for Offshore Wind Energy at the 4th Maritime Conference clearly demonstrates this.

After this memorable event in Bremen the telephone in Udo Paschedag's office in the Federal Environment Ministry in Berlin didn't stop ringing. Everyone was wondering what would happen next. None of the manufacturers was daring to push their way forward. "The Ministry of Economic Affairs was just not interested in offshore development. Every step was a hard one to take", says Paschedag. "We tried again and again to put the subject of offshore wind energy onto the political agenda, but at the end of the day it was in vain."

In the first half of 2005 an "icebreaker" was desperately needed, as Paschedag puts it. All the manufacturers had said during the workshop in Bremen that they would need a test field. Even Aloys Wobben, founder and owner of the German wind-turbine market leader Enercon welcomed the idea. "That's just what we all need", is what he reportedly said. Nevertheless, in spite of this broad agreement in the industry there was one decisive question left unanswered: who's going to do it? At least Paschedag was absolutely sure that only a concerted effort would help. Some kind of organization would be needed so that the risk was spread fairly over several shoulders – the banks, insurers, manufacturers, component suppliers, energy companies, grid operators and not least the project developers should all work together to get the desired test field going. What was to be done? Suddenly the idea of a foundation cropped up. "They create foundations in the USA for anything and everything, so why not for the German offshore industry as well?", was what went through Paschedag's mind.

Hamburg think-tank: unity within a small group

The embers were beginning to flicker into a flame. In the discreetly chic, hanseatic café of the Hyatt Hotel in Hamburg's city centre, on a grey and dreary day in February 2005 an illustrious group of wind energy supporters that Paschedag had brought together met for the first time. All those present were immediately keen on his idea and said they wanted to actively support it. They were Dr. Martin Skiba from turbine manufacturer REpower; Andreas Düser from Enercon; Jörgen Thiele from the tower manufacturer KGW and President of the Schwerin Mecklenburg Chamber of Industry and Commerce (IHK); Jens Eckhoff and Jörg Kuhbier, as well as Dr. Knud Rehfeldt from German company WindGuard GmbH; Dr.-Ing. Joachim Schwarz from the German Association for Maritime Technology (GMT), Dr. Hans Kahle from construction company F+Z Baugesellschaft mbH and Thorsten Herdan from VDMA.

"The bankers were missing." Paschedag drinks a cup of tea while he recalls this noteworthy meeting. Before the pros and cons of the foundation idea were discussed, Paschedag told the informal group that his boss at that time, the Federal Minister for the Environment, Jürgen Trittin, had personally promised him support for the initiative. Then the participants discussed the advantages and disadvantages and at the end of the day they all agreed. Taking up a suggestion by Udo Paschedag, they decided that Professor Martin Schulte, the renowned expert on foundations, should be commissioned to create a suitable concept for the structure, content and objectives of the foundation. In the meantime, the Power Systems section of German industry federation VDMA, with its offshore expert Johannes Schiel had started collating a list of criteria for the choice of a suitable, as it was called then,

und Präsident der IHK zu Schwerin, Jens Eckhoff, Jörg Kuhbier, Knud Rehfeldt von der Deutschen WindGuard GmbH, Dr.-Ing. Joachim Schwarz von der Gesellschaft für Maritime Technik (GMT), Dr. Hans Kahle von der F+Z Baugesellschaft mbH und Thorsten Herdan vom VDMA.

„Banker fehlten", erinnert sich Paschedag Tee trinkend an das denkwürdige Treffen. Bevor das Für und Wider der Stiftungsidee diskutiert wurde, unterrichtete Paschedag den informellen Kreis darüber, dass sein Dienstherr, der damalige Bundesumweltminister Jürgen Trittin, ihm in einem persönlichen Gespräch die Unterstützung für diese Initiative zugesagt hatte. Anschließend diskutierten die Teilnehmer die Vor- und Nachteile. Am Ende war man sich schließlich einig. Auf Anregung von Udo Paschedag wurde entschieden, dass der renommierte Kenner der Stiftungsmaterie Professor Dr. Martin Schulte beauftragt werden sollte, für die zu gründende Stiftung ein passendes Konzept über Struktur, Inhalt und Zielsetzung zu erarbeiten.

Unterdessen machte sich der Verband VDMA Power Systems mit seinem Offshore-Experten Johannes Schiel daran, einen Kriterienkatalog für die Auswahl eines geeigneten, wie es damals hieß, „Offshore Windenergie Test- und Demonstrationsfeld" aufzustellen. Schiel trug sage und schreibe 33 Kriterien zusammen, die ein solches Testfeld bestenfalls erfüllen müsse.

Wichtige Punkte waren unter anderen die Wirtschaftlichkeit und die Bereitstellung einer Infrastruktur. Schiel schrieb: „Um dem Betreiber die Errichtung der Netzinfrastruktur zu ermöglichen, sollte die Bundesregierung die Durchsetzung und Finanzierung der Kabeltrasse und der Netzanbindung für das Testfeld zwischen EVUs, Betreibern und Herstellern sowie Genehmigungsbehörden von Bund, Land und Kommune moderieren." Zudem erhob der VDMA Power Systems einen Anspruch darauf, dass „die Hersteller und Gründungskonstrukteure ein Testfeld in Deutschland fertigen oder zumindest eine Fertigung aufbauen. Ein hoher Anteil deutscher Wertschöpfung bei Anlagen, Komponenten, Gründung, Verkabelung und Logistik ist schon bei der Errichtung des Testfeldes zu berücksichtigen, um den Aufbau der Serienfertigung von Offshore-Anlagen, Gründungsstrukturen, Kabeln, Installations- und Wartungstechnologien und Komponenten in Deutschland sicherzustellen." Ein weiteres wichtiges Kriterium war für Schiel ein Servicehafen, der in 20 bis 25 Seemeilen erreichbar sein sollte. Außerdem sollte es vorzugsweise ein Projekt sein, das in der AWZ der Nordsee liegt.

Doch bevor mit der Auswahl geeigneter Projekte überhaupt begonnen werden konnte, musste die Stiftungsidee zunächst eine juristische Form annehmen. Es galt, den ersten vor dem zweiten Schritt zu machen, um nicht Gefahr zu laufen, gleich am Beginn zu stolpern.

Prof. Dr. Martin Schulte von der Juristischen Fakultät der TU Dresden nahm die Aufgabe sofort an und fertigte ein 27-seitiges Rechtsgutachten über die Gründung einer „Offshore-Testfeld-Stiftung". Auf der Hannover Messe im April trug der Jurist vor der versammelten Windenergie-Branche seine Überlegungen vor. „Über den Entwurf wurde lebhaft diskutiert", blickt Paschedag zurück, „am Ende gab es aber im Plenum eine überwältigende Mehrheit von Befürwortern."

Die Idee war damit in die Windenergiebranche hineingetragen worden. Es wurde eine Arbeitskreis gegründet, der sich in den darauffolgenden Wochen mehrmals traf. Dieser steckte jörg in erster Linie das zukünftige Innenverhältnis zwischen Stiftung, potenziellen Betreibern des Testfeldes und Infrastruktur ab. Nachdem das Konstrukt der zu gründenden Stiftung auf allgemeine Zustimmung getroffen und eine

'Offshore Wind Energy Test and Demonstration Field'. Schiel put together an impressive list of 33 criteria that such a test field should ideally fulfil.

The important aspects were, amongst others, economic viability and availability of infrastructure. Schiel wrote: "In order to enable the operator to set up the grid infrastructure, the Federal Government needs to act as a mediator for the implementation and financing of the cable route and grid connection and talk to the power supply companies, operators and manufacturers as well as to the licencing authorities in the federal government, states and municipalities." Moreover, VDMA Power Systems wanted "turbine manufacturers and foundation suppliers to set up a test field in Germany – or at least to set up a manufacturing process. A large proportion of the turbines, foundation components, cabling and logistics for the test field were to be sourced domestically, putting Germany in a position to enter serial production of the offshore turbines, foundation structures, cables, installation and maintenance technologies and components." According to Schiel a further important criterion was a service port available within 20 to 25 nautical miles. Moreover, it should preferably be a project located within the North Sea EEZ.

However, before anyone could start choosing a suitable project at all, the idea of creating the offshore wind foundation needed to take legal shape. They had to make sure that they walked before they ran, so as not to risk stumbling right from the start.

Prof. Martin Schulte from the Faculty of Law at the Dresden University of Technology immediately accepted the task and prepared a 27-page legal analysis on the formation of an 'offshore test field foundation'. At the Hanover Fair in April the lawyer presented his ideas to the wind-energy community gathered there. "There was a lively discussion about the draft", Paschedag looks back, "At the end, however, there was an overwhelming majority in the plenum which agreed to it."

The idea had thus now been introduced to the wind-energy sector. A task force was created, which met several times in the subsequent weeks. The main task was to look into the future internal structure between the Foundation, potential operators of the test field and the infrastructure. After the organizational form of the Foundation had received widespread support and funding had been agreed in principle by the German Federal Environment Ministry (BMU), the decisive question was which one of the already-permitted offshore projects should be selected for acquiring the licence. There were several projects at their disposal.

Dr. Knud Rehfeldt, CEO of consulting company Deutsche WindGuard GmbH was commissioned by the task force to carry out a brief evaluation to find the most suitable project. According to Paschedag some of the project developers, amongst them the Husum OSB Butendiek GmbH & Co. KG, which was promoting the idea of a 'people's wind farm' from land onto the sea and was planning a project 30 kilometres off the island of Sylt with 80 turbines each rated with three megawatts, turned them down immediately. "A mistake", as Knud Rehfeldt says in retrospect. Wolfgang Paulsen, MD of OSB Butendiek saw the situation somewhat differently. "I doubt, even if we had shown a great degree of interest, that we would have been a serious candidate for the Foundation. I don't believe that they would have got involved in our site that was in a nature conservation area." And there were, in fact, numerous opponents of the North Friesian project, especially amongst the nature conservation associations and also the German Federal Agen-

Ingo de Buhr (Prokon Nord) (li.) hat mit hoher Risikobereitschaft den erfolgreichen Umbau des Industriestandortes Stade vorangetrieben: Wo früher Aluminium gegossen wurde, entstehen heute die Flügel der M5000.
Willing to take high risks, Ingo de Buhr (Prokon Nord) pushed forward the successful redevelopment of Stade as an industrial centre. Today the M5000 rotor blades are made where previously aluminium was cast.

Finanzierung durch das Bundesumweltministerium (BMU) im Grundsatz zugesichert war, stellte sich die entscheidende Frage, von welchem der bereits genehmigten Offshore-Projekte man eigentlich die Genehmigungsrechte erwerben wollte. Mehrere Projekte standen zur Disposition.

Dr. Knud Rehfeldt, Geschäftsführer der Deutschen WindGuard GmbH, erhielt vom Arbeitskreis den Auftrag, das passende Projekt in einem kompakten Gutachten zu sondieren. Einige Projektierer, unter anderem die Husumer OSB Butendiek GmbH & Co. KG, die mit über 8.000 Kommanditisten den Bürgerwindpark-Gedanken vom Land aufs Meer tragen wollte und 30 Kilometer vor Sylt einen Park mit 80 Anlagen à drei Megawatt plante, winkten nach Aussage von Paschedag sofort ab. „Ein Fehler", wie Knud Rehfeldt im Nachhinein sagt. Wolfgang Paulsen, Geschäftsführer von OSB Butendiek, bewertet die Situation etwas anders. „Ich bezweifle, dass wir, selbst wenn wir damals großes Interesse gezeigt hätten, ein wirklich ernsthafter Kandidat für die Stiftung gewesen wären. Ich glaube nicht, dass man an unserem Standort, der in einem Naturschutzgebiet liegt, eingestiegen wäre." Tatsächlich gab es gerade in den Reihen der Naturschutzverbände und auch des Bundesamtes für Naturschutz (BfN) viele Widersacher gegen das nordfriesische Projekt. Sie wollten verhindern, dass die deutsche Offshore-Ära ausgerechnet in einem für den Vogelschutz sensiblen Raum startete.

Das im Juni 2005 von Rehfeldt verfasste Brevier legte dar, dass die Standorte in der Ostsee wenig geeignet schienen, um eine hohe Akzeptanz in Politik und Wirtschaft erreichen zu können. So blieben nur noch vier Projekte übrig, die in die engere Auswahl kamen. Allerdings lagen zwei Projekte innerhalb der Zwölf-Seemeilen-Zone, wo das Genehmigungsverfahren aufgrund der ungeklärten Fragen hinsichtlich des niedersächsischen Wattenmeers und drohender Klagen der Inselgemeinden wegen der Netzanbindung sehr schwierig werden würde. Damit wäre eines der wichtigsten Ziele der Stiftung, eine breite Akzeptanz in der bundesdeutschen Öffentlichkeit gegenüber dem Einstieg in die Offshore-Windenergie, wohl zunichte gewesen. Als dann noch zwei Planungsunternehmen absagten, fiel die Wahl letztlich auf das Projekt, das beim BSH die erste Genehmigung überhaupt erteilt bekommen hatte: Borkum West. Die Lage, die Anzahl der Anlagen und das weit fortgeschrittene Netzanbindungsverfahren sprachen für das Projekt nördlich vor Borkum.

Anfang Juli war es soweit. Die Initiatoren gründeten die Stiftung. Am 26. Juli wurde sie von der Niedersächsischen Stiftungsbehörde offiziell als gemeinnützige Stiftung anerkannt. Zum ersten Präsidenten wählten die Initiatoren Jens Eckhoff, zum Vizepräsidenten Thorsten Herdan, Geschäftsführer im VDMA Fachverband Power Systems. Den Vorstand bildete das Trio Jörg Kuhbier, Jörgen Thiele und Dr. Knud Rehfeldt. Während Rehfeldt als Kenner von Windgutachten einen guten Ruf genoss, engagierte sich Thiele im Vorfeld für die Weiterentwicklung der Offshore-Windenergie in Mecklenburg-Vorpommern und hatte sich an der Gründung der Offshore Technologie Projektgesellschaft (OTP) in Rostock beteiligt. Die OTP wollte vor allem die Offshore-Pläne in der Ostsee nach vorne bringen. Thiele betonte als mecklenburgischer IHK-Präsident immer wieder die industriepolitische Bedeutung der Offshore-Windenergie insbesondere für die norddeutschen Bundesländer und generell für Deutschlands Wirtschaft. „Es wäre töricht, wenn wir im Bereich der Windenergie die technologische Führungsrolle abgeben würden", kritisierte der Maschinenbauer. Ähnlich beurteilte es Jörg Kuhbier als Dritter im Vorstandstrio,

cy for Nature Conservation (BfN). They aimed to hold back the dawn of the German offshore era – above all in an area that is important for bird protection.

The report written by Rehfeldt in June 2005 confirmed that the locations in the Baltic Sea would appear to be less suitable for gaining a high degree of acceptance from politicians and industry. This meant that there were only four projects left on the shortlist. However, two of these projects were within the 12-nautical-mile zone, where the licencing process would prove to be very difficult due to unresolved issues regarding the Lower Saxony Wadden Sea region and the threat of lawsuits from the island communities due to the grid connection. This would have endangered one of the most important goals of the Foundation, i.e. widespread acceptance among the German general public for the start into offshore wind energy. After two more project developers had tendered, the choice finally went to the project which had received the first licence of all from the BSH: Borkum West. The location, the number of turbines and the grid connection – already in a fairly advanced stage – were all reasons for selecting the project to the north of Borkum.

So the time had come early in July 2005: the initiators set up the German Offshore Wind Energy Foundation. It was officially recognized by the Lower Saxony Foundation Authority on the 26th July as a not-for-profit foundation. The initiators elected Jens Eckhoff as the first President and Thorsten Herdan, MD of the VDMA Power Systems section as Vice President. The Board was made up of Jörg Kuhbier, Jörgen Thiele and Dr. Knud Rehfeldt. While Rehfeldt had a good reputation as someone who knows a lot about wind reports, Thiele had been working hard to promote offshore wind energy in Mecklenburg-Western Pomerania and was involved in the creation of the Offshore Technology Project (OTP) in Rostock. In particular the OTP intended to move forward the offshore plans in the Baltic Sea. As President of the Chamber of Commerce (IHK) in Mecklenburg, Thiele emphasized again and again the industrial-political significance of offshore wind energy especially for the federal states in the north of Germany and for Germany's economy in general. "It would be foolhardy if we were to give up the leading technological role in the field of wind energy", criticized the machine constructor. Jörg Kuhbier, as third person in the trio, saw things similarly; his role as skilled moderator was beneficial to the work of the Foundation, both internally as well as to the outside world.

In the meantime, Udo Paschedag was pulling the strings behind the scenes. "He was the one who asked me whether I wanted to accept the position of Foundation President", recalls Eckhoff, who was directly involved in the work to set up the Foundation and who had been a recognized expert in wind energy for a long time. As a very young politician in the CDU he had stood up early on for the subject of offshore energy. Already in 1997, when he was Environmental Spokesperson for the Bremen CDU (conservative party) and the main contact person in the region for the wind-energy sector, the Bremen State Parliament had decided that this Hanseatic city on the Weser should become a centre for wind energy. "Therefore, we deliberately went on to promote Bremerhaven as the place for offshore wind energy. It was a fantastic opportunity for Bremerhaven to attract new jobs". Eckhoff is pleased that numerous companies which are nowadays very successful have located their manufacturing plants there, in particular Multibrid and REpower. That's why he has less patience for the politicians who wanted to "protect the frogs" and prevent the enlargement of the port in

der seine Rolle als geschickter Moderator in die Arbeit der Stiftung nach innen wie außen hineintrug.

Unterdessen zog Udo Paschedag hinter der Bühne die Strippen. „Er war es, der mich fragte, ob ich den Posten des Stiftungs-Präsidenten übernehmen wolle", erinnert sich Eckhoff, der zwar nicht unmittelbar in die Aktivitäten der Stiftungsgründung eingebunden, doch seit langem ein ausgewiesener Kenner der Windenergie war. Er hatte sich als sehr junger Politiker in den Reihen der CDU in einem frühen Stadium für die Offshore-Thematik stark gemacht. Schon im Jahr 1997, damals war er umweltpolitischer Sprecher der Bremer CDU-Fraktion und in der Region der Hauptansprechpartner für die Windenergie-Branche, beschloss die Bremer Bürgerschaft, dass die Hansestadt an der Weser ein Windenergiezentrum werden sollte. „Wir haben dann in der Folgezeit Bremerhaven ganz bewusst für die Offshore-Windenergie positioniert. Es war doch eine wunderbare Chance für Bremerhaven, dadurch neue Arbeitsplätze zu bekommen", freut sich Eckhoff über die mittlerweile erfolgte Ansiedlung von Fertigungsbetrieben von mehreren Firmen, allen voran Multibrid und REpower. Wenig Verständnis habe er deshalb für eine Politik, die „Frösche schützt" und den Ausbau des Hafens in Bremerhaven verhindere. „Mit so einer Haltung wird man in Zukunft keine Atomkraftwerke abschalten", spricht Eckhoff, der inzwischen aus der aktiven Politik ausgestiegen und heute im Immobilien-Geschäft tätig ist, deutliche Worte. Während Eckhoff als CDU-Mann mit klarem Bekenntnis zur Windenergie die Stiftung nach außen repräsentierte, waren in jener schwierigen Phase vor und nach der Gründung vor allem Udo Paschedag und Jörg Kuhbier die treibenden Kräfte im Aufbau der Stiftung. „Die Stiftungsvorbereitungstreffen waren ein bisschen wie Elternabende", erinnert sich Kuhbier lachend an die Anfänge. „Gleichzeitig mussten wir uns mit den Vorurteilen aus dem Wirtschaftsministerium auseinandersetzen, das damals von Wolfgang Clement geleitet wurde. Der hatte nur Kohle, aber nicht die erneuerbaren Energien im Sinn und hielt Offshore offenbar für eine Spinnerei seines Kollegen Jürgen Trittin." Doch die Stiftungsgründer und die Befürworter im BMU, allen voran Udo Paschedag und seine engsten Mitarbeiter Thorsten Falk und Dr. Guido Wustlich, ließen sich trotz der Unkenrufe nicht beirren. Fördergelder dafür einzutreiben, war jedoch nicht leicht. Der designierte Vorstand stellte im Namen der Stiftung, die im Juli gegründet worden war, beim BMU einen Förderantrag zum Erwerb der Genehmigungsrechte für das Offshore-Testfeld. Damals bahnte sich das Ende der rot-grünen Koalition an, und es herrschte in den Ministerien große Skepsis gegenüber dem Vorhaben der Stiftung. Es bedurfte zäher Überzeugungsarbeit, um Mitstreiter zu finden. Die fand Paschedag dann unter anderen auch bei Mitarbeitern des BMU-Haushaltsreferates, das die Mittel für den Erwerb der Rechte am Projekt schließlich absegnete. Noch vor der Bundestagswahl im Herbst 2005 wurde am 2. September der Haushaltsposten in Höhe von fünf Millionen Euro als Stiftungskapital freigegeben. Am 6. September stellte Jens Eckhoff als Stiftungspräsident in der Berlin-Brandenburgischen Akademie der Wissenschaften der Öffentlichkeit im Beisein von Umweltminister Trittin die Intentionen der Stiftung vor. „Zweck der Stiftung ist die Förderung des Umwelt- und Klimaschutzes durch eine verbesserte Erforschung und Entwicklung der Windenergie in der deutschen Nord- und Ostsee. Eckhoff hob vier zu fördernde Kernbereiche heraus:

1. Technologische Forschung, Entwicklung und Innovation der Offshore-Windenergie unter Berücksichtigung des Energietransports bis zum Verbraucher

Bremerhaven. "With such an attitude you won't be able to shut down any nuclear power stations", says Eckhoff in no uncertain fashion. He has left active politics and works now in the real-estate business. While Eckhoff, as a CDU man with a clear commitment to wind energy, represented the Foundation to the outside world, it was Udo Paschedag and Jörg Kuhbier who were the driving forces in building up the Foundation in this difficult period immediately before and after its launch. The meetings to get the Foundation going were a bit like the parents' evenings at school", Kuhbier remembers the beginnings with a smile. "We also had to deal with the prejudices of the Federal Ministry of Economics, which was led at the time by Wolfgang Clement. He only had coal power on his mind but not renewable energies and regarded offshore power as merely the ramblings of his colleague, Jürgen Trittin. "Nevertheless, the initiators of the Foundation and its proponents in the BMU, in particular Udo Paschedag and his closest co-workers, Thorsten Falk and Dr. Guido Wustlich, were not put off by the prophets of doom. However, it was not easy to get a grant. The Board-to-be applied to the BMU for a grant to purchase licence rights for the offshore test field in the name of the Foundation that had been officially set up in July. At the time it seemed the SDP/Green Party coalition was coming to an end, and there was a great degree of scepticism within the ministries towards the intentions of the Foundation. It was tough work convincing anyone to join in. But Paschedag did find people, from the employees of the BMU budget department amongst other groups, who ended up approving the funds for purchasing the rights to the project. Before the German general election in the autumn of 2005, on the 2nd September amounts to the sum of five million euros were released to form the Foundation's capital. On 6th September, President of the Foundation Jens Eckhoff publicly presented the intentions of the Foundation at the Berlin-Brandenburg Academy of Sciences, in the presence of Environment Minister Trittin. "The goal of the Foundation is to promote environmental and climate protection through improved research and development of wind energy in the German North and Baltic Seas. Eckhoff emphasized four core areas to be promoted:

1. Technological research, development and innovation in offshore wind energy – taking into account the transport of the energy to the end consumer.
2. Accompanying ecological research on the impact on the marine environment of the construction, operation and removal of offshore wind turbines, including their cable connection to the grid as well as research into ecological optimization of turbine technology and the turbine systems for offshore wind energy.
3. Research into the suitability and economic feasibility of public instruments for promoting offshore wind energy with regard to improved environmental and climate protection.
4. Exchange of knowledge about offshore wind energy between the scientific and business communities, as well as other public or private institutions.

At this point in time, the Borkum West deal had been negotiated and was ready for signing. The project developers Prokon Nord took up the offer from the Foundation without any great hesitation. They sold their rights to this project for five million euros. "Ingo de Buhr dealt with us very fairly", says Kuhbier about the negotiations. "At the time he was happy not to have to master the offshore experiments alone and simply wanted to benefit from the experiences in the test field."

An interpretation of the situation that the Prokon Nord CEO does not wish to contradict: thanks to the sale of the project rights, the middle-

2. Ökologische Begleitforschung zu den Auswirkungen des Baus, Betriebs und Rückbaus von Offshore-Windenergieanlagen einschließlich ihrer Kabelanbindung auf die Meeresumwelt sowie die Forschung zur ökologischen Optimierung der Anlagentechnik und der Anlagensysteme von Offshore-Windenergieanlagen
3. Forschung zur Eignung und Wirksamkeit staatlicher Instrumente zur Förderung der Offshore-Windenergie im Hinblick auf einen verbesserten Umwelt- und Klimaschutz
4. Austausch und Vermittlung von Wissen über Offshore-Windenergie zwischen Wissenschaft, Wirtschaft und anderen öffentlichen oder privaten Stellen

Zu diesem Zeitpunkt war der Deal mit Borkum West schon unterschriftsreif ausgehandelt. Der Projektentwickler Prokon Nord ging auf das Angebot der Stiftung ohne langes Zögern ein. Für fünf Millionen Euro verkaufte er die Rechte an seinem Projekt. „Ingo de Buhr hat sich uns gegenüber sehr fair verhalten", sagt Kuhbier über die Verhandlung. „Er war zum damaligen Zeitpunkt froh, die Offshore-Experimente nicht im Alleingang meistern zu müssen, und wollte einfach von den Erfahrungen im Testfeld profitieren."

Eine Interpretation, der der Chef von Prokon Nord nicht widersprechen mag, konnte sich doch das mittelständische Unternehmen durch den Verkauf der Projektrechte auf die Weiterentwicklung ihrer eigenen Offshore-Anlage M5000 konzentrieren. Als Prokon Nord die Firma Multibrid von der Pfleiderer AG im Dezember 2003 übernahm, war die Firma damit als einziges Planungsunternehmen in der Branche mutig ins Herstellergeschäft eingestiegen. Es war ein Husarenstück, das bald sichtbare Erfolge zeitigte. Schon im Herbst 2004 konnte das kleine Entwicklungsteam um Martin Lehnhoff den Prototypen der M5000 in Bremerhaven-Weddewarden in Betrieb nehmen und seither eingehend testen. Insofern kam das Angebot von der Stiftung genau zum richtigen Zeitpunkt. „Die Idee, dem potenziellen Kunden in spe die Investition für das Testfeld zu übertragen, war gut", sagt Ingo de Buhr.

Erfolgreiche Moderation durch die Stiftung

Wer nun aber geglaubt hatte, alles Weitere würde wie von selbst laufen, sah sich gewaltig im Irrtum. Wie die Aussage von Ingo de Buhr schon andeutet, mieden die Windenergieanlagenhersteller die Offensive. Und so platzte die ursprüngliche Idee, dass die Hersteller Enercon, REpower und Multibrid den Park von der Stiftung anteilig pachten und dort jeweils vier ihrer 5 Megawattanlagen aufbauen und betreiben würden, schneller als gedacht. Während REpower und Multibrid in Wartestellung verharrten, machte Enercon, trotz anfänglicher Zustimmung aber nach den Erfahrungen einer gescheiterten Offshore-Gründung vor Hooksiel, einen Rückzieher. Enercon-Chef Aloys Wobben entschied sich aus strategischen Gründen konsequent gegen Offshore, um, so die Begründung, die rasante Entwicklung seines Unternehmens auf internationaler Bühne nicht zu gefährden.

Die Absage aus Aurich sorgte in der Stiftung für Irritationen. Zumindest die Bemühungen von Kuhbier und Co. hinsichtlich der Netzanbindung für das geplante Testfeld wurden während dieser turbulenten Phase belohnt. Als unabhängiger Moderator gelang es der Stiftung, sowohl das Bundesland Niedersachsen, die Inselgemeinde Norderney als auch die Planer von mehreren Offshore-Projekten von einer gemeinsamen Trassenführung über Norderney zu überzeugen. Hilfeleistung dazu gab es im Vorfeld von Matthias Machnig, dem damaligen

sized enterprise could now concentrate on further developing their own offshore turbine, the M5000. When Prokon Nord took over the company Multibrid from Pfleiderer AG in December 2003 it became the only developer in the industry brave enough to enter the manufacturing business. It was a daring enterprise that was soon to demonstrate visible success. The small team of engineers gathered around Martin Lehnhoff was able to start up the prototype of the M5000 in Bremerhaven-Weddewarden as early as the autumn of 2004 and since then has been carrying out in-depth tests. In this respect, the offer from the Foundation came at just the right time. "It was a good idea to pass on the investments for the test field to the potential customers-in-waiting", says Ingo de Buhr.

Successful moderation by the Foundation

Anyone who believed that it was to be all easy going from now on was making a huge mistake. As Ingo de Buhr had already feared, the wind-turbine manufacturers ignored these efforts and this is why the original idea failed more quickly than expected. The idea was that each of the three turbine manufacturers, Enercon, REpower and Multibrid would lease their share of the test field from the Foundation and then build and operate four of their 5-megawatt turbines. Whereas REpower and Multibrid waited in the starting blocks, Enercon, however, withdrew in spite of the original agreement after their experience with a failed offshore turbine foundation off Hooksiel. The reason given was that Enercon CEO Aloys Wobben "decided for strategic reasons against offshore energy", so as not to endanger the rapid development of his company on the international stage.

The rebuff from Aurich caused a stir within the Foundation. But at least the efforts of Kuhbier and Co. to get the grid connections for the planned test field were rewarded during this turbulent phase. As independent moderator, the Foundation was able to convince both the Federal state of Lower Saxony, the island community of Norderney and also the developers of several offshore projects north of Borkum that a shared cable line across Norderney would be a good idea. There had been support in the run-up from Matthias Machnig, the State Secretary of the time in the BMU. He invited the squabbling parties to the BMU and "read them the Riot Act", as Paschedag puts it. "Machnig made it unmistakably clear to all those involved that their disagreements would have negative consequences on the whole offshore development in Germany if they didn't stop as soon as possible. After a common cable route had finally been agreed, the offshore developers were able to convince the energy supply companies EWE, E.ON and Vattenfall to take on the planning and construction of this grid connection. Since the search for new cooperation partners for the test field failed in spite of numerous attempts to attract other wind-turbine producers – Siemens amongst others also refused – the three energy suppliers eventually filled the gap. In April 2006, their managers agreed with German Chancellor Angela Merkel at an energy summit in her offices in Berlin to set up and run an offshore test field as soon as possible. A few months later, the lease agreement for a duration of 20 years had been finalized between the German Offshore Wind Energy Foundation and DOTI (Deutsche Offshore-Testfeld und Infra-struktur GmbH & Co. KG), which had been founded by the suppliers E.ON, EWE and Vattenfall. In the words of Thorsten Herdan, Vice President of the Foundation and Chairman of the VDMA Power Systems section, the basis had finally been laid to dem-

Staatssekretär im BMU. Er lud die Streithähne ins BMU ein und las ihnen beherzt, so Paschedag, „die Leviten". Machnig machte allen Beteiligten unmissverständlich klar, welche negativen Konsequenzen der Streit für die gesamte Offshore-Entwicklung in Deutschland haben würde, wenn man ihn nicht alsbald beenden würde.

Nachdem endlich eine gemeinsame Trassenlösung vorlag, konnten die Offshore-Planer die Energieversorgungsunternehmen EWE, E.ON und Vattenfall dafür gewinnen, die Planung und den Bau dieser Netzanbindung zu übernehmen. Als die Suche nach neuen Kooperationspartnern für den Betrieb eines Testfeldes auf Seiten der Hersteller trotz vieler Versuche fehlschlug – unter anderem winkte auch Siemens ab –, füllten die drei Energieversorger schließlich die Lücke. Im April 2006 sagten ihre Manager beim Energiegipfel im Berliner Kanzleramt Angela Merkel zu, alsbald ein Offshore-Testfeld zu errichten und zu betreiben. Einige Monate später war der Pachtvertrag über eine Dauer von 20 Jahren zwischen der von den Versorgern E.ON, EWE und Vattenfall gegründeten Deutsche Offshore-Testfeld und Infrastruktur GmbH & Co. KG, kurz DOTI, und der Stiftung Offshore unter Dach und Fach. Mit den Worten von Thorsten Herdan, Vizepräsident der Stiftung und Geschäftsführer des VDMA Fachverbandes Power Systems, war damit endlich die Grundlage geschaffen, um am Standort Deutschland zu beweisen, dass man in Wassertiefen von bis zu 40 Metern und 40 Kilometer vor der Küste wirtschaftlich Windenergieanlagen mit fünf Megawatt oder mehr betreiben kann. „Mit Hilfe von alpha ventus kann die deutsche Offshore-Technologie ein Exportschlager werden."

onstrate with the test field in Germany that wind turbines with five megawatts and more could be run economically in water depths of up to 40 metres and more than 40 kilometres off the coast: "With the help of alpha ventus, German offshore technology can become a major export industry."

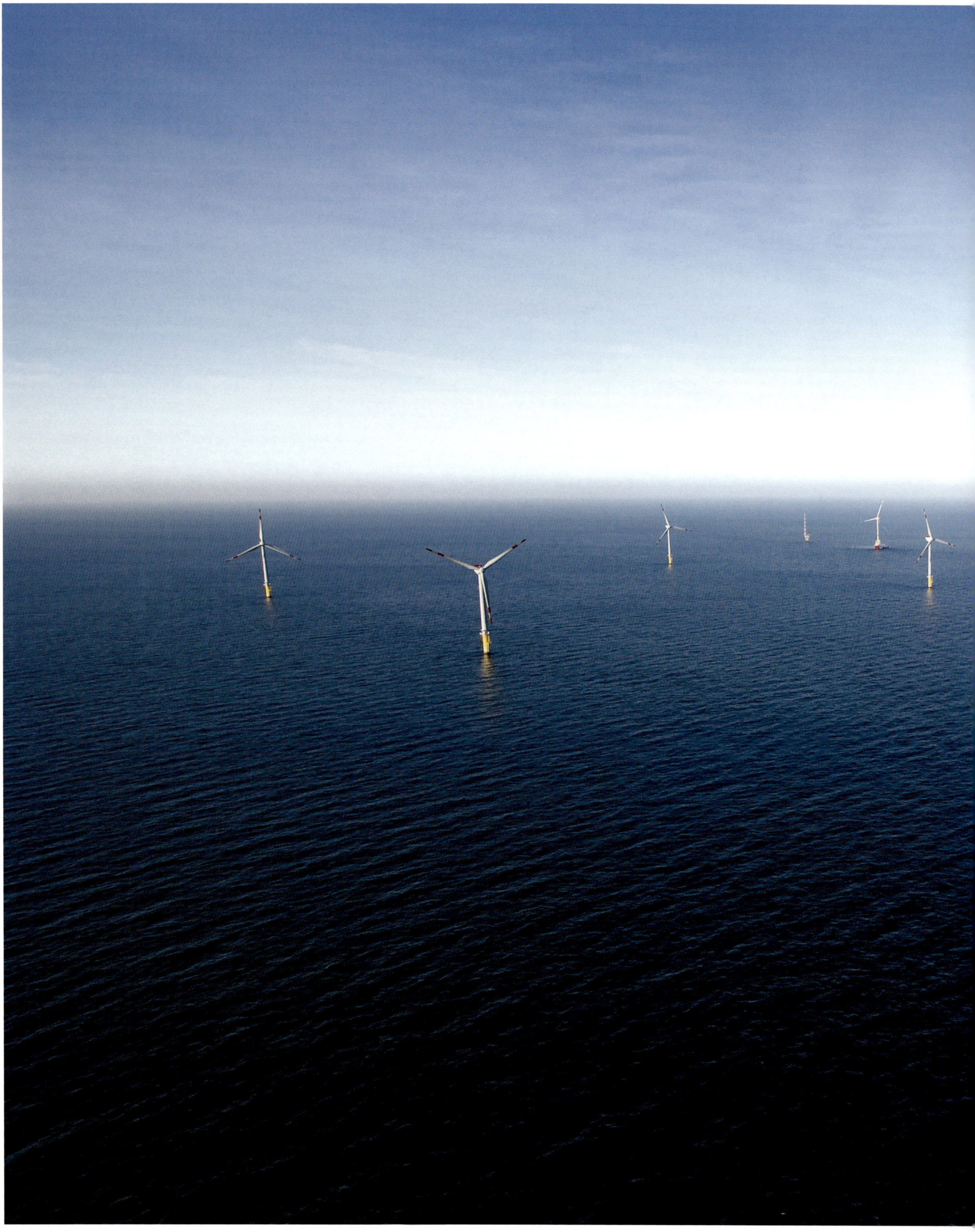

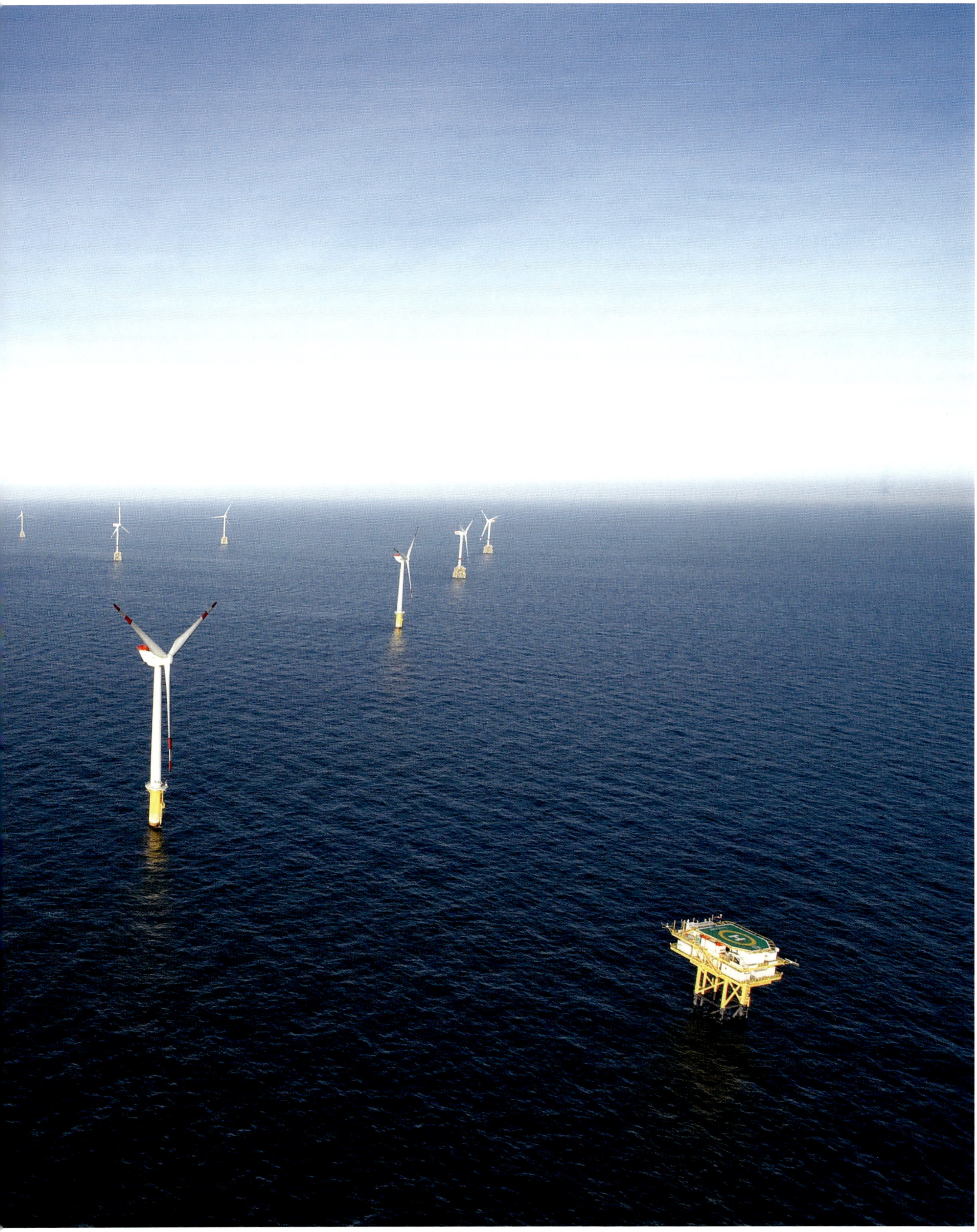

Dialog zwischen Industrie und Politik
Dialogue between industry and politics

KNUD REHFELDT VORSTAND STIFTUNG OFFSHORE WINDENERGIE
BOARD MEMBER OF THE OFFSHORE WIND ENERGY FOUNDATION

Knud Rehfeldt

Dr. Knud Rehfeldt hat auf dem Gebiet der Regelung von Windenergieanlagen in Bremen promoviert. Er war zwischen 1995 und 2001 Mitarbeiter am Deutschen Windenergie Institut (DEWI). Zuletzt hat Knud Rehfeldt die spanische Niederlassung des DEWI in Pamplona aufgebaut. Seit 2001 ist er geschäftsführender Gesellschafter der Deutschen WindGuard, eines international tätigen Dienstleistungsunternehmens der Windenergiebranche mit ca. 70 Mitarbeitern.

Herr Rehfeldt, wie kam es zur Gründung der Stiftung Offshore Windenergie?

Im Lauf der Maritimen Konferenz 2005 wurde unter deutschen Windenergieanlagen-Herstellern der Wunsch geäußert, ein Testfeld auf hoher See zu errichten. In großer Runde haben sich alle beteiligten Akteure überlegt, wie man ein solches Testfeld realisieren könnte. Die ersten Fragen lauteten etwa, wie man an Projektrechte herankommt und welches Konstrukt überhaupt notwendig ist, um ein Testfeld betreiben zu können. Es gab zunächst sehr unterschiedliche Vorstellungen über mögliche und notwendige Strukturen. Viele Varianten standen zur Disposition. Am Ende des Diskussionsprozesses erschien eine gemeinnützige Stiftung als die beste Lösung, um die Rechte eines Offshore-Projektes übernehmen zu können.

Wieso haben die Anlagenhersteller das Testfeld nicht selber in Angriff genommen?

Die Hersteller Enercon, REpower und AREVA Multibrid, damals noch Multibrid, wollten sich zwar in einem Feld zusammentun und dort ihre Anlagen aufstellen. Aber die Erfahrung hat gezeigt, dass es immer schwierig ist, aus drei konkurrierenden Unternehmen eine Gesellschaft zu schmieden, deshalb suchten alle nach einer unabhängigen Instanz. Die jedoch noch nicht existierte. Mit der Stiftung Offshore Windenergie haben wir dieses Defizit ausgeglichen und alle Akteure mit ihren

Dr. Knud Rehfeldt received a PhD in Bremen in the field of wind turbine control. Between 1995 and 2001 he worked at the German Wind Energy Institute (DEWI), during which time he established the DEWI Spanish office in Pamplona. Since 2001 he has been Managing Director of Deutsche WindGuard, an international service provider to the wind-energy industry with some 70 employees.

Mr. Rehfeldt, why was the Offshore Wind Energy Foundation established?

During the Maritime Conference 2005 several German wind-turbine manufacturers expressed their desire to set up a test field on the open sea. All the protagonists came together in a large group to discuss how such a test field could be realized. The first questions were, broadly speaking, "How do we obtain the project rights?" and "What sort of organization would be necessary at all to be able to operate such a test field?" At first there were very differing ideas about the possible and necessary structures, as so many variations were available. At the end of the discussion process it appeared that a non-profit-making foundation would be the best solution to be able to acquire the rights for an offshore project.

Why didn't the turbine manufacturers try to tackle the test field themselves?

The manufacturers – that is, Enercon, REpower and AREVA Multibrid, at the time still named Multibrid, had in fact wanted to get together with a field and set up their turbines there. However, experience has shown that it is always difficult to set up an organization comprising three competing companies, and that's why everyone was looking for an independent body – which didn't yet exist. We were able to fill this gap with the Offshore Wind Energy Foundation and get all partici-pants, with their respective interests, around the same table to

60 alpha ventus

jeweiligen Interessen zusammen an einen Tisch bringen können, um im gemeinsamen Interesse aller das Testfeld in die Tat umzusetzen.

Reduziert sich die Aufgabe der Stiftung allein auf den Erwerb des Testfeldes?
Nein, ganz und gar nicht. Die Stiftung hatte nicht nur die Aufgabe, das Testfeld zu akquirieren und an einen Betreiber zu übertragen, sondern sie will darüber hinaus die Entwicklung der Offshore-Windenergie initiativ fördern und begleiten. Die Stiftung verfolgt zudem das wichtige Ziel, Wissenstransfer zu leisten. Es geht nicht nur um den Aufbau des Testfeldes, sondern auch darum, die Erfahrungen, die im Zuge der Realisierung von alpha ventus gesammelt wurden, möglichst an alle Akteure der Offshore-Windenergie-Industrie weiterzugeben.

implement the test field in everyone's common interest.

Is the task of the Foundation simply to acquire a test field?
No, not at all. The Foundation not only has the task of acquiring a test field and passing it on to an operator, but also intends to take the initiative in promoting the development of offshore wind power. What's more, the Foundation is pursuing the important goal of passing on know-how. It's not just about setting up a test field but also about passing on the experience gathered from realizing alpha ventus wherever possible to all protagonists in the offshore wind-energy industry. On top of this comes the task of intensifying the dialogue between the sector and politics.

The overarching idea of all these activities is the benefit to the public interest, which the Foundation consistently pursues. It does not intend to make any money out of the test field. That was not the original aim and will not be in future, either.

Why did the first German offshore windfarm need to be set up so far away from the coast?
In Germany we find ourselves in the situation that offshore farms near the coast will encounter serious problems in receiving a licence, for numerous reasons. There are four projects planned near the coast; however they will probably not get connected to the grid due to this difficult approval situation until after numerous offshore projects in the Exclusive

Hinzu kommt noch die Aufgabe, den Dialog zwischen Industrie und Politik zu vertiefen. Über allen Aktivitäten steht die Idee der Gemeinnützigkeit, die die Stiftung konsequent verfolgt. Sie will mit dem Testfeld keine Gewinne erzielen. Das war, ist und wird auch in Zukunft nicht das Ziel sein.

Wieso musste der erste deutsche Offshore-Park so weit von der Küste entfernt errichtet werden?

Wir befinden uns in Deutschland in der Situation, dass küstennahe Offshore-Parks aus vielerlei Gründen nur sehr schwer eine Genehmigung bekommen. Es gibt zwar vier Projekte, die küstennah geplant sind, aber sie werden wahrscheinlich aufgrund dieser schwierigen Genehmigungssituation erst nach vielen Offshore-Projekten in der Ausschließlichen Wirtschaftzone (AWZ) ans Netz gehen. Und wie es im Augenblick aussieht, wird es keine weiteren Planungen für küstennahe Standorte mehr geben. Das Thema ist erledigt und damit fällt auch das Konfliktpotenzial mit dem Naturschutz, der Fischerei und dem Tourismus weg. Trotzdem ist es ganz klar, dass es für die Offshore-Windenergie wünschenswert gewesen wäre, wenn man sich von flachen, küstennahen Standorten in tiefere Gewässer langsam hätte vorarbeiten können.

Mit welcher Motivation engagieren Sie sich für die Stiftung Offshore Windenergie?

Ich bin schon seit 1989 in der Windbranche aktiv. Ich kenne den Bereich an Land sehr gut. Für mich stellt sich die Frage, wie wir die klimapolitischen Zielvorstellungen in der Bundesrepublik in Zukunft erreichen können. Windenergie ist sicherlich ein ganz wichtiger Baustein, den es sowohl onshore als auch offshore zu nutzen gilt. Ich gehöre nicht zu denjenigen, die sagen, wir brauchen das eine oder das andere; ich gehöre auch nicht zu denjenigen, die beides gegeneinander ausspielen wollen. Ich denke vielmehr, dass wir den Ausbau von beidem brauchen, um die politischen Zielvorstellungen tatsächlich zu erreichen. Wir planen im Moment 10.000 Megawatt offshore für das Jahr 2020, dann stehen onshore wahrscheinlich schon mehr als 40.000 Megawatt. Mit anderen Worten, wir sind im Onshore-Ausbau in den nächsten zehn Jahren viel schneller und erreichen damit einen viel größeren Energiebeitrag als durch den Ausbau der Offshore-Windenergie. Dies heißt allerdings im Umkehrschluss nicht, dass wir kein Offshore-Engagement brauchen würden. Um diese Erkenntnis weiterzutragen, engagiere ich mich in der Stiftung.

Economic Zone have come on-stream. And at the moment it appears that there will be no further plans for sites near the coast. For now that spells an end to the matter and this avoids any potential for conflict with the nature conservationists, the fishing industry and tourism. Nevertheless, it's obvious that it would have been desirable for offshore wind energy to have been able to start from the shallow areas near the coast and then move slowly into deeper waters.

What is the motivation for your work in the Offshore Wind Energy Foundation?

I have been working in the wind business since 1989 and was already very familiar with the sector on land. For me the question was, "How can we meet the climate policy objectives of the German Federal Government in the future?" Wind power is certainly a crucial component of the energy mix of the future and that needs to be utilized both onshore and offshore. I am one of those people who doesn't say we need the one or the other, or who wants to play the one against the other. Rather, I believe we need to develop both to stand the best chance of achieving these political goals. We're currently planning 10,000 MW offshore by the year 2020; by then there will probably be more than 40,000 MW on land. In other words, we will be a lot quicker in developing onshore power in the next ten years and it will thus make a greater initial contribution to energy supply than offshore wind energy. However, this doesn't mean you can use the converse argument to say we don't require any work on offshore energy. My work in the Foundation is intended to propagate that idea. And when in 2005, people asked around in the wind-energy sector who would like to take on this responsibility, Jörg Kuhbier, Jörgen Thiele and myself declared ourselves willing to accept positions on the Board.

What is the offshore wind industry learning from alpha ventus?

Firstly, it has learned from the process of coming into being itself – with all the difficulties and the conditions with waves and wind on the open sea, that were initially underestimated. It's all about correctly selecting the respective equipment suitable for all weather conditions. The location of alpha ventus has certainly been well chosen; it's representative for the further expansion of offshore wind energy in the North Sea, with regard to the height of the waves, water depths and distance from the coast – and thus the challenges associated with these. In the German North Sea, over 25 offshore wind

Und als im Jahr 2005 in den Reihen der Windenergiebranche gefragt wurde, wer Verantwortung übernehmen wolle, haben sich Jörg Kuhbier, Jörgen Thiele und ich uns bereiterklärt, Posten im Vorstand zu übernehmen.

Was lernt die Offshore-Windindustrie durch alpha ventus?

Sie lernt zunächst vom Entstehungsprozess selbst – mit all den Schwierigkeiten und anfangs unterschätzten Bedingungen von Welle und Wind auf dem Meer. Es geht um die richtige Wahl des entsprechenden Equipments für alle Wetterbedingungen. In jedem Fall ist der Standort von alpha ventus gut gewählt. Er ist für die weitere Nutzung der Offshore-Windenergie in der Nordsee repräsentativ, und zwar was Wellenhöhen, Wassertiefen und Küstenentfernung anbelangt und die damit zusammenhängenden Herausforderungen. In der deutschen Nordsee sind bis Ende 2009 über 25 Offshore-Windparks genehmigt worden, die Initiatoren dieser Projekte haben ganz genau beobachtet, was im Testfeld passierte.

farms had been licenced by the end of 2009 and the initiators of these projects have been watching very carefully what happens in the test field. Now that the test field has been set up we have to make sure we are also successful in operating it.

Windfarms at sea are the one side of the coin. What about the other – connecting them to the grid?

Up to now there has only been a grid connection for the alpha ventus test field and four further subsequent projects in the North Sea with a production capacity of 3,000 megawatts. The cable through Norderney is, however, only one of a total of four clusters planned for bringing North Sea wind power ashore. Nevertheless, their implementation is still a long way off. This situation makes the planning of further development extremely difficult. Moreover, we have to think a step even further: we have to connect up the cluster areas with each other to set up, in the long-term, a transnational offshore grid. Irrespective of this,

I think that with the cable solution over Norderney, that was implemented before the Act on Accelerated Infrastructure Planning, we have a good example of how you can bring various project developers together for a common procedure and establish legal agreements. I believe that particularly the Foundation, as moderator, can make an important contribution there. The cable through Norderney is, up to now, the only approved crossing of the Wattenmeer (North Sea mudflats) National Park. If you intend to install 25,000 megawatts of generating capacity without clustering, however, you'd need a lot more than 100 cables to go through the mudflats. It'd be impossible to get that approved.

And how do you believe can the problem be solved?

With the Act on Accelerated Infrastructure Planning we have had a fundamental tool available since December 2006 to push forward the expansion of the grid at sea. However, we need a master plan for the offshore sector to

Jetzt, wo das Testfeld errichtet ist, müssen wir dafür sorgen, dass es auch im Betrieb ein Erfolg wird.

Parks im Meer sind die eine Seite der Medaille. Wie sieht es mit der anderen Seite, der Netzanbindung, aus?

Bisher gibt es in der deutschen Nordsee nur den Netzanschluss für das Testfeld von alpha ventus und vier Folgeprojekte mit einer Kapazität von insgesamt 3.000 Megawatt Leistung. Diese Trasse über Norderney ist aber nur eines von vier Clustern, die für die Erschließung der Offshore-Windparks in der Nordsee geplant sind. Ihre Realisierung liegt aber leider noch in weiter Ferne. Diese Situation erschwert massiv eine geordnete Weiterentwicklung. Darüber hinaus müssen wir noch einen Schritt weiterdenken. Es geht darum, die Cluster miteinander zu verbinden, sodass langfristig ein transnationales Offshore-Netz entstehen kann. Unabhängig davon denke ich aber, dass wir mit der Trassenlösung über Norderney, die noch vor dem Infrastruktur-Planungsbeschleunigungsgesetz erzielt wurde, ein gutes Beispiel dafür haben, wie man verschiedene Projektentwickler für ein gemeinsames Vorgehen und Vertragswerk gewinnt. Daran hat, so glaube ich, gerade die Stiftung als Moderator einen wichtigen Beitrag leisten können. Die Trasse über Norderney ist bisher die einzige genehmigte Querung durch den Nationalpark Wattenmeer. Wenn Sie aber 25.000 Megawatt installieren wollen, dann brauchen Sie ohne Cluster weit über 100 Leitungen, die durch das Wattenmeer gehen müssen. Das ist genehmigungstechnisch unmöglich.

Und wie soll aus Ihrer Sicht dieses Problem gelöst werden?

Mit dem Infrastruktur-Planungsbeschleunigungsgesetz haben wir nun das Instrumentarium für einen zielstrebigen Netzausbau auf dem Meer. Aber es braucht einen Generalplan offshore, um allen Beteiligten eine Planungssicherheit beim erforderlichen Aufbau der Infrastruktur zu gewähren.

Wie beurteilen Sie die wirtschaftlichen Perspektiven der Offshore-Windenergie?

Aktuell liegt die Vergütung von Offshore-Windstrom bekanntlich bei 15 Cent pro Kilowattstunde. Damit ist der Windstrom vom Meer deutlich teurer als der vom Land. Allerdings lagen die Kosten für Windstrom an Land vor knapp 20 Jahren sogar noch über dem Niveau von 15 Cent. Ich will damit sagen, dass mit der neuen Offshore-Technologie noch deutliche Kostenreduzierungen möglich sind.

Ein solcher Entwicklungsprozess ist aber nicht von heute auf morgen zu bewältigen. Trotzdem glaube ich nicht, dass Offshore-Windstrom unter den deutschen Rahmenbedingungen in zehn Jahren kostengünstiger als Onshore sein wird.

Wie sieht aus Ihrer Sicht die deutsche Nord- und Ostsee im Jahr 2030 aus? Wird sie „verspargelt" sein?

„Verspargelt" klingt so negativ. Wer in einigen Jahren auf der Nordsee unterwegs ist, wird die Anlagen selbstverständlich sehen. An der Küste werden die Anwohner und Urlauber sie jedoch nicht wahrnehmen. Ich glaube aber, dass die wirtschaftliche Nutzung der Nordsee erst durch die Windenergie ins öffentliche Bewusstsein vordringt. Obwohl vielfältige Nutzung schon seit Jahrzehnten praktiziert wird – denken Sie nur an Sandabbau, Fischfang sowie intensive Öl- und Gasbohrungen, die in gigantischen Ausmaßen existieren.

Beginnt mit der Offshore-Windenergie eine neue Ära für die deutsche maritime Wirtschaft?

Durch die aufkommende Offshore-Windenergie wird deutlich, dass die Holländer, Engländer, Norweger und Dänen wesentlich mehr Erfahrungen mit Projekten auf hoher See haben. Die gesamte Öl- und Gas-Industrie in der Nordsee liegt außerhalb der deutschen AWZ, wo sich keine Vorkommen befinden. Das ist der Grund, weshalb sich in Deutschland bislang noch keine Offshore-Industrie entwickelte. Durch die Offshore-Windenergie haben wir nun die Chance, so eine Industrie aufzubauen – wenn wir schnell genug sind. Denn die Nachbarn sind in den Startlöchern und würden unser Geschäft gerne mit übernehmen. Es muss jetzt unser Interesse sein, eine eigene Industrie, quasi als nationale Aufgabe, aufzubauen. Auch dafür brauchen wir das Testfeld.

Kann aus Ihrer Einschätzung heraus Windstrom langfristig Strom aus Kohle und Atomkraft ersetzen?

Da müssen wir hinkommen.

ensure that all involved can rest assured that the necessary infrastructure will be set up – after all, this is essential for their further planning.

How do you see the economic perspectives of offshore wind energy?

As you know, the reimbursement for offshore wind electricity is currently 15 eurocents per kilowatt-hour, which means that wind power at sea is a lot more expensive than that on land. However, the costs for wind power on land were above the 15-cent level almost 20 years ago. What I'm saying is, the new offshore technology and the associated learning curve mean that even greater cost reductions are possible – although such a process does not happen overnight. Nevertheless, given the framework conditions in Germany, I do not believe that offshore wind energy will be cheaper than onshore power in ten years' time.

How do you think the North and Baltic Seas will look in 2030 – something like an asparagus field?

That sounds rather negative! If you're out and about in the North Sea in a few years' time you will, of course, see the turbines. However, the inhabitants and holidaymakers on the coast won't notice them. I believe, however, that people will only slowly become aware of the economic importance that the North Sea has due to wind power. Let's not forget that it has already been exploited very intensively for decades in other ways – just think of the sand dredging, commercial fishing and the drilling for oil and gas.

Does the offshore wind energy mean a new era is starting for the German maritime economy?

The up-and-coming offshore wind energy sector has made it clear that we Germans have not been doing what the Dutch, English, Norwegians and Danes have been doing for a while at sea. The whole oil and gas industry in the North Sea is outside the German Exclusive Economic Zone, in which there are no such reserves. That's why Germany has not yet been able to develop an offshore industry. Through offshore wind energy, however, we now have the unique opportunity to build an industry of our own – if we are quick enough. Because our neighbours are in the starting blocks and would like to do the same business too. It has to be in our interest to build our own industry, basically as a task for the nation. But to do that, we need the test field.

Would you say that wind power can replace electricity produced from coal and atomic power?

In the long term, that's what we have to do.

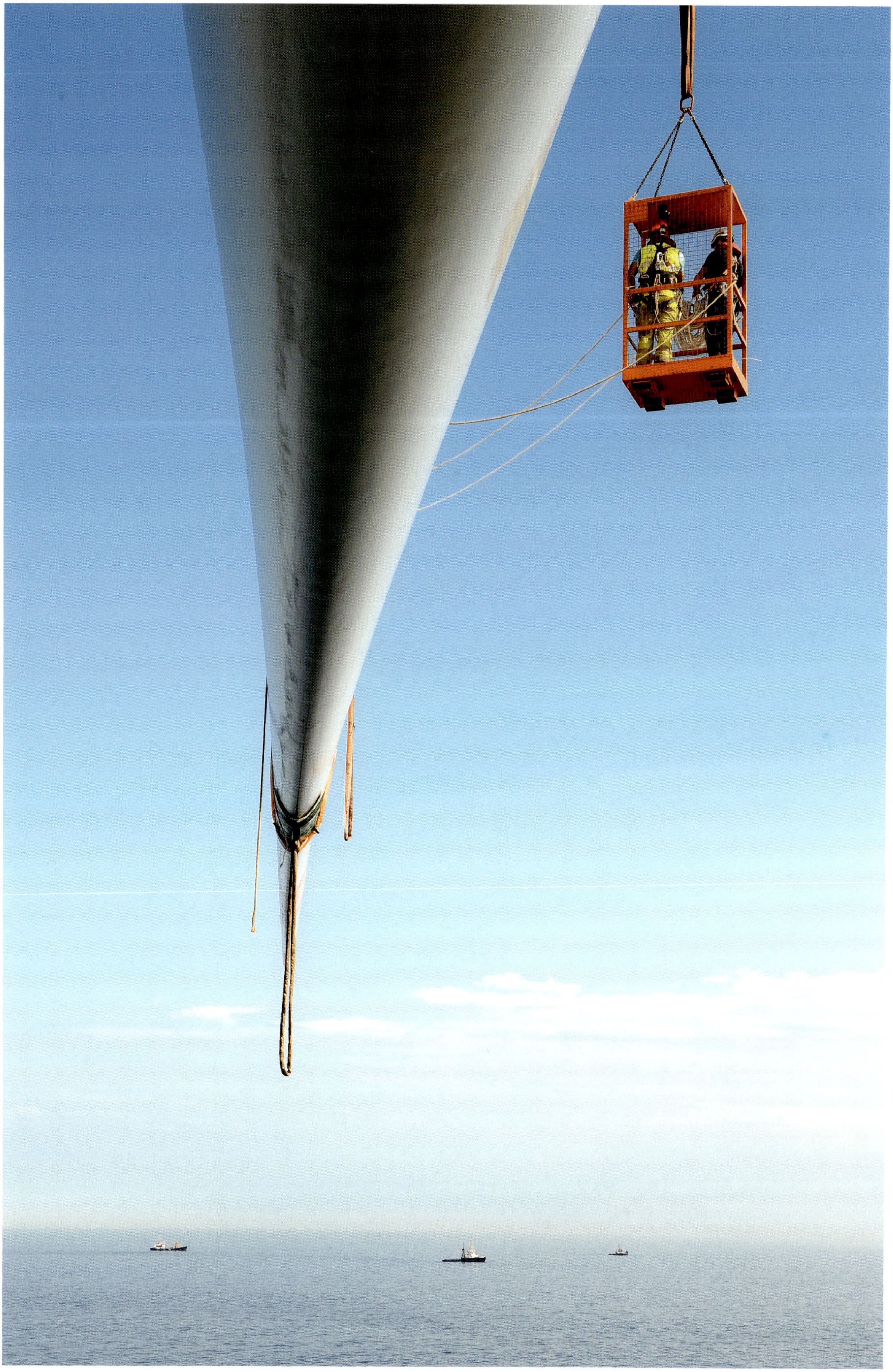

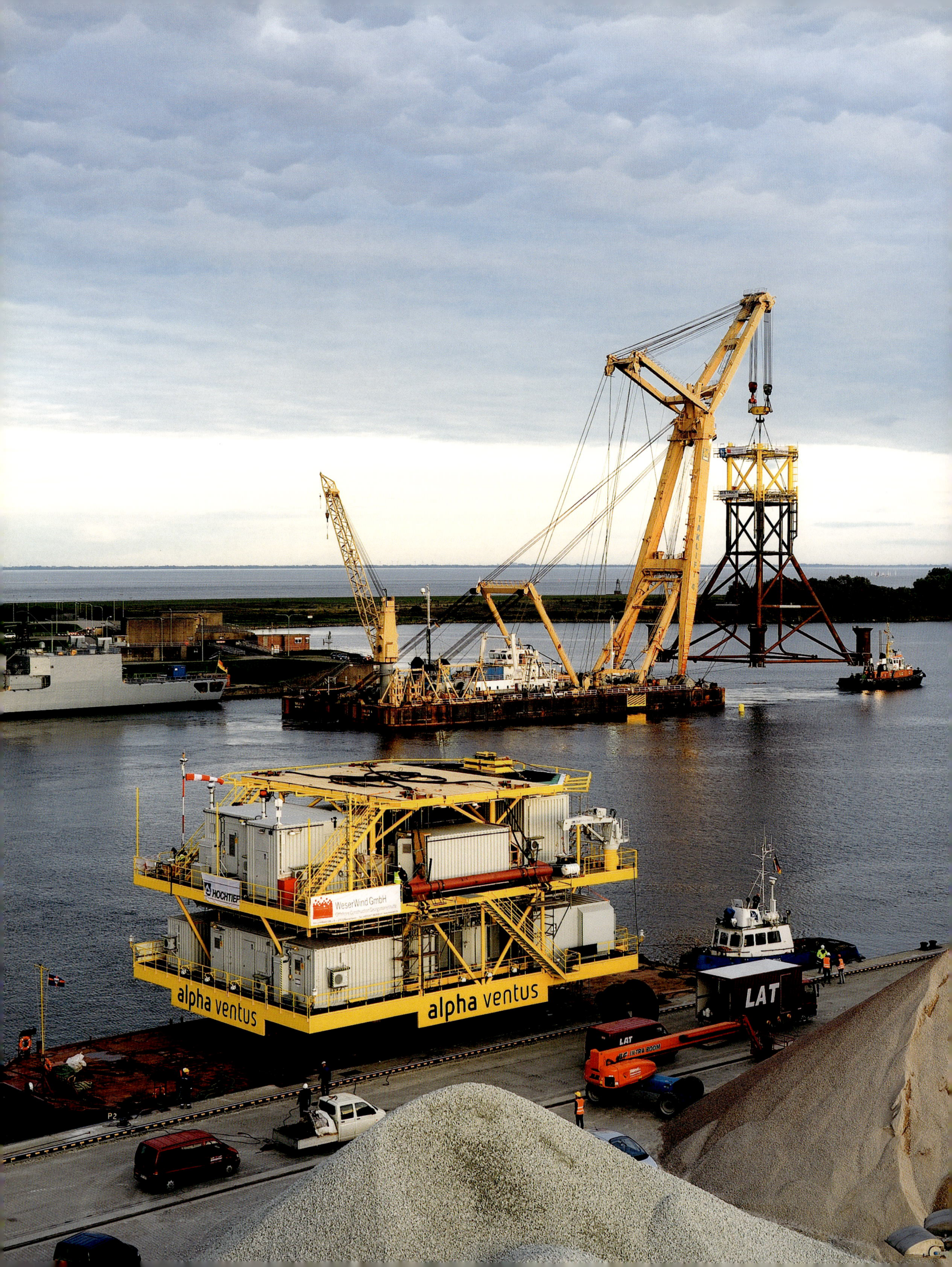
HOCHTIEF
WeserWind GmbH
alpha ventus
alpha ventus
LAT
LAT

Energieversorger steigen ins Offshore-Geschäft ein
Power companies enter the offshore business

Hand aufs Herz: Wer in der Windenergiebranche hätte bei der Gründung der Stiftung Offshore Windenergie im Juli 2005 gedacht, dass der erste Offshore-Windpark Deutschlands schließlich von drei Energieversorgern gemeinsam errichtet und betrieben werden würde? Wohl niemand. Denn die Blicke der unterschiedlichen Akteure waren in der ersten Offshore-Euphorie, als die BSH-Genehmigungen noch eine rasche Realisierung vermuten ließen, zunächst einmal auf den Fortschritt des jeweils eigenen Projektes gerichtet. Der Gedanke, die Entwicklung der Offshore-Windenergie als Gemeinschaftsaufgabe der erneuerbaren Energiebranche, ja der ganzen Energiewirtschaft und sogar des Staates zu begreifen, war wenig ausgeprägt.

Diese Haltung änderte sich jedoch schrittweise, als die Offshore-Pioniere nach eingehender Beschäftigung mit der Materie mehr und mehr erkennen mussten, welche Dimension das Unternehmen Offshore eigentlich einnimmt. Und zwar in vielerlei Hinsicht: technisch, logistisch, planerisch, genehmigungsrechtlich und natürlich auch finanziell. So sahen sich viele begeisterte kleine und mittelständische Projektentwickler, die schwungvoll Offshore-Projekte initiiert hatten, plötzlich Schwierigkeiten gegenüber, die sie in dieser Heftigkeit bei Windenergieprojekten an Land seit den Pioniertagen nicht mehr kannten.

Besonders die Finanzierung erwies sich angesichts des großen Investitionsvolumens mit schlecht kalkulierbaren Risiken häufig als eine unüberwindbar erscheinende Hürde. Viele Projekte kamen deshalb nicht voran und bei so manchem Initiator verflogen die Offshore-Träume fast so schnell wie sie aufgekommen waren. Auch die deutschen Windenergieanlagen-Hersteller wollten sich nicht im Alleingang auf das finanzielle Abenteuer einlassen, in eigener Regie ein Testfeld zu errichten und zu betreiben.

Was tun? Das fragte sich sicherlich auch Bundeskanzlerin Angela Merkel, die im April 2006 zum Energiegipfel nach Berlin ins Kanzleramt lud. Dort wurde im Kreis der wichtigsten Entscheidungsträger der deutschen Energiewirtschaft auch das Thema Offshore-Windenergie angeschnitten. Wie könnte der Einstieg ins deutsche Offshore-Geschäft gestaltet werden? Die Politik drängte und am Ende sagten EWE, E.ON und Vattenfall der Kanzlerin fest zu, gemeinsam ein deutsches Offshore-Testfeld errichten zu wollen.

Drei unter einem Dach

„Endlich!" werden sich insgeheim viele Offshore-Entrepreneure zwischen Oder und Ems gesagt haben. Unterdessen setzte die öffentlich gegebene Zusage der Konzernchefs die drei beteiligten Windenergie-Abteilungen der Unternehmen erst einmal mächtig unter Strom. Immerhin war zu jenem Zeitpunkt schon entschieden, dass das Test-

Let's be honest now: When the Offshore Wind Energy Foundation was formed in July 2005, who in the wind-energy business would have thought that Germany's first offshore wind farm would be jointly built and operated by no less than three power companies? Probably no-one. In that initial euphoria for offshore wind energy, as the approvals by the German Federal Marine and Hydrographic Authority (BSH) seemed to bode rapid implementation, all eyes were on the progress of each company's own projects. The idea of offshore wind energy as a joint effort on the part of the renewable energy industry, the entire energy industry as a whole – or even the state – had not yet gained a toehold.

This attitude changed gradually, as the pioneers in the offshore business got deeper into the practicalities of the matter and began to realise the sheer dimensions of the technical, logistical, planning, approval and financial issues involved. Many of the small and medium-sized project developers who had started offshore projects in the first flush of enthusiasm suddenly faced difficulties of a severity unseen since the earliest days of wind energy on land.

Financing in particular often turned out to be a seemingly insurmountable obstacle, given the large investment volumes and poorly calculable risks. Many projects stalled and many companies' offshore dreams faded away as quickly as they had arisen. The German wind-turbine manufacturers likewise were unwilling to risk the financial adventure of constructing and operating their own test field.

What was to be done? German Chancellor Angela Merkel must have asked herself that question as she invited the key decision-makers of the German energy industry to the Energy Summit in Berlin in April 2006. Offshore wind energy was among the hottest topics on the agenda. What was the best way for Germany to get into the offshore business? This time the government pressed industry to take action, and finally three power companies, EWE, E.ON and Vattenfall, promised the Chancellor that they would join forces to create a German offshore test field.

Three's company

"Finally!" said many German offshore entrepreneurs to themselves. Meanwhile, the promise the three CEOs had publicly made to the Chancellor was putting these three companies' wind-energy departments under severe pressure. At least there was one decision that had already been made – the test field would be built at the Borkum West site, the rights to which the Offshore Wind Energy Foundation had acquired a few months previously. But how the cooperative effort would actually function still needed to be worked out among the three very differently structured companies. Who would take on which

feld am Standort von Borkum West, dessen Rechte die Stiftung Offshore Windenergie einige Monate zuvor erworben hatte, errichtet werden sollte. Doch wie sich in Zukunft die Zusammenarbeit gestalten würde, musste erst einmal geklärt werden. Wer sollte welche Aufgabe übernehmen, damit möglichst schnell eine tragfähige und funktionstüchtige Einheit gebildet werden konnte?

Schon drei Monate nach dem Energiegipfel gründeten im Juli 2006 zwei der drei sehr unterschiedlich strukturierten Energieversorger ein in dieser Konstellation wohl einmaliges Gemeinschaftsunternehmen: die Deutsche Offshore-Testfeld- und Infrastruktur-GmbH & Co. KG, kurz DOTI genannt. Die DOTI setzte sich dabei anfänglich aus der EWE AG und der E.ON-Tochterfirma E.ON Energy Projects GmbH, auf die nach konzerninterner Umstrukturierung die E.ON Climate & Renewables GmbH folgte, zusammen. Wenig später stieß die Vattenfall-Unternehmenstochter Vattenfall Europe New Energy GmbH dazu, die operativ schon von Beginn involviert war. Deren Anteile gingen im Frühjahr 2009 auf die Vattenfall Europe Windkraft GmbH über.

Die EWE AG ist seit einer Kapitalaufstockung im Herbst 2008 mit 47,5 Prozent der größte Anteilseigner. Firmensitz ist formal in Oldenburg, wenngleich die DOTI von Beginn an dezentral operierte und neben den Standorten Oldenburg und Westerstede noch Projektbüros in Hamburg und München unterhielt. „Wir waren von der ersten

tasks, so that a robust, functional unit could be formed as quickly as possible?

Just three months after the Energy Summit, in July 2006 two of the three power companies founded a joint company that is probably the only one of its kind – the Deutsche Offshore-Testfeld- und Infrastruktur-GmbH & Co. KG, or DOTI for short. DOTI was initially formed by EWE AG and the E.ON subsidiary E.ON Energy Projects GmbH, which later became E.ON Climate & Renewables GmbH after internal restructuring. Shortly thereafter the Vattenfall subsidiary Vattenfall Europe New Energy GmbH joined the group, having been involved at the operational level right from the beginning. Its shares were transferred to Vattenfall Europe Windkraft GmbH in the spring of 2009.

Following an injection of capital in the autumn of 2008, EWE AG became the largest shareholder with 47.5 percent of DOTI's capital. The headquarters is officially in Oldenburg, northwest Germany, but DOTI operated decentrally right from the start, with project offices in Hamburg and Munich besides the Oldenburg and Westerstede locations. "From the very first we were a virtual team, spread throughout Germany," says Wilfried Hube, who functioned as CEO of DOTI and in the autumn of 2008 was named overall Project Director of alpha ventus. Hube was one of the people at EWE who had been working on transmission-grid planning for the first offshore wind farms even

Stunde an ein virtuelles Team, das über ganz Deutschland verstreut war", erzählt Wilfried Hube, der in der DOTI die Geschäftsführung von Seiten der EWE übernahm und im Herbst 2008 zum Gesamtprojektleiter von alpha ventus ernannt wurde. Hube gehörte zu den EWE-Mitarbeitern, die sich schon vor der Gründung der DOTI mit der Netzplanung für die ersten Offshore-Parks beschäftigten; für ihn kam die Dreier-Kooperation nicht überraschend. Hinter den Kulissen waren schon vor dem Berliner-Energiegipfel intensive Gespräche darüber geführt worden, wie man den Bau eines Offshore-Testfeldes gemeinsam anpacken könnte. Insofern war die DOTI für Hube in gewisser Weise die Fortsetzung einer längst begonnenen Arbeit. Allerdings bot die DOTI jetzt eine solide Grundlage für das ganze Projekt: die finanzielle und technische Zusammenarbeit für den Netzanschluss, die Logistik, die Errichtung und die Inbetriebnahme des Testfeldes.

Die Aufgaben wurden geteilt: Während die EWE alle Aufgaben rund um Seekabel, Umspannstation und Leittechnik übernahm, kümmerte sich die E.ON Climate & Renewables um sämtliche Fragen rund um die Windenergieanlagen. Vattenfall verantwortete schließlich die Gründung und Logistik. Darüber hinaus galt es, für sämtliche Offshore-Tätigkeiten ein vollkommen neues Arbeits-, Umweltschutz- und Sicherheitskonzept (Health, Safety and Environment – kurz HSE) zu erarbeiten, was das BSH als Genehmigungsauflage mit auf den Weg

Die Topside des Umspannwerks von alpha ventus wird im Hafen von Wilhelmshaven vom Schwimmkran Taklift 4 am Haken genommen und aufs Meer hinaus transportiert.

The alpha ventus transformer station's topside is taken by the hook from Taklift 4 floating crane in the port of Wilhelmshaven and moved out into the open sea.

Energieversorger steigen ins Offshore-Geschäft ein Power companies enter the offshore business

gegeben hatte. Verantwortlich für diese komplexe Materie war Irina Lucke von der EWE. Mit Unterstützung des externen Experten Andreas Stutz, der für die Offshore-Industrie als erfahrener Berufstaucher tätig ist, entwarf sie federführend ein HSE-Konzept, das sich während der Bauphase bewährte und den kommenden Offshore-Projekten sicherlich als Vorbild dienen wird.

Die erste Amtshandlung für die DOTI nach ihrer Gründung war es dann, die Genehmigungsrechte an dem Testfeld von der Stiftung Offshore Windenergie zu pachten. Außerdem wurde für das Vorhaben ein neuer Name gesucht. „alpha 12" stand zur Debatte, doch fehlte diesem Vorschlag nach dem Geschmack der Beteiligten noch der letzte Pfiff. Der entscheidende Dreh gelang dann E.ON-Manager Sven Utermöhlen und seinen Kollegen. Sie warfen die lateinisch-griechische Wortschöpfung „alpha ventus" – was frei übersetzt so viel heißt wie „Erster Wind" – in den Ring. Alle Beteiligten fanden den Namen passend und so wurde Borkum West kurzerhand in alpha ventus umgetauft. „Wir wollten der Öffentlichkeit signalisieren, dass wir mit dem Testfeld einen gemeinsamen Neustart in Sachen Offshore-Windenergie beabsichtigten", erklärt Lutz Wiese von der Vattenfall-Kommunikation und Pressesprecher der DOTI zur symbolträchtigen Namensgebung.

Nomen est omen. Tatsächlich war es ein Neustart. Allerdings dauerte es noch rund dreieinhalb Jahre, bis das weltweit einmalige Testfeld Ende 2009 endlich errichtet war. Auch wenn Außenstehenden die Zeitspanne ziemlich lang erscheint, hält Wilfried Hube klipp und klar dagegen: „Für einen Offshore-Windpark ist das verdammt wenig!" So verschlangen allein die Ausschreibungen und die darauf folgenden akribischen Auswertungen der Angebote für die Windenergieanlagen, die Gründungen, die Spezialschiffe und die übrigen Gewerke viel Zeit und auch Manpower. Auch das Personal-Karussell drehte sich. Vor allem während des ersten Findungsprozesses kam es zu Umbesetzungen, nicht zuletzt, weil innerhalb der Konzerne die Strukturen auf das Geschäft mit den erneuerbaren Energien ausgerichtet wurden. Trotzdem beschreiben im Nachhinein fast alle Mitarbeiter im DOTI-Team, das sich über die gesamte Planungs- und Bauzeit zweimal im Monat im Hamburger Projektbüro zu Arbeitssitzungen traf, die gute, ja „erstaunlich gute" Kooperation miteinander und einen sehr guten Teamgeist. Da konnten selbst Störfeuer von außen, die gerade dann, wenn es im Baufeld mal wieder nicht so lief wie gewünscht, keine Unruhe entfachen. Ohnehin ließen die drei beteiligten Unternehmen der DOTI zu keinem Zeitpunkt den geringsten Zweifel daran aufkommen, dass sie an dem Projekt alpha ventus festhalten würden. Wieso auch? EWE, E.ON und Vattenfall knüpfen hohe Erwartungen an die Offshore-Windenergie. Das ist ihr gemeinsamer Nenner beim Pionierprojekt alpha ventus, obgleich die unternehmerischen Strategien kaum unterschiedlicher sein könnten, wie der genaue Blick auf die zurückliegenden, aktuellen und kommenden Aktivitäten der drei Unternehmen demonstriert.

EWE setzt auf die Faszination des Machbaren

Die „Energieversorgung Weser-Ems", die EWE AG, beschränkt sich seit Langem nicht mehr nur auf ihr Stammland in Nordwestdeutschland, sondern hat ihr Versorgungsgebiet deutlich ausgeweitet. Inzwischen ist die Oldenburger Aktiengesellschaft auch in Brandenburg, auf Rügen und in Nordvorpommern aktiv, außerdem in Polen und der Türkei. Der EWE-Konzern ist in drei Geschäftsbereichen tätig.

before DOTI came into being. The triple partnership did not come as a surprise for him, as even before the Berlin Energy Summit there had been much discussion behind the scenes of how to go about building a joint offshore test field. Thus, for Hube DOTI was just the continuation of something he had long since begun working on. However, DOTI now offered a solid foundation for the entire project – financial and technical cooperation for the grid connection, the logistics, and the construction and commissioning of the test field.

The work was divided up among the partner companies. EWE took on all tasks connected with undersea cables, the transformer station and control systems. E.ON Climate & Renewables concentrated on all matters concerning the wind turbines. Vattenfall was in charge of the turbine tower foundations and logistics. On top of all this, the German Federal Marine and Hydrographic Authority (BSH) needed to see a completely new Health, Safety and Environment (HSE) concept before it would grant approval. Irina Lucke of EWE was put in charge of the complex task of developing this. With the assistance of external expert Andreas Stutz, an experienced professional diver for the offshore industry, she and her team drafted an HSE manual that proved its value during the construction phase and will doubtlessly serve as a model for future offshore projects.

The first official act of DOTI after its founding was to lease the approval rights for the test field from the Offshore Wind Energy Foundation. And of course the project needed a name. 'alpha 12' was mooted, but the parties involved felt that although this was promising, it lacked that certain something. E.ON-Manager Sven Utermöhlen and his colleagues found the answer – they contributed the Greco-Latin neologism 'alpha ventus' (freely translated as 'First Wind') to the pool of ideas. Everyone felt the name was appropriate, and so Borkum West was renamed 'alpha ventus' without further ado. "We wanted the name to be an outward symbol of our intention for this test field to represent a shared new beginning for offshore wind energy," says Lutz Wiese of Vattenfall Communications and DOTI Press Spokesman.

And it is indeed a new beginning – although it was to take until late 2009, another three-and-a-half years – to complete the test field, still the only one of its kind in the world. 42 months might seem a long time to some outside observers, but Wilfried Hube sees it differently: "That's really very fast for an offshore wind farm!", he enthuses, "especially given the amount of time and manpower required just to prepare the bid tenders, and then evaluate in painstaking detail the resulting bids for wind turbines, foundations, special vessels – and all the other components of this massive project." Personnel changes also brought challenges, especially during the initial phases as the partner companies restructured internally in order to focus better on renewables. This resulted in a series of changes in the staff assigned to various tasks. Nevertheless, in retrospect almost all of the employees on the DOTI team that met twice monthly in the Hamburg project office over the entire course of the project described the inter-company cooperation as "astoundingly good," and spoke of the "excellent team spirit." Even outside interference and problems on the construction site could not unsettle this increasingly tight-knit team. In fact, at no point did any of

Im Herbst 2008 wurde das Umspannwerk im Testfeld alpha ventus errichtet. The transformer station was set up in the test field in autumn 2008.

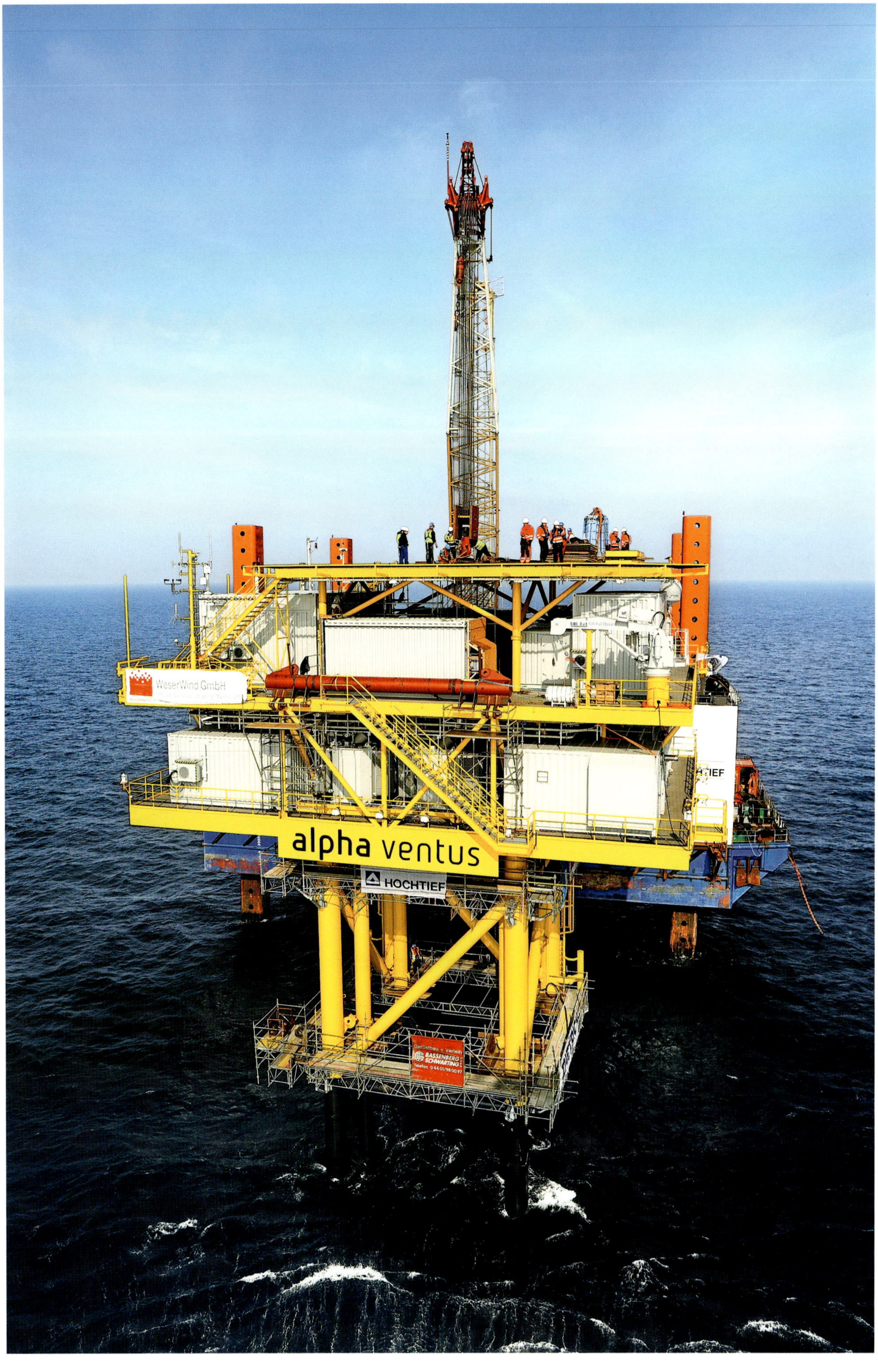

WeserWind GmbH
alpha ventus
HOCHTIEF

Die beiden klassischen Bereiche Energie und Netz werden seit 1996 durch einen dritten Geschäftsbereich ergänzt, der Telekommunikation und Informationstechnologie umfasst. Das Oldenburger Unternehmen versorgt rund eine Million Stromkunden und 1,2 Millionen Erdgaskunden mit Energie.

Erneuerbare Energien spielen für die EWE eine wachsende Rolle und die Stromerzeugung aus Windenergie, Biomasse, Biogas und Solarenergie wird stetig ausgebaut. Das vielleicht populärste Projekt in dieser Hinsicht ist die Solaranlage an der Fassade des Bremer Weserstadion. Sie leistet 1,2 Megawatt und ist eine der größten ihrer Art. In Emden betreibt das Unternehmen gemeinsam mit zwei Projektpartnern ein Biomasseheizkraftwerk mit 20 Megawatt elektrischer Leistung. Außerdem ist die EWE in die Biogaserzeugung eingestiegen. Am stärksten investierte die EWE AG bisher in die Stromerzeugung aus Windenergie. Das Unternehmen kann auf eine über 20-jährige

the three companies involved in DOTI express the slightest doubt that they would stay on board with the alpha ventus project. And why should they? EWE, E.ON and Vattenfall all continue to have very high expectations for offshore wind energy. This is their common interest in this pioneering project, although otherwise their company strategies could hardly be more different, as a close examination of the past, present, and upcoming activities of the three companies reveals.

EWE's commitment to the fascination of the possible

'Energieversorgung Weser-Ems' (EWE AG) has long looked beyond its home territory in northwest Germany and has greatly extended the area to which it supplies power. From its base in Oldenburg, the group is now active in Brandenburg, Rügen and North Pomerania in Germany, and as far afield as Poland and Turkey.

RESPEKT VOR DEN GEFAHREN AUF SEE
RESPECTING THE DANGERS OF THE HIGH SEAS
von Dierk Jensen by Dierk Jensen

Das Arbeitsschutz-, Sicherheits- und Umweltschutzkonzept im Testfeld alpha ventus leistet wertvolle Vorarbeit für kommende Offshore-Projekte.

„Hast du auch das Seepferdchen machen müssen?" Zuerst wusste ich gar nicht, was der Monteur auf der Hubinsel meinte. Wollte er mich auf den Arm nehmen? Doch im zweiten Moment verstand ich. „Ja, ja, habe ich absolviert, in Rotterdam, drei Tage lang", antwortete ich. „Da war ich auch", entgegnete der Kollege, „du hast bestimmt den Bosiet-Kurs belegt, mit simuliertem Helikopterabsturz unter Wasser, Feuerlöschtraining und Rettung auf See, das volle Programm." Ich stimmte zu: „Ja, ja, das volle Programm", erwiderte ich und hatte in diesem Augenblick wieder die aufregendste der vielfältigen Übungen vor Augen, bei der man nämlich angeschnallt unter Wasser um die eigene Achse gedreht wird, dabei die Luft anhält und einen Augenblick gar nicht mehr weiß, wo links und rechts und wo der Ausstieg nach oben an die rettende Wasseroberfläche ist.

Dieses Offshore-Training ist für alle verpflichtend, die in der Bauphase im Testfeld von alpha ventus gearbeitet haben, und auch für die, die während des zukünftigen Betriebes dort im Einsatz sein werden. Die Teilnehmer lernen durch den mehrtägigen Offshore-Kurs, wie sie sich in Notfällen lebensrettend verhalten sollen. Es wird in diesen Trainingscenter ein großer Aufwand betrieben, um etwaige Notfälle so realistisch wie möglich zu simulieren und alle im Offshore-Bereich Arbeitenden mit praktischen Tipps so zu präparieren, dass sie im Katastrophenfall handlungsfähig bleiben.

Diese praktischen Übungen ironisch als Seepferdchen abzuwerten, könne nur aus dem Munde von jemandem kommen, der noch nicht lange auf dem Meer gearbeitet hat und die Tücken auf hoher See nicht kennt. Das ist zumindest die Einschätzung von Andreas Stutz.

The alpha ventus health, safety and environment programme is a valuable resource for future offshore projects

"Did you also have to do the seahorse?" At first I didn't know what the fitter on the jack-up platform meant. Was it some kind of joke? But then I got it. "Oh, yes, I took the course, in Rotterdam – three days," I answered. "So did I," he said. "I bet you had to do the Bosiet course, the simulated helicopter crash underwater, fire-extinguisher training, high-seas rescue, the whole thing." "Yes," I said, "the whole thing," and thought of the most challenging of the many exercises we did – the one where they turn you around underwater in a flooded compartment while you're strapped in and holding your breath, so you don't know right from left, or which direction to go to get to the hatch and escape to the surface.

This offshore training is mandatory for everyone working in the construction phase of the alpha ventus test field, and will be required for everyone who works there when it's operational. The course takes several days and teaches participants how to stay alive in emergency situations. The training centres place great emphasis on simulating emergency situations as realistically as possible, and on giving offshore workers the practical knowledge they need in order to be able to react appropriately in case of emergency. Only somebody who hasn't been at sea for long and doesn't know how dangerous it can be, would refer to this highly practical training as "seahorse."

Er hat als Berufstaucher mit langjährigen Offshore-Erfahrungen im Auftrag der DOTI unter der Leitung von Irina Lucke (EWE AG) das Arbeitsschutz-, Sicherheits- und Umweltschutzkonzept (HSE) für alpha ventus in wesentlichen Zügen mit erarbeitet. „Wir von der Offshore-Branche wissen um die Gefahren bei der Arbeit auf dem Meer und haben aus diesem Grund sehr hohen Respekt davor. Die Sicherheit offshore spielt für uns die allererste Rolle", unterstreicht Stutz. „Die Sicherheitsvorschriften hier erfordern komplett andere Standards als an Land. Nur wer die genau definierten Qualifikationen im Voraus aufweist, darf auf See. Wer die Papiere im Ausgangshafen nicht vollständig vorlegen kann, der bleibt an Land. Koste es, was es wolle. Da gibt es gar keine Kompromisse", sagt Stutz. So muss jeder neben dem Offshore-Training auch einen Gesundheitscheck mit Lungentest und EKG, einen Erste-Hilfe-Kurs sowie Abseilübungen absolviert haben. „Alles, was schiefgehen kann, wird auch schiefgehen", verweist Stutz in diesem Zusammenhang auf die berühmte Kernaussage von Murphys Gesetz.

Irina Lucke, verantwortlich für die Bereiche Genehmigung und HSE, spricht von einem „Riesenglück", dass man Andreas Stutz für die Erarbeitung des Sicherheitskonzeptes und als Sicherheitskoordinator hat gewinnen können. Die große Herausforderung in der Planungsphase von alpha ventus lag darin, dass Lucke, Stutz und Co. für das erste deutsche Offshore-Projekt auf keinerlei Vorgaben zurückgreifen konnten. Wohin sie auch Kontakt aufnahmen, Fehlanzeige. „Im Gegensatz zu den Deutschen verfügen die übrigen Nordsee-Anrainerstaaten über langjährige Erfahrungen mit Öl und Gas und haben Richtlinien entwickelt, die es in Deutschland nicht gab."

Mit alpha ventus hat sich das nun grundlegend geändert. Denn mit dem 75-seitigen Arbeits- und Sicherheitskonzept, ohne das das BSH keinen Bau zugelassen hätte, liegt jetzt eine „Bedienungsanleitung" für ein Gefahren vermeidendes Verhalten vor, auf die alle weiteren Offshore-Projekte zurückgreifen und das sie gegebenenfalls weiterentwickeln können. In dem Regelkonvolut ist jeder einzelne Aspekt, von „Verantwortlichkeiten" über „Persönliche Schutzausrüstung" bis hin zu „Seilunterstütztes Zugangs- und Positionierungsverfahren" minutiös berücksichtigt. „Für jede Arbeit, die Sie draußen auf dem Meer umsetzen, muss im Vorfeld eine genaue Arbeitsprozedur mit Gefährdungsbeurteilung und Risikoanalyse erstellt werden. Jede Arbeit wird genau beschrieben, auch wenn es nur um das Streichen einer Wand geht. Es wird abgebildet, welche Geräte, welche Ausrüstung, wie viele Personen gebraucht werden, aber auch, welche Gefahren damit verbunden sind und welche Maßnahmen man im Vorfeld ergreifen muss, um diese Gefahren zu reduzieren beziehungsweise ganz auszuschalten", erklärt Irina Lucke zur umfassenden Dokumentation.

Letztlich hat sich der Aufwand für die Sicherheit mehr als gelohnt. Trotz einiger Unfälle, die sich immer wieder auf Offshore-Baustellen ereignen können, hat sich das HSE-Konzept bewährt. Dennoch wird Andreas Stutz nicht müde, in der Windenergie-Branche weiterhin für mehr Verständnis für die sehr hohen Sicherheitsansprüche im Offshore-Bereich zu werben.

At least, that's what Andreas Stutz thinks. As a professional diver with extensive offshore experience, he was engaged by DOTI under the supervision of Irina Lucke (EWE AG) to work out the major features of the occupational health, safety and environment (HSE) scheme for alpha ventus. "Those of us in the offshore industry know the hazards of working at sea, and have the greatest respect for them. Safety offshore is our first priority," said Stutz, adding: "Safety requirements at sea have a completely different standard than on land. Nobody goes to sea unless they can prove ahead of time that they fulfil rigorously defined qualifications. If your papers aren't in order, you're staying on land, regardless of cost. No compromises." In addition to the offshore training course, everyone has to have a thorough health check, including a lung check and ECG, and must have completed a first aid course and rappel (abseiling) training. "If something can go wrong, it will, and you have to be ready for it," notes Stutz, in a reference to Murphy's famous law.

Irina Lucke, the person in charge of Approvals and HSE, calls it "great luck" that she was able to get Andreas Stutz to prepare the safety programme and to accept the post of Safety Coordinator. The biggest challenge during the alpha ventus planning phase was that Lucke, Stutz and their colleagues on this first German offshore project had no guidelines to turn to. Wherever they looked, they came up empty. "Unlike Germany, the other nations bordering the North Sea have many years' experience with oil and gas platforms and have developed guidelines that simply didn't exist in Germany."

Now alpha ventus has changed all that. The health, safety and environment programme, without which the German Federal Maritime and Hydrographic Agency would not have approved construction, provides an Operating Manual for hazard prevention that all future offshore projects can refer to and develop further as necessary. This 75-page manual covers in minute detail every individual aspect, from 'Responsibilities' to 'Personal safety equipment' to 'Rope-supported access and positioning.' Irina Lucke says of the comprehensive documentation, "For every task that is done out at sea, there must be a precisely predefined working procedure, with hazard assessment and risk analysis. Each task is described in exhaustive detail – even if it's just painting a wall. The Manual lays out what tools, what equipment, and how many people are needed for each task, as well as which hazards are involved and what measures must be taken in advance in order to minimize or eliminate these hazards", Lucke explains.

In the final analysis, the safety effort paid off. Despite a few accidents, of the kind that can always happen on an offshore construction site, the HSE concept more than proved its value. And Andreas Stutz does not tire of further publicising the need for the highest safety requirements in the offshore wind industry.

Safety first: Übungen für den Notfall sind für jeden, der im Offshore-Bereich arbeitet, Pflicht. Dazu gehört das Abseiltraining vom Helikopter auf die REpower 5M, die auf dem Testfeld der DEWI-OCC in Cuxhaven steht.
Safety is first priority for anybody working in the offshore field. That's why emergency exercises are compulsory, including rapelling training from the helicopter and from a REpower 5M, located on the DEWI-OCC test field in Cuxhaven.

Erfahrung auf diesem Gebiet zurückblicken. Der erste Windpark der EWE entstand bereits 1988 in der Nähe von Cuxhaven. In kurzen Abständen folgten weitere Windparkprojekte, vorwiegend in Ostfriesland. Der bislang größte Windpark der EWE steht im Wybelsumer Polder. Rund ein Drittel der dort installierten Gesamtleistung (79 Megawatt) wurde von dem Energieversorger in den Jahren 1997 bis 2002 ans Netz gebracht.

Erste Schritte ins Wasser

Im Oktober 2004 errichtete EWE im flachen Wasser der Emsmündung, in der Nähe des Emder Hafens, eine Windenergieanlage mit 4,5 Megawatt Leistung. Es war die erste Windenergieanlage in deutschen Küstengewässern – zwar noch nicht „offshore", aber immerhin schon „nearshore". Damit sammelte EWE erste Erfahrungen auf dem Weg in Richtung Offshore-Windenergie. Ein Jahr später ließ das Unter-

EWE works in three business fields. Traditionally a power-generation and grid utility, in 1996 it added telecommunications and information technology to its portfolio. Today, the company supplies electricity to around a million customers and natural gas to 1.2 million customers. Renewable energy plays a growing role for EWE and the company is steadily expanding its generation capacity in wind, biomass and solar power. Perhaps its most popular renewable energy project is the solar array on the façade of the Bremen Weser Stadium: this can produce 1.2 megawatts and is one of the largest of its kind anywhere. In Emden the company operates a 20-megawatt biomass power plant jointly with two project partners. EWE is also involved in biogas generation.

EWE AG's greatest renewables investment so far has been in electricity generation from wind energy, and the company has over 20 years of experience in the field. The first EWE wind farm was built in 1988 near Cuxhaven and was quickly followed by other wind farms, mostly in the East Friesia region of northwest Germany. EWE's largest wind

nehmen eine 6-Megawatt-Windenergieanlage auf dem Testfeld in Cuxhaven errichten, um diesen Anlagentyp unter „offshore-ähnlichen" Bedingungen zu erproben. Auf diesem Erfahrungshintergrund lag die Beteiligung am Projekt alpha ventus nahe. Seit Inbetriebnahme des Windparks ist EWE für dessen ordnungsgemäßen Betrieb zuständig. Einen eigenen Offshore-Windpark plant das Unternehmen in der Zwölf-Seemeilen-Zone, rund 15 Kilometer nordwestlich von Borkum. In wenigen Jahren werden im Windpark Riffgat 24 Windenergieanlagen in der Nordsee stehen und eine etwa doppelt so hohe Leistung wie alpha ventus erbringen. Um eines Tages den aus Windenergie erzeugten Strom in ausreichender Menge zwischenspeichern zu können, sollen Elektrofahrzeuge in das Energiesystem integriert werden. Die EWE AG entwickelt deshalb gemeinsam mit dem Osnabrücker Fahrzeughersteller Karmann ein Elektroauto, dessen Prototyp auf der Hannovermesse 2009 vorgestellt wurde. In wenigen Jahren sollen die Elektroautos ins Stromnetz integriert werden und sich als mobile

farm to date is in the Wybelsum Polder. Around a third of the installed capacity of 79 megawatts there was brought on-stream between 1997 and 2002.

Venturing into the water

In October 2004 EWE sited a 4.5-megawatt wind-energy converter in the shallow water of the Ems Estuary, near the port of Emden. It was the first in German coastal waters – if not quite offshore, then certainly 'inshore' – and it gave EWE the opportunity to gain experience it could apply to later offshore projects. A year later the company set up a 6-megawatt turbine in the test field in Cuxhaven, in order to test this type of turbine under offshore-like conditions. This wealth of experience made EWE's participation in the alpha ventus wind-farm project an easy decision to take, and since the farm was brought on-stream the company has been responsible for ensuring its correct operation.

Ansicht Süd-Ost **View from south east**

Position: N4 00´, E6 37,40´
Position: N4 00´, E6 37,40´

30 m Helideck
30 m Helicopter deck

25 m Hauptdeck
25 m Main deck

21 m Kabeldeck
21 m Cable deck

Hochwasser **High tide**

Niedrigwasser **Low tide**

Kabelführungsrohr
J-tube

1. Leittechnik
   Control systems
2. Sternpunktbildner
   Three-phase earthing transformer
3. GIS-Schaltanlage
   Gas insulated switchgear (GIS)
4. GS- und NS-Anlage
   DC and low-voltage equipment
5. Feuerlöschanlage
   Firefighting equipment
6. Transformator
   Transformer
7. GIS-Schaltanlage
   Gas insulated switchgear (GIS)
8. MVAr-Drossel
   MVAr reactor coil
9. Kran
   Crane
10. Geräteraum
    Equipment room
11. Aufenthaltsraum/Notunterkunft
    Staff room/emergency accommodation
12. Werkstatt
    Workshop
13. Batterie/Gleichrichter
    Battery/ rectifier
14. Leckölsammeltank
    Leakage oil collection tank
15. Notstromaggregat
    Emergency back-up generator
16. Dieseltank
    Diesel tank
17. Dieseltank
    Diesel tank

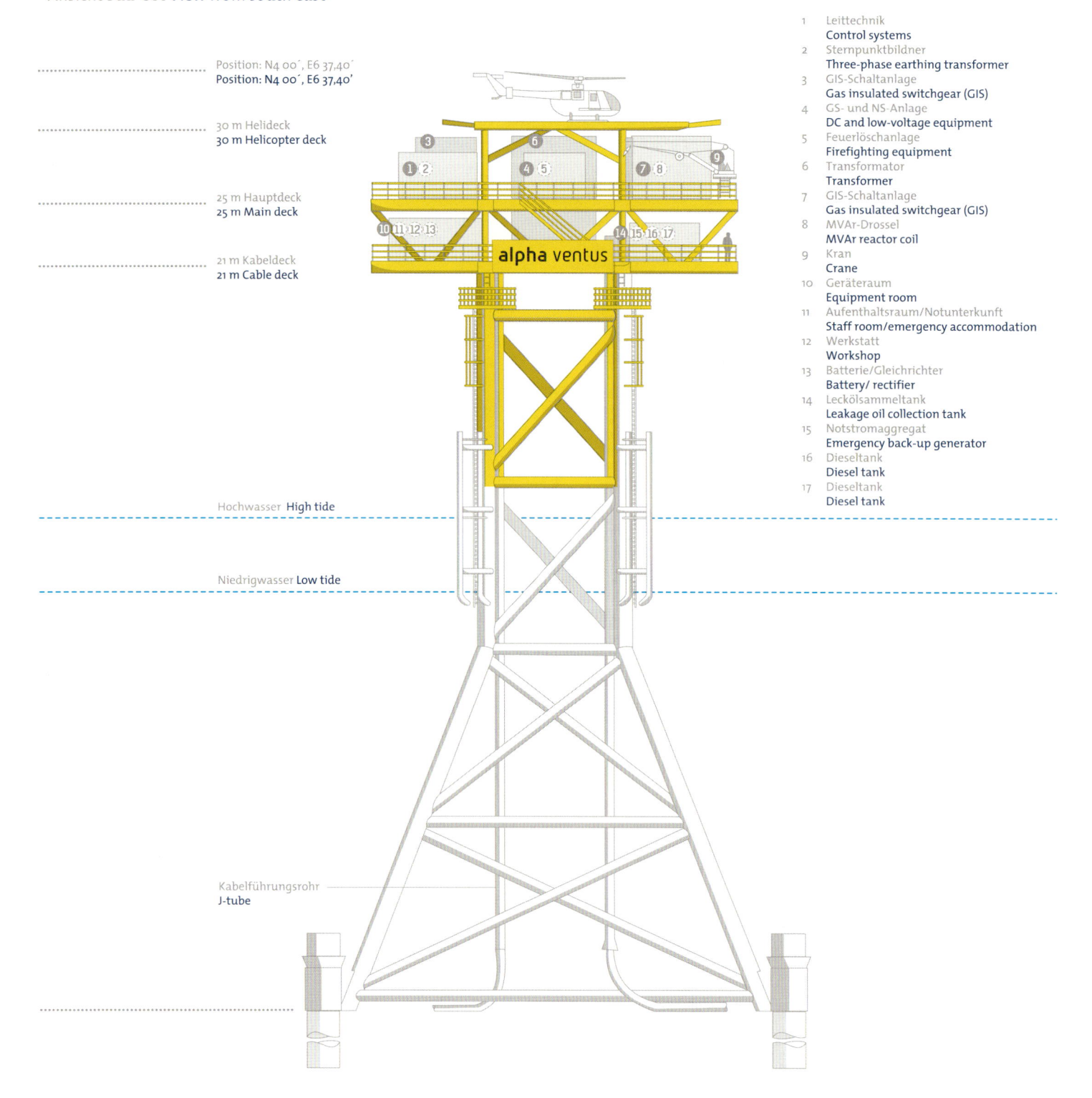

Stromspeicher bewähren. Um das Engagement in Zukunft auf wissenschaftlicher Grundlage fortsetzen zu können, gründete die EWE unter dem Namen „Next Energy" ein Forschungszentrum für Energietechnologien an der Universität Oldenburg. Forschungsschwerpunkte sind erneuerbare Energien, Energieeffizienz und Energiespeicherung.

Kompetenzen in der Region nutzen

„Das Engagement der EWE wird nach wie vor getragen von der Faszination des Machbaren", erklärt Unternehmensvorstand Thomas Neu-

The company plans to build its own offshore wind farm in the 12-nautical-mile zone, some 15 kilometres northwest of Borkum on the North Sea coast. In a few years the 24 turbines that are to be erected in the Riffgat wind farm will deliver about twice as much power as alpha ventus. In order to create intermediate storage capacity for the electricity generated by wind power, electric cars need to be integrated into the energy-supply system. EWE AG is working with Osnabrück automaker Karmann on an electric car, a prototype of which was presented at the 2009 Hanover Fair. In a few years, electric cars will become part of the electrical grid, acting as mobile intermediate storage devices. To provide a sound scientific basis for further progress, EWE

ber. „Wir setzen große Erwartungen in die Offshore-Technologie, auch wenn wir in Deutschland damit weit draußen auf dem Meer schwierigen Bedingungen ausgesetzt sind." Dabei ist sich Neuber bewusst, dass der erste Schritt meist der schwierigste ist, was sich auch in der ersten Bauphase von alpha ventus zeigte.

Trotz aller Widrigkeiten ist der Ausbau der erneuerbaren Energien ein fester Bestandteil der EWE-Strategie. An Land sind die Ausbaumöglichkeiten im Stromversorgungsgebiet der EWE zwischen Ems, Weser und Elbe allerdings inzwischen stark begrenzt, sodass EWE auch das enorme Potenzial auf dem Meer nutzen will.

„Wir wollen den Umbau der Energieversorgung in Richtung Nachhaltigkeit und Klimaschutz aktiv mitgestalten", sagt Thomas Neuber. alpha ventus ist ein wichtiges Signal dafür, dass die Offshore-Windenergie einen erheblichen Beitrag zum Umbau der Energieversorgung leisten kann. Dieser Beitrag ist dringend erforderlich, damit die Bundesregierung die gesetzten Klimaziele erreichen kann.

Darüber hinaus sieht EWE die Offshore-Technologie als Zukunftsthema mit großem Innovations- und Wachstumspotenzial. Thomas Neuber: „Deutschland hat die Chance, das hohe Exportpotenzial im Offshore-Markt in enorme Wertschöpfungs- und Beschäftigungsimpulse umzusetzen. Unser Land ist führend in der Windenergie, in der Offshore-Technologie muss es dagegen erst noch führend werden. Zwar haben wir die weltweit leistungsfähigsten Offshore-Anlagen im Angebot, aber wir konnten sie bisher noch nicht unter realen Bedingungen demonstrieren. Deshalb ist es so wichtig, mit alpha ventus und den nachfolgenden Offshore-Windparks ein Exportschaufenster zu haben. Wir müssen um unsere Führungsrolle in der Windenergie-Technologie kämpfen."

Um dieses Ziel zu erreichen, ist es sinnvoll, die vorhandenen Kräfte zu bündeln. Als ein in der Region verwurzeltes Unternehmen setzt sich die EWE AG dafür ein, die in Nordwestdeutschland vorhandenen starken Kompetenzen auszubauen. „Die EWE ist bereit, sich auch weiterhin für eine erfolgreiche Offshore-Zukunft zu engagieren", betont Thomas Neuber.

Vattenfall will klimaneutral produzieren

Diese Bereitschaft ist auch bei Vattenfall deutlich zu erkennen. Bester Beweis dafür ist das Nordsee-Projekt Dan Tysk, dessen Rechte der schwedische Energieversorger im April 2007 erwarb. Hergen Stolle, der als Vattenfall-Mitarbeiter seit 2007 im Auftrag der DOTI im Projekt alpha ventus für Gründung und Logistik verantwortlich zeichnet, wird auch an den Planungen und der stufenweisen Errichtung von Dan Tysk mit einem Endausbau von 1.500 Megawatt rund 70 Kilometer vor der Insel Sylt integriert sein. Die Windturbinen und das Umspannwerk dazu befinden sich zurzeit im Ausschreibungsprozess. Der erste Bauabschnitt mit 400 Megawatt soll 2011 beginnen. „Ich werde viele Erfahrungen von alpha ventus mit in dieses Projekt hineintragen können", zieht Stolle ein positives Resümee aus der Pioniertat. „Gerade im Jahr 2009, als im Baufeld Gründungsarbeiten und die Errichtung von Anlagen zugleich stattfanden, hatten wir logistisch schon einige heikle Herausforderungen zu meistern. Oft haben wir uns die Haare gerauft", erzählt Hergen Stolle von den kritischen Phasen im „sehr anstrengenden und intensiven Aufbaujahr". Doch haben ihn die Erfahrungen für die kommenden Aufgaben bestens präpariert. Deshalb sieht der Bauingenieur Stolle der Zukunft – nach überstandener Reifeprüfung – gelassen entgegen.

has founded a research centre by the name of 'Next Energy' at Oldenburg University. The centre is focused on renewable energy, energy efficiency and energy storage.

Making use of regional expertise

"EWE's commitment is based on our fascination for the possibilities," says CEO Thomas Neuber. "We have great expectations for offshore technology, even if for us in Germany it means that we have to cope with difficult conditions far out to sea." Neuber is aware that the first step is usually the hardest, as the first construction phase of alpha ventus showed.

But despite all the difficulties, expansion of renewable energies is a firm part of EWE's strategy. On land, however, the scope for the company to expand in its power supply area between the Ems, Weser and Elbe rivers is severely limited, and therefore EWE is looking to make use of the enormous potential at sea.

"We want to play an active role in the shift of energy production to sustainability and climate protection," notes Thomas Neuber. alpha ventus is an important demonstration that offshore wind energy can make a substantial contribution to this shift in the way energy is generated. This contribution is urgently needed if Germany is to meet the climate protection targets set by the government.

In addition, EWE sees offshore technology as having great future potential for innovation and growth. As Thomas Neuber says, "Germany has the opportunity to use the high export potential in the offshore market to create enormous growth in value creation and jobs. Our country leads in wind energy overall, but not yet in offshore technology. We offer the world's most powerful offshore turbines, but have not yet had the opportunity to demonstrate their effectiveness under real-life conditions. That is why it is so important to have an export shop window in the form of alpha ventus and future offshore wind farms. We must fight for our leadership role in wind-energy technology."

To reach this goal, it makes sense to bundle existing assets. As a company with strong roots in the region, EWE AG intends to help to make sure that the substantial expertise already present in Northwest Germany will be expanded and extended. "EWE is committed to continued effort on behalf of a successful offshore future," Thomas Neuber emphasises.

Vattenfall aims for carbon neutral generation

The same forward-looking attitude is also evident at Vattenfall. The best proof is the Dan Tysk project about 70 kilometres off the island of Sylt in the North Sea, the rights to which this Swedish energy company acquired in April 2007. Vattenfall construction engineer Hergen Stolle, responsible at DOTI since 2007 for the foundations and logistics of the alpha ventus project, will also be involved in the planning and step-by-step construction of Dan Tysk, which will have a total capacity of 1,500 megawatts when completed. The wind turbines and the transformer station are currently in the bid tender process and the first construction phase for 400 megawatts of the total is slated to begin in 2011. "I'll be able to bring very relevant experience from alpha ventus to bear on this project," notes Stolle as a positive result of the pioneering project. "In 2009, when the foundation work and the installation of the turbines were going on simultaneously, we had no shortage of logistical challenges – in fact we were often tearing our hair out!"

Unterdessen beabsichtigt Vattenfall mit seiner Strategie „Making Electricity Clean", die CO_2-Emissionen seiner Energieerzeugung bis zum Jahr 2030 um die Hälfte zu senken. Bis 2050 soll das Erzeugungsportfolio komplett klimaneutral sein. Dass die Windenergie dabei eine wichtige Rolle spielen wird, liegt auf der Hand. Vattenfall kann bei der Realisierung der ambitionierten Ziele auf langjährige Erfahrungen mit der Windenergie zurückgreifen. Das Unternehmen begann schon vor 30 Jahren, die Stromerzeugung aus Windenergie zu erproben. Am Anfang stand die Errichtung einer Versuchsanlage. Sie leistete 60 Kilowatt, das entsprach der Leistungsklasse der damals serienmäßig hergestellten Windenergieanlagen.

Anfang der achtziger Jahre gründete Vattenfall auf der Insel Gotland das Testfeld Näsudden und errichtete dort die Windenergieanlage Näsudden I. Mit 2 Megawatt Leistung gehörte sie damals zu den wenigen sehr großen Versuchsanlagen. Sie wurde 1993 durch die noch größere Näsudden II (3 Megawatt) ersetzt, die rund 15 Jahre lang in Betrieb blieb und weltweit die erste Windturbine war, die insgesamt mehr als 60 Millionen Kilowattstunden Strom produzierte. 2008 wurde Näsudden II durch den Prototyp einer 2,5-Megawatt-Anlage ersetzt.

Insgesamt hat Vattenfall in Nordeuropa heute Windenergie-Kapazitäten von mehr als 900 Megawatt onshore und offshore installiert, mit denen jährlich mehr als zwei Milliarden Kilowattstunden erzeugt werden. Bis 2030 will Vattenfall rund zwölf Prozent seiner Stromproduktion aus Windenergie erzeugen.

Das von Vattenfall im Jahr 2008 veröffentlichte „Market Stimulation Program"(Marktanreizprogramm) hat das Ziel, die jährliche Stromerzeugung aus erneuerbaren Energien bis 2016 auf zehn Milliarden Kilowattstunden zu steigern. Neue Wasserkraftwerke sollen zwei Milliarden Kilowattstunden liefern, Biomassekraftwerke 0,5 Milliarden und Windparks sieben bis acht Milliarden. Das setzt die Installation von neuen Windenergieanlagen mit 2.500 bis 3.000 Megawatt Gesamtleistung voraus. Um dieses Ziel zu erreichen, verfolgt Vattenfall eine Strategie, die sich unter anderem auf die nächste Generation der Offshore-Windturbinen (Nennleistung von 3,5 bis fünf Megawatt und mehr) sowie auf Onshore-Windturbinen mit einer Nennleistung von zwei bis drei Megawatt und mehr stützt.

Seit einigen Jahren schon erzeugt Vattenfall Strom auf dem Meer. Dem Unternehmen gehören die drei schwedischen Offshore-Windparks Utgrunden, Yttre Stengrund und Lillgrund sowie der britische Windpark Kentish Flats. Am dänischen Windpark Horns Rev ist Vattenfall zu 60 Prozent beteiligt, an alpha ventus zu 26,25 Prozent. Ende 2008 erwarb Vattenfall die Rechte am britischen Offshore-Projekt Thanet. In der Themsemündung werden 100 Windenergieanlagen mit einer Nennleistung von jeweils drei Megawatt errichtet werden. Die letzten der 100 Fundamente für die Windturbinen wurden im Januar 2010 aufgestellt, die Errichtung der Turbinen ist noch in 2010 vorgesehen. Wenn alles so klappt, wie sich die Strategen in der Konzernspitze es wünschen, dann wird Vattenfall schon in wenigen Jahren mit einer Kapazität von rund 1000 Megawatt auf dem Meer Strom erzeugen.

E.ON investiert Milliarden

Bei all den Aktivitäten des schwedischen Mitwettbewerbers mag der Energieversorger E.ON nicht untätig bleiben. Ganz im Gegenteil, man strebt mit Macht an die Spitze: Das Unternehmen bündelte im Mai 2007 alle Ökostrom-Aktivitäten in der neu geschaffenen E.ON Climate & Renewables. Seitdem hat E.ON die eigenen Erzeugungskapazitäten

recounts Hergen Stolle of the critical phases in what he terms a "very difficult and intense construction year." But that experience was the perfect preparation for his upcoming challenges and Stolle can look ahead to the future with confidence.

Meanwhile, Vattenfall plans to halve the CO_2 emissions of its electricity generation by 2030, through its 'Making Electricity Clean' strategy. By 2050 the company intends its electricity generation portfolio to be entirely carbon-neutral and it is clear that wind energy will play an important part in this. In moving ahead towards this ambitious goal, Vattenfall can draw on long experience with wind energy, having begun experimenting 30 years ago with electricity generation from wind. The company's first step was a 60-kilowatt test turbine, which was the power class of the wind turbines then in series production.

In the early 'eighties Vattenfall set up the Näsudden test field on the Swedish island of Gotland, and built the Näsudden I wind energy converter. At 2 megawatts output, it was one of only a very few large test turbines in existence at the time. In 1993 it was replaced by the even larger Näsudden II (3 megawatts), which remained in operation for some 15 years and was the world's first wind turbine to produce a total of over 60 million kilowatt hours of electricity. In 2008 Näsudden II was replaced by a 2.5-megawatt turbine.

Vattenfall now has installed onshore and offshore wind energy capacity totalling over 900 megawatts in northern Europe, generating over two billion kilowatt hours every year. By 2030 Vattenfall plans to draw around twelve percent of its electricity generation from wind energy.

In 2008 the company publicised its 'Market Stimulation Programme' aimed at ramping up annual renewable energy generation to ten billion kilowatt hours by 2016. New hydroelectric plants will supply two billion kilowatt hours, biomass power plants 0.5 billion, and wind farms seven to eight billion kilowatt-hours. This will require the construction of new wind energy capacity totalling 2,500 to 3,000 megawatts. To reach this goal, Vattenfall is pursuing a strategy that includes the next generation of offshore wind turbines (rated at 3.5 to five megawatts or more) and onshore wind turbines rated at two to three megawatts or more.

Vattenfall has been generating electricity at sea for some years and owns the three Swedish offshore wind farms Utgrunden, Yttre Stengrund and Lillgrund, as well as the British wind farm Kentish Flats. Vattenfall has a 60 percent share in the Danish wind farm Horns Rev, and 26.25 percent in alpha ventus. In late 2008 Vattenfall acquired the rights to the British offshore project Thanet, which will consist of 100 wind turbines rated at 3 megawatts each in the mouth of the Thames. The last of the 100 foundations was completed in January of 2010 and the turbines are also to go up in 2010. If everything goes as intended by company strategists, in just a few years Vattenfall will be producing electricity at sea with a capacity of around 1,000 megawatts.

E.ON investing billions

With all the activity of its Swedish competitor, energy supplier E.ON cannot remain idle. On the contrary, the company is aiming to claim the top spot. In May 2007 E.ON bundled all of its green power activities in the newly created subsidiary E.ON Climate & Renewables. Since then the company has increased its own generation capacity five-fold and now produces almost 2,400 megawatts from wind energy, biomass and small hydropower plants. In the first four years, i.e. from 2007 to 2011, a total investment of eight billion euros in renewable

versechsfacht und produziert mittlerweile Strom aus Windenergie, Solaranlagen, Biomasse und Biogas mit rund 3.000 Megawatt Leistung. In den ersten vier Jahren, von 2007 bis 2011, werden insgesamt acht Milliarden Euro in den Ausbau der erneuerbaren Energien fließen, um diesen Sektor gezielt aufzubauen und ihn zu einem der Hauptgeschäftsfelder des Konzerns zu machen. Bis zum Jahr 2015 will E.ON mit erneuerbaren Energien die 10-Gigawatt-Schwelle erreichen.

Dieser schnelle Ausbau der erneuerbaren Stromerzeugungskapazitäten stellt einen Kraftakt dar, der nur mit sehr großen Projekten zu bewältigen ist. Sven Utermöhlen, Geschäftsführer der E.ON Climate & Renewables Central Europe GmbH, beschreibt das Kernelement der Strategie so: Es sei das Ziel, „vom Boutique- zum Industriemaßstab zu gelangen" und von kleinen Projekten zur industriellen Größenordnung überzugehen. Dabei zähle nicht allein die Projektgröße, sondern es gehe auch darum, die Wertschöpfungskette dieser jungen Branche über Partnerschaften zu verbessern, die Effizienz zu steigern und damit letztlich die erneuerbaren Energien wettbewerbsfähiger zu machen.

Zur Strategie gehören auch Sonnenenergie und Biomasse. Doch die Windenergie wird auf absehbare Zeit den weitaus größten Teil des Stroms liefern, den E.ON aus erneuerbaren Energien erzeugt. Im August 2007 kaufte der Konzern mehrere Windparks in Spanien und Portugal, indem er einen großen Windparkbetreiber übernahm, und stei-

energy is planned in order to expand this sector and make it one of the E.ON Group's main business areas. By 2015 the group hopes to have reached the 10-gigawatt mark with renewable energy.

This rapid expansion of renewable electricity generation capacity is a major effort and will be possible only through very large projects. Sven Utermöhlen, CEO of E.ON Climate & Renewables Central Europe GmbH, describes the central element of the strategy: "The goal is to get from 'boutique' to industrial scale, and from small projects to industrial dimensions. This is not just a matter of project size, but also depends on improving the value-adding chain of this young industry through partnerships that boost efficiency, and ultimately make renewable energies more competitive."

Naturally, solar power and biomass are part of this strategy. But for the foreseeable future, wind power will supply by far the greatest part of the electricity that E.ON gets from renewable energy sources. In August 2007 the group acquired several wind farms in Spain and Portugal through the takeover of a large wind farm operator, thereby increasing its installed capacity to reach around 700 megawatts.

In October 2007 E.ON acquired the North American business of Irish wind farm operator Airtricity, in order to open a strong market position with high growth potential outside Europe. This move gave the E.ON Group wind farms with 210 megawatts' capacity. By the end

gerte dadurch die installierte Leistung auf rund 700 Megawatt. Im Oktober 2007 erwarb E.ON das Nordamerikageschäft des irischen Windparkbetreibers Airtricity, um sich eine starke Marktposition mit großem Wachstumspotenzial außerhalb Europas zu erschließen, und sicherte sich Windparks mit 210 Megawatt Leistung. Bis Ende 2008 wurden weitere Windparks mit 880 Megawatt in Nordamerika fertiggestellt.

Zwei Projekte verdeutlichen die Größenordnung, die gemeint ist, wenn E.ON vom Industriemaßstab spricht. Im September 2009 ging in Texas der Windpark Panther Creek ans Netz. Er besteht aus 305 Windturbinen mit einer Gesamtleistung von 458 Megawatt. Schon einen Monat später folgte der 400 Quadratkilometer große Windpark Roscoe, der ebenfalls in Texas steht und zurzeit der größte der Welt ist. E.ON erzeugt dort mit 627 Windturbinen und einer Gesamtleistung von 780 Megawatt sauberen Strom für rechnerisch rund 230.000 Haushalte.

Diese beeindruckenden Windenergie-Projekte, die inzwischen eine Gesamtleistung von 2.200 Megawatt erreichen, wurden sämtlich an Land verwirklicht, sie sollen aber bald von Offshore-Windparks in den Schatten gestellt werden. Für E.ON spielt die Offshore-Windenergie aufgrund ihres enormen Potenzials eine besondere Rolle. Weil der Wind über dem Meer bei weitem stärker und stetiger als an Land weht, ist die Windausbeute wesentlich höher. Außerdem kann ein Energieversorger die auf See erzeugte Elektrizität besser in die Stromversorgung integrieren als den an Land erzeugten Windstrom.

Offshore-Windenergie besitzt für E.ON strategische Priorität. So wird der Windpark London Array, der in der Themsemündung entstehen soll, ein Gigawatt (1.000 Megawatt) leisten und neue Maßstäbe setzen. Um dieses gigantische Projekt zu verwirklichen, kooperiert E.ON mit dem dänischen Energieversorger DONG und der Masdar-Initiative (Abu Dhabi). Der erste Bauabschnitt mit 630 Megawatt soll im Jahr 2012 fertiggestellt werden. Zurzeit laufen unter E.ON-Regie fünf Offshore-Windparks mit insgesamt knapp 300 Megawatt.

alpha ventus spielt auf diesem Weg eine Schlüsselrolle für E.ON, denn es ist ein wichtiger Schritt in größere Wassertiefen und hin zu Küstenentfernungen, die vor allem vor der deutschen Nordseeküste maximale Herausforderungen darstellen. Aus den bisherigen Erfahrungen mit den Offshore-Projekten hat E.ON einen 20:20-Aktionsradius definiert. Er markiert den Offshore-Bereich bis zu 20 Kilometern Küstenabstand und bis zu 20 Metern Wassertiefe und kennzeichnet in etwa die Grenze zwischen den Projekten, die bisher erfolgreich realisiert wurden, und den Projekten, die nun in Angriff genommen werden sollen. Die Errichtung von Windparks, die außerhalb dieses Radius liegen (zum Beispiel alpha ventus), erfordert einen größeren technischen Aufwand sowie eine weitaus komplexere Logistik und stellt zugleich erhöhte Anforderungen ans Prozess- und Risikomanagement.

Die Strategie von E.ON besteht darin, zunächst Erfahrungen mit dem Bau von Windparks unter weniger kritischen Bedingungen zu sammeln. Diese Windparks liegen nahe der Küste in seichteren Gewässern, vor allem in Dänemark oder Großbritannien. Das gilt für die Projekte Blyth, Scroby Sands und Nysted, aber auch für den Windpark Robin Rigg, der im September 2009 erstmals Strom lieferte, und den noch im Bau befindlichen Windpark Rødsand 2. In keinem dieser Parks ist das Wasser mehr als 15 Meter tief.

Frank Mastiaux, CEO der E.ON Climate & Renewables, zieht eine positive Bilanz: „E.ON hat bereits mehr als 1.000 Megawatt Offshore-Windkraft im Betrieb und im Bau. Wir haben mit diesen Projekten die praktische Erfahrung und das Know-how aufgebaut, um die großen Herausforderungen des Offshore-Geschäfts zu meistern." E.ON hat

of 2008 more wind farms were completed in North America, totalling 880 megawatts.

Two projects illustrate what E.ON means by 'industrial scale'. In September 2009 the Panther Creek wind farm in Texas came on-stream. It consists of 305 wind turbines with a total output of 458 megawatts. Only a month later it was followed by the 400-square-kilometre Roscoe wind farm, likewise in Texas and currently the largest wind farm in the world. At this site, E.ON generates clean power for the equivalent of 230,000 households, with 627 wind turbines and a total capacity of 780 megawatts.

These impressive wind power projects, which have a combined capacity of 2,200 megawatts, are all onshore. However, they will soon be eclipsed by offshore wind farms. For E.ON, the enormous potential of offshore wind energy gives it a special role: the wind blows stronger and steadier at sea than on land, allowing an energy utility to integrate offshore electricity into its transmission system better than the less consistent power generated by onshore wind turbines.

Offshore wind energy is a strategic priority for E.ON. Its offshore projects up until now have been relatively small, but the London Array wind farm planned for the mouth of the Thames will then produce one gigawatt (1,000 megawatts) and in doing so will set a new standard. To handle this gigantic project, E.ON is working together with the Danish energy supplier DONG and the Masdar Initiative (Abu Dhabi). The first construction phase (630 megawatts) is planned for completion in 2012. Currently E.ON operates five offshore wind farms with just under 300 megawatts capacity, so there is still a long way to go to reach the first gigawatt at sea.

The alpha ventus project plays a key role for E.ON in this effort. It is a major step towards the deeper water and greater distances from shore that present such extreme challenges, especially off the German North Sea coast. From its experience with existing offshore projects E.ON has defined a 20:20 radius of action, marking the zone up to 20 kilometres from shore and 20 metres water depth that is the approximate dividing line between the projects that have been successful thus far, and the projects that will now be started. Building wind farms outside this radius (such as alpha ventus) is technically more challenging and places higher demands on process and risk management.

E.ON's strategy is to first gain experience with the construction of wind farms under less demanding conditions. These farms are in shallower water nearer the coast, primarily in Denmark and Great Britain. Examples are the Blyth, Scroby Sands und Nysted projects, the Robin Rigg wind farm that generated its first electric power in September 2009, and the Rødsand 2 wind farm currently under construction. In none of these farms is the water deeper than ten metres.

Frank Mastiaux, CEO of E.ON Climate & Renewables, has a positive outlook: "E.ON already has over 1,000 megawatts of offshore wind power in operation or under construction. With these projects we have gradually gained the practical experience and expertise we need to meet the great challenges of the offshore business." In May 2007 E.ON committed itself to halving its specific CO_2 emissions from the 1990 level by 2030. If it is possible to achieve a global reduction goal of at least 50 percent by 2050 from the 1990 level, accompanied by medium-term reduction goals for 2020 and 2030 at the international level and including all industrialised countries, E.ON will move its 50 percent reduction in specific emissions goal to 2020.

In 2030, renewable energy will then have a 36 percent share and will be the largest single position within E.ON's energy portfolio. These

sich im Mai 2007 verpflichtet, die spezifischen CO_2-Emissionen von 1990 bis 2030 zu halbieren. Sollte es gelingen, ein globales Reduktionsziel von mindestens 50 Prozent bis 2050 gegenüber 1990 zu vereinbaren, flankiert von mittelfristigen Reduktionszielen bis 2020 bzw. 2030, die auf internationaler Ebene verankert werden und alle Industrieländer einschließen, will E.ON die Reduzierung der spezifischen Emissionen um 50 Prozent bereits in 2020 erreichen.

Im Jahr 2030 werden die erneuerbaren Energien dann mit 36 Prozent den Hauptanteil am E.ON-Energiemix stellen. Der Energiekonzern ist entschlossen, in Zukunft auch beim Klimaschutz eine international führende Rolle einzunehmen.

Klein – aber von großer Bedeutung

Große Ziele, die sich die Energieversorger gesetzt haben. Wenn sie erreicht sein werden, wird alpha ventus mit seinen lediglich 60 Megawatt Leistung wahrscheinlich schon in Vergessenheit geraten sein. Was ganz im Sinne aller Initiatoren und Beteiligten sein müsste, denn sie wollen der Offshore-Windenergie mit dem Testfeld in Deutschland, aber auch über die Grenzen hinweg, zum Durchbruch verhelfen. Diese Perspektive sollte aber nicht darüber hinwegtäuschen, dass sich die drei Energieversorger mit dem vermeintlich kleinen Projekt alpha ventus wohl die schwierigste Aufgabe gestellt haben, die zumindest bis heute jemals von Windenergie-Projektentwicklern zu bewältigen war. Keiner wagte sich vorher an so extreme Bedingungen in dieser Entfernung zur Küste in Kombination mit den großen Wassertiefen. Aus diesem Grund setzt der Park, den man im Verhältnis zu zukünftigen Dimensionen wahrscheinlich als klein bezeichnen muss, trotzdem ein großes Zeichen in der Debatte um die Machbarkeit.

Ein Standort in der Ostsee wäre gewiss leichter gewesen. „Doch die größten deutschen Offshore-Potenziale liegen nun mal auf der Nordseeseite", stellt Gesamtprojektleiter Wilfried Hube nach dem Bau zufrieden fest. „Deshalb ist das jetzige Testfeld in der Nordsee genau richtig angesiedelt."

Nach gelungener Errichtung des ersten Dutzends einer neuen Generation von Multi-Megawattanlagen in Pioniergewässern ist Hube ohnehin mehr denn je davon überzeugt, dass mit alpha ventus „Erkenntnisse gesammelt wurden, die für zukünftige Projektentwickler ganz entscheidend sein werden". Diese Erkenntnisse beziehen sich zum einen auf die Planung des Umspannwerks im Speziellen (unter anderem die Notstromkonzepte) und der Netzanbindung im Ganzen. „Zum anderen haben wir wertvolle Erfahrungen mit den Fundamenten und ihrer Errichtung auf hoher See gewinnen können", sagt Hube. Für den Versorgungsingenieur besteht beim Abenteuer Offshore die mit Abstand anspruchsvollste Herausforderung ohnehin darin, „die Fundamente ins Wasser zu lassen und auf dem Meeresgrund sicher zu verankern. Schon bei recht kleinen Windgeschwindigkeiten haben wir in der Nordsee Wellenhöhen, die es unmöglich machen, mit den heute gängigen Spezialschiffen zu arbeiten." Doch wird sich das schon bald ändern, weiß Hube, denn eine neue, größere Schiffsgeneration wird in naher Zukunft die Werften verlassen. Hube selbst steckt inzwischen bereits in den Planungen für den Offshore-Windpark Borkum Riffgat, wo alle bisherigen Erfahrungen mit einfließen werden. Routine wird es trotzdem noch lange nicht geben. Die wird vielleicht erst im Jahr 2029 eintreten, dann nämlich, wenn die Windenergieanlagen von alpha ventus ihr erstes Soll erfüllt haben, und die Betreiber möglicherweise beginnen, über ein Repowern auf dem Meer nachzudenken.

commitments emphasize that the company is determined to play a leading international role in future climate protection.

Small size – large importance

These energy suppliers have set themselves ambitious goals. When they reach them, alpha ventus with its mere 60 megawatts of output will probably be long forgotten. But that is actually in the interests of all involved, because they want this test field to help offshore wind energy achieve a breakthrough, in Germany and elsewhere. This optimistic outlook should not conceal the fact that as modest as alpha ventus may seem in terms of wattage, the three energy companies building it have taken upon themselves what may be the toughest assignment ever attempted by any wind energy project developers. No one has ever before ventured out into this combination of extreme conditions, distance from shore and water depth. Although the project may be small-scale when compared with the dimensions of future farms, it is making a very big impact on the feasibility debate.

A site in the Baltic would certainly have been easier. "But the biggest German offshore potential just happens to be in the North Sea," pointed out overall project leader Wilfried Hube with satisfaction after construction was completed. "So, by being in the North Sea, this test field is right where it needs to be."

In any case, after the successful installation of the first dozen new-generation, multi-megawatt turbines at this pioneering site, Hube is more convinced than ever that with alpha ventus "we'll gain experience that will be absolutely critical for the success of future projects." This experience relates to the planning of the transformer station in particular (including the emergency power concept) and to the grid connection as a whole. "We've also gained invaluable knowledge about foundations and how to construct them on the high seas," said Hube. As a power engineer, he considers far and away the greatest challenge within the entire adventure of offshore technology to be "getting foundations into the water and anchoring them securely to the sea-floor. Even relatively low wind speeds kick up wave heights in the North Sea that make it impossible to work with the specialised ships currently available." But that will change soon, as Hube knows, because a new generation of larger ships will soon leave the shipyards. Hube himself is already busy with the planning for the Borkum Riffgat offshore wind farm, where all of the experience gained at alpha ventus will be put to good use. However, it won't be a routine process for a long time yet. That might start to happen in 2029, when the turbines at alpha ventus have reached the end of their planned lifetime and the operators may begin to think about repowering at sea.

Mitarbeiter der WeserWind GmbH fertigen die Jacket-Konstruktion des Umspannwerks am Braunschweigkai in Wilhelmshaven.
WeserWind GmbH employees assemble the transformer station's jacket structure at Braunschweigkai in Wilhelmshaven.

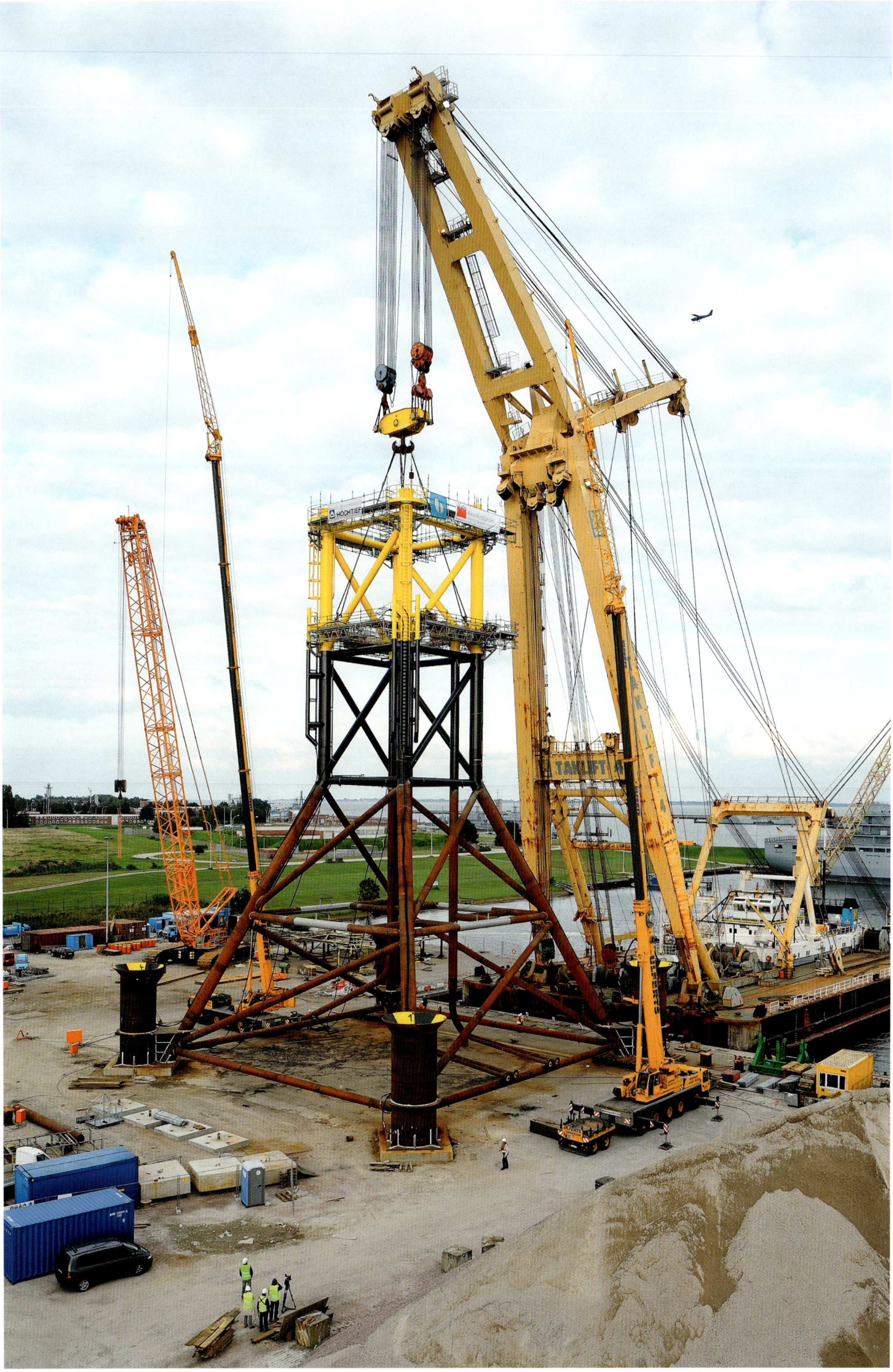

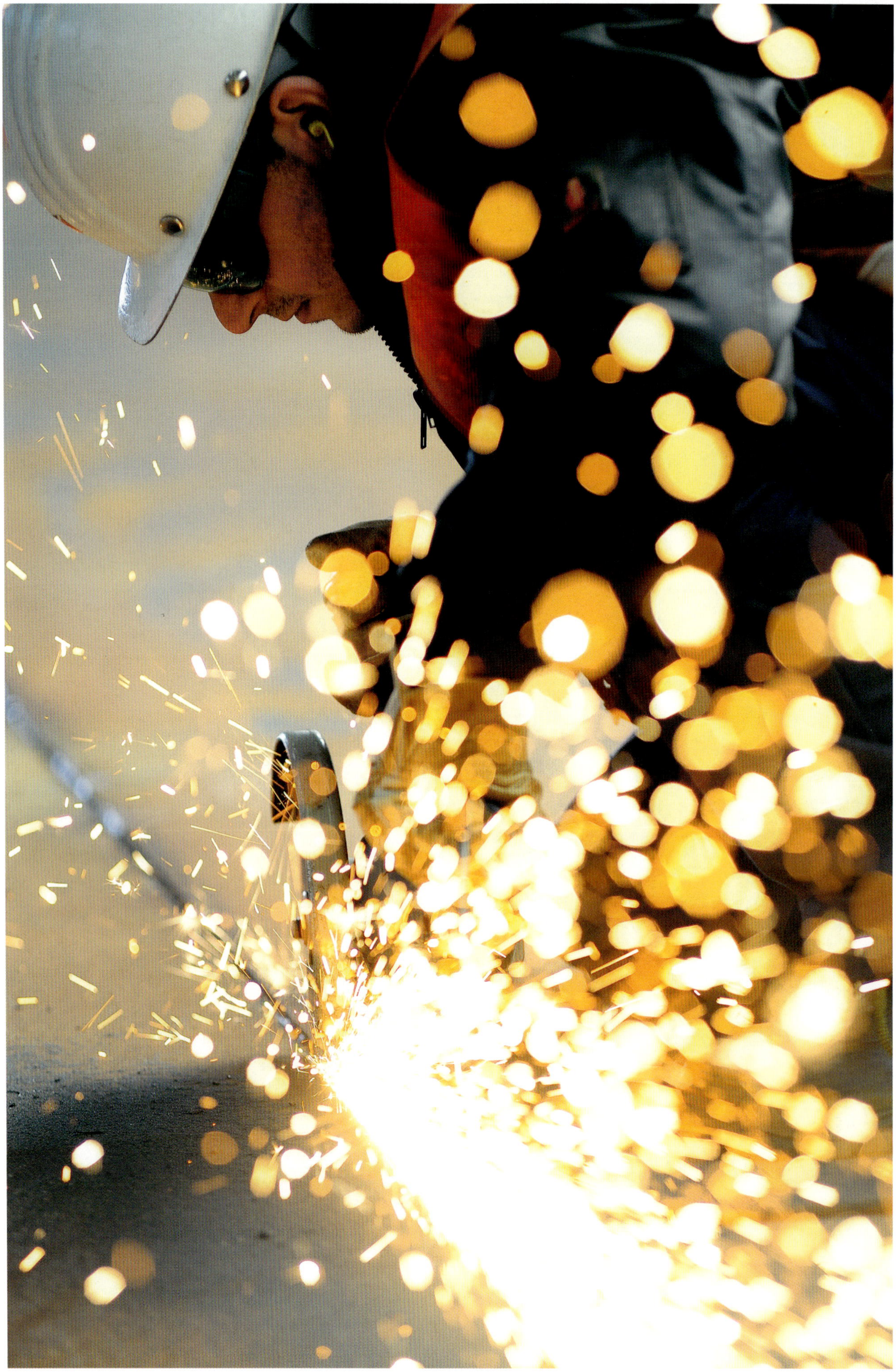

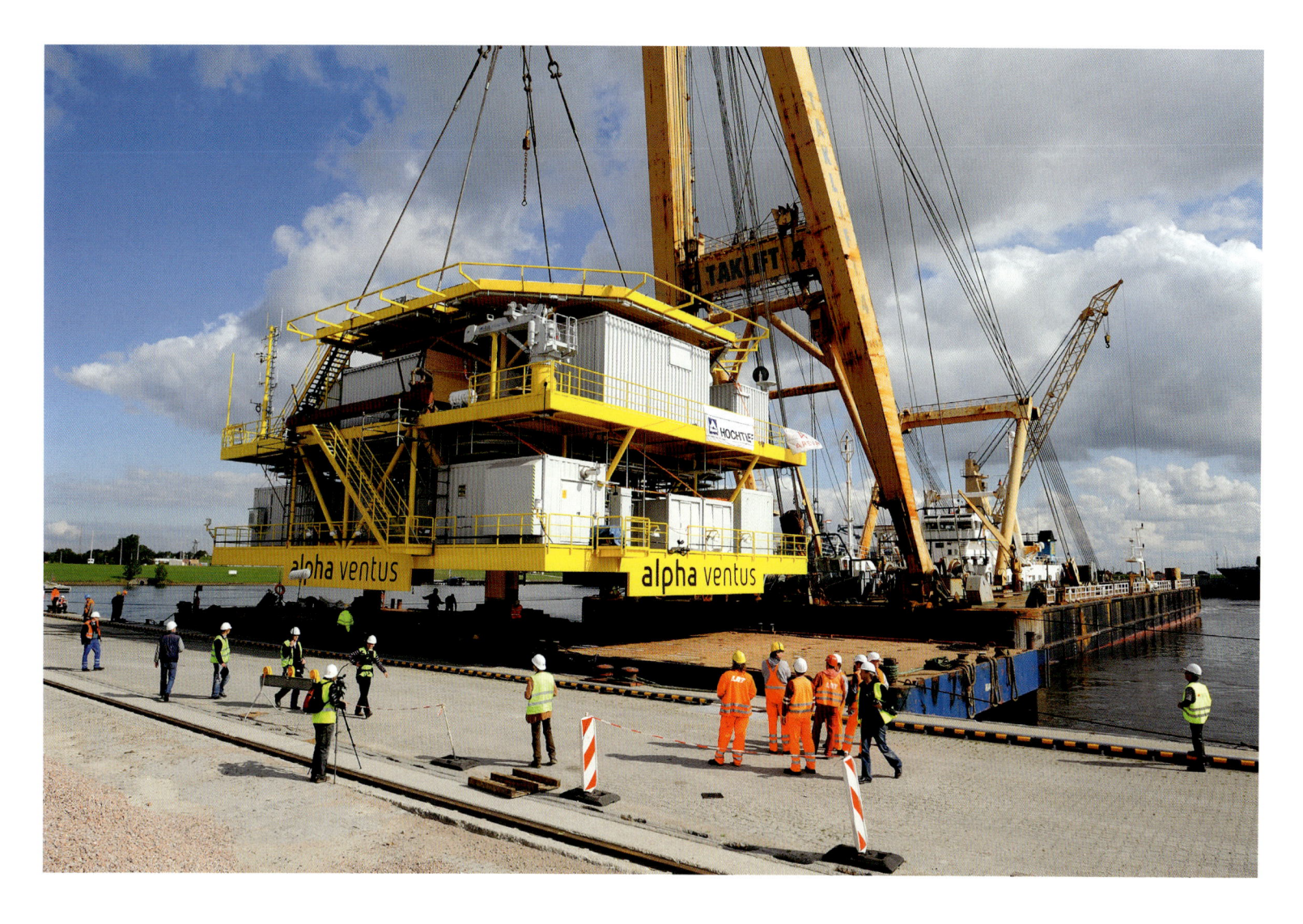

Das Transformatormodul (Topside) des Umspannwerks wird für den Transport auf See startklar gemacht.
The transformer module (topside) of the transformer station is made ready to go to sea.

Von oben sieht alles so kinderleicht aus: Die Hubinsel Odin bei Aufbauarbeiten am Umspannwerk von alpha ventus. Techniker von DOTI erreichen das Bauwerk mit dem Hubschrauber oder mit dem Service-Katamaran „Windforce I".
No big deal when you see it from above. The Odin jack-up barge is working at the alpha ventus transformer station. Technicians from DOTI reach the building by helicopter or by the catamaran "Windforce I".

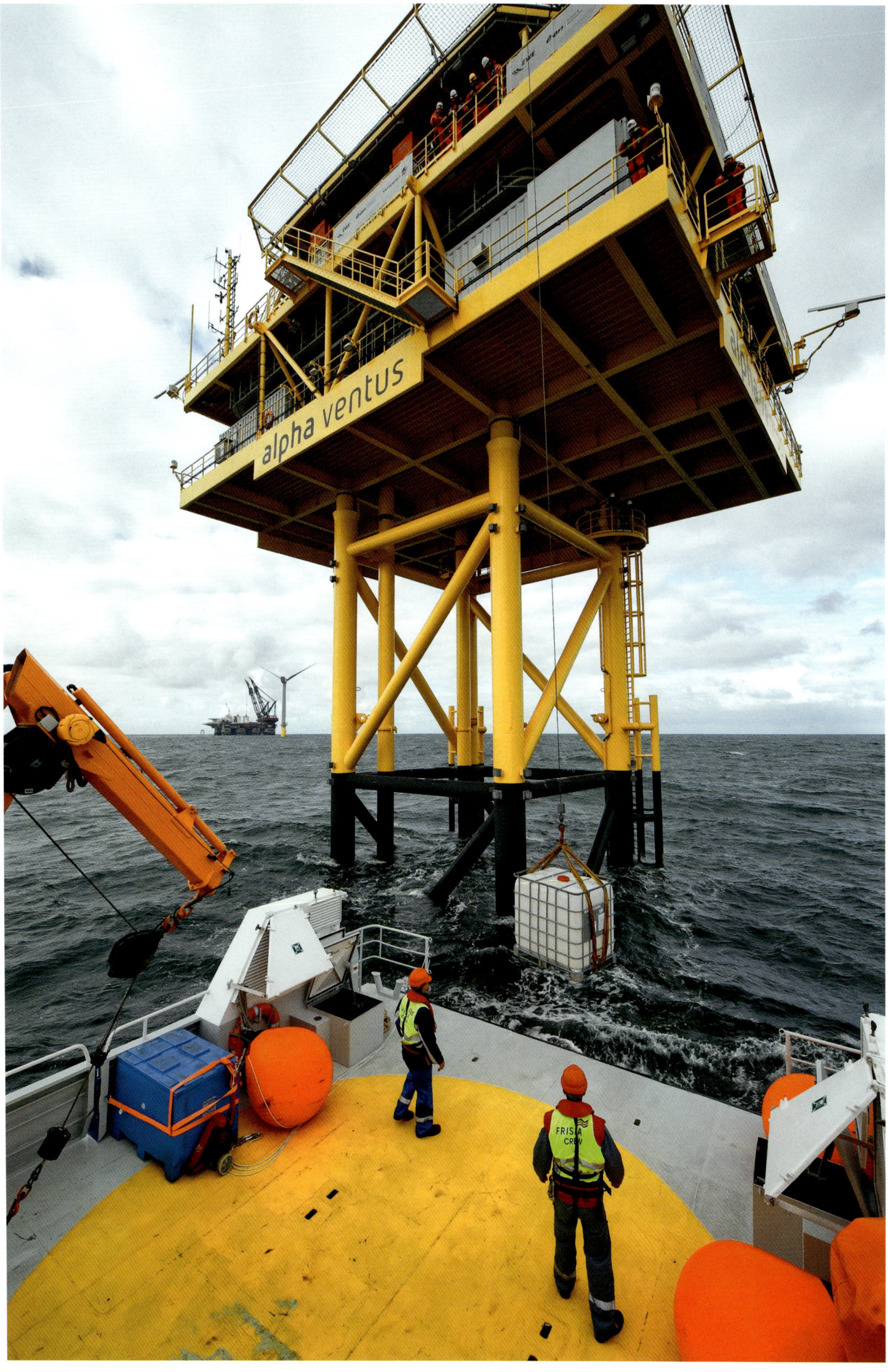
alpha ventus

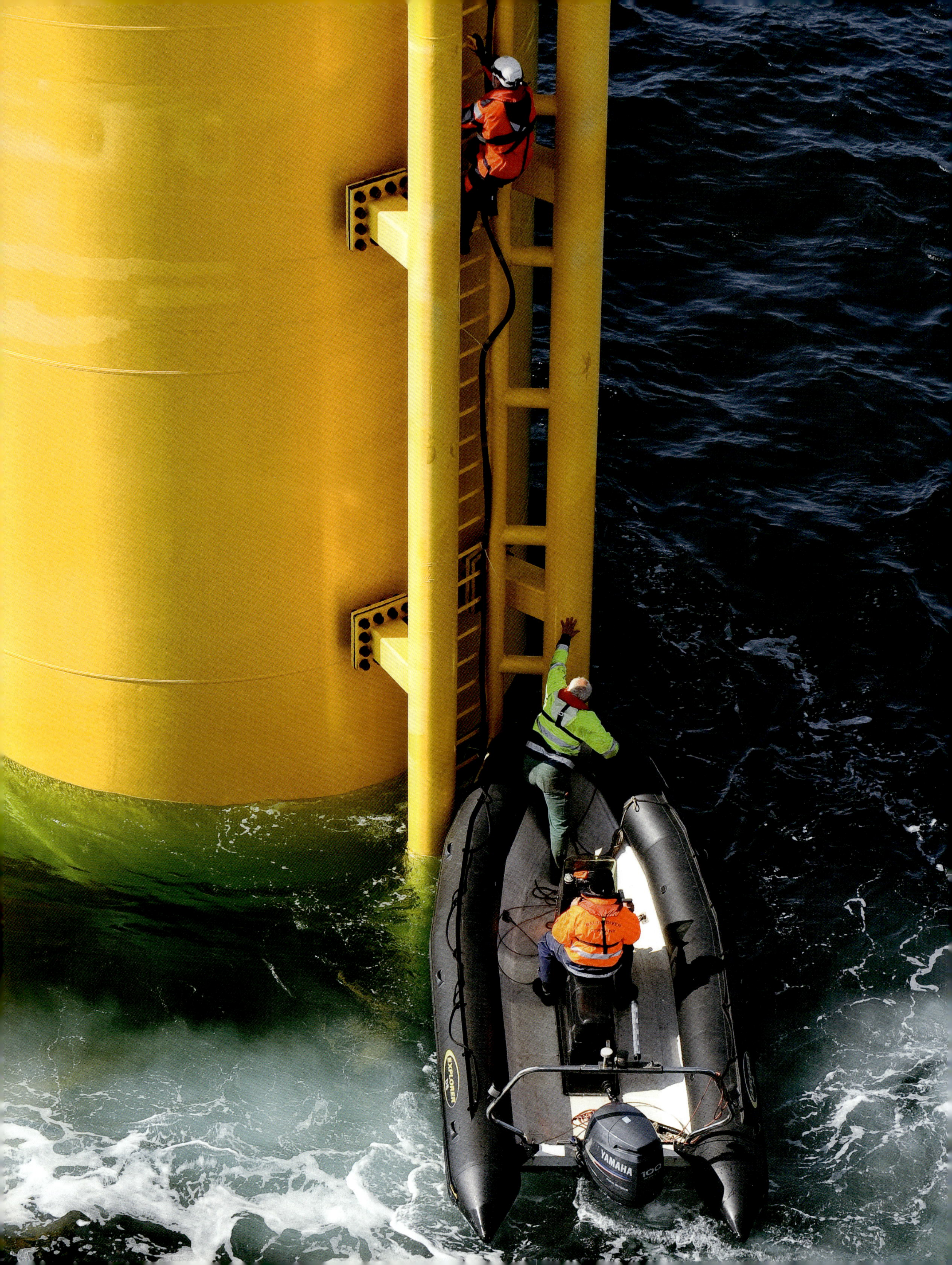
EXPLORER
YAMAHA
100

Forschung und Messtechnik
Research and metrology

Windenergie auf hoher See ist eine neue Technologie. Die Offshore-Anlagen, die vor der dänischen, schwedischen und englischen Küste stehen, haben zwar mittlerweile schon ein paar Jahre auf dem Buckel, doch sind diese Pionierprojekte allesamt küstennah, in relativ flachen Wassertiefen gesetzt und mit vergleichsweise kleinen Turbinen bewerkstelligt worden. Dagegen gibt es noch so gut wie keine Erfahrungen mit der neuen Generation von Multimegawattanlagen jenseits von fünf Megawatt. Wie werden sich diese Anlagen, die weit entfernt von den Küstenlinien bei tobenden Wellen draußen auf dem Meer, in tiefem Wasser und in einem rauen Klima mit extremen Temperaturschwankungen auf Dauer bewähren? Welchen Belastungen sind Material und Maschine unter diesen Bedingungen tatsächlich ausgesetzt?

Bisher gibt es darüber allenfalls vage Prognosen oder einige vorsichtige Einschätzungen. Die Offshore-Windenergiebranche steht im Augenblick erst am Anfang einer längeren Lernkurve. Ähnlich verhält es sich mit all den Fragen, die die Wechselbeziehung zwischen Offshore-Windparks und dem Naturraum Meer beschäftigen. Welchen Einfluss haben die neuen Giganten des Meeres auf die Vogelwelt, die Meeresfauna und auf das Leben im und auf dem Meeresboden?

Bereits die vielfältigen Erfahrungen während der Bauphase von alpha ventus boten den Ingenieuren, Monteuren, Logistikern und Projektmanagern viele Erkenntnisse, die sicherlich in neue technische Ideen und Methoden einfließen, die wiederum für die Errichtung zukünftiger Offshore-Anlagen von großem Nutzen sein werden. Dies gilt auch für die Betriebsphase, die mindestens 20 Jahren dauern soll. Der erste deutsche Offshore-Windpark ist bei Weitem nicht nur ein wichtiges wirtschafts- und energiepolitisches Demonstrationsobjekt in einem der führenden Windenergieländer der Welt, sondern zugleich auch Objekt intensiver Forschung über einen langen Zeitraum hinweg. Forscher vieler Institute sitzen ungeduldig in den Starlöchern, um all diese Fragen in den nächsten Jahren wissenschaftlich fundiert beantworten zu können. Wie sind die realen Witterungsbedingungen? Wie werden Gründung, Türme, Gondel und Flügel auf Wind und Wellen dauerhaft reagieren? Bewährt sich die erfolgreich erprobte Anlagentechnik an Land auch auf dem Meer? Wie häufig treten tatsächlich extreme Wettersituationen auf? Wie beeinflussen Wind und Wetter den Zugang für das Servicepersonal? Leidet der Schweinswal, ein marines Säugetier, das in der Nordsee rund 1,80 Meter groß wird und zur Familie der kleinen Zahnwale gehört, unter dem Aufbau und Betrieb der Offshore-Windparks? Stören die Turbinen die Vogelwelt? Verändern sich Wind- und Strömungsverhältnisse? Wie verhalten sich die Sedimente? Spülen die Meereskräfte die Fundamente womöglich frei? Außerdem wirft der Betrieb auf hoher See neben technischen und ökologischen Aspekten auch eine Reihe ökonomischer Fragen auf.

Wind energy at sea is a new technology. The wind farms off the Danish, Swedish and British coasts are just a few years old. But all these groundbreaking projects are nearshore in relatively shallow waters and they have used comparatively small turbines. On the other hand, virtually no experience has been gained with the new generation of multi-megawatt wind turbines with a capacity of five megawatts and more. These wind-energy converters are located far off the coasts in deep waters, subjected to rough seas in harsh climates and exposed to extreme fluctuations in temperature. So how will they stand the test of time? What stresses will materials and machines have to cope with under these conditions?

To date, only vague guesses or cautious expectations have been made at best. The offshore wind-energy industry is still at the very beginning of a long learning curve. The same applies to issues concerning the relationship between offshore wind farms and the sea as a natural habitat. What impact will these new giant structures in the sea have on bird life, the wildlife that inhabits the sea and the flora and fauna living in and on the seabed? During the construction phase of alpha ventus, the engineers, fitters, logistics experts and project managers gained a huge range of experience. The expertise acquired will definitely shape new ideas and methods which again will be of huge benefit when constructing offshore turbines in the future. This also applies to the operational phase, which is scheduled to last for at least 20 years.

The first German offshore wind farm is not just an important model in business and energy policy terms for one of the world's premier wind energy nations, but will also be the subject of intensive research over a long period of time. Researchers from many institutes are waiting impatiently in the wings to provide scientifically verified answers to the several key questions over the next few years. What really are the weather conditions? How will the foundations, towers, nacelles and rotorblades react to wind and waves in the long term? Will the wind-turbine technology, proven onshore, also prove itself at sea? How often do extreme weather conditions actually occur? How do wind and weather affect access for service personnel? Will the porpoise, a marine mammal that grows to around 1.80 metres in the North Sea and belongs to the family of small-toothed whales, be adversely affected by the expansion and operation of the offshore wind farms? Will the turbines bother birds? Will wind and tidal stream conditions change? How will sediments behave? Could the force of the sea possibly wash away the foundations?

In addition to technical and ecological aspects, operating wind farms at sea also throws up a number of business-related questions. Which material will perform best? How can downtimes be minimised? How can the transportation of personnel and material to the offshore wind

Welches Material wird sich bewähren? Wie gelingt es, die Ausfallzeiten zu minimieren? Wie organisiert man den raschen Transport von Personal und Material zu den Offshore-Windparks? Wie sieht die Aufbaulogistik in Zukunft aus? Wo lassen sich Kosten einsparen? Und zu guter Letzt stellt sich die Frage, wie der erzeugte Strom vom Meer so übertragen werden kann, dass er wirtschaftlich ins Verbundnetz kommt.

Breitgefächerte Forschungsinitiative

Um die komplexe Materie im Testfeld strukturiert zu erforschen, hat das Bundesumweltministerium (BMU) im Vorfeld sämtliche Forschungsvorhaben im so genannten Programm „Research at Alpha VEntus", kurz RAVE, zusammengefasst. Der Bund finanziert über einen Zeitraum von fünf Jahren die zumeist interdisziplinäre Arbeit von RAVE mit insgesamt 50 MillionenEuro. Biologen, Geografen, Geologen, Ornithologen, Materialforscher, Strömungstechniker, Physiker, Ozeanografen, Ökonomen, Maschinenbauer und Elektrotechniker werden in dieser Zeit messen, Daten sammeln und auswerten. Nie zuvor hat man einen Windpark so gründlich untersucht. Umfangreiche Messtechnik wurde schon vor der Errichtung an den einzelnen Anlagen angebracht. So sind rund 1.200 Sensoren im Einsatz, die rund um die Uhr Daten liefern. Nichts bleibt unbeobachtet. Die meisten Messwerte (beispielsweise Wind- und Wellen- sowie Strömungsdaten, Schallmessungen, außerdem die an den Windenergieanlagen gemessenen Lastdaten, Leistungswerte und andere Betriebsdaten) werden den im Rahmen von RAVE akkreditierten Forschern direkt zur Verfügung gestellt.

Das BMU hat den Projektträger Jülich (PtJ) mit der administrativen Abwicklung des Forschungspaketes beauftragt, während die Koordinierung des RAVE-Programms beim Fraunhofer-Institut für Windenergie und Energiesystemtechnik (IWES) liegt, ist das BSH verantwortlich für die ökologische Begleitforschung. „Die Absicht des BMU war es von Anfang an, dieses Testfeld nicht allein zum Aufstellen von Anlagen zu nutzen, sondern so viele Ergebnisse wie möglich für die künftigen Offshore-Windparks zu gewinnen", unterstreicht der bei der PtJ für RAVE und der Forschungsplattform in Nord- und Ostsee, kurz FINO 1, verantwortliche Dr. Joachim Kutscher.

Fünfzehn Forschungsprojekte

Mit Stand von Februar 2010 sind insgesamt 15 RAVE-Projekte (www.rave-offshore.de) in Arbeit:
1. Foundations (Gründungen) untersucht die Effekte von Wind, Wellen und Anlagenbetrieb auf das Fundament.
2. GIGAWIND alpha ventus soll durch ein ganzheitliches Dimensionierungskonzept die Tragstrukturen verbessern. Das Ziel ist es, diese Strukturen zu einem wirtschaftlichen Massenprodukt zu entwickeln.
3.- 6. Bevor der Bau von Offshore-Windparks in der Nordsee auf breiter Front beginnt, sollen die Erfahrungen und Erkenntnisse aus der Planung, dem Aufbau und dem Betrieb des Testfeldes alpha ventus in die Weiterentwicklung der Technologie eingebracht werden. Für die Rotorblätter geschieht dies im Projekt REpower Blades (Rotorblätter), für die Wechselwirkungen im Gesamtsystem im Projekt REpower Components (Komponenten) und für die innovative Weiterentwicklung der Multibrid

farms be organised quickly? What will installation logistics look like in the future? How can costs be saved? And finally: how can the electricity generated at sea be transported and fed into the interconnection grid most economically?

A wide-ranging research initiative

In order to research these complex matters in the test field in a structured way, the German Federal Ministry for the Environment (BMU) has combined all related research projects in a programme called 'Research at alpha ventus', or RAVE for short. The German government is funding RAVE's primarily inter-disciplinary work over a five-year period to the tune of 50 million euros. During this period, biologists, geographers, geologists, ornithologists, material researchers, ocean current engineers, physicists, oceanographers, economists, as well as mechanical and electrical engineers will carry out measurements, collect and analyse data. Never before has such detailed research been carried out on a wind farm. Extensive measuring devices were fitted to selected turbines before they were installed. As a result, around 1,200 sensors are in operation delivering data around the clock. Nothing goes unobserved. The majority of data collated (for example wind, wave and ocean current data, acoustic measurements, as well as the load data, performance characteristics and other operational data measured on the wind turbines themselves) are delivered to accredited researchers as part of the RAVE initiative.

The BMU has appointed the Projektträger Jülich (PtJ) as Administrative Project Sponsor to supervise the research activities. The RAVE programme is being co-ordinated by the Fraunhofer Institute for Wind Energy and Systems Studies (IWES) in Kassel, whereas the German Federal Maritime and Hydrographic Agency (BSH) is in charge of providing and organising ecological research. "Right from the outset, it was the BMU's intention not to use this test field only to set up wind farms, but to obtain as many results as possible for future offshore wind farms", emphasises Dr. Joachim Kutscher, the Jülich manager responsible for RAVE and the research platform FINO 1.

Fifteen research projects

As of February 2010, work on a total of 15 RAVE projects (www.rave-offshore.de) is in progress:
1. The Foundations project examines the effects of wind, waves and turbine operation on the foundations.
2. The aim of GIGAWIND alpha ventus is to improve the support structures using holistic dimensioning concepts. The project aims to develop these structures into an economically viable mass product.
3.- 6. Before large-scale installation of offshore wind farms in the North Sea begins, experience gained and lessons learnt from planning, setting up and operation of the alpha ventus test field are to be applied in developing the technology. The REpower Blades project will look at the rotor blades. REpower Components will investigate interactions in the overall system and the AREVA Multibrid M5000 Improvement project will conduct research on how selected components of the wind turbine can be improved. The OWEA project will verify key aspects required for the reliable design and operation of offshore wind-energy converters.

Oben: Der Tripod ist Objekt einer ganzen Reihe von Forschungsprojekten – u. a. wird ein aktiver Korrosionsschutz getestet. **Unten:** Taucher überprüfen nach der erfolgreichen Gründung die Funktionstüchtigkeit der installierten Messinstrumente.
Top: The tripod is object of various research projects such as corrosion protection testing.
Bottom: After successful anchoring of the foundation, divers check to make sure if the measurement equipment is in good working condition.

M5000 unter erschwerten Offshore-Bedingungen. Im Projekt OWEA (Offshore-Windenergieanlagen) sollen Schlüsselaspekte für einen zuverlässigen Entwurf und Betrieb von Offshore-Windenergieanlagen verifiziert werden.

7. Im Projekt LIDAR wird der Einsatz moderner Windfeldmessverfahren (LIDAR = Light Detection And Ranging) an Offshore-Anlagen untersucht, zugleich will man möglichen Verbesserungen der Betriebsführung auf die Spur kommen.
8. Die mit dem Monitoring seit Jahren vertrauten Forscher des IWES in Kassel sammeln wesentliche Betriebsdaten (Energieerträge, Ausfallzeiten, Verfügbarkeit etc.) der Windenergieanlagen, um sie anschließend auszuwerten. Grundlage ist das Wissenschaftliche Mess- und Evaluierungsprogramm (Offshore-WMEP) im Rahmen der RAVE-Initiative. Das Offshore-WMEP soll möglichst alle Windenergieanlagen erfassen, die in den nächsten Jahren in der Nord- und Ostsee installiert werden.
9. Im Projekt Grid Integration (Netzintegration) werden Strategien zur Integration der Offshore-Windenergie in das deutsche Übertragungsnetz entwickelt, implementiert und demonstriert. Ziel ist es, die zukünftige Stromversorgung mit einem hohen Anteil Offshore-Windenergie mit gleicher Qualität und gleich hoher Zuverlässigkeit wie beim konvetionellen Kraftwerksbetrieb sicher zu stellen.
10. Ziel der ökologischen Begleitforschung im Projekt Ecology (Ökologie) ist es, Erkenntnisse der bau- und betriebsbedingten Auswirkungen auf die Meeresumwelt (Benthos, Fische, Rastvögel, Zugvögel, marine Säugetiere) zu gewinnen.
11. Wichtige ozeanografische und geologische Daten werden im Rahmen des Projektes Geology (Geologie) gemessen, um die Sedimentdynamik im Bereich der Anlagen und im gesamten Windpark zu erfassen und zu bewerten. Die Sedimentdynamik macht sich vor allem in Form von Ausspülungen (Kolkbildung) an den Tragstrukturen bemerkbar. Aus den Untersuchungen soll eine verlässliche Basis für die Planung von Offshore-Konstruktionen entwickelt werden.
12. Der Schall, den die Anlagen unter Wasser abstrahlen, ist Gegenstand der Untersuchungen im Projekt Operational Noise (Betriebsschall). Dabei wird die gesamte Schallbelastung für Meereslebewesen, insbesondere Meeressäuger, ermittelt.
13. Das Projekt Noise Reduction (Hydroschall) untersucht, inwieweit der Schall während der Bauphase gedämpft werden kann. Erprobt werden Luftblasenschleier, die aus Schläuchen aufsteigen und während des Rammens das Bauwerk einhüllen.
14. Die Vermeidung von Kollisionen von Unterseebooten mit Gründungen steht im Rahmen des Projektes Sonar-Transponder im Fokus. Mit Hilfe von Sonar-Transpondern, die an den Windenergieanlagen angebracht werden, sollen in Gefahrensituationen mögliche Kollisionen von U-Booten mit den Anlagen vermieden werden.
15. Außerdem gibt es eine Arbeitsgruppe an der Universität Halle-Wittenberg, die sich mit der gesellschaftlichen Akzeptanz von Offshore-Windparks beschäftigt. Das Forscherteam erarbeitet Handlungsempfehlungen für politische Entscheidungsträger, um den Ausbau der Offshore-Windenergienutzung möglichst konfliktarm zu gestalten und zur Verbesserung der Akzeptanz der Windenergienutzung beizutragen.

7. The LIDAR project (Light Detection and Ranging) will investigate the use of modern wind field measurement techniques on offshore turbines. At the same time, it will try to discover any improvements that are possible in operational management.
8. With their years of experience in wind-plant monitoring, Fraunhofer IWES researchers in Kassel, Germany, collect essential operational data (such as energy yields, downtimes, availability etc.) of wind energy converters for subsequent evaluation. As part of the RAVE initiative, the Wind Measurement and Evaluation Programme (Offshore WMEP) provides the cornerstone for their work. The aim of the Offshore WMEP is to cover all wind turbines which are to be set up in the North Sea and the Baltic Sea over the next few years.
9. The Grid Integration project develops, implements and demonstrates strategies for integrating offshore wind energy into the German grid. Its goal is to reduce the backup and balancing reserve capacities by using new forecasting tools, without having a negative impact on the safety and availability of the interconnection grid.
10. to obtain information on the impact of construction and operation on the marine environment (benthos, i.e. marine snails, worms and crabs, fish, resting and migrant birds, marine mammals).
11. Part of the Geology project is to measure key oceanographic and geological data in order to collect and evaluate sediment dynamics in the immediate vicinity of the turbines and across the whole wind farm. Sediment dynamics can become particularly noticeable as washing-outs (scour) on the support structures. The goal of the research is to provide a reliable basis for the design of offshore structures.
12. Underwater noise emissions from the turbines are measured in the Operational Noise project. The project looks into all noises that affect marine life, marine mammals in particular.
13. The Noise Reduction project ('Hydrosound') examines how noise can be reduced during the construction phase. Bubble curtains have been tested which emerge from hoses and cover the structure during ramming work.
14. The Sonar Transponder project focuses on avoiding collisions of military submarines with turbine foundations. Sonar transponders, fitted to wind energy converters, should help prevent any collisions of submarines with turbines in dangerous situations.
15. Furthermore, a work group from the German Halle-Wittenberg University is looking into the acceptance of offshore wind farms by society at large. The research team will draft recommendations for political decision makers to help expand offshore wind power use so that as few disputes as possible are caused and the acceptance of wind energy usage is enhanced.

In addition to the 15 already approved projects, another one is in the pipeline. It is a research project called UFO, in short, "Impact of ambient conditions on offshore wind energy converters". The project has been applied by fk-wind, the Institute for Wind Energy at Bremerhaven University of Applied Sciences.

FINO 1 Research platform

While RAVE will only really get going once alpha ventus goes online, FINO 1, the research platform in the North Sea and Baltic Sea was

Neben den 15 bereits bewilligten Projekten ist noch ein weiteres in Planung. Es handelt sich um das Forschungsprojekt namens UFO. Dieses Kürzel steht für „Umgebungseinflüsse auf Offshore-Windenergieanlagen" und ist von der fk-wind, dem Institut für Windenergie an der Hochschule Bremerhaven, beantragt worden.

Forschungsplattform FINO 1

Während RAVE erst nach der Inbetriebnahme von alpha ventus richtig auf Hochtouren kommt, ist die Forschungsplattform kurz FINO 1, schon 2003 am Rand des jetzigen Offshore-Testfelds errichtet worden. Seither liefern die Instrumente auf der Plattform eine Reihe von wertvollen Daten. Am wichtigsten ist die Messung der Windgeschwindigkeit und der Windrichtung in acht verschiedenen Höhen. Darüber hinaus erfassen die installierten Apparate das gesamte Wettergeschehen und ozeanografische sowie ökologische Parameter.

FINO 1 war die erste Messeinrichtung in der deutschen AWZ; später folgten weitere Stationen in Ost- und Nordsee, die alle vom BMU finanziert wurden. FINO 1 war auf jeden Fall ein wichtiger Vorposten für alpha ventus. Eine Webcam informierte fortlaufend über den Stand der Dinge. Dieser Service wurde insbesondere während der heißen Bauphase gerne und oft genutzt.

Die Gründungsstruktur der Forschungsplattform FINO 1 ist inzwischen mit Miesmuscheln und Seenelken bewachsen. Wie reagieren Flora und Fauna auf Offshore-Windenergieanlagen?
The FINO 1 research platform's foundation structure has become covered with a growth of mussels and sea anemones. How do flora and fauna respond to offshore wind energy converters?

Der Auftrag für den Bau der FINO 1 wurde an die Arbeitsgemeinschaft der F + Z Baugesellschaft mbH, Hamburg, und der Bugsier Reederei- und Bergungsgesellschaft mbH & Co, Bremerhaven, vergeben. Der Germanische Lloyd (GL) koordinierte Bau, Aufstellung und Inbetriebnahme. Das Plattformdeck ruht auf einer stählernen Fachwerkkonstruktion, die den Fundamenten der Jackets ähnelt, auf denen die sechs REpower-Windenergieanlagen stehen. Die Jacket-Struktur der FINO 1 ist jedoch „ausladender". Sie besteht aus Stahlrohrprofilen mit einer Basisfläche am Meeresboden von 26 mal 26 Metern und einer Kopfbreite unterhalb des Plattformdecks von 7,5 mal 7,5 Metern. Auf der 20 Meter hohen Plattform steht ein 80 Meter hoher Messmast.

Im Juni 2003 brachte der Schwimmkran ENAK das Jacket von Bremerhaven zum Standort und setzte es dort ab. Anschließend wurden die vier Pfähle in die Pile Sleeves eingefädelt und 30 Meter tief in den Meeresboden gerammt.

Übernachten nur im Notfall

Die Instrumente auf der Plattform, die vom Germanischen Lloyd (GL) betreut werden, laufen vollautomatisch. FINO 1 ist unbemannt und wird nur besucht, wenn beispielsweise etwas repariert oder ausgetauscht werden muss. Die Anfahrt geschieht je nach Wetterlage auf dreierlei mögliche Art: Bei Windstille und spiegelglatter See bringt ein Schiff die Forscher zur FINO 1. Unter diesen sehr günstigen Wetterbedingungen können sie vom Schiff aus eine der beiden Leitern erreichen, die an den Beinen der Jacket-Gründung zur Plattform hinaufführen. Voraussetzung ist allerdings, dass das Fahrzeug an der Stahlkonstruktion anlegen kann – was nur mit kleinen Schiffen oder Schlauchbooten möglich ist.

Alternativ kann man eine zweite Möglichkeit wählen: Das Schiff hält in einigen Metern Abstand vor dem Jacket, während der ferngesteuerte Kran der Plattform einen Personenkorb hinablässt, mit dem die Besucher anschließend nach oben befördert werden. Diese Zugänge stellen jedoch die seltene Ausnahme dar. Schon bei wenig Wind und leichtem Seegang kann der Überstieg vom Schiff gefährlich sein.

Die dritte und teuerste Möglichkeit ist eine Option für jedes Wetter: der Anflug mit dem Hubschrauber zur FINO 1. Dafür benötigt man von Bremerhaven aus nur 40 Minuten, während der Schiffstransfer sieben bis acht Stunden dauert. Eine Übernachtung auf der FINO 1 ist nur im Notfall möglich. Für die eigentliche Arbeit auf der Plattform bleibt also nur wenig Zeit. Deshalb wird in den meisten Fällen der Helikopter genutzt, um die Plattform zu erreichen.

Starke Winde, extreme Wellen

Die Meteorologen können inzwischen – nach mehr als sechs Jahren Messungen auf der FINO 1 – die durchschnittliche jährliche Windgeschwindigkeit am Standort alpha ventus mit ziemlich großer Genauigkeit angeben. Sie liegt bei 10,06 Meter pro Sekunde und lässt erwarten, dass der Windpark die erhofften hohen Erträge bringen wird. Doch auch auf See schwankt die Windgeschwindigkeit stark, weshalb auch die zeitliche Verteilung der Windgeschwindigkeitsklassen so wichtig ist. Die Auswertung hat ergeben, dass an 8.000 Stunden des Jahres mit mindestens vier Metern pro Sekunde (Windstärke 3) gerechnet werden kann. Das ist die Windgeschwindigkeit, bei der sich die Rotoren der Windenergieanlagen in Bewegung setzen. Zum Vergleich: Das Jahr hat 8.760 Stunden. Die Rotoren im Windpark alpha ventus wer-

already set up at the rim of today's offshore test field in 2003. The instruments on the platform have been providing a host of valuable data since that time. Top priority is measuring wind speed and wind direction at eight different heights. The installed devices collect and record the entire meteorological and oceanographic conditions as well as ecological parameters.

FINO 1 was the first measuring facility in the German EEZ, followed later on by further platforms in the Baltic Sea and North Sea, all funded by the German Federal Ministry for the Environment (BMU). At any rate, FINO 1 was an important outpost for observing alpha ventus, as a webcam constantly showed the changing status quo. This service was very popular, especially during the critical construction phase.

A consortium of F + Z Baugesellschaft mbH, Hamburg, and the Bugsier Reederei- und Bergungsgesellschaft mbH & Co, Bremerhaven, was commissioned with installing FINO 1. Germanischer Lloyd (GL) coordinated construction, setting up and commissioning. The platform deck is based on a steel construction similar to the jacket foundations that support the six REpower wind-energy converters. However, the FINO 1 jacket structure protrudes further. It consists of steel-tube profiles with a 26 x 26-metre base on the sea floor and a head width of 7.5 x 7.5 metres beneath the platform deck. A measuring mast 80 metres in height is located on the 20-metre high platform.

In June 2003, the ENAK floating crane moved the jacket out from Bremerhaven and positioned it on site. Subsequently, the four piles were threaded through the pile sleeves and rammed thirty metres deep into the seabed.

Overnight stays only in emergencies

The instruments on the platform are looked after by Germanischer Lloyd (GL) and operate fully automatically. FINO 1 is unmanned and only visited if anything needs to be repaired or replaced. Depending on weather conditions, the platform can be approached in three different ways. When there is a lull in the wind and the sea is dead calm, a ship brings the researchers to FINO 1. In these very favourable weather conditions, they can reach one of the two ladders from the ship that lead from the legs of the jacket foundation up to the platform. The condition is, however, that the vehicle can moor alongside the steel construction – which is only possible for small ships or dinghies.

There is also a second alternative: the ship moors at several metres' distance from the jacket, while the remote-controlled crane lets down a personnel lift cage from the platform to convey visitors to the top. These forms of access are rarely possible, however. Even if there is just light wind and a slight swell, transfer from the ship can be dangerous. The third and most expensive option, but possible in any weather, is to fly by helicopter to FINO 1. From Bremerhaven the flight takes just 40 minutes, while the passage by ship takes seven to eight hours. Overnight stays on FINO 1 are only possible in emergencies. Consequently, there is very little time to actually work on the platform. Therefore, the helicopter is used to reach the platform in the majority of cases.

Strong winds, extreme waves

After six years of taking measurements at FINO 1, meteorologists are now able to identify the annual mean wind speed at the alpha ventus site with fairly high accuracy: it's 10.06 metres per second on average,

den also – hohe technische Verfügbarkeit vorausgesetzt – voraussichtlich nur selten stillstehen.

Erfreulich ist auch ein weiteres Ergebnis: An mehr als 2.000 Stunden wurden zwölf bis 13 Meter pro Sekunde (Windstärke 6) gemessen. Bei dieser Windgeschwindigkeit erreichen die Windenergieanlagen ihre Nennleistung. Aus den gemessenen Daten ergibt sich, dass jede der zwölf 5-Megawatt-Anlagen voraussichtlich 22,5 Millionen Kilowattstunden pro Jahr liefern wird. Das entspricht 4.500 Stunden mit Nennleistung (4.500 Volllaststunden), mehr als doppelt so viel, wie diese Anlagen an einem guten Standort an Land liefern würden.

Diese Ergebnisse sind erfreulich, aber nicht überraschend, denn die Nordsee ist für hohe Windgeschwindigkeiten bekannt. Für mehr Verblüffung sorgte dagegen die Messung der Wellenhöhen. Am 1. November 2006 und am 9. November 2007 zogen zwei schwere Stürme über die Nordsee, die extrem hohe Wellen auftürmten. Wie hoch die höchsten Wellen waren und mit welcher Wucht sie gegen die Forschungsplattform anrollten, lässt sich erahnen, wenn man die Schäden an der Gründungsstruktur der Forschungsplattform FINO 1 betrachtet: Sowohl 2006 als auch 2007 verursachten 15 Meter über Normalnull reichende Wogen Schäden an der umlaufenden Arbeitsplattform. Dass die stählernen Geländer verbogen werden könnten, hatte man nicht erwartet.

and the wind farm is expected to generate the high yields hoped for. However, wind speeds fluctuate heavily, even at sea. Which is why the wind-speed distribution over time into wind-speed classes is so essential. The analysis showed that for 8,000 hours per year, wind speeds of at least four metres per second (Beaufort Force 3) can be expected. The wind turbine's rotor blades are set in motion at this wind speed. By comparison, there are 8,760 hours in a year. Subject to high levels of technical availability, the rotor blades at the alpha ventus wind farm will probably hardly ever stop turning.

There is also more good news to report: for more than 2,000 hours, 12 to 13 metres per second (Force 6) were measured. At this wind speed the turbines reach their rated capacity. The data indicates probable production of 22.5 million kilowatt hours per year by each of the twelve 5-megawatt turbines. This is equivalent to 4,500 hours at rated capacity (i.e. 4,500 full load hours), more than double than what these turbines would produce at good onshore sites.

These results are pleasing, but not surprising because the North Sea is known for its high wind velocities. On the other hand, the measurement of wave heights produced astonishing results. On November 1, 2006 and on November 9, 2007, two heavy storms raged across the North Sea whipping up the waves to extreme heights. The damage to the FINO 1 research platform hints at just how high the highest

Die unbemannte Forschungsplattform FINO 1 war lange Zeit einsamer Vorposten von alpha ventus. Sie wurde im Jahr 2003 errichtet, liefert seither wichtige Wetterdaten und wird regelmäßig gewartet. Udo Paschedag (li., unten) vom BMU beim Besuch der Plattform.
The unmanned FINO 1 research platform has been alpha ventus's lonely outpost for a long period. Set up in 2003, it provides vital weather data and is regularly checked by experts. Udo Paschedag (left bottom), member of the BMU, is visiting the platform.

Die höchsten Wellen hatten etwa eine Höhe von 16,5 Metern. Das bedeutet, dass die Arbeitsplattform um etwa 1,5 Meter überspült wurde und dass die Wellenkämme bis etwa 3,5 Meter unterhalb der Hauptarbeitsplattform reichten. Bemerkenswert ist, dass ein Sturm- und Seegangsereignis dieser Größenordnung in zwei aufeinanderfolgenden Jahren auftrat.

Christian Nath, der als Vizepräsident Industriedienste des Germanischen Lloyd für die Zertifizierung der FINO 1 verantwortlich war, hat trotz der beeindruckenden Sturm- und Wellenereignisse keine Bedenken: „Die Plattform ist ausreichend ausgelegt." Beschädigt wurden nur sekundäre Anbauten, „die bewusst so ausgelegt waren, dass sie bei bestimmten singulären Stürmen beschädigt werden können. Das hat zu einer günstigeren Gesamtkostenschätzung geführt."

Laserstrahlen erforschen die Windströmung

Neben den bisherigen, mit klassischen Methoden durchgeführten Windmessungen auf der FINO 1 kommt nun im Rahmen von RAVE auch der Laserstrahl zum Einsatz. Gemessen wird die Rückstreuung des gebündelten Laserlichtes durch die in der Luft stets vorhandenen Staubpartikel und Aerosole. Das Verfahren heißt Light Detecting And

Ranging (LIDAR) und hat eine Reichweite von mehreren hundert Metern. Es handelt sich also um eine Methode der Fernerkundung. Man braucht dafür keinen Messmast, sondern kann das Messgerät neben eine Windenergieanlage auf den Boden stellen und den Laserstrahl senkrecht nach oben aussenden, um die Windgeschwindigkeit in mehreren Höhen zu messen. Die Ergebnisse sind deshalb interessant, weil die Windgeschwindigkeit mit wachsender Höhe über Grund zunimmt. Das macht sich vor allem in dem Bereich bemerkbar, den der Rotor überstreicht, also etwa zwischen 50 und 150 Metern über Grund. Der Rotor erlebt während eines Umlaufs ganz unterschiedliche Windgeschwindigkeiten, was zu Materialbelastungen führt. Über dem Meer ist dieser Effekt zwar nicht so stark ausgeprägt wie an Land, dennoch ist es wichtig, das vertikale Windgeschwindigkeitsprofil im Bereich der gesamten Rotorfläche zu kennen.

Um zu erproben, ob sich das Verfahren auch für Messungen auf See eignet, steht im Zuge des RAVE-LIDAR-Projekts seit Juni 2009 ein LIDAR-Messgerät auf der Forschungsplattform FINO 1. Die Messungen werden vom DEWI durchgeführt. Mit dem Laserstrahl kann man auch in horizontaler Richtung messen. Diese Messrichtung ist das aktuelle Forschungsgebiet einer Arbeitsgruppe am Stiftungslehrstuhl Windenergie (SWE) der Universität Stuttgart. Der Wind, der einen

waves were and the force at which they hit the platform. In 2006 and 2007, waves towering up to 15 metres caused damage to the peripheral work platform: nobody had expected it was possible for these to bend the heavy steel railings.

The highest waves reached some 16.5 metres in height. Consequently, the work platform was submerged by about 1.5 metres of water and the wave crests towered up to 3.5 metres beneath the main work platform. It is remarkable that storm and swell incidents of such magnitude could happen within two successive years. In spite of such critical incidents, Christian Nath, Vice President of Germanischer Lloyd Industrial Services, who was responsible for the FINO 1 certification, had no reservations and commented: "The platform's design is adequate." Only auxiliary extensions were damaged and he went on to say that these had been purposely designed to cope with damage in certain rare storms and as a result had led to a more cost-effective total cost of ownership. The main level of the research platform protrudes 20 metres over the sea.

Laser beams investigate the wind flow

In addition to the traditional wind measurements carried out on FINO 1, laser beams are now also being used as part of RAVE. Backscatter-

Windpark durchströmt, ist nicht stetig, sondern oftmals böig und von Turbulenzen durchsetzt. Für die Konstrukteure von Windenergieanlagen ist es wichtig, möglichst viel Wissen über die Anströmung wie auch über die Nachlaufströmung des Windes zu haben.

Der SWE hat zunächst ein LIDAR-Messgerät auf der Gondel einer Multibrid M5000 installiert, die in der Nähe von Bremerhaven, also an Land steht. Die Erkenntnisse und Messmethoden sollen 2010 auf See im Offshore-Testfeld alpha ventus (RAVE-Projekt OWEA) umgesetzt werden. Gemessen wird von der Gondel aus nach vorn, um den anströmenden Wind zu erfassen und Böen im Voraus erkennen zu können. Man hofft, die Effekte der Böen auf die Drehzahl des Rotors schneller ausregeln zu können, um dadurch die Belastungen der Rotorblätter, des Triebstranges und des Turms zu vermindern.

Außerdem soll die horizontale Messung des einströmenden Windfeldes zur Leistungskurvenmessung herangezogen werden. Die Messung der Windgeschwindigkeiten und die daraus resultierende Verteilung über die gesamte Rotorfläche erlauben Aussagen über das Verhältnis der erzeugten Leistung zum Wind sowohl onshore als auch offshore. Um viele Messpunkte über der Fläche anzuvisieren, wurde hierzu eigens ein Scanner entwickelt, der eine beliebige Führung des Laserstrahls erlaubt. Außerdem wird von der Gondel aus nach hinten gemessen, um die Nachlaufströmung zu erfassen. Der Rotor beeinflusst natürlich die Windströmung, in der er sich bewegt. Hinter einer Windturbine bildet sich eine Wirbelschleppe, so dass Mindestabstände zu beachten sind, um andere Windenergieanlagen im Windpark nicht zu stark zu belasten. Numerische Nachlaufmodelle werden nun dank der Fernerkundung mittels der LIDAR-Technologie verbessert und können für die zukünftige Planung von Windparks eingesetzt werden.

Blasenschleier soll Lärm vermindern

Das lauteste Geräusch, das während des Baus des Windparks die Lebewesen im Meer belasten könnte, entsteht beim Rammen der Gründungspfähle. Jeder der sechs Tripods, auf denen die Multibrid-Windturbinen stehen, wird mit drei Pfählen im Meeresgrund verankert. Die Jacket-Gründungen der REpower-Anlagen brauchen sogar jeweils vier Pfähle. Insgesamt musste also 42-mal gerammt werden. Um einen einzigen Pfahl 30 bis 40 Meter tief in den Meeresboden zu treiben, waren bis zu 14.000 Rammschläge erforderlich. Die Rammgeräusche werden im Wasser schneller und über viel weitere Strecken geleitet als in der Luft – mit der Folge, dass der Schall noch in Entfernungen von mehr als 20 Kilometern zu hören ist.

Dieser Lärm stört vor allem die Schweinswale. Je nach Abstand von der Schallquelle kann die Kommunikation der Tiere untereinander oder ihre Echoortung bei der Jagd behindert werden. Auch ist die Gefahr, dass die Tiere reversible oder irreversible Hörschäden erleiden, bisher nicht sicher auszuschließen. Auf Populationsebene steht zu befürchten, dass die Meeressäuger bei gehäuft auftretenden Rammarbeiten ihre Vorkommensgebiete mittel- bis langfristig verlassen werden.

Um das Verhalten der Schweinswale im Blick zu behalten, wurden die Säugetiere in der südlichen Nordsee vor, während und nach den Rammarbeiten von Meeresbiologen von Flugzeugen und Schiffen aus gezählt und mit Unterwassermikrofonen erfasst. Aufgrund der Empfindlichkeit des Schweinswalgehörs hat man vor Beginn der lauten Hammerschläge so genannte Vergrämungsmaßnahmen eingesetzt, um die Tiere aus dem Nahbereich zu vertreiben. Der Unterwasser-

ing of the bundled laser light by the ever-present dust particles and aerosols is measured. The technique is called Light Detecting and Ranging (LIDAR) and has a range of several hundreds of metres. In other words, this is a remote sensing technique.

A measuring mast is not required, but the measuring device can be placed next to a wind turbine: it directs the laser beam vertically upwards to measure the wind speed at several heights. The results are interesting because the wind picks up speed with increasing height above ground. This is particularly obvious in the area swept by the rotor, or between about 50 and 150 metres above ground. The rotor encounters very different wind speeds during a rotation, resulting in material stresses. While this is not as pronounced at sea as on land, knowing the vertical wind speed profile within the area swept by the rotor is still important.

During the RAVE LIDAR project, a LIDAR measuring device has been placed on the FINO 1 research platform since June 2009 to verify whether the technique is also suitable for measurements at sea. Measurements have been conducted by the German Wind Energy Institute DEWI. Laser beams can also measure horizontally. This direction of measurement is what a wind-energy Working Group at Stuttgart University (SWE) is working on. The wind flowing through a wind farm is not constant, but often gusty with occasional turbulence. For designers of wind turbines, it is therefore essential to gain as much insight into the oncoming wind flow as well as the wake flow as possible.

The SWE initially installed a LIDAR measuring device on the nacelle of a Multibrid M5000 located onshore near Bremerhaven. In 2010, the findings and measuring techniques gained are to be put into practice at the alpha ventus offshore wind test field (RAVE project Offshore Wind Energy Converter – OWEA). Measurements are made from the front of the nacelle in order to capture the incident wind and to be able to detect gusts in advance. Researchers hope to compensate for the impact of gusts on the rotor speed more quickly in order to reduce the loads on the rotor blades, drive train and tower.

Horizontal measurements of the inflow wind field are also to be applied when measuring the power curve. Measuring wind speeds and the resulting distribution across the entire rotor area provides information about the ratio of the power produced per wind inflow – both onshore and offshore. A scanner has been specifically developed to focus the laser beam as required to target several measuring points across the surface area. Measuring is also performed from the nacelle towards the rear to capture the wake flow. The rotor does of course affect the wind flow it is moving in. Wake turbulence forms beneath a wind turbine, so that minimum distances must be kept in order to avoid placing too much load on other wind turbines in the wind farm. Thanks to remote sensing using LIDAR, numerical wake models will be improved and used for future wind-farm planning.

Bubble curtain to cut noise

The loudest noise to disturb marine life is created when ramming in the foundation piles. Each of the six tripods on which the Multibrid wind turbines are mounted is anchored to the seabed by three piles. REpower turbine jacket foundations even need four piles each. Ramming had to be done a total of 42 times. A pile needed to be hit some 14,000 times just to sink it 30 to 40 metres into the seabed. Noise caused by ramming is transmitted faster and over much longer dis-

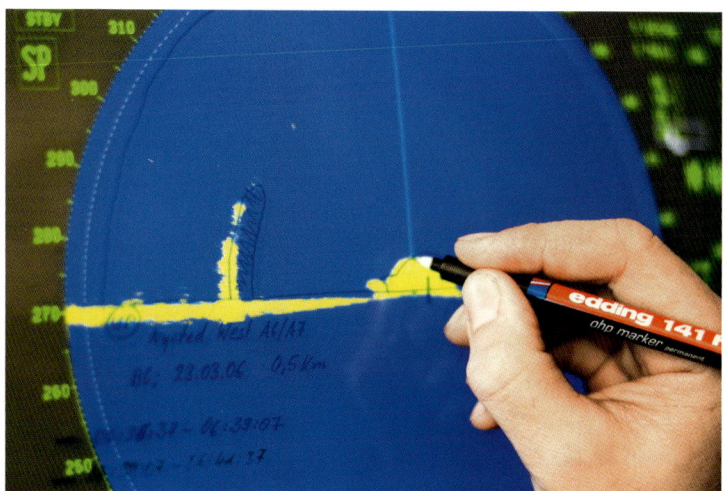

Der Vogelschutz auf dem Meer ist ein wichtiges Thema. Ornithologen erfassen, welche Vogel-Populationen und welcher Vogelzug an potentiellen Standorten für Offshore-Windparks anzutreffen sind.
Bird protection at sea is a key issue. Ornithologists find out which bird populations and which migrant birds can be encountered at potential offshore wind farm locations.

tances through water than through the air. Therefore, the noise can be heard even at distances of more than 20 kilometres. This noise particularly disturbs porpoises. Depending on the distance from the source, the noise impairs communication between the animals, or their navigation system called echolocation while hunting. The risk that the animals suffer reversible or irreversible damage to their hearing cannot be ruled out either. In terms of population, there is reason to fear that these marine mammals will abandon their habitats in the medium or long term when ramming work is performed more frequently.

In order to keep a close watch on the porpoises' behaviour, marine biologists on planes and ships counted the mammals in the southern part of the North Sea during and after ramming and recorded them with underwater microphones. Because porpoises have such sensitive hearing, steps were taken to scare the animals away before loud hammering started. Measuring underwater sound at distances of up to 20 kilometres has confirmed that the noise travels great distances.

Tests using a bubble curtain were conducted to reduce the noise produced during ramming. The Institut für Statik und Dynamik (ISD) at the University of Hanover oversaw these tests. The principle is straightforward: they made small air bubbles rise from thin tubes surrounding the noise source to form a curtain. This purpose of this Little Bubble Curtain (LBC) is to reduce the noise spreading. To put the principle to the test, they surrounded the tripod base of Multibrid turbine AV09 with four tubes forming a ring. These tubes enclose the pile sleeve and are welded to the base point like a cage.

When first implemented in May 2009, the bubble curtain started to rise while the ram pile was driven through the pile sleeve. The noise emitted was measured at a distance of about 500 metres using hydrophones to verify the curtain's ability to cut noise. It emerged that reducing the noise caused by the bubble curtain heavily depended on the strength and direction of the ocean current. During the ramming process, the bubble curtain rising in the water body was driven away with the direction of the current. So on one side the bubble curtain had virtually no effect, while on the other, noise reduction of twelve decibels (dB) and more was measured. More tests based on a bubble curtain concept are soon planned. The concept means it is possible to maintain a greater distance from the noise source and has already been successfully used while installing the FINO 3 research platform.

Impact on the marine environment

Ecological research has to be done in the test field by the operator and monitored by the German Federal Maritime and Hydrographic Agency (BSH). The standard investigation concept on the effects of offshore wind farms on the marine environment was applied for the first time at alpha ventus. The concept will be compulsory in future and is known officially as StUK3. The BSH also coordinated a project on secondary ecological research (called StUKplus) in which specific associated research issues are looked at. Based on the results, StUK3 is to be checked and thus evaluated for its level of adequacy and effectiveness.

The goal of this ecological research is to increase knowledge on the impact of wind-farm construction and operation on the marine environment and to make the expansion of offshore wind energy as environmentally friendly as possible. Biologists use before-and-after comparisons to identify the effect of the wind farm on benthos (snails, worms and crabs), fish, resting and migratory birds, as well as marine

sionen mit den Rotorblättern ebenso zu erfassen wie Ausweichbewegungen. Diese Geräte werden erstmalig auf hoher See eingesetzt. Unterwasserfotos zeigen, dass sich die Gründungsstruktur der nahe gelegenen Forschungsplattform FINO 1 in nur kurzer Zeit zu einem künstlichen Riff mit Bewuchs von Miesmuscheln, Seenelken und sogar Austern entwickelt hat. Ähnliches wird voraussichtlich mit den zwölf Fundamenten der Windenergieanlagen geschehen. Das Gewicht der Anlagen wird daher in nur wenigen Jahren um bis zu sechs Tonnen in den Sommermonaten „anwachsen". Auf dem ursprünglich feinsandigen Boden im Nahbereich um die Anlagen werden sich Taschenkrebs und Samtkrabbe ansiedeln, die sonst nur auf Riffen und Wracks zu finden sind.

Auch für Fische, Rastvögel und marine Säuger ändert sich der Lebensraum. Der Windpark stellt einerseits durch Licht- und Geräuschemissionen einen Eingriff in die Meeresumwelt dar, andererseits bietet er einen Schutzraum vor der Fischerei, die einige Fischarten und möglicherweise sogar die Schweinswale dazu bewegen wird, den Windpark zukünftig bevorzugt zu nutzen. Auch dies wird Gegenstand der Forschung in den nächsten Jahren sein.

Messergebnisse dienen ganz Europa

„alpha ventus wird sicherlich nicht das letzte Wort der Offshore-Windenergieforschung sein", kündigt Dr. Joachim Kutscher (PtJ) an. Er erwartet, dass in den nächsten Jahren weitere technische Entwicklungen einsetzen werden, die die Sicherheit der Windenergieanlagen erhöhen, Kosten reduzieren sowie Betriebsführung und Umweltverträglichkeit verbessern helfen. „Die wissenschaftliche Begleitung wird sich daher nicht auf alpha ventus beschränken." Nichtsdestoweniger gibt RAVE die wissenschaftliche Vorlage für kommende Projekte in ganz Europa. „Diese Messergebnisse von alpha ventus sind dort übertragbar, wo wir auf ähnliche naturräumliche Verhältnisse stoßen. Wassertiefen, Wind- und Wellenverhältnisse, wie sie draußen in der Deutschen Bucht vorliegen, sind auch im Bereich der britischen Ostküste und des spanischen Festlandsockels anzutreffen", ergänzt Christian Nath vom Germanischen Lloyd. Das bedeutet: Die durch FINO 1 und die RAVE-Initiative gesammelten Erkenntnisse werden den Offshore-Planungen in ganz Europa nützen. Sie tragen dazu bei, dass eines Tages ein großer Teil des klima- und umweltfreundlichen Stroms, den Europa dringend braucht, vor den Küsten produziert wird.

mammals. "Temporary disruptions occurred during the construction phase", comments Dr. Georg Nehls of Bioconsult SH, who observed the behaviour of the porpoises when alpha ventus was being set up. "The porpoises clearly avoided the site, keeping a distance of 15 to 20 kilometres". Nevertheless, Nehls expects the porpoises to "use the marine environment during the operational phase of alpha ventus, just as they did before". However, long-term research is still required to observe the precise reactions of the animals to the wind farm in their natural habitats.

As part of the migratory bird projects, new video and thermal imaging cameras as well as radars are used to record any collisions with the rotor blades, or any attempts made by the birds to avoid them. This equipment is being used for the first time on the high seas.

Underwater photos show that the foundation structure of the neighbouring FINO 1 research platform developed an artificial reef of mussels, sea anemones and even oysters within just a short space of time. The same will also probably happen to the 12 foundations of the wind turbines. As a result, in just a very few years, the weight of the installations will increase by up to six tonnes in the summer months. Edible crabs and velvet crabs will settle on the fine sandy seabed near the installations; these crabs are usually otherwise only found on reefs or wrecks.

The habitat will also change for fish, resting birds and marine mammals. During operation, the wind farm will create a disturbance due to light and noise emissions. On the other hand it will offer protected areas from commercial fishing operations. Therefore, some species of fish and possibly even porpoises might prefer to come to the area near the wind farm. This issue will also be the subject of research over the next few years.

Research results to benefit all of Europe

"alpha ventus will definitely not be the last word in offshore wind energy research", comments Dr. Kutscher from project sponsor Jülich. Over the next few years he expects further technical developments to increase the safety of wind-energy installations, cut costs and help enhance operational management and the eco-friendliness of the wind farms. "Therefore, scientific studies will not just be limited to alpha ventus". Nevertheless, RAVE will become a scientific role model for upcoming projects in the whole of Europe. "The scientific findings at alpha ventus can be applied to wherever we find similar natural parameters. Water depths, wind and wave conditions, such as those we experience out in the German Bight, can also be encountered on the east coast of Britain and the Spanish continental shelf", adds Christian Nath of Germanischer Lloyd.

Therefore, the findings gained from FINO 1 and the RAVE initiative will benefit offshore planning right across Europe. The results will help to ensure that a major proportion of the climate- and environmentally-friendly electricity that Europe so urgently needs is produced offshore.

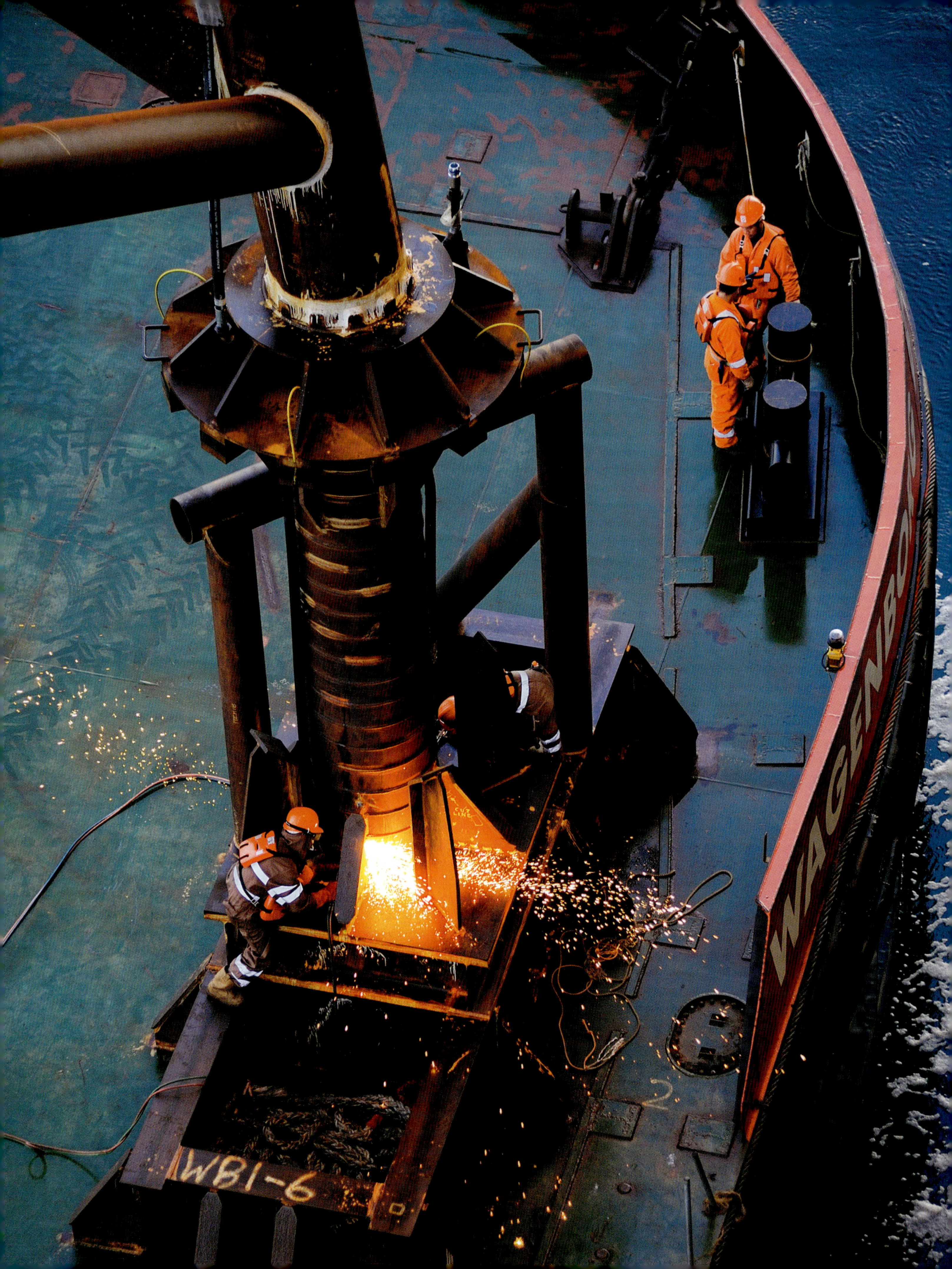
WB1-6

Arbeit an Land – Technik auf See
Work on land for technology at sea

Jedes Offshore-Vorhaben beginnt an Land. Während die Hersteller von Offshore-Windenergieanlagen in ihren Fabrikhallen, die im optimalen Fall an der Kaikante stehen, Gondeln, Türme und Flügel bauen, fügen andere Unternehmen meist in Hafennähe Stahlkomponenten zu Gründungsstrukturen zusammen. Wieder andere Firmen kümmern sich um die umfangreiche Logistik, damit die einzelnen Produktionsteile in den Häfen verschifft und mit einer ganzen Reihe von Spezialschiffen auf die Meeresbaustelle gebracht werden. Wiederum andere Akteure sorgen dann für die Errichtung der stählernen Riesen im Meer. Und dies alles am besten just in time.

Dieser komplexe Produktionsprozess setzt jedoch Strukturen voraus, die es in der Vergangenheit zumindest an den deutschen Küsten nicht gab. Der weitere Ausbau der norddeutschen Hafenstädte muss ganz oben auf der Agenda stehen bleiben, um die Herausforderungen der jungen Offshore-Windenergie-Ära meistern zu können. Genauso wichtig ist aber auch die Weiterentwicklung einer maritimen Logistikkette mit neuen Spezialschiffen, die mit den gewaltigen Dimensionen, die die Offshore-Anlagen mit fünf und mehr Megawatt Leistung sowie den dazugehörigen Fundamenten inzwischen angenommen haben, umgehen können. Es braucht in den nächsten Jahren eine logistische Offensive in Häfen und Schiffsbauindustrie, damit die Wertschöpfung in der norddeutschen Region bleibt und neue Arbeitsplätze hinzukommen. Mit anderen Worten: Herstellung und Transport der Offshore-Komponenten benötigen eine eigene Industrie und eine eigene Logistik. Beides befindet sich noch in den Anfängen. Will man jedoch die ambitionierten deutschen Offshore-Pläne tatsächlich mittelfristig verwirklichen, führt kein Weg daran vorbei, noch mehr als bisher in die Infrastruktur zu investieren, um die anvisierten Ziele erreichen zu können.

Netzwerk für Offshore-Industrie

Wie der Auf- und Ausbau dieser Offshore-Industrie und -Logistik aussehen könnte, lässt sich besonders gut in Bremerhaven beobachten. Die Stadt hat sich in wenigen Jahren zum größten Offshore-Stützpunkt an der deutschen Nordseeküste entwickelt. Vorausgegangen war eine langjährige und systematische Investitionsförderung, die mit einer vorausschauenden Stadtentwicklung einherging. In den vergangenen Jahren sind dadurch in Bremerhaven 4.000 neue Arbeitsplätze vor allem im Bereich des Hafenumschlags sowie im Container- und Automobil-Terminal entstanden. Aber auch die Windenergie-Industrie leistet inzwischen einen erheblichen Beitrag zur dynamischen Wirtschaftskraft des Standortes. Vorangetrieben und koordiniert wurde dieser Prozess vor allem durch die Bremerhavener Gesellschaft für Investiti-

All offshore projects start onshore. Manufacturers of offshore wind energy converters build nacelles, towers and rotor blades in their factories, which are ideally located dockside. Steel fabricators, usually near the harbour, assemble steel components into foundation structures. Other companies handle the complex logistics involved in getting the individual components to port and from there to the offshore site, using a variety of specialised vessels. Finally, specialist construction firms set up the steel giants out on the open sea. Naturally, all this should happen 'just in time' and without delays.

This complex production process requires an infrastructure that formerly did not exist on the German coasts. Further extension of the northern German ports must be a priority, if the challenges of the new offshore wind energy era are to be met and mastered. No less important is the further development of a maritime logistics chain, with new vessels that can handle the huge dimensions of offshore turbines of five or more megawatts capacity, plus their foundations. In the next years there will need to be a logistics offensive in harbours and the shipbuilding industry in order to keep the value-creation process and its jobs in the north German region. The manufacture and transportation of offshore components requires its own industrial and logistical basis, which is still in its infancy. If Germany's ambitious offshore plans are truly to come to fruition in the coming years, the country will have to boost its investment in the infrastructure needed to make it happen.

A network for the offshore industry

The German port city of Bremerhaven on the River Weser gives a good example of how expansion of the offshore industry and logistical infrastructure might look. In recent years the city has developed into the largest offshore wind-energy support base on the German North Sea coast. This was preceded by a long and systematic investment process and accompanied by forward-looking urban development which created 4,000 new jobs in Bremerhaven, primarily in cargo handling and at the container and road-freight terminal. The wind-energy sector is also making a significant contribution to the port's dynamic economic growth. This expansion was driven and coordinated in large part by the Bremerhaven Economic Development Company Ltd. (Bremerhavener Gesellschaft für Investitionsförderung und Stadtentwicklung mbH, BIS). Back in 2000, even before initial approval was granted for development of the first offshore wind farm, the BIS read the signs of the times. It was obvious even at that early date that the existing port facilities and conventional logistics were not up to the manufacture and transportation of offshore wind energy components on a regular basis.

onsförderung und Stadtentwicklung mbH (BIS). Schon im Jahr 2000, also noch bevor der erste Offshore-Windpark genehmigt war, nutzte die BIS die Gunst der Stunde. Denn schon damals zeichnete sich ab, dass die Herstellung und der Transport von Komponenten der Offshore-Windenergie mit der vorhandenen Ausstattung der Häfen und der gängigen Logistik dauerhaft nicht funktionieren würden.

Um nun Bremerhaven frühzeitig für das Zukunftsgeschäft Offshore-Windenergie ins Spiel zu bringen, eruierte die BIS die Marktpotenziale am Standort an der Weser. Argumente für Bremerhaven waren damals vor allem die vorhandenen Gewerbeflächen und das industrielle Know-how mit qualifizierten Arbeitskräften in der maritimen Wirtschaft. Als die Standortpolitiker im November 2001 die Windenergiebranche und ihre Zulieferindustrie zu einer standortpolitischen Tagung einluden, wurden sie von der großen Resonanz überrascht. Zur Veranstaltung kamen 200 Besucher – etwa viermal so viel wie erwartet. Und sie kamen nicht nur aus der Region, sondern aus ganz Deutschland. Dieses große Interesse ermutigte die BIS, die Windenergie-Agentur Bremerhaven/Bremen e.V. (wab) zu gründen, um das vorhandene Potenzial auszuschöpfen. In der Tat gelang es den Mitarbeitern der wab, in nur wenigen Jahren ein umfassendes Kompetenznetzwerk für Windkraft in der Weserregion zu aufzubauen. Dabei brachte die wab die Akteure in der Windenergie-Industrie mit denen aus der maritimen Industrie in der Region sowie den vorhandenen wissenschaftlichen Einrichtungen zusammen. Mit Erfolg – dem Verein gehören heute über 220 Unternehmen und Institute an.

Der Sogeffekt entstand zusätzlich auch aufgrund der historisch gewachsenen Strukturen einer Hafenstadt, die neben der – wenn auch in den letzten Jahrzehnten arg gebeutelten – Fischereiwirtschaft seit jeher vom Schiffsbau und der maritimen Wirtschaft lebt und über große Freiflächen verfügt. Des Weiteren gibt es Ausbildungs- und Qualifizierungspotenziale, die dafür sorgen, dass geeignete Arbeitskräfte in kurzer Zeit für neue Aufgaben bereitstehen. „Bis Ende 2008 hat die Stadt Bremerhaven etwa 40 Millionen Euro investiert, um den Standort auszubauen. Davon sind 25 Millionen Euro zu Infrastrukturmaßnahmen zu rechnen, die ohnehin erforderlich waren. Gezielt für die Windenergie haben wir 15 Millionen investiert", zieht Nils Schnorrenberger, Leiter des BIS-Geschäftsbereiches Wirtschafts- und Technologieförderung, eine überaus positive Bilanz. Die städtischen Mittel waren klug angelegtes Geld, denn insgesamt hat die Windenergie-Industrie mit Unterstützung von Bund und Land bis Ende 2008 etwa 250 Millionen Euro am Standort Bremerhaven investiert.

So haben sich in Bremerhaven inzwischen mehrere Hersteller und Zulieferer angesiedelt: AREVA Multibrid, REpower Systems und PowerBlades, die alle am Bau von alpha ventus beteiligt waren. Allein durch diese drei Firmen sind über 1.000 neue Arbeitsplätze entstanden. Darüber hinaus wird die Firma WeserWind in Kürze eine Fertigungshalle am Fischereihafen errichten, um dort Fundamente für Offshore-Windturbinen und Plattformen für Offshore-Umspannwerke zu bauen. Hinzu kommen am Standort Bremerhaven noch zwei Forschungseinrichtungen: Das Fraunhofer-Institut für Windenergie und Energiesystemtechnik (IWES), das über einen Rotorblattprüfstand verfügt und die Deutsche WindGuard GmbH, die einen Windkanal gebaut hat. Last but not least siedelten sich im Lauf der letzten Jahre zahlreiche kleinere Lieferanten und Dienstleistungsunternehmen an, die attraktive Arbeitsplätze schufen und an dem beginnenden Offshore-Boom in der Region Bremerhaven-Bremen teilhaben. Es ist rund um den alten Fischereihafen also schon viel passiert. Doch abgeschlossen

In order to position Bremerhaven early on for the promising offshore wind energy business, the BIS investigated the market potential of the port. In its favour from the beginning were existing industrial real-estate and expertise, including a good supply of skilled maritime workers. In November 2001 the local government invited the wind-energy industry and its suppliers to an economic development conference. The response was overwhelming – 200 visitors came, about four times more than expected. They came not just from the region, but from all over Germany. This lively interest encouraged the BIS to found the Wind Energy Agency Bremerhaven/Bremen e.V. (wab) to maximise the potential of the area. In just a few years, the wab was able to create a comprehensive wind energy expertise network in the Weser region, bringing wind-energy companies together with local maritime industry and scientific institutions. This was a success and today over 220 companies and institutes belong to the association.

The attractiveness of the area was enhanced by the character of Bremerhaven as a port city, which had previously always lived from fishing, shipbuilding and the maritime economy, and had ample available space. The city also had the education and training facilities to qualify workers for new jobs in a short time. "By late 2008 about 40 million euros had been invested in Bremerhaven as a business location. Of this, 25 million euros went to infrastructure projects that were necessary in any case. 15 million were earmarked directly for wind energy," notes Nils Schnorrenberger, Director of the BIS Department for Economic and Technology Promotion. The money the city spent was a wise investment, as the wind energy industry, with state and German federal support, had invested about 250 million euros in Bremerhaven by the end of 2008.

Several manufacturers and suppliers have opened facilities in Bremerhaven – AREVA Multibrid, REpower Systems and PowerBlades, all of which were involved in the construction of alpha ventus. These three companies alone created over 1,000 new jobs. In addition, the WeserWind company will soon open a plant in the 'Fischereihafen', Bremerhaven's fishing harbour, for the manufacture of foundations for offshore wind turbines and platforms for transformer stations. The city is also receiving two research institutes, the Fraunhofer Institute for Wind Energy and Energy System Technology (IWES), with a rotor-blade test facility, and Deutsche WindGuard GmbH, which has built a wind tunnel. Last but not least, over the past few years numerous small suppliers and service providers have settled in the area, creating attractive job opportunities in the incipient offshore boom in the Bremerhaven-Bremen region. Much has happened – but much still remains to be done before the conversion to an offshore support base is complete. The logistics and pre-assembly of offshore wind farms will require much additional space for the intermediate storage of components such as foundation structures, tower segments, nacelles and rotor blades. The harbour, currently reachable only through locks, needs unhindered access to the sea if Bremerhaven is to become a base for the construction of offshore wind farms. The lack of this free access to the sea when construction started on alpha ventus forced the project leaders to use Eemshaven in Holland for all the logistics. This meant that the nacelles for the turbines, which were manufactured in two dockside production facilities in Bremerhaven's Fischereihafen, first had to be shipped through the double lock to the River Weser, then to the North Sea and finally to Eemshaven on the west side of the River Ems. This very time-consuming manoeuvre will become completely uneconomical when 100 or even 200 wind turbines

Am Schwerlastkai im Labrador-Hafen in Bremerhaven werden die Maschinenhäuser der Repower 5M verladen. Die Fertigungshalle für die 5M befindet sich unmittelbar am Kai.
At the heavy-load quayside in Bremerhaven's Labrador-harbour the Repower 5M nacelles are loaded. The production hall is right next to the quayside.

ist der Ausbau zum Offshore-Stützpunkt noch lange nicht. Für die Logistik und die Vormontage von Offshore-Windparks werden zusätzlich große Flächen benötigt, um alle Komponenten wie Gründungsstrukturen, Turmsegmente, Maschinenhäuser und Rotorblätter zwischenlagern zu können. Ebenso braucht der Hafen, der bisher nur über Schleusen erreichbar ist, einen freien Zugang zum Meer. Nur mit dieser Maßnahme kann Bremerhaven auch Basishafen für die Errichtung von Offshore-Windparks werden. Weil es diesen freien Meereszugang zum Zeitpunkt des Baubeginns von alpha ventus noch nicht gab, waren die Bauherren gezwungen, auf das niederländische Eemshaven als Basishafen für die gesamte Logistik auszuweichen. So mussten etwa die Gondeln der Windturbinen, die in den beiden Produktionshallen direkt am Kai von Bremerhavens Fischereihafen produziert wurden, auf ihrem Weg nach Eemshaven zunächst per Schiff durch die Doppelschleuse, um dann die Weser und die Nordsee in Richtung Eemshaven an der Westseite der Ems zu erreichen. Ein sehr zeitraubendes Manöver, das wirtschaftlich nicht mehr zu vertreten ist, wenn schon bald jährlich 100 oder sogar 200 Windturbinen von Bremerhaven aus in die Nordsee verschifft werden. Die Offshore-Komponenten müssen, so die Forderung der Offshore-Akteure, ohne Schleusen und damit „auf kurzem Wege" auf die Weser verschifft werden können. Kurzum: Ein neuer Hafen ist sinnvoll.

Doch nicht nur Bremerhaven möchte von der Offshore-Windenergie profitieren. Auch andere Küstenorte und Hafenstädte haben die Chancen dieser neuen Industrie bereits erkannt. Emden, Cuxhaven und Stade ist es mit Infrastrukturmaßnahmen im Wettbewerb mit anderen Orten gelungen, Firmen aus der Offshore-Windenergieindustrie rechtzeitig an ihre Standorte zu locken. So unternahm Cuxhaven große Anstrengungen, um die Fundamente, die dort von den Firmen CSC und Züblin gebaut werden, möglichst zügig verschiffen zu können. Um einen Zugang zur Elbmündung zu schaffen, wurde eine neue Deichquerung gebaut. Zudem wird die Hafenfläche deutlich erweitert, damit die Fundamente auf möglichst kurzem Wege die Schiffe erreichen. Emden hat sich nicht weniger angestrengt und sich Stück für Stück zu einem weiteren wichtigen Produktionsstandort der Offshore-Industrie gemausert. Nach der Ansiedlung der Bard-Gruppe, die dort Maschinenhäuser und Rotorblätter herstellt, wurde der Emdener Hafen auch für einen Turmhersteller interessant: Die Schaaf Industrie AG (SIAG) übernahm im September 2009 die Thyssen Nordseewerke. Seither werden auf der Werft keine Schiffe mehr gebaut, sondern Türme und Fundamente für Offshore-Windturbinen. Nicht zu vergessen ist Stade, auf dessen Industriegebiet Bützfleth mit dem gleichnamigen Hafen am Südufer der Elbe innerhalb von wenigen Jahren ein atemberaubender Strukturwandel gelang. Wo früher Atomenergie und Aluminiumerzeugung ihren Platz hatten, wird heute Energie aus Ersatzbrennstoffen erzeugt, Bioethanol hergestellt und die PN Rotor GmbH fertigt die Flügel für die M5000 von AREVA Multibrid.

Tripods und Jackets aus dem Ausland

Obwohl einzelne Kommunen, Pioniere und mancher Politiker große Anstrengungen unternommen haben, zeigte der Bau von alpha ventus, dass in Deutschland noch Produktionskapazitäten fehlen. Positiv gewendet könnte man nun sagen, dass dieses Defizit vielleicht von anderen Hafenstädten, ob sie nun Rostock, Stralsund, Lübeck, Kiel, Flensburg oder Brunsbüttel heißen, als Chance gesehen werden kann, bald selbst ein neues Kapitel in der Offshore-Story zu schreiben. Auf

per year soon begin leaving Bremerhaven for the North Sea. The offshore companies require components to get from the harbour to the Weser directly, i.e. without going through locks. A new harbour is needed.

But Bremerhaven is not the only port hoping to benefit from offshore wind energy. Other German coastal towns and ports also see opportunities in this new industry. Emden, Cuxhaven and Stade have made infrastructure improvements that have succeeded in attracting offshore wind energy companies early on. For example, Cuxhaven went to great lengths so that the foundations built there by the companies Cuxhaven Steel Construction (CSC) and Züblin could be shipped out as fast as possible. The city built a new dyke crossing to improve access to the River Elbe, and considerably enlarged the harbour so that the foundations could be shipped to the dock by the most direct route possible.

Emden went to no less effort, and has step by step become another important production centre of the offshore industry. The Bard Group has located there to fabricate nacelles and rotor blades, and a tower manufacturer has also taken up residence, through the September 2009 acquisition by Schaaf Industrie AG (SIAG) of the Thyssen North Sea Works. Now the former shipyard no longer builds ships, but instead makes towers and foundations for offshore wind-energy converters. Stade, meanwhile, has undergone a breathtaking structural change in just a few years, with the Bützfleth industrial zone at the harbour of the same name on the south bank of the Elbe. Where formerly atomic energy and aluminium were produced, today alternative energy is generated from other fuels, bioethanol is produced and PN Rotor GmbH manufactures rotor blades for the AREVA Multibrid M5000.

Tripods and jackets from other countries

Although municipalities, pioneers and politicians have gone to great lengths, the construction of alpha ventus has showed that production capacity is still lacking in Germany. Viewed positively, this unmet need can also be interpreted to mean that other port cities such as Rostock, Stralsund, Lübeck, Kiel, Flensburg and Brunsbüttel have the opportunity to write their own new chapters in the offshore story. But initially, the alpha ventus leaders had to look outside Germany for manufacturers, because WeserWind in Bremerhaven was still under construction and therefore not yet able to fabricate the foundation structures. Instead, the Aker Kværner shipyard in Verdal, Norway, built the tripods, and the Burntisland shipyard in Scotland fabricated the jackets. This meant that the foundations travelled great distances across the North Sea and then back out to the construction site. In the end, five production sites in five countries were involved in building the alpha ventus wind farm, although in future component construction will be concentrated to a much greater degree in Germany – at least according to politicians in Germany's five coastal states. Of course, over the long

Das Maschinenhaus der M5000 wird in Bremerhaven auf das Spezialschiff Mega-Motti verladen.
The nacelle of the M5000 are loaded onboard the Mega-Motti pusher barge in Bremerhaven.

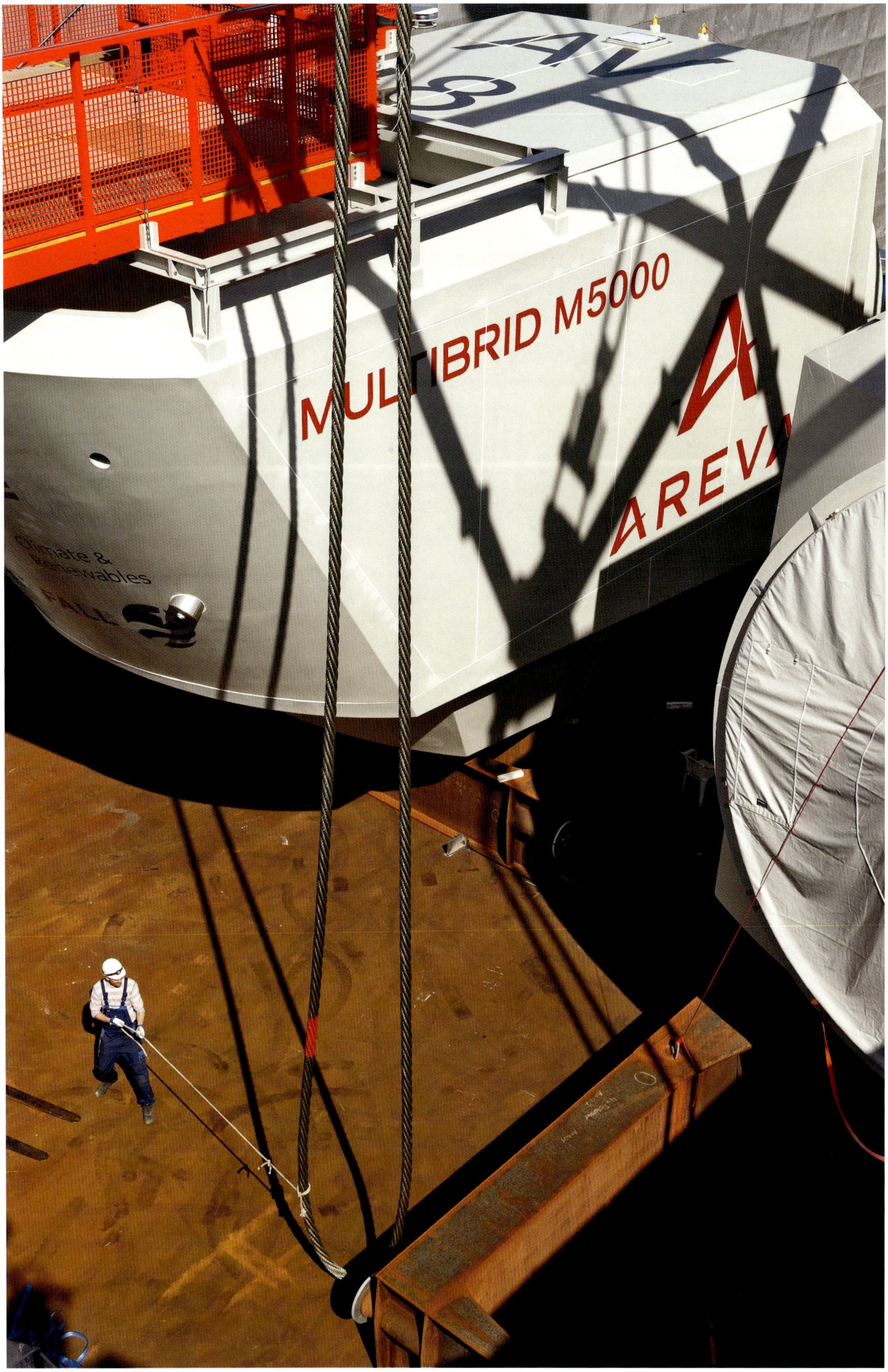
MULTIBRID M5000
AREVA
Climate &
Renewables

jeden Fall mussten die Bauherren von alpha ventus auf Hersteller im Ausland ausweichen, weil sich die Fertigung der Gründungsstrukturen durch WeserWind in Bremerhaven noch im Aufbau befand. Deshalb stellte die Aker Kværner Werft in Verdal (Norwegen) die Tripods und die schottische Burntisland-Werft die Jackets her. Die Gründungen legten also eine weite Reise quer durch die Nordsee zur Baustelle zurück. Am Ende waren fünf Produktionsstandorte in drei Ländern an der Errichtung des Windparks alpha ventus beteiligt, obgleich zukünftig, so zumindest die Beteuerungen der Wirtschaftspolitik der fünf Küstenbundesländer, die Fertigung der Komponenten stärker in Deutschland konzentriert werden soll. Allerdings wird, langfristig gesehen, die Nutzung der Nord- und Ostsee-Windenergie eine Aufgabe aller Anrainerstaaten sein.

Spezialschiffe für die Arbeit auf dem Meer

Um einen Windpark im Meer zu bauen, muss man vor allem schnell sein. Das gilt besonders unter den rauen Klimabedingungen auf der Nordsee. Zwischen den Stürmen im Frühjahr und im Herbst steht nur ein Zeitraum von etwa Mitte April bis Mitte September zur Verfügung. Nur in diesen Monaten kann auf See bei guten Wetterbedingungen gearbeitet werden. Geringe Windgeschwindigkeiten und niedrige Wellenhöhen sind die wichtigsten Voraussetzungen. Aber auch im Hochsommer kann es passieren, dass der Wind stark auffrischt und eine Arbeitspause erzwingt. Die Zeitfenster, in denen ein ungestörter Aufbau möglich ist, haben oft nur eine Ausdehnung von wenigen Tagen.

Um diese knappe Zeit optimal auszunutzen, müssen alle im Hafen liegenden Fundamente, Türme, Gondeln und Rotorblätter über einen schnellen, direkten Zugang zum Meer verfügen. Überdies sollte ein solcher Hafen nah an der Baustelle liegen: Je kürzer die Distanz, desto schneller die Transporte. Von Eemshaven aus brauchten die von Schleppern gezogenen Hubinseln nur etwa zwölf bis 14 Stunden bis ins Testfeld von alpha ventus. Darüber hinaus braucht so ein Basishafen Platz, zum Beispiel für die Montage von Blättern und Nabe zum Rotorstern, die die Hersteller REpower und AREVA Multibrid an Land durchgeführt haben, um kostbare Zeit auf dem Meer zu sparen. Dennoch dauerte der Aufbau der zwölf Windturbinen von Mitte April bis Mitte November 2009, also rund sieben Monate. Diese Zeitspanne brauchte es, um die besagten Zeitfenster mitzunehmen, die ein Arbeiten auf See bei schwachem Wind und mäßiger Wellenhöhe erlaubten. Um in Zukunft zehnmal so viele Windturbinen in der gleichen Zeit aufbauen zu können, müssen nicht nur wesentlich mehr Transport- und Montageschiffe eingesetzt, sondern auch die Zeitfenster ausgedehnt werden. Das kann man in erster Linie nur erreichen, indem man größere Spezialschiffe einsetzt, die auch bei höherem Seegang noch arbeiten können. Um mit passenden Gerätschaften und Spezialschiffen für die kommenden Herausforderungen präpariert zu sein, ist die Auswertung der Arbeitsabläufe im Baufeld von alpha ventus von so großer Bedeutung.

Bis dato war die Auswahl der Schiffe, die für die Offshore-Windenergie zur Verfügung standen, noch relativ gering. Die Zeitplanung für die Errichtung von alpha ventus war unter anderem auch davon abhängig, wann Schwimmkräne und Hubinseln vom Einsatz für Öl- oder Gasförderung freigestellt werden konnten. Da die Offshore-Windenergie in Zukunft aber nicht mehr nur „Lückenfüller" sein möchte und mit dem Aufbau der Windparks schneller vorankommen will als bisher, braucht sie so bald wie möglich eigene große Schiffe, die speziell für

term, exploitation of North Sea and Baltic wind energy will be a task for all coastal countries.

Special ships for construction at sea

To build a wind farm out at sea you have to work quickly. This is especially true under the rough weather conditions in the North Sea. The spring and autumn storm seasons leave a window of good weather from mid-April to mid-September. This is the only time wind speeds and wave heights are low enough for construction. Of course, even in high summer the wind can freshen sharply and force a cessation of work. The periods during which construction work can proceed without interference are often a matter of just a few days.

To make the best use of the short time available, all of the foundations, towers, nacelles and rotor blades need to get from harbour to offshore site as quickly and directly as possible. The port should be close to the site – the shorter the distance, the faster components can get there. For example, from Eemshaven, tugs needed only about 12 to 14 hours to tow the jack-up platforms to the alpha ventus test field. The harbour needs enough space to permit the assembly of rotor blades and hubs, which the manufacturers REpower und AREVA Multibrid did on land for alpha ventus in order to save precious time at sea. Nevertheless, setting up the twelve turbines took from mid-April to mid-November 2009, or around seven months. This was the time needed to accumulate enough good-weather periods of low wind and moderate wave height during which work could proceed. Future wind farms, involving the construction of ten times as many turbines in the same amount of time, will require not only many more transport and assembly vessels, but also longer time windows. The only way to achieve this is with larger, specialised vessels that can work in rougher weather. Assessment of the work processes for alpha ventus is of great importance because it will assist in creating the right equipment and vessels to be prepared for future challenges.

Up until now the number of vessels available for offshore wind energy work has been relatively low. One of the factors in planning the construction of alpha ventus was the limited availability of floating cranes and jack-up barge platforms, which are normally contracted for offshore oil and gas work. If the offshore wind industry doesn't want to just be a gap-filler, and wants to ramp up the pace of wind-farm construction, it will need its own large ships as soon as possible, specially designed for the needs and dimensions of the industry. Shipbuilders have already responded to the demand; the first specialised vessels are under construction and will be available in 2010.

Offshore power on a long haul from sea to mainland

Offshore wind-energy converters (WECs) are in the public eye. They can be seen from afar as they rotate spectacularly above the sea. While turbine manufacturers win admiration for their engineering skills, it is easily forgotten that manufacturers can only garner the glory because their turbines are connected by cables that bring the power to shore. Escaping the notice of the observer because they lie hidden on the seabed or are even buried in it. Subsea cables are the bottleneck of offshore wind-power operations. No electric power would ever reach the shore without them. However, the effort required for planning and laying the cables far exceeds what some might think. Next to WECs and

Oben: Die von der AMBAU GmbH gefertigten Turmsegmente für die M5000 werden in Bremen verladen.
Above: The M5000 tower sections fabricated by AMBAU GmbH are loaded onboard in Bremen.
Unten: Arbeiten an der Gründungsstruktur des Umspannwerks von alpha ventus in Wilhelmshaven.
Work proceeds on the transformer station's foundation structure for alpha ventus in Wilhelmshaven.

Im Stader Elbehafen werden
Rotorblätter für die M5000 auf
die Mega-Motti verladen.
The blades of the M5000 are
loaded onboard the Mega-Motti
pusher barge in the Elbe port
of Stade.

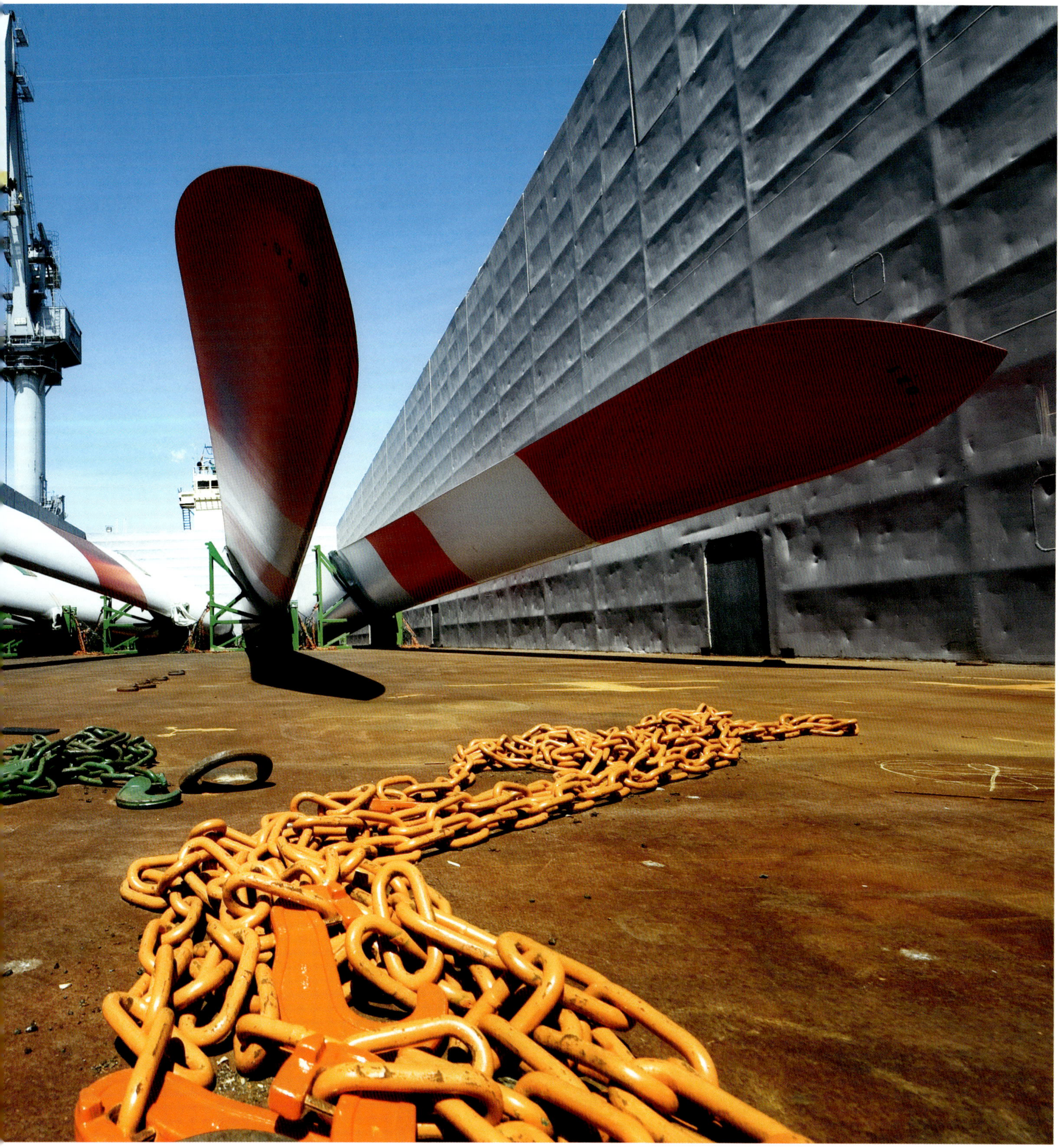

ihre Zwecke und Dimensionen konstruiert sind. Die Schiffsindustrie hat inzwischen auf den angemeldeten Bedarf reagiert: Die ersten Spezialschiffe sind im Bau und können schon ab 2010 eingesetzt werden.

Der lange Weg des Stroms vom Meer zum Festland

Die Offshore-Windenergieanlagen stehen im Rampenlicht der Aufmerksamkeit. Sie sind weithin sichtbar und drehen sich telegen über dem Meer. Die Bewunderung für die Ingenieurstechnik ist den Turbinenherstellern sicher. Gerne wird dabei vergessen, dass die Hersteller der Turbinen den Ruhm letztlich nur einheimsen können, weil die Anlagen mit Kabeln verbunden sind, die den Strom an Land bringen. Auch wenn sie für den Betrachter kaum in Erscheinung treten, weil sie versteckt auf dem Meeresboden liegen oder sogar in den Meeresgrund eingebuddelt werden, sind die Kabel das Nadelöhr der Operation Offshore-Windenergie: Ohne Kabel gibt es keinen Strom an Land. Dabei ist der Aufwand für Planung und Bau der Kabeltrassen wesentlich größer, als manche denken mögen. Neben den Windenergieanlagen und den Gründungsstrukturen ist die Stromübertragung der dritte große Investitionsposten beim Offshore-Geschäft.

Dass die Netzanbindung des Testfeldes von alpha ventus rechtzeitig fertig gestellt werden konnte, ist letztlich einem Gesetz zu verdanken, foundation structures, power transmission is the third-largest investment factor in the offshore business.

Ultimately, it was thanks to a law passed by the German Parliament (Bundestag) in October 2006 that grid connection of the alpha ventus test field could be completed in time. The law has achieved some notoriety because of its unwieldy name – the Infrastructure Planning Acceleration Law. Politicians went to great lengths in framing and formulating this law to enable implementation of major projects such as federal highways, railway lines, waterways and airports faster than had previously been possible. It was not until the final reading in the Bundestag that a section was incorporated into the law which was of key significance for offshore wind energy. In this section, grid operators were obliged to provide for the connection of wind farms to the grid in their balancing zone. This meant that transmission system operators were bound by law to install the 'outlets in the sea.'

This law turned the tables in one fell swoop. No more did the planners have to arrange for their own line to the grid connection point for each offshore project, as had previously been common practice. All of a sudden, on this legal basis it became possible to connect several offshore wind farms to the grid, bundled via one cable. The optimised route planning is not only supposed to cut costs but also considerably mitigate the impact on nature and the environment.

KABEL DURCH WATT UND INSEL
A CABLE THROUGH MUDFLATS AND ISLAND

Das Seekabel durchquert die ostfriesische Insel Norderney.
The subsea cable crosses the North Sea island of Norderney.

Zuhauf stapeln sich die Ordner im Büro von Ludwig Salverius. Auf den Aktenrücken stehen Begriffe wie „Eon Netz Offshore", „Plambeck Godewind" oder „Naturschutzfachlicher Teil". Als Bürgermeister der Inselgemeinde Norderney musste sich Salverius jahrelang mit der komplexen Thematik der Offshore-Windenergie beschäftigen, die unter den Insulanern heftig und zuweilen auch kontrovers diskutiert wurde. Verläuft doch mitten durch die Insel die Kabeltrasse, die den Windstrom aus dem Testfeld von alpha ventus und später von weiteren Windparks zur ostfriesischen Küste bringt.

Alles begann im Jahr 1999. Damals kam ein gewisser Ingo de Buhr von der Firma Prokon Nord auf die Insel. Er berichtete über das Vorhaben seiner Firma, 45 Kilometer vor Borkum ein paar Windmühlen aufzustellen. Die sehe man gar nicht, soll der Mann aus Leer versprochen haben. „Für mich war sofort klar, dass wir als Inselgemeinde aufpassen müssen, um nicht plötzlich zu Zuschauern des ganzen Verfahrens zu werden", erinnert sich Salverius an die erste Begegnung. Besonders die geplante Querung der Kabeltrasse über die Ferieninsel war ein heikles Thema. Viele Fragen waren offen. „In den ersten Diskussionen mit den Beteiligten herrschte oft Chaos", blickt der Bürgermeister auf eine „spannende Zeit" zurück. Alle betraten technisches Neuland. So wurde sogar überlegt, ob man die vom Kabel abgegebene Wärme nutzen könne.

Es herrschte Skepsis unter den Insulanern, weil viele meinten, dass die Offshore-Wind-

das im Oktober 2006 vom Bundestag verabschiedet wurde. Es hat den gewöhnungsbedürftigen Namen Infrastrukturplanungsbeschleunigungsgesetz. An diesem Gesetz arbeiteten und formulierten die Politiker lange herum, um Großprojekte – wie Bundesfernstraßen, Eisenbahntrassen, Wasserstraßen und Flughäfen – schneller zu verwirklichen, als es in der Vergangenheit möglich war. Erst kurz vor den entscheidenden Lesungen im Bundestag wurde eine Passage ins Gesetzeswerk aufgenommen, die für die Offshore-Windenergie von zentraler Bedeutung war. In dieser Passage wurden nämlich die Netzbetreiber verpflichtet, für den Netzanschluss der Offshore-Windparks in ihrer Regelzone zu sorgen. Die Netzbetreiber bekamen damit qua Gesetz den Auftrag, „die Steckdosen ins Meer zu legen".

Dieses Gesetz veränderte auf einen Schlag die ganze Situation. Die vorher gängige Praxis, dass sich die Planer jedes einzelnen Offshore-Projektes um eine eigene Leitung zum Netzanschlusspunkt kümmern mussten, war nun obsolet. Auf der Grundlage des neuen Gesetzes wurde plötzlich die gebündelte Anbindung mehrerer Offshore-Windparks durch eine Kabeltrasse möglich. Diese optimierte Trassenplanung soll nicht nur die Kosten, sondern auch die Eingriffe in Natur und Umwelt erheblich vermindern.

Die transpower stromübertragungs gmbh (vormals E.ON Netz) ist als zuständiger Übertragungsnetzbetreiber besonders stark in der Pflicht.

As the responsible system operator, transpower stromübertragungs gmbh (formerly E.ON Netz) is under close scrutiny. The company established a subsidiary for this task, transpower offshore gmbh, which was commissioned by its parent company to take on the planning and laying of connection lines at sea to the grid node-point on land. The first project was to connect the alpha ventus test field to the grid. This connection could not be made in just a few weeks. With a transmission capacity of 60 megawatts, the approximately 70-kilometre-long cable starts at the transformer station next to the alpha ventus offshore wind farm. It then runs southeast to the resort island of Norderney, crosses the island, and then passes through the Lower Saxony Wadden Sea National Park, to finally terminate at the Hagermarsch transformer station where the wind power produced at sea is fed into the 110-kilovolt grid. Three construction sections had to be managed: crossing the island of Norderney, laying the submarine cables in the Wadden Sea and continuing at sea to the transformer station at the alpha ventus test field.

Crossing Norderney

The extensive works started with the crossing of the coastal resort island of Norderney. At a very early stage, planners considered how the impact on nature could be reduced to a minimum, in spite of the multiple

In Ludwig Salverius' office the ring binders are piled high. Their spines are neatly labelled 'Eon Grid Offshore', 'Plambeck Godewind' or 'Nature conservation part'. As Mayor of the island community of Norderney, Salverius has had to deal with the complicated subject of offshore wind power for years, a controversial topic often hotly discussed by the islanders. The cables carrying wind power from the alpha ventus test field run right through the middle of his island, soon to be joined by others from more wind farms on the East Frie-sian coast.

It all began in 1999, when a certain Ingo de Buhr from the company Prokon Nord in nearby Leer came to the island and spoke of his company' intention to set up a few wind turbines some 45 kilometres off the neighbouring island of Borkum. "You won't even see them", he promised. These first encounters are still fresh in Mayor Salverius' memory: "It immediately became clear to me that we, as an island community, had to be very careful that we didn't all of a sudden become mere spectators watching all this going on around us." With numerous questions left unanswered, the planned laying of the cable over this holiday island was a particularly touchy subject: "The initial discussions with those involved were frequently chaotic". Nevertheless Salverius remembers this as an "exciting period", when the community was breaking new technological ground. It was even discussed whether the heat emitted from the cables could be used.

The island's inhabitants were sceptical,

energie den touristischen Nerv der Insel empfindlich treffen würde. Doch heute ist das Thema Windenergie in der Öffentlichkeit grundsätzlich positiv besetzt. Die Erfahrungen, die auf der Insel gemacht wurden, haben zur Beruhigung beigetragen. „Sanfter Tourismus" und „sauberer Strom" scheinen durchaus vereinbar.

Trotzdem verging noch viel Zeit, bis dann Entscheidungen fielen. „Wir leben hier eben auf einem sehr kleinen Raum, da bleibt nichts verborgen und was auch immer hier passiert, es lässt sich kein Vorhaben vertuschen. Deshalb haben wir auch immer wieder um die bestmögliche Lösung für die Kabelverlegung durch Watt und Insel gerungen", erklärt der Bürgermeister den zurückgelegten Diskussionsmarathon um ein für alle Seiten akzeptables Verfahren. Alle sprachen sich für eine sensible, vorsichtige Verlegung aus – und unbedingt unterirdisch sollte sie sein.

Am Ende haben sich alle Beteiligten geeinigt. „Wir haben uns inzwischen mit der Windenergie auf See arrangiert", zeigt sich Salverius in den Dünen von Norderney zufrieden. „Da verläuft die Trasse", sagt er, dreht sich um die eigene Achse und zeichnet mit dem ausgestreckten Finger eine Line in die Luft. Es ist eine imaginäre Linie, denn die Trasse, die nach Angaben vom Netzbetreiber transpower maximal 3.000 Megawatt Leistung abführen kann, liegt rund drei Meter unter dem Boden. So tief, dass auch die Erwärmung der Kabel für Mensch und Tier nicht zu spüren ist.

as many of them believed that offshore wind energy would have a negative impact on tourism on the island. Nowadays, however, the subject of wind power has fundamentally positive connotations. The experience gained on the island contributed to calming the islanders' initial fears, as they began to accept that sustainable tourism and 'clean energy' seemed to fit together very well.

Nevertheless, a lot of time passed until the key decisions could be taken. "There's not a lot of space to live on here – nothing stays hidden for long, and whatever happens on this island you can't keep plans like these under wraps. That's why we didn't stop fighting until we got the best-possible solution for laying the cable through the mudflats and our island", is how Salverius describes the discussion marathon needed to reach an agreement acceptable to all sides. Everyone wanted a low-impact, cautious laying of the cable – meaning it definitely had to go underground.

All involved were able to finally reach an agreement. Happily looking out to sea with his feet planted firmly in the sand of the Norderney dunes, Salverius states: "We've come to accept wind power at sea. That's where the route goes", he says, tracing an arc across the terrain with his outstretched arm. But this is an imaginary line, as the cable – which according to grid operator transpower can carry a maximum of 3,000 megawatts – is three metres underground. So deep that no person or animal would ever notice any heat from the cable.

Arbeiten zwischen Ebbe und Flut:
Seekabelverlegung auf der Seeseite Norderneys.
Between high and low tide: cable-laying work
proceeds on Norderney's seaward side.

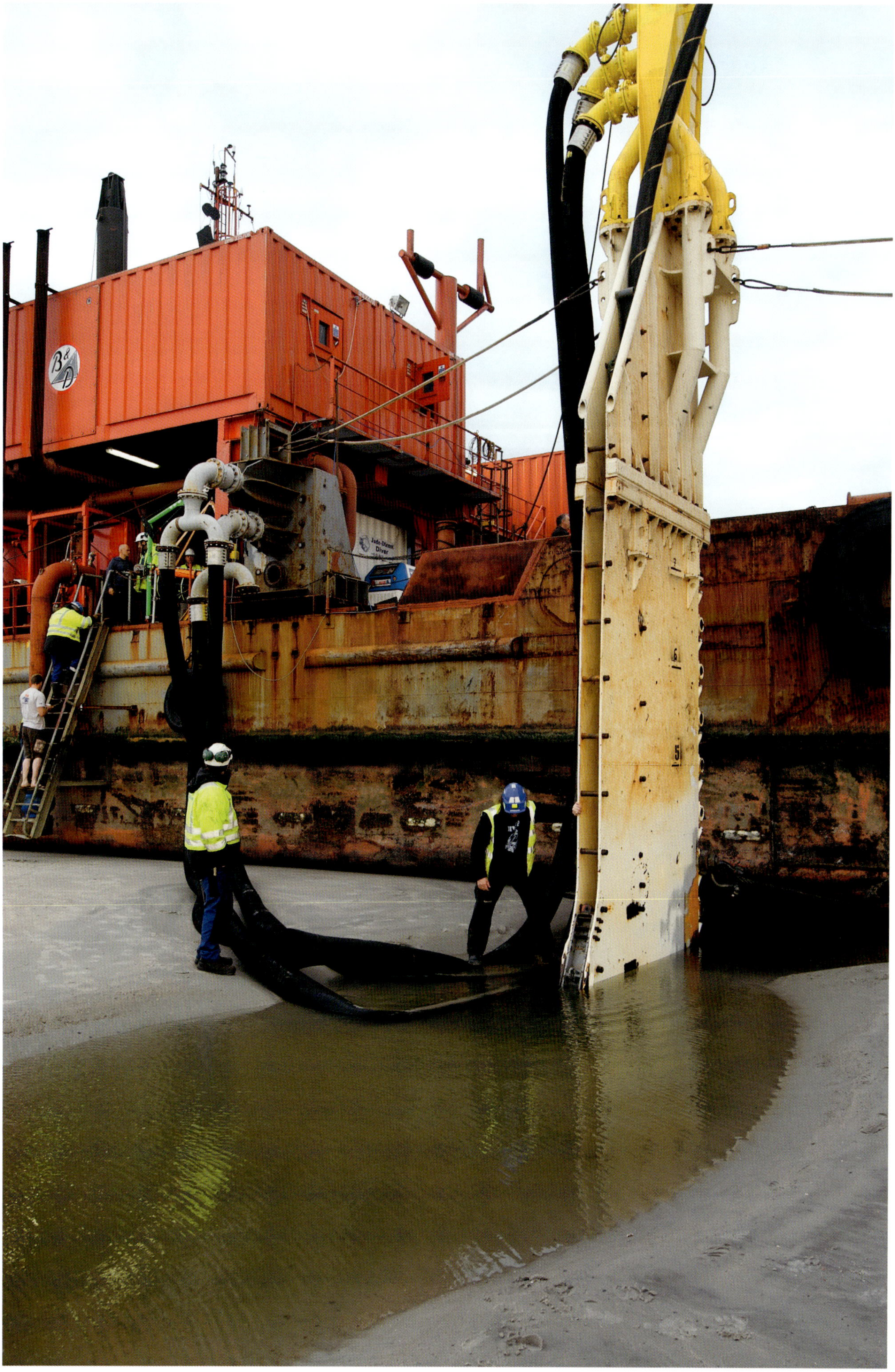

Das Verlegen des Seekabels durch den Nationalpark Niedersächsisches Wattenmeer unterstand strengen naturschutzrechtlichen Auflagen. Es galt, den Eingriff in den sensiblen Naturhaushalt so gering wie nur möglich zu gestalten.

To minimise the impact on the ecosystem, subsea cable laying through the "Lower Saxony Wadden Sea National Park" was subject to strict nature conservation conditions.

Das Unternehmen hat für diese Aufgabe eine Tochtergesellschaft gegründet, die transpower offshore gmbh, die im Auftrag ihrer Muttergesellschaft die Planung und den Bau von Anschlussleitungen auf See bis zum Netzknotenpunkt an Land übernimmt. Das erste Projekt bildete der Netzanschluss des Testfeldes von alpha ventus. Diese Netzanbindung war nicht in wenigen Wochen zu meistern. Das rund 70 Kilometer lange Kabel mit einer Übertragungskapazität von 60 Megawatt beginnt beim Umspannwerk direkt neben dem Offshore-Windpark alpha ventus, verläuft dann nach Südosten in Richtung Norderney, durchquert die Urlaubsinsel, führt anschließend durch den Nationalpark Niedersächsisches Wattenmeer und endet schließlich im Umspannwerk Hagermarsch, wo der auf See erzeugte Windstrom in das 110-Kilovolt-Netz eingespeist wird. Es waren drei Bauabschnitte zu bewältigen: die Querung der Insel Norderney, die Verlegung des Seekabels im Wattenmeer und die Verlegung des Seekabels bis hin zur Umspannstation unmittelbar am Testfeld von alpha ventus.

Die Querung der Insel Norderney

Die aufwändigen Arbeiten begannen mit der Querung der Insel Norderney. Schon zu einem sehr frühen Zeitpunkt gab es Überlegungen,

grid connections that were to be built. The solution was hollow ducts which were laid beneath an existing road. No fewer than 35 hollow ducts were integrated into this 1.5-kilometre-long structure, in order to be prepared for future projects as well. According to state regional planning procedure, a total of around 3,000 megawatts can be connected via Norderney. The first work started in early 2007 and the companies involved completed construction of the hollow ducting in early 2008.

In addition, in the summer of 2007 transpower carried out four horizontal subterranean drillings under the dunes and dykes of Norderney and near Hilgenriedersiel on the mainland. This procedure, commonly called horizontal direct drilling (HDD procedure), consists of three steps. First a pilot drilling is performed with a measuring probe in the drill head, which finds its way through the ground at depths of more than 20 metres. Then a further drilling follows using a bigger drill head: this leaves a borehole in which, in the third step, workers lay the cable ducts and then insert the cables. Transport vessels brought materials and equipment from the port of Norddeich through the shipping lane to Baltrum. The first cable entry for the line to alpha ventus was laid in May 2008. At the same time, in April 2008, transpower started building the feed-in point on land, the new Hagermarsch transformer station, to which a 4.5-kilometre buried cable was laid from Hilgenriedersiel.

wie trotz mehrerer geplanter Netzanbindungen ein möglichst geringer Eingriff in die Natur zu bewerkstelligen wäre. Die Lösung waren Leerrohre, die unter einer bestehenden Straße verlegt wurden. Um auch für künftige Projekte gerüstet zu sein, wurden gleich 35 Leerrohre in dieses 1,5 Kilometer lange Bauwerk eingebettet. Denn entsprechend des Landesraumordnungsverfahrens können insgesamt rund 3.000 Megawatt über Norderney angeschlossen werden. Schon im Frühjahr 2007 begannen die ersten Arbeiten und im Frühjahr 2008 stellten die beteiligten Baufirmen das Leerrohrbauwerk fertig.

Im Sommer 2007 nahm transpower zudem vier unterirdische Horizontalbohrungen unter den Dünen und Deichen von Norderney und bei Hilgenriedersiel auf dem ostfriesischen Festland vor. Dieses so genannte Horizontal-Direct-Drilling-Verfahren (HDD-Verfahren) besteht aus drei Schritten: Als erstes folgt eine Pilotbohrung mit einer Sonde im Bohrkopf, die auch in Tiefen von über 20 Metern den richtigen Weg durchs Erdreich findet. Danach erfolgt eine weitere Bohrung mit einem größeren Bohrkopf, der einen Erdkanal hinterlässt, in den die Bauarbeiter im dritten Schritt die Kabellehrrohre hineinlegen und später die Kabel einziehen. Transportschiffe brachten Materialien und Gerätschaften vom Hafen Norddeich durch die Fahrrinne nach Baltrum. Der erste Kabeleinzug für die Trasse nach alpha ventus erfolgte schließlich im Mai 2008. Parallel dazu begann transpower im April 2008 mit dem Bau des Einspeisepunktes an Land, dem neuen Umspannwerk Hagermarsch, zu dem von Hilgenriedersiel aus ein 4,5 Kilometer langes Landkabel gelegt wurde.

Die Kabelverlegung im Watt und auf hoher See

Das Zipfelchen Landkabel war sicherlich die leichteste Übung beim Bau der gesamten Stromübertragungstrasse. Die Verlegung des Seekabels im Watt und auf hoher See bis hin zum Umspannwerk gestaltete sich wesentlich aufwändiger. Bei einem Kabeldurchmesser von 18 Zentimetern und knapp 53 Kilogramm Gewicht pro Meter kann man sich leicht vorstellen, dass für dieses Unterfangen Spezial-Equipment erforderlich war. Zudem sind je nach Untergrund unterschiedliche Arten der Kabelverlegung notwendig. So wurde auf See das Kabel von der Zehn-Meter-Wassertiefen-Linie aus mit zwei Schiffen verlegt und eingespült. Doch bevor es damit losgehen konnte, machte schlechtes Wetter den Crews einen Strich durch die Rechnung. Erst nach fünf Tagen geduldigen Wartens hatten sich Wogen wieder soweit geglättet, dass die Mannschaft vom Kabelverlegeschiff Team Oman bei ruhiger See ein fünf Kilometer langes Kabel auf das Spezialschiff Installer

umspulen konnte. Danach startete die Installer in Richtung Norderney, während die Team Oman das Seekabel in Richtung Windpark auslegte. Mittels eines Spülschwertes beziehungsweise einer Fräse wurde das Kabel in den Meeresboden eingespült. Weit draußen auf dem Meer schlossen die Kabelleger dann das Seekabel ans Umspannwerk an.

Insbesondere die Arbeiten im Naturpark Niedersächsisches Wattenmeer waren sehr sensibel zu handhaben, da sie strengen Auflagen unterliegen. Normalerweise sind Bautätigkeiten hier gänzlich verboten. Erst nachdem die geplanten Bauarbeiten und ihre genaue Ausführung für die Netzanbindung des Testfeldes von alpha ventus im Detail beschrieben waren, erteilten die zuständigen Behörden innerhalb eines eng definierten Rahmens die Befreiung vom Bauverbot. Um den Auflagen in jedem Stadium der Arbeiten im Watt gerecht zu werden, beauftragte transpower das Landschaftsplanungsbüro Ecoplan aus Leer mit der naturschutzfachlichen Baubegleitung. Ecoplan dokumentierte die Baumaßnahmen, beriet den Bauherrn und die Baufirmen in allen Fragen des Naturschutzes und vermittelte zwischen transpower und den Naturschutzbehörden. Zudem kontrollierte Ecoplan alle Maßnahmen zum Biotop- und Vogelschutz sowie zum Boden- und Wasserschutz.

In der Tat erwies sich die Kabelverlegung im Watt als schwierig, weil möglichst wenige Baggerfahrten durchgeführt werden sollten. Allerdings machten Reparaturen und technische Probleme mehr Fahrten als geplant erforderlich. Zudem hielt die eingesetzte Verlegetechnik nicht das, was sie versprach. Weil die Kabel bei Hochwasser verlegt wurden, sah man die Ergebnisse erst bei der nächsten Tide. Nicht zuletzt aufgrund dieser Erfahrungen wurde bereits im Folgejahr für die Kabelverlegung in einem anderen Netzanbindungsprojekt eine alternative Technik gewählt. Künftig kommt ein Vibrationspflug zum Einsatz. „Wir brauchen ungefähr die halbe Zeit und nehmen auch wesentlich weniger Raum in Anspruch, sodass die Beeinträchtigungen des Nationalparks deutlich geringer ausfallen", zieht Gesamtprojektleiter Matthias Mensing Bilanz.

Mensing hat die Erfahrung gemacht, dass Touristen die Bauarbeiten durchaus neugierig wahrnehmen: „Generell sind die Menschen sehr wissbegierig und stellen erstaunlich detaillierte Fragen", berichtet er, „und wenn man erklärt, was gerade gemacht wird, erntet man meist auch Akzeptanz, verbunden mit der Hoffnung, dass hinterher auch alles funktionieren möge."

Aber nicht nur die richtige Technik macht's, auch der Zeitrahmen ist im Nationalpark besonders eng. Zwar hat das Wetter nicht den Einfluss wie auf hoher See, doch sind vor allem Deich- und Vogelschutz zu beachten. Die Deichschutzgesetze schreiben vor, dass nur zwischen dem 15. April und dem 31. August eines Jahres überhaupt gearbeitet werden darf. Überlagert wird dieser Zeitraum von der Schutzzeit für die Brutvögel, die bis zum 15. Juli dauert. Übrig bleibt also die Spanne zwischen dem 15. Juli und dem 31. August, in der im Schutzgebiet gearbeitet werden darf. Mit einer Ausnahmegenehmigung kann dieser Zeitraum im Notfall bis maximal 30. September verlängert werden. Außerhalb dieses Zeitraumes ist es verboten, landgestützte Arbeiten im Wattgebiet durchzuführen. Fazit: Es bleiben anderthalb, maximal zweieinhalb Monate Zeit für die Bauarbeiten im Nationalpark.

Transformator auf hoher See

Bevor der von den Windenergieanlagen erzeugte Strom an Land fließen kann, wird er über eine Innerparkverkabelung zum Umspann-

Laying cable across tidal flats and under the sea

The short length of cable on land was certainly the easiest section to build of the entire power transmission line. Laying undersea cable across the tidal flats and on the sea floor to the transformer station was much more involved. With a cable measuring 18 centimetres in diameter and weighing almost 53 kilograms per metre, it's easy to see why special equipment would be necessary. In addition, different types of seabed require different cable-laying methods. At sea, the cable was laid and buried from the 10-metre depth line with two ships. But before they could even get started, bad weather forced a delay. Only after five days' patient waiting did the sea again become calm enough for the crew of the cable-laying ship 'Team Oman' to wind five kilometres of cable onto the ship 'Installer'. Then 'Installer' set out towards the island of Norderney, while 'Team Oman' laid the cable towards the wind farm. The cable was injected into the seabed with a vertical injector or plow. Far out to sea, the installers connected the cable to the transformer station.

Cable laying in the Lower Saxony Wadden Sea National Park required special care due to the special restrictions in force there. In fact, normally no construction of any kind is allowed in the Park. The responsible authorities granted permission to lay cable within a very tightly defined route, and then only after a detailed description of the planned work and its exact procedure had been submitted. In order to comply with the restrictions at every phase of the work in the Wadden Sea, transpower tasked landscape planning company Ecoplan from Leer, Germany, with environmental protection consulting to accompany construction. Ecoplan documented the construction processes, advised the project leaders and construction companies on all questions surrounding environmental protection and acted as a go-between for transpower and the authorities. Ecoplan also monitored all measures for biotope, bird, soil and water protection.

Cable laying across the tidal flats of the Wadden Sea proved difficult, since the crew had to keep heavy machinery movement to a minimum, while repairs and technical problems necessitated more traffic than planned. In addition, the laying technique used did not work as well as projected. Since the cables were laid at high tide, the results were visible only at the next low tide. Based in large part on this experience, for another grid connection project the following year an alternative technology was chosen, the vibration plow. "It takes only about half the time and uses much less space, so it has considerably less environmental impact on the National Park," says overall project leader Matthias Mensing.

Mensing's experience is that tourists are quite curious about the work. "Generally people are interested in what's going on, and ask astonishingly detailed questions," he reports. "And when you explain what you're doing, most people express their approval, combined with the hope that it all works properly when finished."

But it's not just a matter of the right technology. The time window is particularly narrow in the National Park. The weather doesn't have quite the same influence as on the high seas, but dyke and bird protection are priorities. Dyke protection legislation prohibits any work before the 15th of April and after the 31st of August of any given year. This time period is overlapped by the protected breeding season for birds, which lasts until the 15th of July. That leaves the period between the 15th of July and the 31st of August for work in the Park. In exceptional cases an extension can be granted, but only until the 30th of

werk unmittelbar neben dem Windpark zusammengeführt und dort von 30 Kilovolt auf 110 Kilovolt transformiert.

Federführend beim Bau und der Errichtung dieser Offshore-Umspannplattform waren die Bilfinger Berger AG, die Hochtief Construction AG und die WeserWind GmbH. Das Trio bildete für dieses Projekt eine Arbeitsgemeinschaft. Die Jacket-Konstruktion für die Gründungsstruktur und die Aufbauten der Topside – also des Helikopter-, des Haupt- und des Kabeldecks – wurden von März bis September 2008 am Braunschweigkai in Wilhelmshaven vormontiert. Der Transformator selbst wurde Anfang August 2008 von der AREVA Energietechnik GmbH geliefert und auf dem Hauptdeck der Topside installiert.

Der Schwimmkran Taklift 4 brachte das Gittermastfundament (Jacket), auf dem später das Umspannwerk montiert wurde, bereits Mitte September 2008 zur Baustelle und setzte es dort ab. Das Jacket ist 45 Meter hoch und wiegt 650 Tonnen. Wie bei den anderen Jacket-Konstruktionen auch (Gründung der FINO 1 und der sechs REpower 5M) ist an jedem der vier Beine eine senkrechte, nach oben hin ausgeweitete Rohrhülse (Pile Sleeve) angeschweißt, in die ein 35 Meter langes Rohr eingeführt und in den Meeresgrund gerammt wird.

Nachdem der Schwimmkran das Transformatormodul (Topside) auf das Jacket gesetzt hatte, war die Umspannstation Ende September einsatzbereit. Zu diesem Zeitpunkt waren jedoch noch keine Windenergieanlagen aufgestellt. Der Anschluss des Seekabels an die Plattform erfolgte daher erst im Frühjahr 2009. Nach einem Projektzeitraum von 24 Monaten konnte der Netzanschluss nach der Prüfung aller Komponenten schließlich im Mai 2009 in Betrieb gehen.

Das auf See errichtete Umspannwerk muss vor allem vor der aggressiven Salzluft geschützt werden. „Das ganze Umspannwerk ist in Containerbauweise errichtet worden", berichtet Irina Lucke, die für die Errichtung und Installation des Umspannwerks im Auftrag der DOTI verantwortlich war. „Es handelt sich um Offshore-Container, die im Innenraum klimatisiert sind." Beim Betreten der Container lässt sich zwar nicht vermeiden, dass feuchte, salzhaltige Luft eindringt, aber die eingebauten Klimageräte sorgen für einen aktiven Luftaustausch, sodass die salzhaltige Luft relativ schnell wieder aus dem Container entfernt wird. Außerdem sind die Außenwände der Container und auch des Trafos durch ein spezielles, vierfaches Beschichtungssystem geschützt, das sich schon in der Öl- und Gasindustrie als sehr wetter- und witterungsbeständig bewährt hat.

Ein Ausfall der Umspannstation wäre der schwerwiegendste Störfall überhaupt, denn dann würde kein Strom mehr an Land fließen. Deshalb wird alles getan, um diesen Störfall zu vermeiden: „Wir überwachen das ganze Umspannwerk mittels Kamera- und Fernwirktechnik", vermittelt Irina Lucke Zuversicht, „darüber hinaus werden wir routinemäßig ein- bis zweimal im Monat draußen sein, um alles zu kontrollieren."

Fazit: Alles wird gut.

September. Outside this period it is illegal to do any land-based work in the tidal flat zone. In other words, only one-and-a-half months, or at the very most two-and-a-half, are available for cable-laying work in the National Park.

Transformer on the high seas

Before the electric power produced by wind turbines can flow to the shore it is bundled via intra-farm cabling to the transformer station at the wind farm, and there transformed from 30 to 110 kilovolts.

Bilfinger Berger AG, Hochtief Construction AG and WeserWind GmbH were the companies in charge of construction and installation for this offshore transformer platform. The trio formed a consortium for this project. The jackets for the foundation structure and the topside superstructure including the helicopter, main and cable decks were pre-assembled at Braunschweigkai in Wilhelmshaven, Germany, from March to September 2008. The transformer itself was delivered from AREVA Energietechnik GmbH in early August 2008 and installed on the topside's main deck.

As early as mid-September 2008, the Taklift 4 floating crane moved out the jacket foundation, onto which the transformer station was later mounted, and positioned it at its installation site. The jacket is 45 metres high and weighs 650 tonnes. As is the case with other jacket structures (FINO 1 and the six REpower 5Ms), a vertical pile sleeve that widens upwards was welded to each of the four legs, into which a pile 35 metres in length was inserted and rammed into the seabed.

The transformer station was ready for service in late September, after the floating crane had placed the topside transformer module onto the jacket. At that point in time, no wind-energy converters had yet been set up. It was therefore not until early 2009 that the submarine cable was connected to the platform. At last, in May 2009, the platform went online after a project development period of 24 months and thorough inspection of all components.

The transformer station at sea must be protected from the corrosive salt air. "The entire transformer station was installed in a container-type structure", reports Irina Lucke, who was in charge of construction and installation of the transformer station commissioned by DOTI. "In other words, climate-controlled offshore containers." Humid salt air cannot be prevented from entering the container when a person comes in. But the air conditioning ensures an active air exchange that removes the salty air relatively quickly from the container. A special four-layer coating system protects both the container's and the transformer's outer walls. This system has already proved to be very weather-resistant in the oil and gas industry.

A breakdown of the transformer station would be the worst-case scenario, because it would bring the electric power flowing to the mainland to a halt. Therefore all possible measures are taken to prevent this from happening. "We monitor the entire transformer station via camera and telecontrol engineering", Irina Lucke conveys confidently, "and in addition, we will routinely be out at sea once or twice a month to check everything."

In short, prospects for the future look bright.

Rechtes Foto: Der Blick in die Werkshalle der Burntisland Fabrication Ltd in Methil verrät die wahre Dimension des Jackets: Das Fußende, das später in den Meeresboden gerammt wird, sieht aus wie ein riesiger Pfeil.
Photo on the right: A look at Burntisland's production site in Methil reveals the jacket's true dimension. The base which will be rammed into the seabed later on resembles a huge arrow.

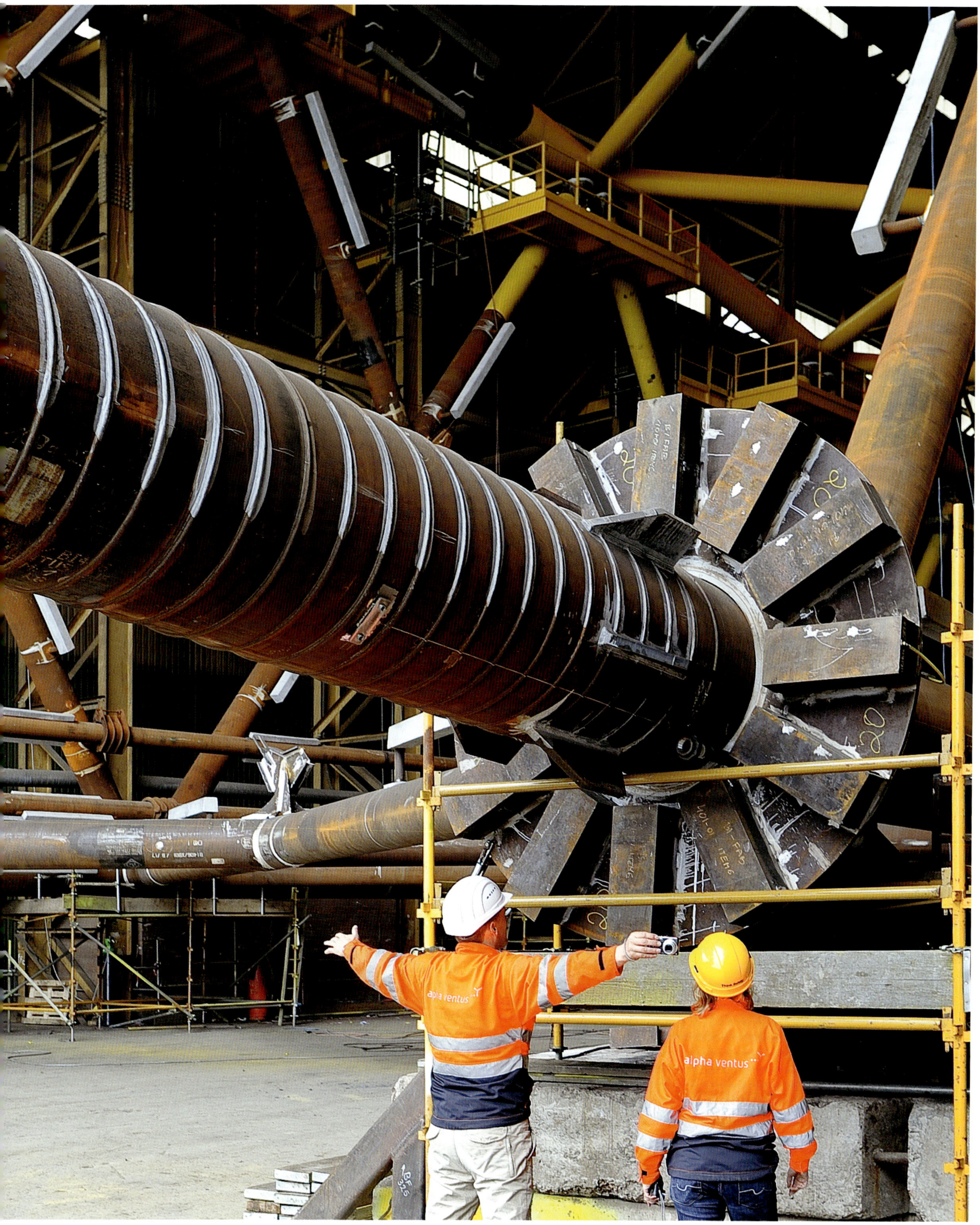
alpha ventus
alpha ventus

Rechts: Das Jacket, die Gründungsstruktur für die 5M, wird vom Kran des Hochsee-Arbeitsschiffes Thialf ins Wasser abgesetzt.
Right: The 5M jacket foundation structure is positioned by the heavy-lift crane of the Thialf special vessel.

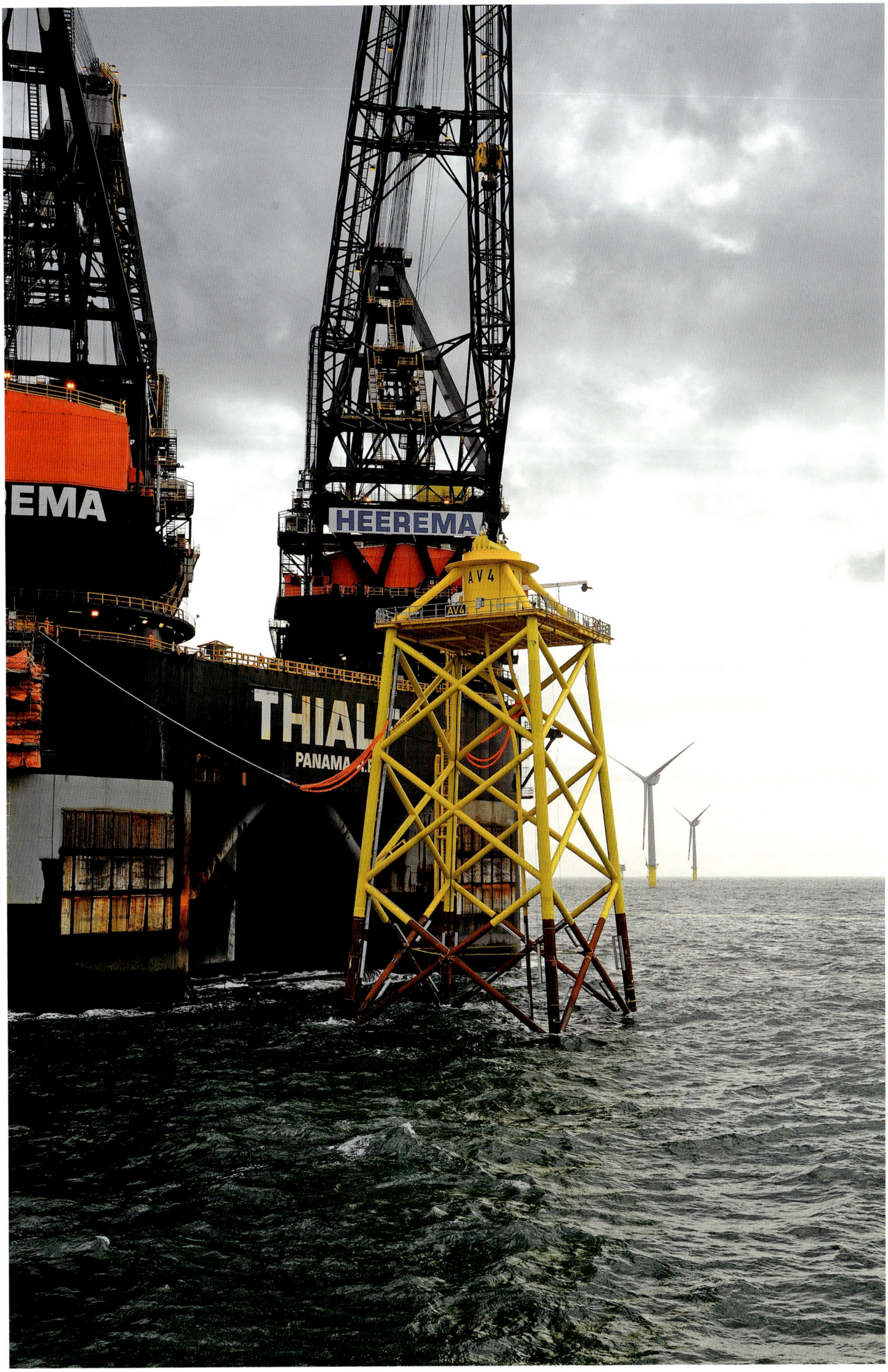
EMA
HEEREMA
AV4
THIAL
PANAMA

Ein Schlepper zieht die im norwegischen Verdal hergestellten Tripods nach Wilhelmshaven.
A tug tows the tripods manufactured in Verdal, Norway, to Wilhelmshaven.

Oben links: Robert Nuglisch und Patrick Bernhardt von AREVA Multibrid.
Top left: Robert Nuglisch and Patrick Bernhardt from AREVA Multibrid.

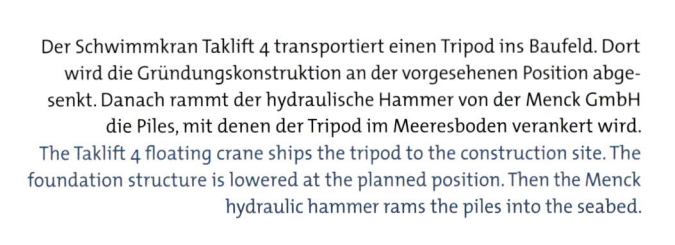

Der Schwimmkran Taklift 4 transportiert einen Tripod ins Baufeld. Dort wird die Gründungskonstruktion an der vorgesehenen Position abgesenkt. Danach rammt der hydraulische Hammer von der Menck GmbH die Piles, mit denen der Tripod im Meeresboden verankert wird.
The Taklift 4 floating crane ships the tripod to the construction site. The foundation structure is lowered at the planned position. Then the Menck hydraulic hammer rams the piles into the seabed.

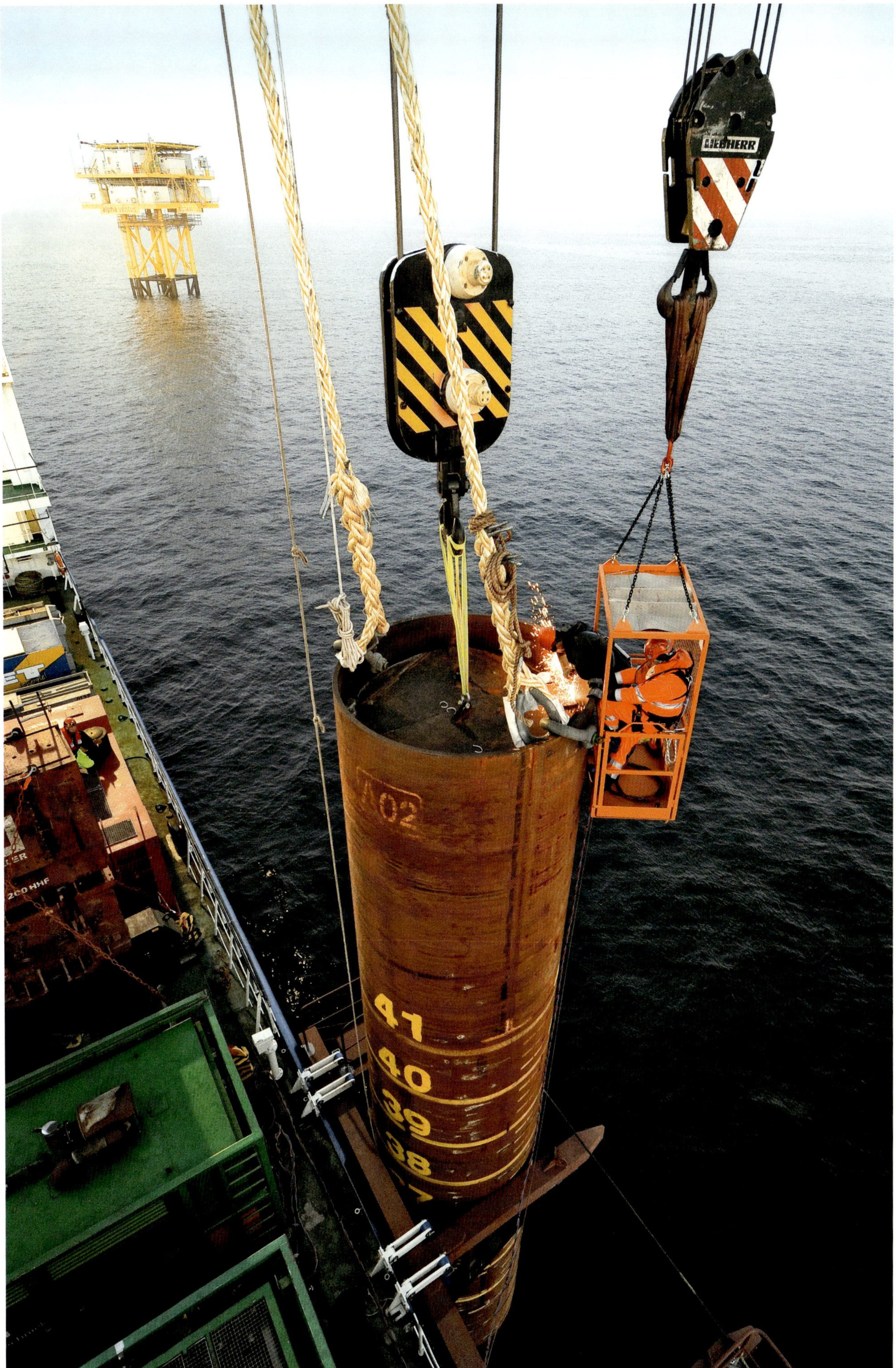
LIEBHERR
102
41
40
39
38

Großes Foto: Michael Klingele und Alexander Klemt stehen unter dem Tripod.
Kleine Fotos: Schwerstarbeit und High-tech beim Einfädeln der Piles in den Tripod.
Big photo: Michael Klingele and Alexander Klemt standing beneath the tripod.
Small photo: Hi-tech and hard work are required when introducing the piles into the tripod.

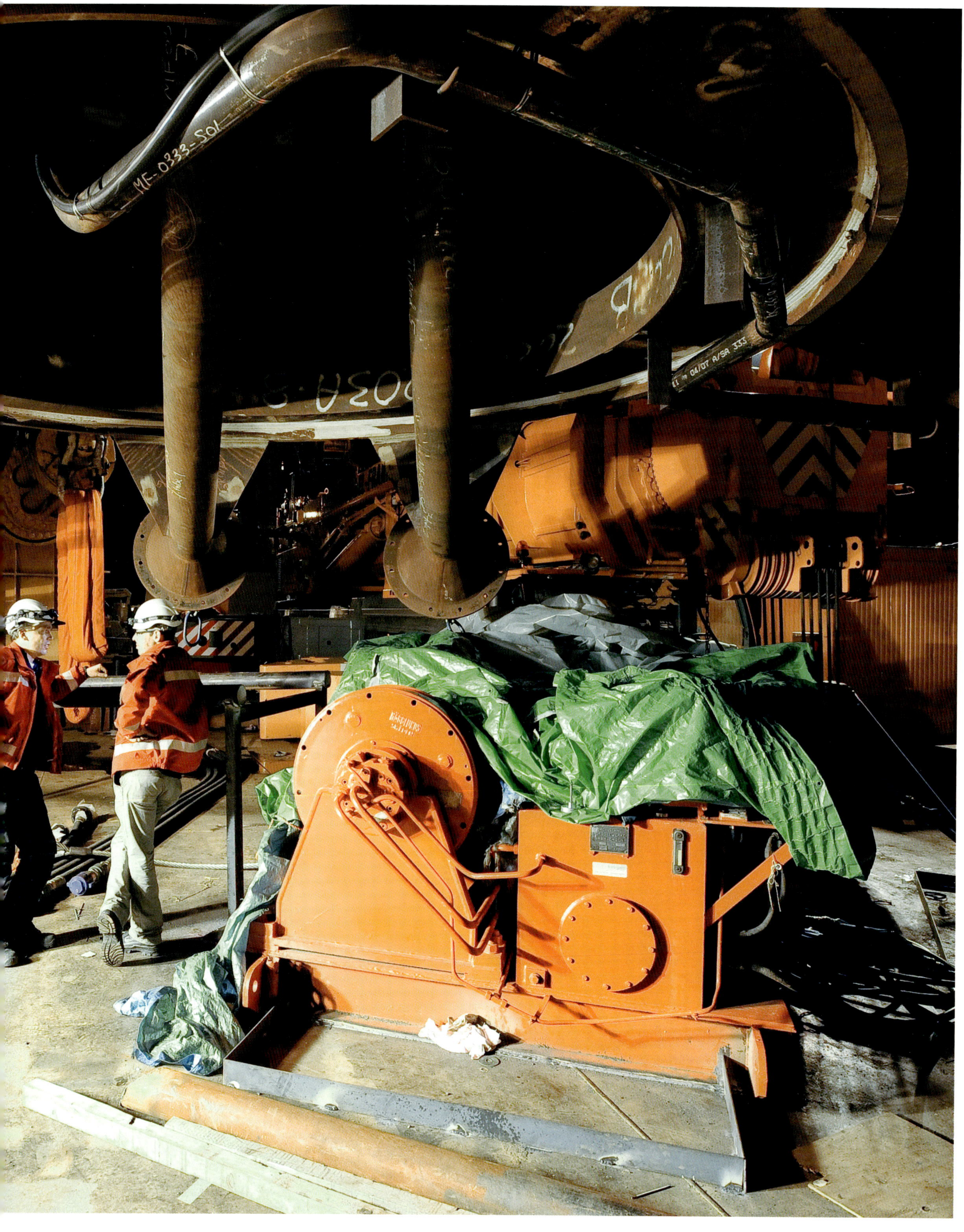

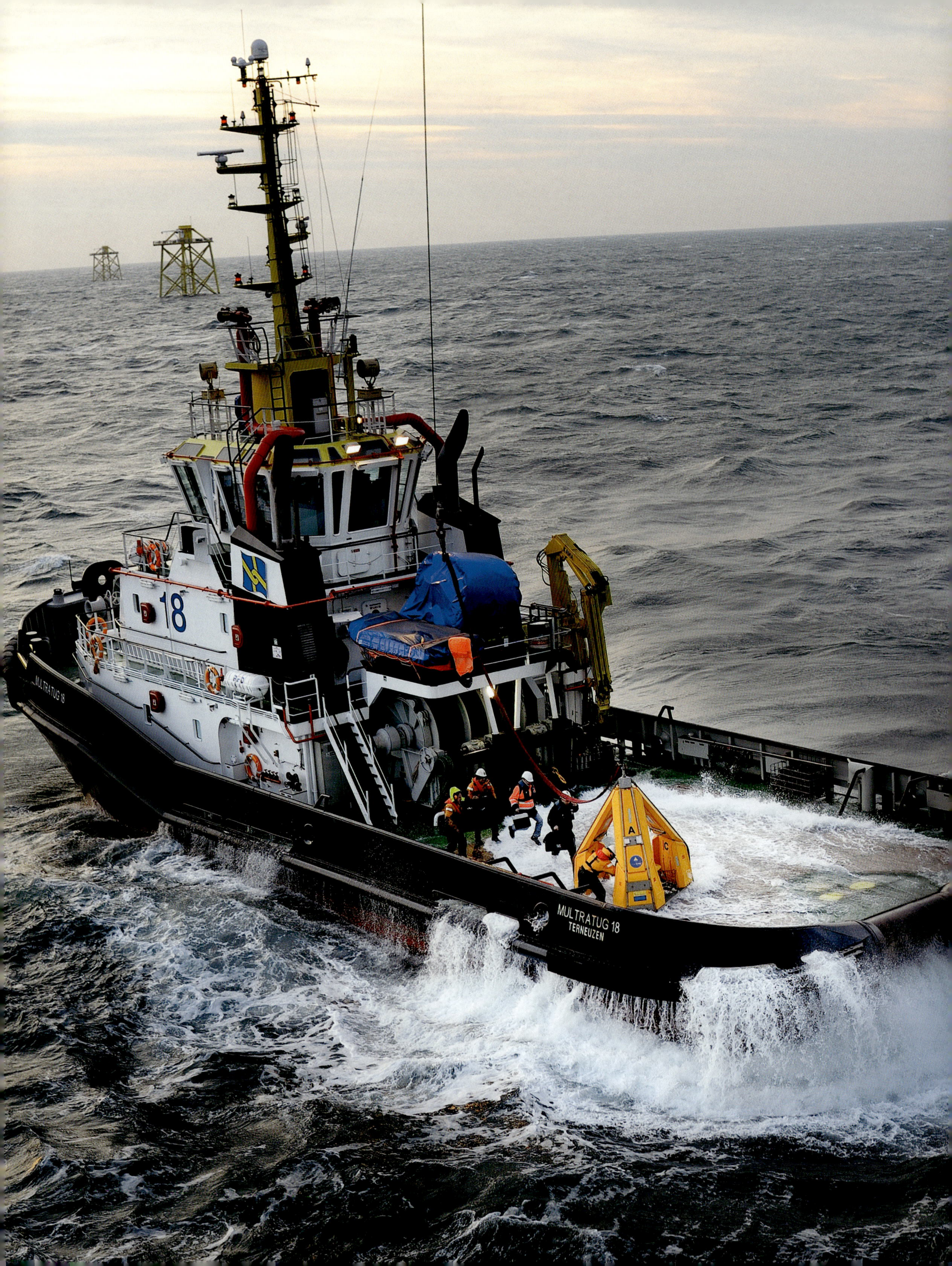

18
MULTRATUG 18
TERNEUZEN

Packendes Finale zwischen Herbststürmen
Exciting finish between autumn storms

Superintendent Dirk Rolland springt vom Schreibtisch auf, schaut aus dem kleinen Fenster, öffnet es. Frische Meeresluft strömt in den überheizten Arbeitsraum auf der Jack-up Barge Buzzard. Der Superintendant beobachtet aufmerksam, was der Schlepper Multratug auf der Backbordseite in der wogenden Nordsee unternimmt. „Ich habe noch keinen Satellitenempfang", murmelt Rolland, Mitarbeiter der belgischen Firma GeoSea. „Deshalb nähern wir uns der Goliath bisher noch ohne GPS." Sein Singsang verrät es sofort: Der Mann kommt aus dem Ruhrpott. Bedächtig schiebt er die Brille über die hohe Stirn. „Elektronik ist gut, Auge aber auch."

Derweil quillt dunkler Qualm aus dem Schornstein des Schleppers Multratug. Dessen Kapitän geht immer wieder volle Kraft voraus, um das Ankerseil gespannt zu halten. Den gleichen Job macht der Schlepper Sea Bravo auf der Steuerbordseite mit einem weiteren Seil, an dessen Ende sich der Anker befindet. Beide Schlepper ziehen, per Funk gut abgestimmt, die Buzzard in die richtige Richtung. Was so tänzelnd leicht aussieht, ist Kraft pur: 5.000 und 3.500 PS ziehen jeweils an den Seilen, um die Buzzard mit ihrer wertvollen Fracht, einer 5M des Windenergieanlagenherstellers REpower, bis auf etwa 100 Meter an den großen Hubinsel-Bruder Goliath, nomen est omen, zu bugsieren. Immerhin sind es 2.000 Tonnen, die an die Goliath bewegt werden müssen. Die Hubinsel hat sich schon am Vortag direkt neben dem Jacket-Fundament 50 Meter über den Meeresspiegel der Nordsee gehoben.

Das Positionieren der Buzzard braucht Geduld. Und Professionalität. Pascal Soeteway, ebenfalls Mitarbeiter der GeoSea und als Working Manager Rollands Pendant auf der Goliath, ist inzwischen per Abseilen und anschließendem Schlepper-Transfer auf die Buzzard gestiegen, um zusammen mit Rolland und seiner fünfköpfigen Crew eine Punktlandung hinzubekommen. Als der Abstand zur Goliath nur noch etwa 100 Meter beträgt, werden die Anker von den Schleppern ins Meer geworfen. Jetzt übernimmt die Buzzard allein die Steuerung. Zu Rollands Freude empfängt die Satellitenschüssel zwischenzeitlich wieder Signale aus dem Weltraum, sodass wieder alle Navigationsinstrumente für die endgültige Positionierung zur Verfügung stehen. Alles muss nach Plan laufen, damit die Windenergieanlagen aufgebaut werden können. Über Kameras, die auf die Winden gerichtet sind, hat die Crew die Ankerseile genau im Blick. Gerade die letzten Meter, ja Zentimeter dieser Annäherung der beiden Hubinseln sind für die verantwortlichen Männer auf der Brücke keine leichte Aufgabe. Der Kapitän der Buzzard, der Belgier Johan van den Berghe, und seine Männer haben nicht nur breite Kreuze, sondern beweisen auch viel Feingefühl. Konzentriert steht er vor einem Pult mit vier Joysticks, mit

Superintendent Dirk Rolland jumps up from behind his desk, looks out of the small window and then opens it. Fresh sea air floods into his overheated cabin-office on the jack-up barge 'Buzzard'. The Superintendent watches carefully to see what the tug 'Multratug' is doing on the port side in the billowing North Sea. "I still haven't got any satellite reception", mumbles Rolland, employee of the Belgian company GeoSea. "That's why we've had to approach the 'Goliath' up to now without any GPS." His singsong voice is an immediate giveaway: he's a Ruhr Valley man. He slowly slides his glasses over his high forehead. "Electronics are good – eyes too, though."

Meanwhile the funnel of the 'Multratug' is belching dark smoke as her skipper keeps her engines on full ahead to keep the anchoring cable tight. The tug 'Sea Bravo' is doing the same job on the starboard side. Coordinating perfectly by radio, both tugs are pulling the 'Buzzard' in the right direction. What looks like child's play is, in fact, pure force: 5,000 und 3,500 HP respectively are pulling on the cables to manoeuvre the 'Buzzard' with her valuable freight, a REpower 5M wind turbine, up to about 100 metres from her enormous sister jack-up barge 'Goliath' – whose name says it all. After all, there are 2,000 tonnes that need moving over to the Goliath. The jack-up platform had already lifted itself the day before 50 metres above the waves of the North Sea, directly next to the jacket foundation.

Getting the 'Buzzard' in the right position requires patience. And professionalism. Pascal Soeteway is also a GeoSea employee and, as Working Manager, is Rolland's counterpart on the 'Goliath'. Soeteway has abseiled down and with a subsequent tug transfer has boarded the 'Buzzard' in order to achieve a precision landing together with Rolland and his five-man crew. Now that the distance to the 'Goliath' is only about 100 metres the tugs drop anchor, leaving the 'Buzzard' in sole control of its destiny. To Rolland's delight his satellite dish is once again receiving signals from space, meaning he has all navigation instruments available for the final positioning. Everything has to go exactly to plan before the wind turbines can be set up. Using cameras pointed at the winches, the crew keeps a clear eye on the anchoring cables. Particularly the last few metres, even centimetres, of bringing the two jack-up barges together are no easy task for the men responsible on the bridge. Aboard the 'Buzzard', Belgian skipper Johan van den Berghe and his men not only have strong backs but also great sensitivity. Deep in concentration in front of his console, he gently nudges its four joysticks to pull, stop and control the total of four anchoring cables to the centimetre.

It's been pitch-black for a while now as the 'Buzzard', on this last evening of October 2009, lowers her long legs in exactly the right

denen er die insgesamt vier Ankerseile zentimetergenau zieht, stoppt und steuert.

Es ist längst stockdunkel, als die Buzzard an diesem 31. Oktober 2009 mit ihren langen Stelzen genau an der richtigen Stelle auf dem Meeresboden im Testfeld alpha ventus aufsetzt. Dann beginnt sich die Hubinsel langsam nach oben zu schieben. Um zehn Uhr abends wird von der 20 Meter höher gelegenen Goliath die Gangway ausgefahren. Der Wind hat derweil kräftig zugenommen. Es nieselt. Mondgrau reflektiert die kabbelige Nordsee im Licht der Scheinwerfer. Pascal Soeteway ist froh, dass die Operation gut geklappt hat. In roter Regenjacke und mit dem Walkie-Talky in der Hand steht er für einige Momente vollkommen allein auf dem Deck. Kurz blickt er in die Höhe, in den nachtdunklen Himmel. Nach einer Weile gönnt er sich schließlich ein kleines Lächeln, sein jungenhaftes Gesicht entspannt sich. „In der letzten Woche lief alles super. Wir haben Glück gehabt, die Logistik stimmte, die Crew war toll und dann spielte auch noch das Wetter mit, einfach Klasse", erzählt der Anfang Dreißiger etwas später in der kleinen, wenig gemütlichen Kantine der Buzzard von den Erfolgserlebnissen in der vorangegangenen Woche. Gelang es doch in Rekordzeit, die vierte REpower-Anlage im Testfeld aufzustellen. Vom Laden bis zur Rückkehr der entladenen Buzzard dauerte es nur vier Tage! Eine große Leistung, die allerdings ihren Tribut fordert. Unrasiert und mit müden Augen sagt Pascal Soeteway nach dem letzten Schluck Kaffee einfach nur noch „Gute Nacht" und klettert danach langsam die Gangway zur Goliath hinauf.

Für den einen ist die Arbeit getan, für die anderen fängt sie an. Kurz nach zehn Uhr abends kommen das Monteur-Team von REpower und die Kletterspezialisten der Berliner Firma Seilpartner von der Goliath hinunter aufs Deck der Buzzard. Obwohl der Wind merklich aufgefrischt hat, will das Team sofort mit dem Aufbau des ersten Turmsegments beginnen. "Wir haben zehn Meter pro Sekunde, das kriegen wir hin", sagt einer der Mitarbeiter von Seilpartner in voller Klettermontur. Wenn es geht, wird rund um die Uhr gearbeitet – solange das Wetter mitmacht. Tatsächlich wird das erste Turmsegment um zwei Uhr morgens vom Kranführer auf der Goliath angehoben, auf das Jacket gesetzt und vom Installationsteam festgeschraubt. Gegen fünf Uhr morgens ist der erste Schritt zur Errichtung der fünften Anlage erledigt.

Eine Nacht zuvor, exakt um null Uhr legt die Buzzard im Hafen von Eemshaven ab. Beladen mit der der fünften 5M für das Testfeld alpha ventus geht es viel früher los als ursprünglich geplant. Gegen Mittag hieß es noch, man würde erst am frühen Morgen loslegen, aber entgegen den Wettervorhersagen konnte der Rotorstern doch innerhalb eines kleinen, aber ausreichenden Zeitfensters noch vor Mitternacht an Bord gehievt werden. Also Leinen los und, gezogen vom Schlepper Multratug, schwimmt die Buzzard mit ihrer sorgfältig festgezurrten Fracht, zwei Turmsegmenten, dem Maschinenhaus und dem Rotorstern, dessen Flügel zu drei Seiten über die Reling hinausragen, zuerst aus dem Hafen, dann auf die Ems und schließlich auf die offene Nordsee.

Apropos „Zeitfenster": für die deutsche Offshore-Windenergie-Industrie sicherlich das Wort des Jahres. Kein anderer Terminus fiel im Zusammenhang mit dem Aufbau des 60 Megawatt großen Offshore-Windparks alpha ventus wahrscheinlich häufiger. Wind und Wellen sind die Parameter, die das viel zitierte Zeitfenster für die gesamte Logistik und die Errichtung definieren. „Sei die maritime Logistik noch so gut, seien die offshore-tauglichen Schiffe und Hubinseln noch so

place onto the sea floor of the alpha ventus test field. Then the jack-up platform starts slowly pushing itself up. At ten o'clock in the evening the gangway is slid out from the 'Goliath', which is 20 metres higher. In the meantime the wind has picked up strength and an all-pervasive drizzle sets in, with the lurching North Sea moon-grey in the spotlights. Pascal Soeteway is pleased: the operation went very well. In a red cagoule, walkie-talkie in hand he stands there for a few moments on the deck completely alone. He briefly looks up into the darkness of the night. After a while he finally allows himself a little smile, his youthful face relaxes. "In the past few weeks everything has gone superbly. We've been lucky, they got the logistics right, the crew were fantastic and the weather even played along – simply great", beams the thirty-something a bit later in the small, not-so-cosy canteen of the 'Buzzard', recounting the successes of the past week. After all, it has now been possible to set up the fourth REpower turbine in the test field in record time: just four days from loading to the return of the empty 'Buzzard'! An outstanding performance – which, however, has taken its toll. Unshaven and with tired eyes Pascal Soeteway says a brief "Good night" and takes his last swig of coffee before slowly climbing up the gangway to the 'Goliath'.

For some work has been completed, for others it is just about to start. Shortly after ten in the evening the assembly team arrives from REpower and the climbing specialists from Berlin-based firm Seilpartner come down onto the deck of the 'Buzzard' from the 'Goliath'. Although the wind has picked up noticeably, the team intends to start fitting the first tower section immediately. "It's ten metres a second, we'll manage", says one of the Seilpartner employees in his full climbing gear. Wherever possible, work is carried out around the clock – weather permitting. And the first tower segment really is lifted at two o'clock in the morning by the crane operator on the 'Goliath', lowered into its foundation jacket and bolted down tightly by the installation team. At about five in the morning the first step in the assembly of the fifth turbine has been completed.

One night earlier, at exactly midnight, the 'Buzzard' had put to sea from the Dutch port of Eemshaven. Loaded with the fifth 5M turbine destined for the alpha ventus test field, it started off a lot earlier than had been originally planned. At about midday it seemed that it would not be possible to set off until early morning, but contrary to the weather forecasts the rotor hub was able to be lifted on board in a small, but sufficient time-window before midnight. The 'Buzzard' then cast off. Pulled by the 'Multratug' it floated first out of the port, then onto the River Ems estuary and finally onto the open North Sea. Its cargo was carefully secured: two tower sections, the nacelle and the rotor hub, with the rotor blades protruding on three sides over the railings.

On the subject of 'time windows', this is certainly the term of the year for the German offshore wind-power industry. There have probably been no other words used more frequently in the context of the construction of the 60-megawatt offshore wind farm alpha ventus. Wind and waves are the parameters that define the much-quoted time window for the complete logistics and construction. "As good as maritime logistics may be, and as large as the offshore ships and jack-up barges are, we humans still can't turn off the weather", says Dirk Rolland looking into his small booklet of tide tables for this area of the North Sea; this contains all the high and low tides all so critical to every offshore operation. "And it's good that we can't change the weather and tides", he adds, philosophically.

groß, der Mensch kann das Wetter trotzdem nicht abschalten", sagt Dirk Rolland und schaut dabei ins kleine Heft „Getijtafels voor Delfzijl en Eemshaven 2009". Es ist der für diesen Bereich der Nordsee relevante Tidekalender, der die für alle Offshore-Operationen so eminent wichtigen Hoch- und Niedrigwasserzeiten anzeigt. „Und dass wir das Wetter und die Gezeiten nicht beeinflussen können, ist auch gut so", fügt er in beinahe philosophischer Stimmung hinzu.

Am frühen Sonntagabend peitscht der Wind übers Deck, pfeift um die Ecken der Aufbauten. Regen liegt fast waagerecht in der Luft. Den ganzen Tag über war es grau-neblig und die anderen, bereits im Testfeld errichteten Anlagen sind nur schemenhaft zu erkennen. Jeder Schritt an Bord ist ein kleiner Kampf gegen den Wind. Gekrümmt und in Regenzeug gehen die Mitglieder der Crew nur den notwendigsten Arbeiten nach. Der erste Novembersturm ist da. Wahrlich ungemütlich, wenngleich es noch nicht schneidend kalt ist, da die Nordsee ihre im Sommer aufgetankte Wärme abgibt. Zu dieser Jahreszeit ist es auf dem Meer für gewöhnlich wärmer als an Land. Temperatur hin oder her: Der Wind bläst kräftig über die beiden dicht aneinanderliegenden Jack-Up Barges hinweg. „Wir haben jetzt Windstärke acht. Ich habe vorhin mit einem Anemometer nachgemessen", sagt Diplom-Bauingenieur Thomas Schramm. Er ist Mitarbeiter der Ingenieurfirma IMS aus Hamburg, die vom Bauherrn DOTI den Auftrag bekommen

Startklar für den Ausflug aufs Meer. Festes Schuhzeug, warme Kleidung, Schutzanzüge und Helm sind ein unbedingtes Muss – es ist eben kein harmloser Ausflug in Grüne.
Getting ready to go to sea. Firm footwear, warm clothing, protective outerwear and helmets are essential. It is not a pleasure boat trip.

Herbst 2009: Eemshaven im Morgengrauen.
Eemshaven at daybreak in autumn 2009.

hat, alle Arbeiten an Bord der Goliath zu koordinieren. Um dies zu gewährleisten, gibt es täglich eine Arbeitsbesprechung, bei der Schramm, der Bauleiter von REpower, die Kapitäne der Barges und der Work Manager Pascal Soetewey von GeoSea das gemeinsame Vorgehen abstimmen. Obwohl der Aufbau von Windenergieanlagen für den 48-jährigen Schramm eine neue Unternehmung ist, ist er doch ein Experte in Sachen Offshore. In der Vergangenheit hat er schon diverse Sperrwerke geplant und gebaut. Auch bei der Bergung der Starthilfe-Raketen der Ariane vor der Küste Französisch-Guayanas hat er mitgewirkt.

Was Windstärke acht auf offener See bedeutet, beschreibt die Beaufort-Skala ganz genau: „Mäßig hohe Wellenberge mit Kämmen beträchtlicher Länge. Gischt beginnt von Kämmen abzuwehen. Ausgeprägte Schaumstreifen in Windrichtung." Und gewiss kein Wetter, um eine Fünf-Megawatt-Anlage aufzubauen. So ruhen die Arbeiten und in den kleinen Kabinen der Monteure laufen die Heizradiatoren auf Hochtouren.

Schramm sitzt in einem von grellem Neonlicht beleuchteten Raum auf der mehrstöckigen Brücke der Goliath. Zwei der Wände sind mit zahlreichen Konstruktionszeichnungen des Krans, der Anlage und der Jack-up-Barge regelrecht tapeziert. Vom Fenster seines Arbeitsplatzes aus hat er einen Rundumblick über das ganze Geschehen auf dem

The first November storm has come. Early on Sunday evening the wind is beating over the deck, whistling around the corners of the superstructure and the rain is almost horizontal. The whole day long it has been grey and foggy, with only the dim outlines of the other turbines already erected in the test field visible. Every step on board is a small battle against the wind. Bent over and in their rain gear the crew members are only doing the work that absolutely has to be done. Truly unpleasant, even if it is not yet that bitingly cold, as the North Sea is still giving off the heat that it has gathered over the summer. During this season it's usually warmer at sea than on land. But irrespective of the temperature, the wind is blowing powerfully through and over the two jack-up barges sitting close to each other. "Wind-force Eight. I measured it just now with an anemometer" says Civil Engineer Thomas Schramm. He works for the Hamburg-based engineering company IMS that has been commissioned by DOTI to coordinate all the work on board the 'Goliath'. To make sure that it is done properly there is a works meeting every day, at which Schramm, the Superintendent Engineer from REpower, the captains of the barges and Works Manager Pascal Soeteway from GeoSea all coordinate their operations. Although the construction of wind turbines is new to 48-year-old Schramm he is, after all, the expert in all things offshore. In the past he has planned and built various flood barriers. He also

Mitarbeiter von REpower fixieren den Rotorstern der 5M auf der Buzzard vor der Abfahrt aufs Meer. Repower staff attach the 5M's rotor star on the Buzzard before going to sea.

Baufeld. Zur Rechten die Buzzard, zur Linken das 20 Meter aus dem Meer hinausragende Jacket mit dem ersten, am Vortag montierten Turmsegment. Direkt vor seiner Nase steht – mittig auf dem Deck der Goliath – der mächtige Liebherr-Kran LR 1800 in Diensten der belgischen Firma Sarens. „Ich habe immer Respekt vor Offshore-Arbeiten", betont Schramm hinter seinem Computer sitzend. „Dabei ist es egal, ob eine Tonne oder ganz viele am Haken sind. Man kann hier draußen immer nur mit dem Wetter arbeiten."

Immer wieder das Wetter. Auch Schramm nimmt nicht nur einmal das Wort Zeitfenster in den Mund. Er zeigt auf die fünftägige Wettervorhersage des englischen Wetterdienstes MET Office, die er sich mehr als einmal ausdrucken lässt: Es sind Kolonnen von Zahlen, die in vielen Zeilen und Spalten aufgefächert sind. Mittendrin ein kleiner Strich, den Schramm mit einem Marker gezogen hat. Der Strich markiert in der Zeile Windstärke alle Werte ab Mittwochabend. Laut Vorhersage wird dann der Wind abschwächen und bis Freitag unter zehn Metern pro Sekunde bleiben. „Das ist unser Zeitfenster. Wie es jetzt ausschaut, werden wir dann das zweite Turmsegment, das Maschinenhaus und den Rotor in einem Rutsch aufbauen können", erklärt Schramm zuversichtlich. Um den Rotor ziehen zu können, darf der Wind zwölf Stunden nacheinander nur mit maximal acht Metern pro Sekunde wehen.

worked on the salvage of the Ariane launch rockets off the coast of French Guyana

What Force Eight means on the open seas is described by the Beaufort Scale very precisely: "Moderately high waves with breaking crests forming spindrift. Well-marked streaks of foam are blown along wind direction. Considerable airborne spray." Certainly no weather for assembling a 5-megawatt turbine. So they stop work and the radiators in the mechanical fitters' cabins are turned on full.

Schramm is sitting in a cabin on the multi-storey bridge of the 'Goliath', lit with bright neon light. Two of the walls have been completely wallpapered with numerous construction plans of cranes, the turbine and the jack-up barge. From his desk here he can see everything that is happening on the construction field. To the right the 'Buzzard', to the left the jacket protruding 20 metres out of the sea with the first tower segment that was fitted to it the day before. Right in front of his nose – in the middle of the deck of the 'Goliath' – there is the powerful Liebherr crane LR 1800 run by Belgian company Sarens. "I have always held offshore work in high esteem", emphasizes Schramm from behind his computer. "It doesn't matter whether you have a tonne or several on the hook. You can only work out here with the weather." Always the weather. Even Schramm mentions the words "time window" more than once. He points to the five-day weather forecast from

Ein Schlepper zieht die Hubinsel Buzzard ins Baufeld.
A tug tows the Buzzard jack-up barge to the installation site.

Sollte sich die Vorhersage der Meteorologen bewahrheiten, wird von Sonntag bis Mittwoch, drei Tage lang, Stillstand auf der Baustelle herrschen. Keine leichte Übung. Denn Warten ist eine echte Herausforderung für die Crews der beiden Hubinseln und auch für das Monteurteam von REpower. Weniger physisch, dafür umso mehr psychisch. „Es gibt hier keine Ablenkung, für diese Situation muss man geschaffen sein", weiß Schramm. Der Kontakt mit der Außenwelt, mit Freunden und Familien, ist dürftig, weil es draußen auf dem Meer keinen Mobilfunk gibt, und auch die Internetverbindung funktioniert nicht immer und wenn, dann nur superlangsam. Einige überbrücken die Langeweile mit endlosem Filmegucken, andere versinken in Lektüre, wiederum andere daddeln am Computer. In solchen Warteschleifen ist die Versorgung das A und O für die Stimmung. Während der Rheinländer Guido auf der Goliath Kulinarisches zaubert, gibt auch der peruanische Koch Lara Zarate auf der Buzzard sein Bestes und serviert zum sonntäglichen Abendessen Saté-Spieße mit süßer Erdnusssoße. In der Warteschleife werden sicherlich auch mehr Zigaretten als gewöhnlich geraucht. Die ausgedrückten Kippen in den Ascheimern vor den Türen zeugen davon.

Für Crew-Mitglied Donald van Torre wird es in dieser Nachtwache auf der Brücke der Buzzard wohl nur wenig Spannendes zu beobachten geben. Aber das ist der erfahrene belgische Seemann gewohnt,

the British MET Office, which he prints out more than once: there are loads of numbers, split into numerous lines and columns. In the middle a small line that Schramm has drawn with a marker pen. He has highlighted all the wind strength values from Wednesday evening onwards. According to the forecast the wind will drop then and remain under 10 metres per second until Friday. "That's our window in time. As it looks at the moment we will be able to install the second section of the tower and the rotor in one go", explains Schramm confidently. In order to lift the rotor the wind should only have a speed of maximum eight metres per second in 12 consecutive hours.

Should the meteorologists' predictions turn out to be true there will be 3 days of standstill on the construction site from Sunday until Wednesday. Not an easy exercise. Because waiting represents a real challenge for the crews of the two jack-up barges and the team of mechanical fitters from REpower. Not so much in a physical sense, but all the more in a psychological one. "There's nothing to do instead, you have to be made for such a situation", is what Schramm knows. There is hardly any contact to the outside world, with friends and family, as there is no mobile phone communication out there at sea, and the Internet does not always work – and if it does it is extremely slow. Some get through the boredom by continually watching films, others get down to their reading, others in turn play on the computer. During such a waiting

Mechaniker Andy Schröder verschnauft nach erfolgreicher Montage um fünf Uhr morgens in der Kantine der Hubinsel Goliath. Fitter Andy Schröder has a break in the Goliath jack-up barge canteen after successful assembly at 5 o'clock in the morning.

denn er hat schon unzählige Nächte auf dem Meer verbracht. Über 30 Jahre war er Fischer und fuhr mit einem Trawler auf die Nordsee und bis in den Atlantik hinaus, um Kabeljau, Seeteufel, Seewolf, Seezunge, Rotbarsch und Seelachs zu fangen. Doch nahmen die Fischbestände in den letzten Jahren dramatisch ab. Als die Löhne immer mickriger wurden, hängte er schließlich seinen Job an den Nagel und heuerte vor Kurzem bei der Geo Sea BV an. „Die Fangquoten sind nicht ohne Grund verringert worden", sagt van Torre auf der Brücke seufzend. Für den 54-Jährigen ist der Einsatz im Baufeld von alpha ventus der erste hautnahe Kontakt zur Offshore-Windenergie-Industrie. „Früher habe ich solche Anlagen nur von Weitem gesehen, hatte keine Idee davon, wie das Ganze überhaupt funktioniert", räumt er ein. „Jetzt weiß ich aber, was das eigentlich bedeutet, auf dem Meer solche Anlagen aufzustellen." Ob die Offshore-Windparks in Zukunft fangfreie Rückzugsgebiete für Fischschwärme sein könnten, hält van Torre für möglich, „doch ist es noch viel zu früh, darüber wirklich etwas Hieb- und Stichfestes sagen zu können".

In der Nacht zum Montag flaut der Wind entgegen aller Vorhersagen doch ab. Alle Überlegungen vom Vortag sind hinfällig. Schon am frühen Morgen nähert sich der Schlepper Multratug der Goliath. An Bord befinden sich zwölf ausgeruhte Monteure von REpower und der Firma SSC Montage, die ihre Kollegen, die schon 14 Tage im Dauer-

period the supplies are the be-all-and-end-all for the atmosphere. While Guido, who comes from the Rhineland, conjures up culinary delights on the 'Goliath', the Peruvian chef on the 'Buzzard', Lara Zarate, also does his best and for the Sunday evening meal serves sate kebabs with sweet peanut sauce. During the waiting period you can rest assured that there will be more cigarettes smoked than normal, as demonstrated by the piles of butts in the ashcans in front of the doors.

There won't be much exciting to see for crewmember Donald van Torre during his night watch on the bridge of the 'Buzzard'. But that's what the experienced Belgian seaman is used to, as he's spent countless nights at sea. He spent 30 years as a fisherman and sailed the North Sea on a trawler, right out into the Atlantic to catch cod, monkfish, sea bass, sole, redfish and pollack. However, fish stocks have fallen dramatically in the past few years. As the wages became more and more miserly he finally gave up his job and was recently hired by Geo Sea BV. "The fishing quotas have been reduced for a reason", says van Torre on the bridge with a small sigh. The deployment in the construction field of alpha ventus is the first time the 54-year-old has had close contact with the offshore wind power industry. "I used to see turbines like this from a distance, I knew nothing about them, nothing about how it all worked at all", he admits. "However, now I know what it means to install these turbines at sea." Van Torres sees the possibility

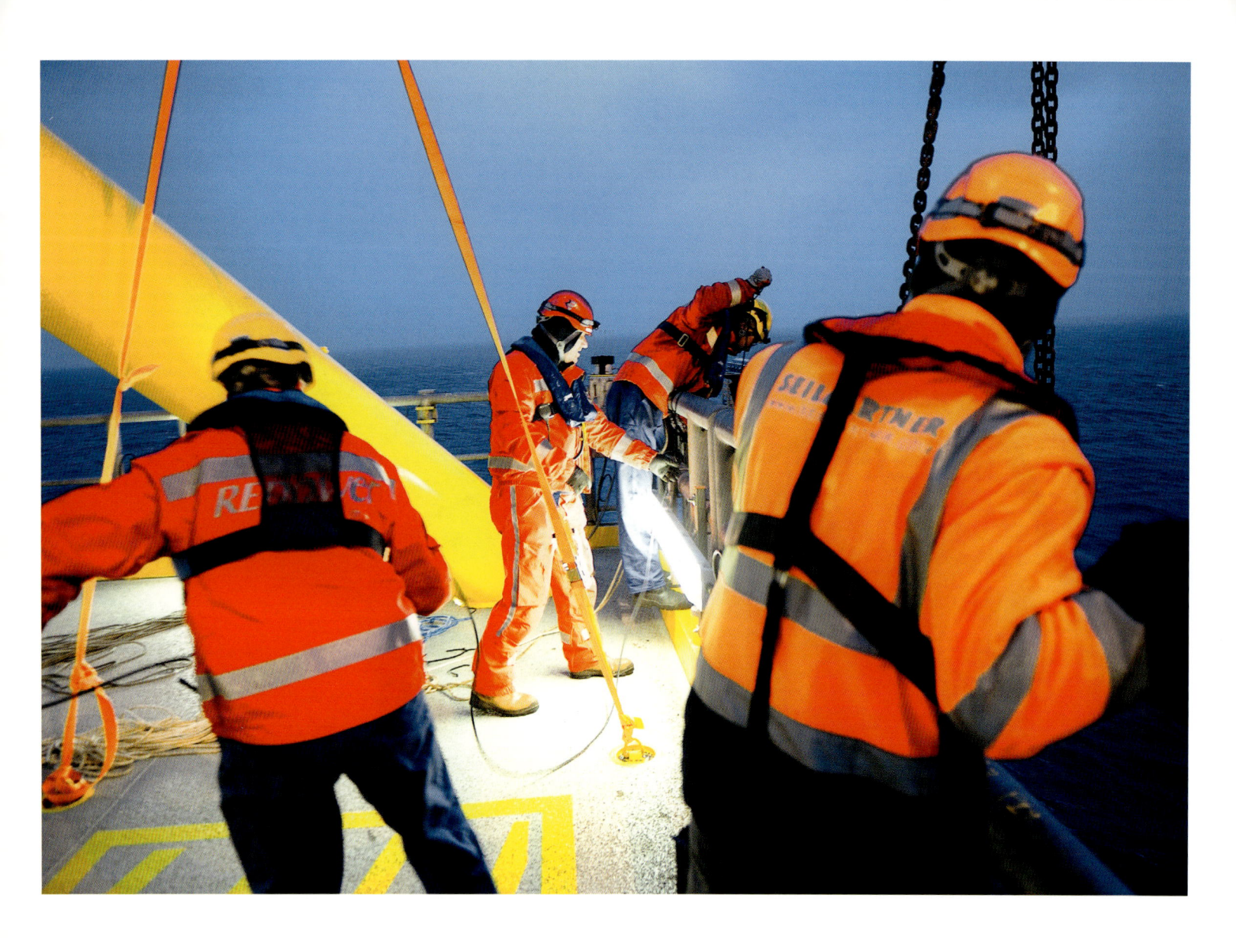

Kurz vor Beginn der Errichtung der AV 3 werden die Schläuche, mit denen das Jacket-Fundament vergossen wurde, demontiert.
Shortly prior to starting the AV 3 installation, the hoses with which the jacket foundation was moulded, are dismantled.

of the offshore wind farms becoming fishing-free havens for schools of fish to retreat to, "however, it is still too early to be able to say anything definite about that yet."

Contrary to all predictions the wind does abate in the night before Monday – which changes all plans from the day before. Early in the morning the 'Multratug' approaches the 'Goliath'. On board there are twelve well-slept mechanical fitters from REpower and the company SSC Montage to take over from their colleagues who have already been working for 14 days. Amongst the newcomers there is Finn Kleinwort from REpower, who is to take over the job of Superintendent Engineer from Jens Fricke for the next two weeks. The atmosphere is good, as the weather conditions mean that all of a sudden a promising time window has opened up. All those responsible on the bridge of the 'Goliath' agree and decide to start assembling the second section of the tower and nacelle as early as midday.

The sun's rays break through the clouds, as the Sarens crane operator lifts the second tower section, manoeuvring it between bridge and crane safely over the deck of the 'Goliath' and places it onto the first section as if it were routine work. Everything seems to be going smoothly; some are even secretly expecting the 'Buzzard' to be able to set off for Eemshaven in thirty-six hours to pick up the last 5M from land and bring it into the construction field.

einsatz sind, ablösen sollen. Unter den Neuankömmlingen ist auch Finn Kleinwort von REpower, der für die nächsten zwei Wochen die Aufgaben des Bauleiters von Jens Fricke übernimmt. Die Stimmung ist gut, weil sich durch die Wetterlage ein vielversprechendes Zeitfenster abzeichnet. Alle Verantwortlichen auf der Goliath-Brücke sind sich einig und beschließen, bereits gegen Mittag mit dem Aufbau des zweiten Turmsegments und des Maschinenhauses zu beginnen.

Die Sonne blinzelt zwischen den Wolken hindurch, als der Kranführer von Sarens das zweite Turmsegment hochhebt, zwischen Brücke und Kran sicher über das Deck der Goliath bugsiert und routiniert auf das erste Segment setzt. Alles läuft wie am Schnürchen, manche rechnen schon im Stillen darauf, dass in anderthalb Tagen die Buzzard Richtung Eemshaven ablegen kann, um die letzte 5M ins Baufeld zu holen.

Doch dann kommt plötzlich alles anders. Auf Zuruf eines Monteurs bemerkt der Kranführer, dass eines seiner stählernen Zugseile beschädigt ist. Ein paar Litzen kräuseln sich auf der Oberseite. Sofort wird der Work Manager Pascal Soeteway informiert, der die schlechte Nachricht augenblicklich an Schramm, Fricke, Kleinwort und den Kapitän der Barge weitergibt. Eine äußerst schwierige Situation. Um keinerlei Risiken einzugehen, wird die Montagearbeit sofort eingestellt. Der Working Manager blickt sorgenvoll in die Runde. Aleksandrs Karakulovs, der im Auftrag des Germanischen Lloyds als Marine Warranty Surveyor Verladung, Transport und Errichtung der REpower 5M minutiös beobachtet, schaut sich den Schaden aus der Nähe an, fotografiert die beschädigte Stelle. Allen Beteiligten ist klar: Jede Entscheidung über den Fortgang der Arbeiten muss vor allem die Sicherheit aller an Bord Arbeitenden gewährleisten. Wenn so ein Seil bei einer Hubarbeit reißen würde, hätte das unkalkulierbare, wahrscheinlich katastrophale Folgen.

Zuerst wird die belgische Zentrale der Kranfirma Sarens über das Malheur unterrichtet. Sie soll entscheiden, ob angesichts der angerissenen Litzen eine Weiterarbeit mit dem viel schwereren Maschinenhaus zu verantworten ist. „Der Schaden sieht von außen betrachtet nicht sonderlich schwerwiegend aus, doch jedes Material hat ein langes Gedächtnis." Schramm nimmt den Vorfall sehr ernst. Zugleich wird die Zentrale von DOTI in Oldenburg benachrichtigt. Nach einigem Hin und Her wird schließlich entschieden: Das Turmsegment wird sicherheitshalber wieder auf die Buzzard zurückgehoben. Für Finn Kleinwort steht zu diesem Zeitpunkt fest, dass ohne ein repariertes Kranseil mit seiner Mannschaft „nichts mehr geht". Diese Auffassung teilen nach einigen Mails und Telefonaten über Satellit auch alle anderen. Auch für den badischen Kranführer Falko Söhner gibt es keine zwei Meinungen. „Was glauben Sie, wenn das Maschinenhaus dranhängt und so ein Seil reißt, dann haut es das Deck weg und wir saufen hier alle zusammen ab", erklärt er und schüttelt seinen Kopf. Was denn mit dem Seil passiert sei? „Von der Logik her passt ein Elefant auch nicht durch ein Schlüsselloch – trotzdem passiert es …"

Die Köpfe rauchen. Auf den Fluren der Brücke diskutieren die Verantwortlichen aufgekratzt alle möglichen Szenarien. Die Losung „Stopp. Take five" hängt mahnend auf dem Flur vor der Tür von Schramms Büro: Laufende Arbeiten beenden, dann nüchtern und überlegt den nächsten Arbeitsschritt angehen. Mehr als 50 Mann, ein riesiger Kran, eine Multimegawatt-Anlage und zwei gewaltige Barges stehen in der Nordsee einsatzbereit. Und nun werfen ein paar millimeterdicke Litzen alle Hoffnungen auf ein zügiges Finale des Aufbaus der letzten beiden Anlagen im Testfeld alpha ventus über den Haufen. Doch hilft Klagen wenig. Die Sicherheit der Mannschaft steht an oberster Stelle

Then suddenly everything takes an unexpected turn. One of the mechanical fitters calls out and the crane operator notices that one of his steel hauling cables is damaged: there are a few strands twisting out on the upper edge. Works Manager Pascal Soeteway is informed immediately, who then passes on the bad news straight away to Schramm, Fricke, Kleinwort and the barge skipper. It's an extremely difficult situation. So as to avoid any risk whatsoever, the assembly work is immediately halted. Soeteway looks worriedly at the others. Aleksandrs Karakulovs, who has been commissioned by Germanischer Lloyd as Marine Warranty Surveyor, has been meticulously monitoring the loading, transport and set-up of the REpower 5M; he moves closer to inspect and take photographs of the damage. It is clear to all involved that any decision made on whether to continue work must ensure, in particular, the safety of all on board. Should such a cable break during lifting work it would have unpredictable and probably catastrophic consequences. First the Belgian head office of the crane company Sarens is informed of the problem. With regard to the torn cable strands they are to decide whether they can accept responsibility for continuing work with the heavy nacelle. Schramm is taking this incident very seriously: "From the outside, the damage doesn't look particularly bad. However, all materials have a long memory." At the same time the head office of DOTI in Oldenburg is informed. After animated discussion a decision is finally taken: to keep things safe the tower section is to be lifted back onto the 'Buzzard'. At this point in time Finn Kleinwort knows that there is "nothing more to do" for his team until the crane cable is repaired. Following e-mails and telephone calls via satellite, everyone else agrees. The decision has the full support of the crane operator from Baden, Falko Söhner. "What do you think would happen if we winched up the nacelle and then that cable broke? It would crash right through the deck and we'd all drown together", he explains. So what exactly has happened to the cable, then? Söhner gently shakes his head: "From a purely logical point of view you can't get an elephant through a keyhole either … but somehow this sort of thing seems to happen anyway."

There is a flurry of activity. Those responsible are discussing all possible scenarios, somewhat annoyed, in the corridors of the bridge. The solution: "Stop. Take five." is hanging as a clear warning in the corridor in front of Schramms' office door: suspend current work, and then coolly and thoughtfully tackle the next step. More than fifty men, one whopping crane, a multi-megawatt turbine and two huge barges are standing there in the North Sea ready to do their job. And now a few millimetre-thick strands of cable have dashed any hopes of a quick end to the construction of the last two turbines in the alpha ventus test field. But moaning won't help. The safety of the crew takes precedence – no matter what it costs. The priority is finding a well-considered, constructive way out of a tricky situation.

On the evening of this cursed Monday all decision-makers get together. They discuss in great detail the two options that are available: either the cable is shortened on site or the 'Goliath' has to go back to Eemshaven to get the repairs to the crane carried out there. The former would be a first and therefore, in insurance terms, questionable; however, it would be less time-consuming and thus probably also less expensive. It is late that evening when a final decision is reached: the 'Goliath' has to go back to port. They were so close to the finishing line – and now all of a sudden the goal vanishes into the distance. Everyone's patience is tested again on Tuesday, as a storm is brewing from the west. Waves are building to reach up to three meters in height. Jacking up the barge

– koste es, was es wolle. Es geht jetzt darum, überlegt und konstruktiv nach Auswegen aus der verfahrenen Situation zu suchen.

Am Abend des vermaledeiten Montags setzen sich alle Entscheidungsträger zusammen. Sie diskutieren im Detail über die zwei Optionen, die im Raum stehen: Entweder wird das Seil vor Ort gekürzt oder die Goliath muss nach Eemshaven zurück, um dort die Reparatur am Kran vornehmen zu lassen. Ersteres wäre eine Novum und deshalb versicherungstechnisch ein heikles Unterfangen, allerdings weniger zeitraubend und daher wahrscheinlich auch kostengünstiger. Zu später Stunde fällt dann die klare Entscheidung: Die Goliath muss in den Hafen zurück. Das schon so nah geglaubte Ziel rückt in diesem Moment wieder in die Ferne. Am Dienstag wird die Geduld aller wieder auf die Probe gestellt, denn es braust ein Sturm von Westen heran. Wellen von bis zu drei Metern Höhe türmen sich auf. An das Up-Jacken der Barge ist nicht zu denken, weil es viel zu gefährlich wäre. Die wogende See bringt die Goliath ins Schaukeln, beizeiten rumst es metallisch. Derweil überprüft die Crew alle Gerätschaften, Container und sonstigen Gegenstände an Bord, ob sie auch seetauglich festgemacht sind. Gegen 18 Uhr dröhnt Alarm. Alle eilen bei steifer Böe zur Übung an Deck, bei der das Überziehen des Überlebensanzugs exerziert wird.

Am nächsten Morgen hat sich der Sturm gelegt. Das Wetter ist aufgeklart, die Sonne scheint, es gibt weite Sicht und das Meer zeigt sich im satten Blau. Überdies spielt die Tide mit. Die kommende Flut

is out of the question, as this would be much too dangerous. The choppy sea rocks the 'Goliath', causing occasional metallic bangs. In the meantime the crew is testing all the gear, containers and other equipment on board, and checking that everything is fastened in a seaworthy manner. At around 6 in the evening an alarm goes off: everyone rushes in the heavy gusts of wind to take part in an exercise on deck, in which they practice getting into the survival suits.

The storm has dropped the next morning. The weather has cleared up: the sun is shining, there is a clear view to the horizon and the sea is a deep blue. What's more, the tide is playing along too. The rising high tide pushes the jack-up barge away from the jacket, meaning that the 'Buzzard' can be repositioned at a safe distance. It will have a lonely existence there until the return of the 'Goliath'. Squeaks are heard as the latter lifts her steel stilts until the jack-up platform is floating on the calm North Sea. After the hauling cable has been fastened the 'Multratug' pulls the assembly platform slowly away from the farm. And it's already long past midnight before it makes fast at the quay in back in Eemshaven.

The 1,300-metre long replacement cable is already there, waiting ready for the crane. Under time pressure the workers on shore get ready to make the replacement. The task is completed within a day, the crane is now ready for use again and the 'Goliath' can be tugged back to her place of deployment in the alpha ventus test field.

GROSSE DURCHLÄSSIGKEIT

Ein Jacket ist, salopp gesagt, ein Gittermast unter Wasser. Nur das obere Endstück ragt mit seiner fachwerkartig gebauten Stahlstruktur über den Meeresspiegel hinaus. Obenauf liegt eine stählerne Plattform mit einem himmelwärts gerichteten Rohrstumpf, auf den der Turm der 5M montiert wird. Am unteren Ende, auf dem Meeresboden, wird das viereckig konstruierte Jacket an jeder Ecke auf Stahlpfähle gesetzt, die vorher in den Meeresboden gerammt wurden, und anschließend mit Spezialmörtel fest vergossen. Wie standfest ein Jacket ist, ist von zwei Faktoren abhängig: von der Standfläche und von der Rammtiefe der Pfähle.

Die von der REpower Systems AG favorisierte Gründungskonstruktion wird seit vielen Jahren auch für den Bau von Förderplattformen in der Öl- und Gasindustrie eingesetzt. Die Jackets, auf denen die sechs Anlagen der 5M im Testfeld alpha ventus stehen, wurden von der schottischen Firma Burntisland gefertigt und vom norwegischen Ingenieurbüro OWEC Tower konzipiert.

„Die Geometrie des Jackets bewirkt eine hohe Steifigkeit, das heißt, dass die Konstruktion dem Druck der Wellen einen besonders hohen Widerstand entgegenbringt", erklärt Experte Dr. Marc Seidel. Er konstruiert, berechnet und zertifiziert in einem kleinen Ingenieur-Team die Tragstrukturen für die Offshore-Turbinen vom Hamburger Windenergieanlagen-Hersteller.

Die fachwerkartige Bauweise des Jackets zeichnet sich zudem durch eine hohe Durchlässigkeit gegenüber dem Wellendruck aus – was auch für Laien leicht nachvollziehbar ist. Diese Durchlässigkeit ist besonders bei Stürmen mit turmhohen Wellen, die am Standort von alpha ventus sage und schreibe 17 Meter erreichen können, ein großer Vorzug: Wellen dieser Größenordnung durchrauschen zu lassen, ist sicherlich besser, als sich ihnen entgegenzustemmen.

Das Jacket ist relativ leicht. Die tragende Struktur für das im Testfeld alpha ventus verwendete Modell wiegt bei einer Gesamthöhe von 55 Metern inklusive aller Anbauten rund 500 Tonnen. Hinzu kommen rund 200 Tonnen für die vier Stahlpfähle, die das gitterhafte Gebilde im Meeresboden verankern.

Das im satten Gelb lackierte Jacket besteht aus Rohren mit einem Durchmesser von etwa 60 Zentimetern für die Verstrebungen beziehungsweise 90 Zentimetern für die Beine. Diese Rohrdurchmesser entsprechen den heutigen industriellen Standards – Pipeline-Hersteller etwa bauen sie in Serie. Um die Fertigungsprozesse noch mehr zu optimieren, hat REpower in Zusammenarbeit mit der Firma WeserWind GmbH eine eigene Jacket-Variante entwickelt, bei der mit so genannten Stahlgussknoten gearbeitet wird: Die Schweißnähte liegen in dieser Fertigungsvariante nicht direkt in den Knotenbereichen, also dort, wo die Rohre aufeinandertreffen, sondern ein Stück entfernt, sodass am Rohr mit reinen Rundnähten automatisch geschweißt werden kann. Eine Wissenschaft für sich, kein Zweifel.

LIGHT YET STRONG

A jacket is, simply put, a subsea lattice tower. Only its upper end with its trusslike structure rises above sea level. A steel platform is located on top. From this extends a short tubular section on which the 5M tower is mounted. On the seabed, at the bottom, the rectangular jacket is attached at each corner to steel piles driven into the seabed and firmly grouted using special mortar. The stability of the jacket's footing is based on the footprint and pile-drive depth.

This foundation structure favoured by REpower Systems AG has already been used to install rigs in the oil and gas sector for many years. The six 5M turbines in the alpha ventus test field are mounted on jackets manufactured in Scotland by the Burntisland company and designed by the Norwegian OWEC Tower engineering bureau.

"The jacket geometry translates into high rigidity, which means that the structure is especially resistant to wave pressure," explains expert Marc Seidel. As part of a small engineering team, he designs, calculates and certifies the support structures for the offshore wind turbines of Hamburg-based manufacturer REpower.

The trusswork-like jacket structure lets wave pressure pass through readily, as is immediately evident even to non-specialists. This feature is an advantage especially in gales with towering waves. At the alpha ventus site, rogue waves can reach incredible heights of up to 17 metres. Letting waves of such magnitude pass through is certainly better than trying to resist them directly.

The jacket is relatively lightweight. The support structure for the version used in the test field weighs 500 tonnes and has an overall height of 55 metres, including all extensions. The four steel piles anchoring the latticework structure to the seabed add another 200 tonnes.

The jacket is painted bright yellow and consists of 60 cm-diameter pipes at the bracings, and 90 cm-diameter pipes at the legs. These pipe diameters are industrial standard, and pipeline manufacturers can mass-produce them easily. In order to further smooth the production process, REpower and WeserWind GmbH have worked together to develop their own jacket variant, which is assembled using special cast steel nodes. In this design, the welded joints are located not directly at the node sections where the pipes meet, but instead at some distance from them. This permits the use of straightforward automatic circumferential seam welding. It's clear that jackets are a science unto themselves!

drückt die Hubinseln vom Jacket weg, sodass die Buzzard in sicherer Entfernung neu positioniert werden kann. Dort führt sie für einige Tage ein einsames Single-Dasein, bis die Goliath wieder zurückkehrt. Unterdessen hebt die Goliath ihre stählernen Stelzen quietschend an, bis die Hubinsel schließlich auf der ruhigen Nordsee schwimmt. Nachdem das Zugseil vertäut ist, zieht der Schlepper Multratug die Montageinsel langsam aus dem Park-Ensemble heraus. Es ist schon nach Mitternacht, als sie am Kai von Eemshaven festgemacht werden kann. Dort steht schon das 1.300 Meter lange Ersatzseil für den Kran bereit. Unter Hochdruck bereiten die Mitarbeiter an Land das Auswechseln vor. Innerhalb eines Tages ist die Austauscharbeit erledigt, und der Kran wieder einsatzbereit. Die Goliath kann wieder zu ihrem Einsatzort im Testfeld alpha ventus zurückgeschleppt werden.

Nun ist das Glück auf der Seite der Tüchtigen. Alles geht jetzt Schlag auf Schlag. Schon nach zwei Tagen, am späten Sonntagabend, hängt der Rotorstern fest am Maschinenhaus. Während die Buzzard nun die letzte Anlage aus Eemshaven holt, fiebern Mitarbeiter, Politiker, Ehefrauen, Freundinnen und viele Windenergiebegeisterte via der Webcam, die auf der FINO 1 installiert ist, dem nahen Finale entgegen. Gewinnen die Seemänner und Monteure den Wettlauf mit der Zeit? Wird es noch ein Zeitfenster zwischen immer neuen atlantischen Tiefausläufern geben? Der Blick in die Webcam wird zum täglichen Ritual.

It's time for fortune to favour the bold. All necessary tasks are now completed like clockwork – and after just two days, late on Sunday evening the rotor hub stands fixed firmly to the nacelle. While the 'Buzzard' now goes to fetch the last turbine from Eemshaven, employees, politicians, wives, girlfriends and numerous wind power enthusiasts watching via the webcam installed on the FINO 1, tensely await the final act. Will the seamen and fitting engineers win their race against time? Will there be another time-window between repeated Atlantic low-pressure troughs? In fact, everyone wants to see for themselves live what is happening at sea and it has become a daily ritual to have a look at the scene from the webcam. And finally, early morning on the 16th November, 2009, it's time: the last bolt is tightened on the REpower 5M at exactly 7.13 a.m. "An Even Dozen", is the title of the press release from the DOTI consortium of operators that same day. At this moment of success all the sweat, frustration and costs recede into the background: the first German offshore wind farm is up and running. "We have climbed a very steep learning curve", beams Oliver Funk, Managing Director at DOTI. And most importantly, everyone involved in the project has come home safely. There was no accident victim during the construction phase, no disaster, no irreparable damage. alpha ventus has also become a role model for the nascent offshore industry, not least thanks to the strict safety precautions implemented.

Alle wollen live miterleben, was auf dem Meer geschieht. Und dann ist es am frühen Morgen des 16. November 2009 endlich soweit: Die letzte Schraube an der 5M wird exakt um 7.13 Uhr festgezogen. „Das Dutzend ist voll", titelt eine Pressemitteilung des Betreiber-Konsortiums DOTI am gleichen Tag. Im Moment des Erfolgs rücken alle Mühen und Kosten in den Hintergrund: Der erste deutsche Offshore-Windpark steht. „Wir haben eine steile Lernkurve durchlaufen", freut sich der Geschäftsführer der DOTI, Oliver Funk. Und das Allerwichtigste: Alle, die beim Projekt im Einsatz waren, sind heil nach Hause gekommen. Es gab während der Bauphase keine Unfallopfer, keine Havarie, keine irreparablen Schäden. Nicht zuletzt wegen der strengen Sicherheitsvorkehrungen ist alpha ventus auch ein Vorbild für die zukünftige Offshore-Industrie.

Die lehrreiche Bauzeit ist beendet. Nun beginnt eine nicht minder interessante Betriebsphase, in der die Forschung im Mittelpunkt steht. Ökologen, Ingenieure, Techniker, Physiker und Ozeanographen erhoffen sich wichtige neue Erkenntnisse. Angesichts dessen wird fast vergessen, dass alpha ventus zukünftig grünen Strom für mehr als 50.000 Haushalte liefert. Der Stromabnehmer an Land sieht die sich drehenden Windflügel dank Entfernung und Erdkrümmung nicht. Die Stromerzeugung findet draußen auf dem Meer statt, da wo Vergänglichkeit und Ewigkeit näher zusammenrücken als irgendwo anders.

The richly informative construction period has been completed. Now the operation phase starts, one that is just as fascinating, in which research will be the focal point. Ecologists, engineers, technicians, physicists and oceanographers are all hoping for important new findings. In this respect, it has almost been forgotten that this offshore pioneering farm will provide renewable energy to more than 50,000 households. However, due to the distance and the curvature of the Earth, those electricity consumers on land won't see the rotating blades of the turbines. The power is being generated out there on the open sea, where transience and eternity come closer together than anywhere else in the world.

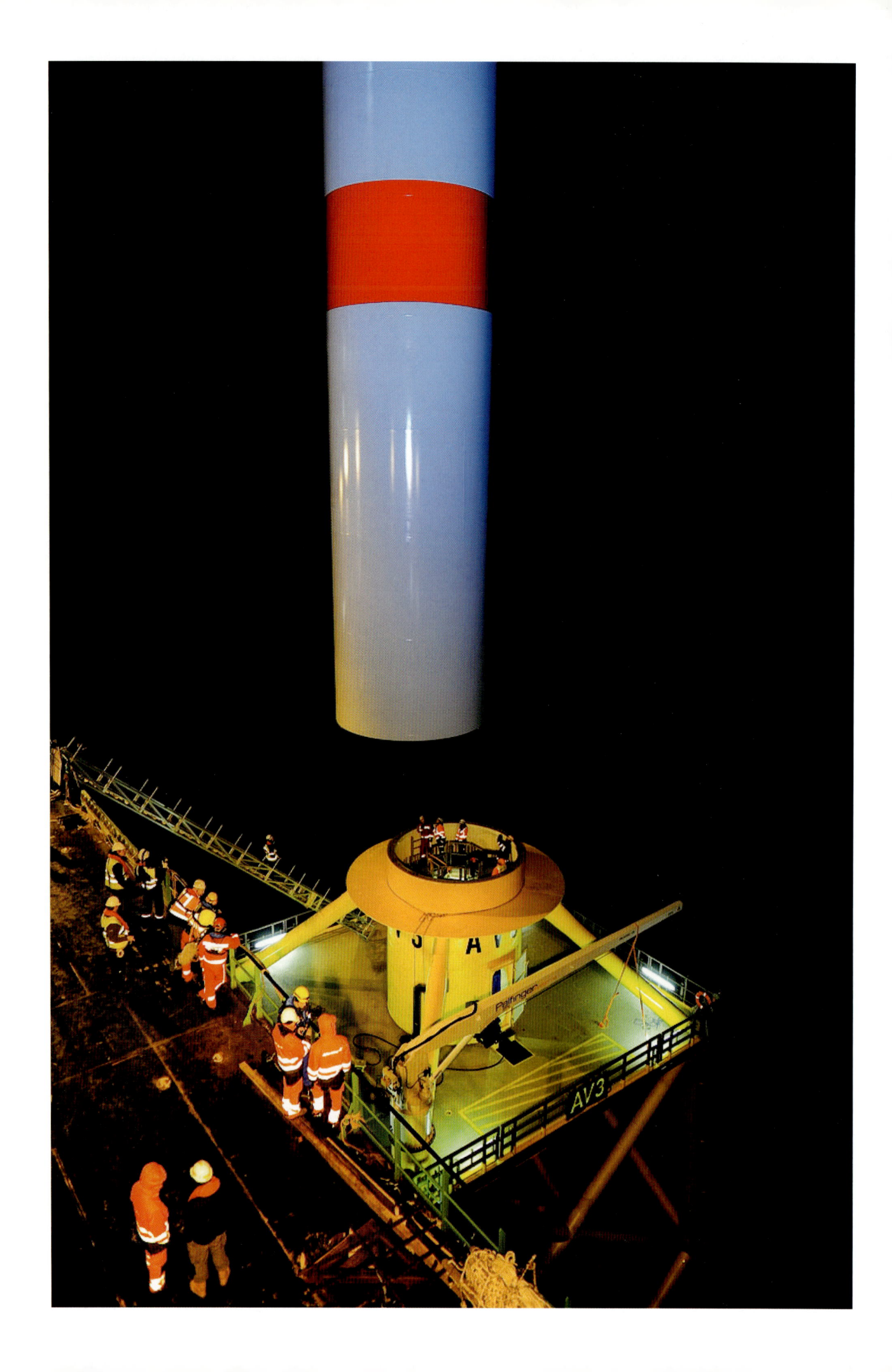
AV3
Palfinger

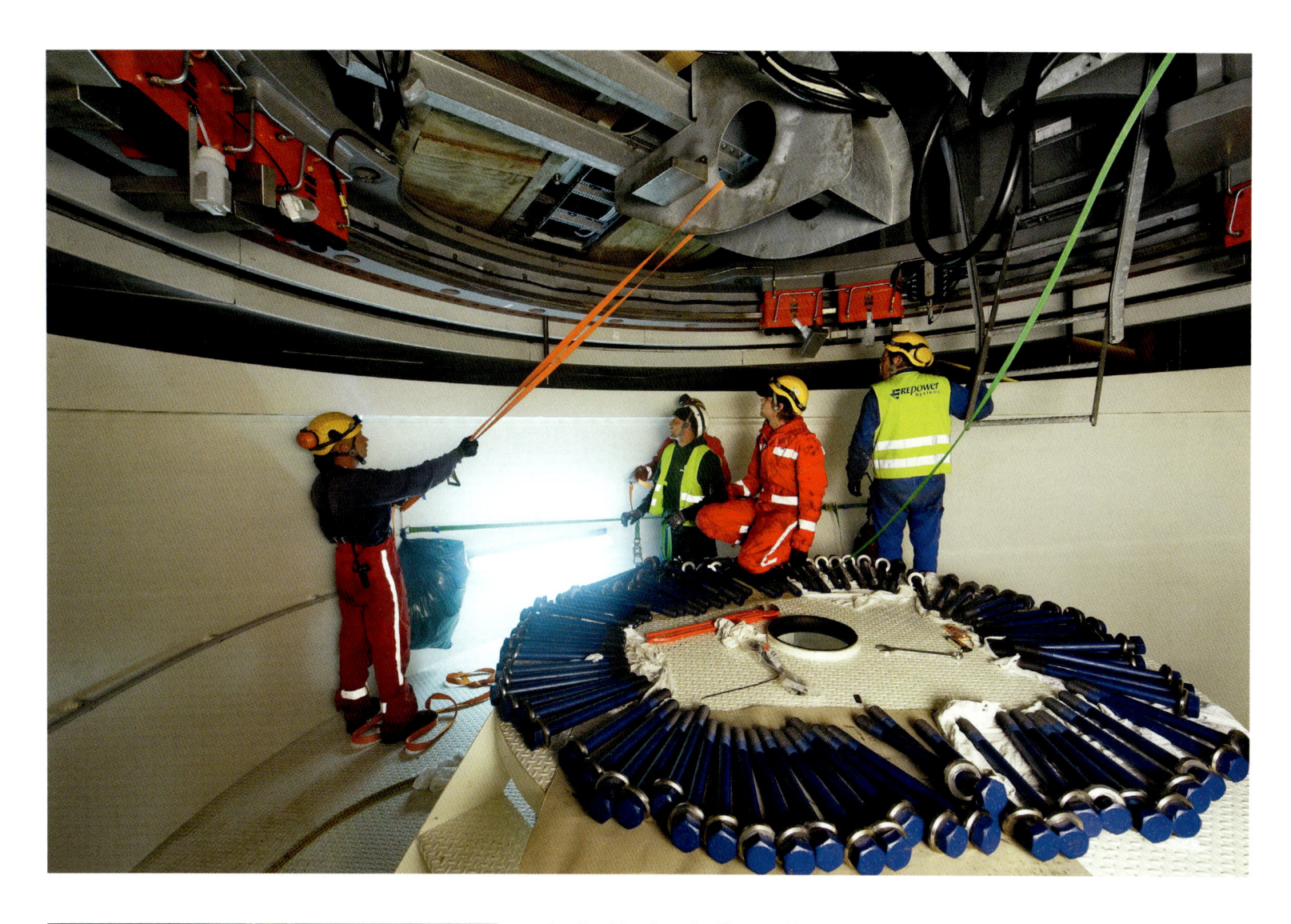

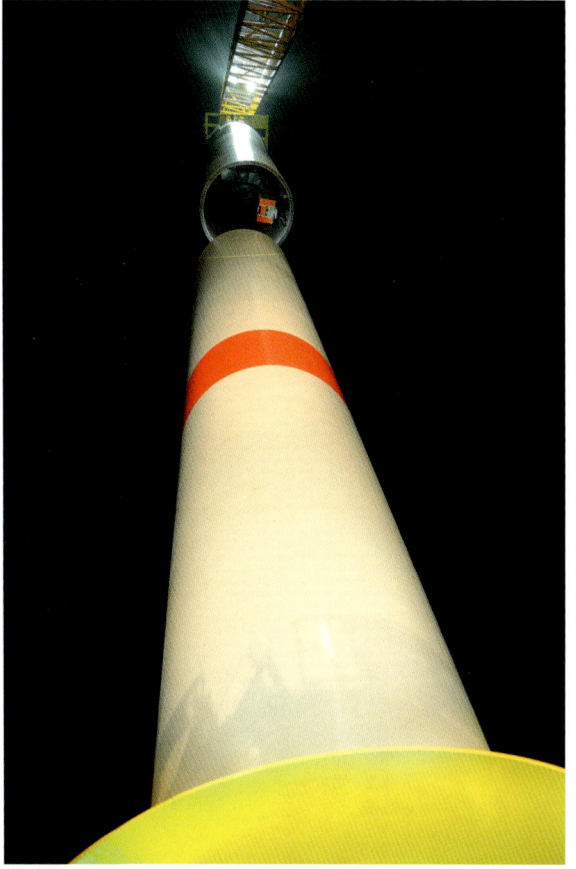

Das Maschinenhaus der REpower 5M wird auf den Turm gesetzt. Die Bolzen liegen für das Verschrauben schon bereit.
The M5 nacelle is mounted on top of the tower. The bolts are ready to attach the nacelle to the tower.

Und immer wieder Nachtschichten. Das Aufbau-Team von REpower und Kletterspezialisten der Berliner Seilpartner Windkraft GmbH nutzen die wenigen Zeitfenster und setzen in der Dunkelheit das Maschinenhaus der 5M auf den Turm.
Kleines Foto unten: Sven Winkler von der Seilpartner Windkraft GmbH auf der Baustelle.
Night shifts time and again. The REpower fitter team and "Seilpartner" climber-experts from Berlin use the short time-windows and erect the 5M in the darkness.
Small photo below: Sven Winkler from Seilpartner Windkraft GmbH on the construction site.

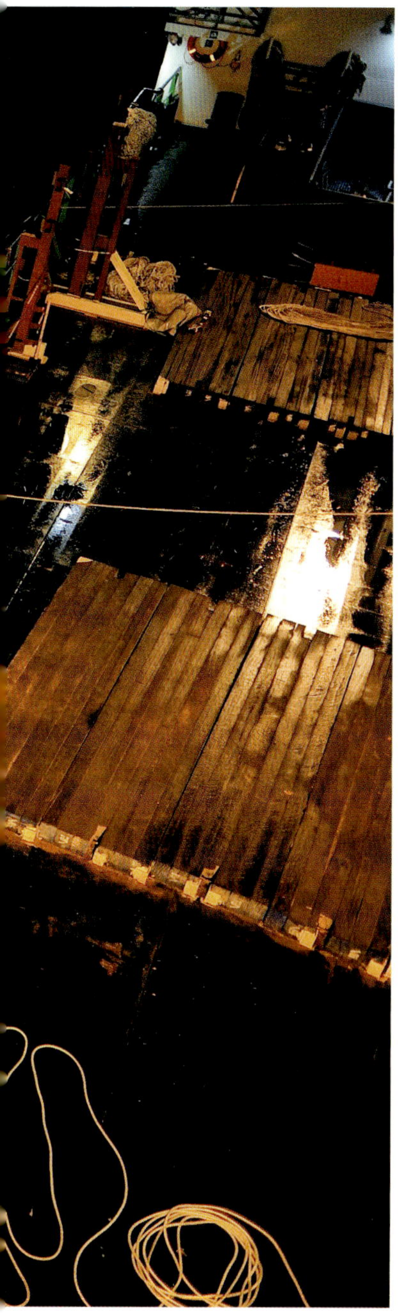

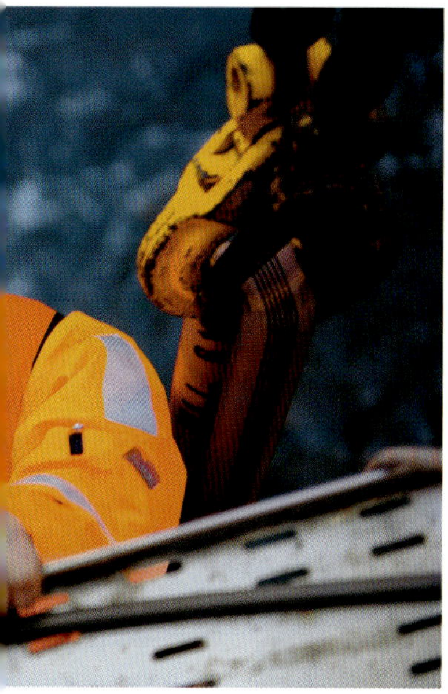

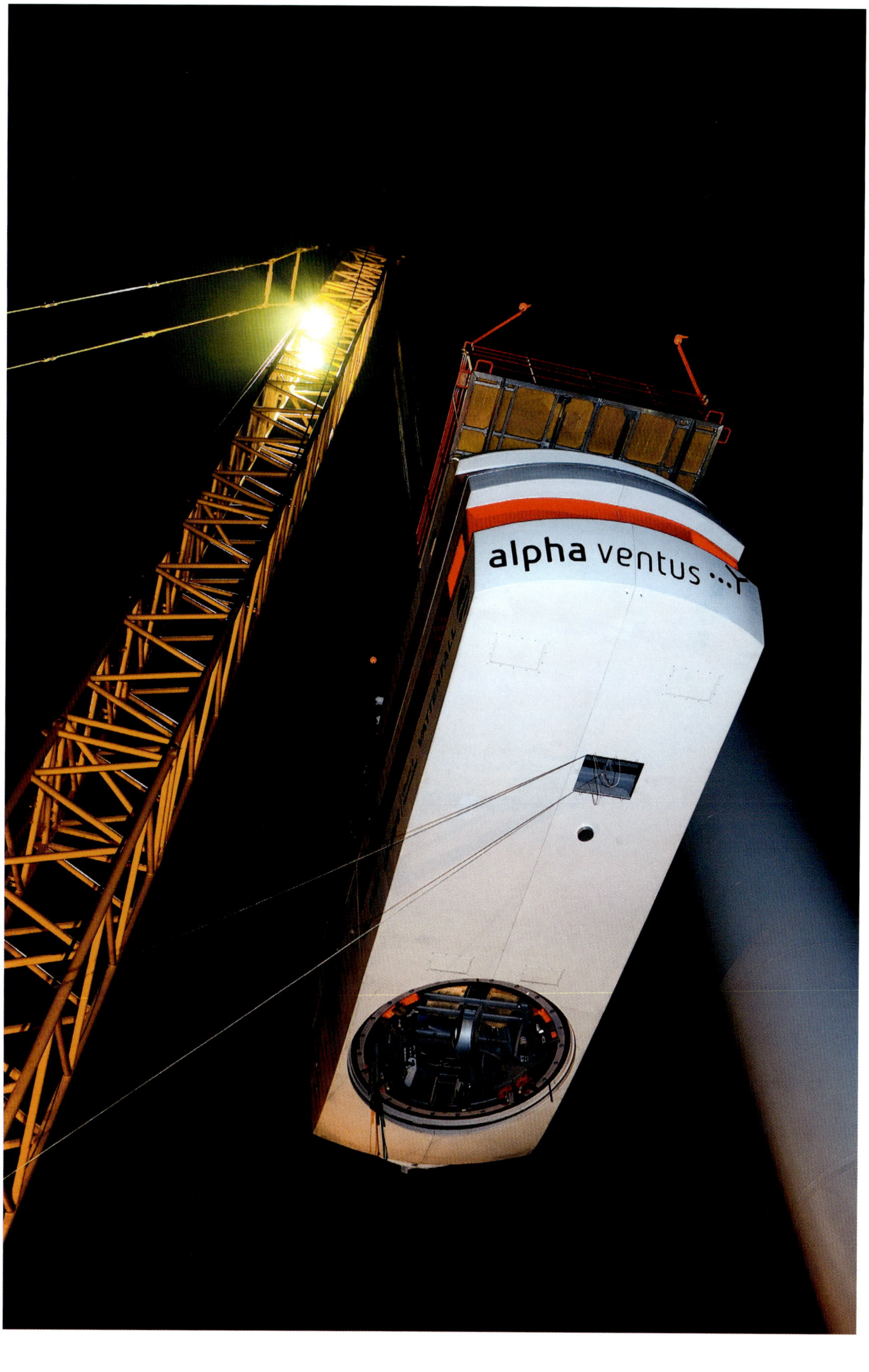
alpha ventus

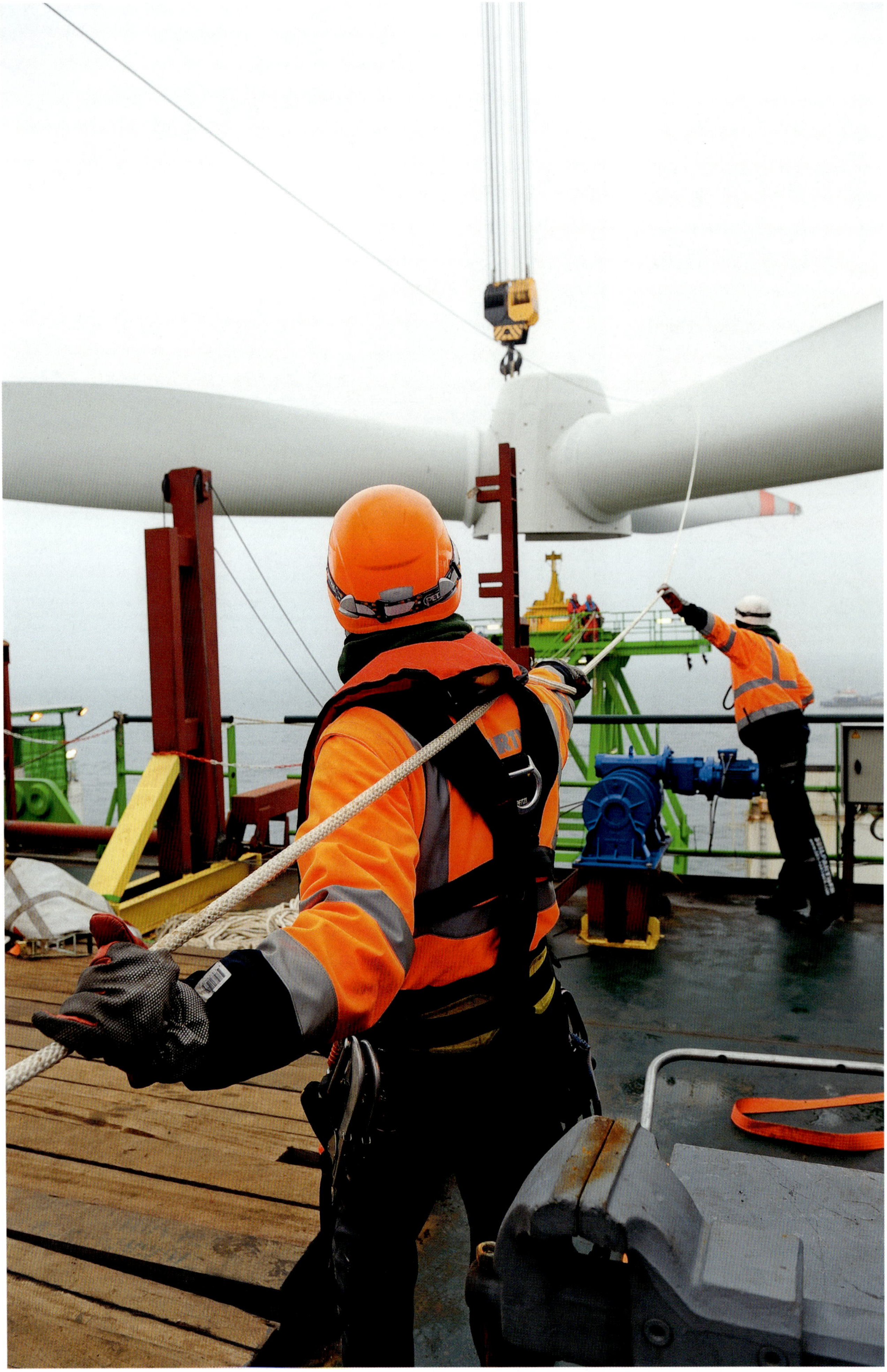

Das Ziehen des Rotorsterns ist der heikelste Arbeitsschritt beim Aufbau. Die Flügel werden von der Montage-Mannschaft mit mehreren Seilen in die richtige Position gebracht, damit der Kran den Rotor unbeschadet in die Höhe ziehen kann. Dies ist nur bei geringen Windstärken möglich.

Hoisting the rotor star is the most complex operation during the offshore wind-energy converter's installation. The rotors are brought into the right position by the fitter crew so that the crane can hoist the rotor up high without any damage. This can only be done when there is low wind speeds.

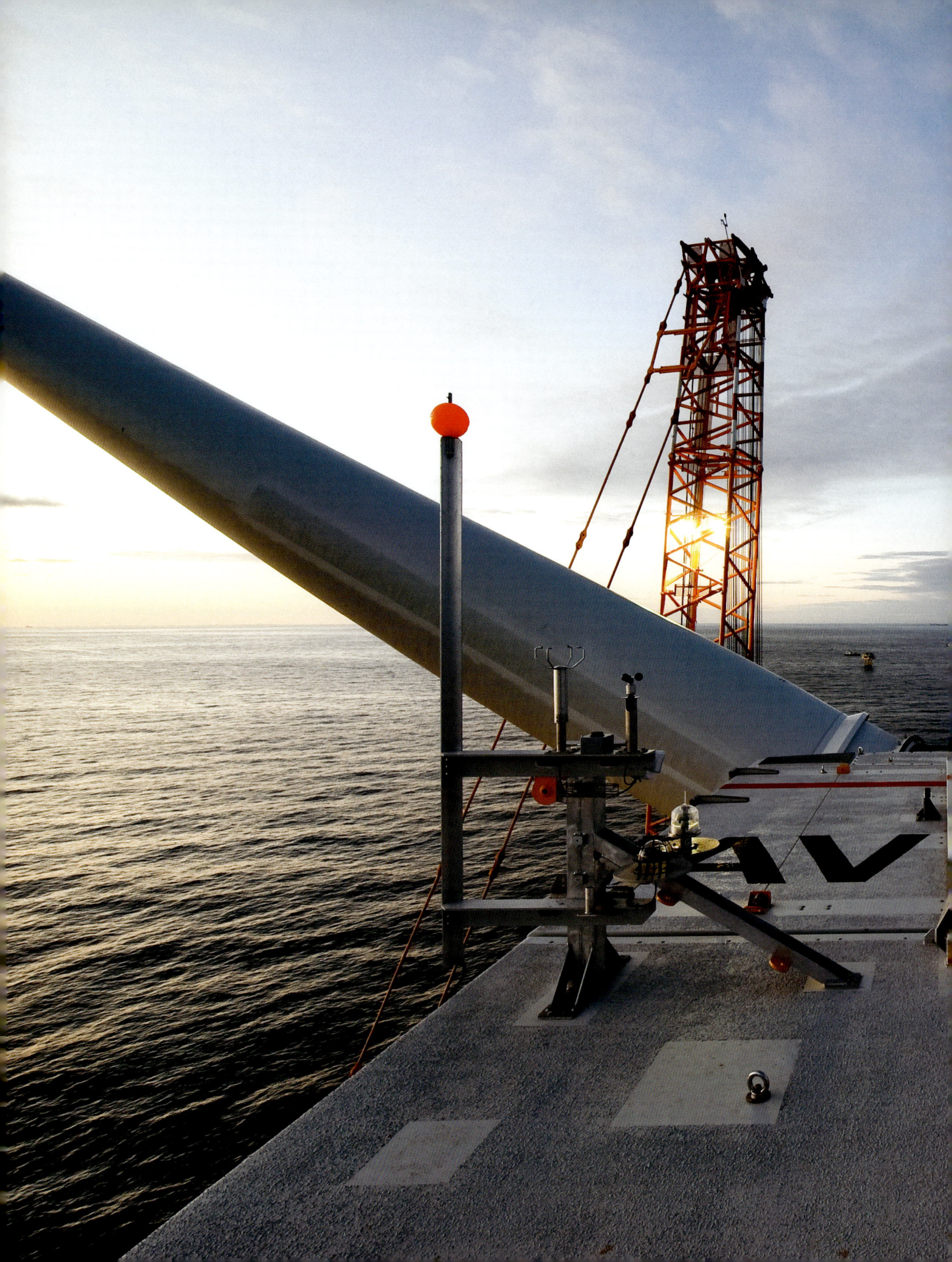

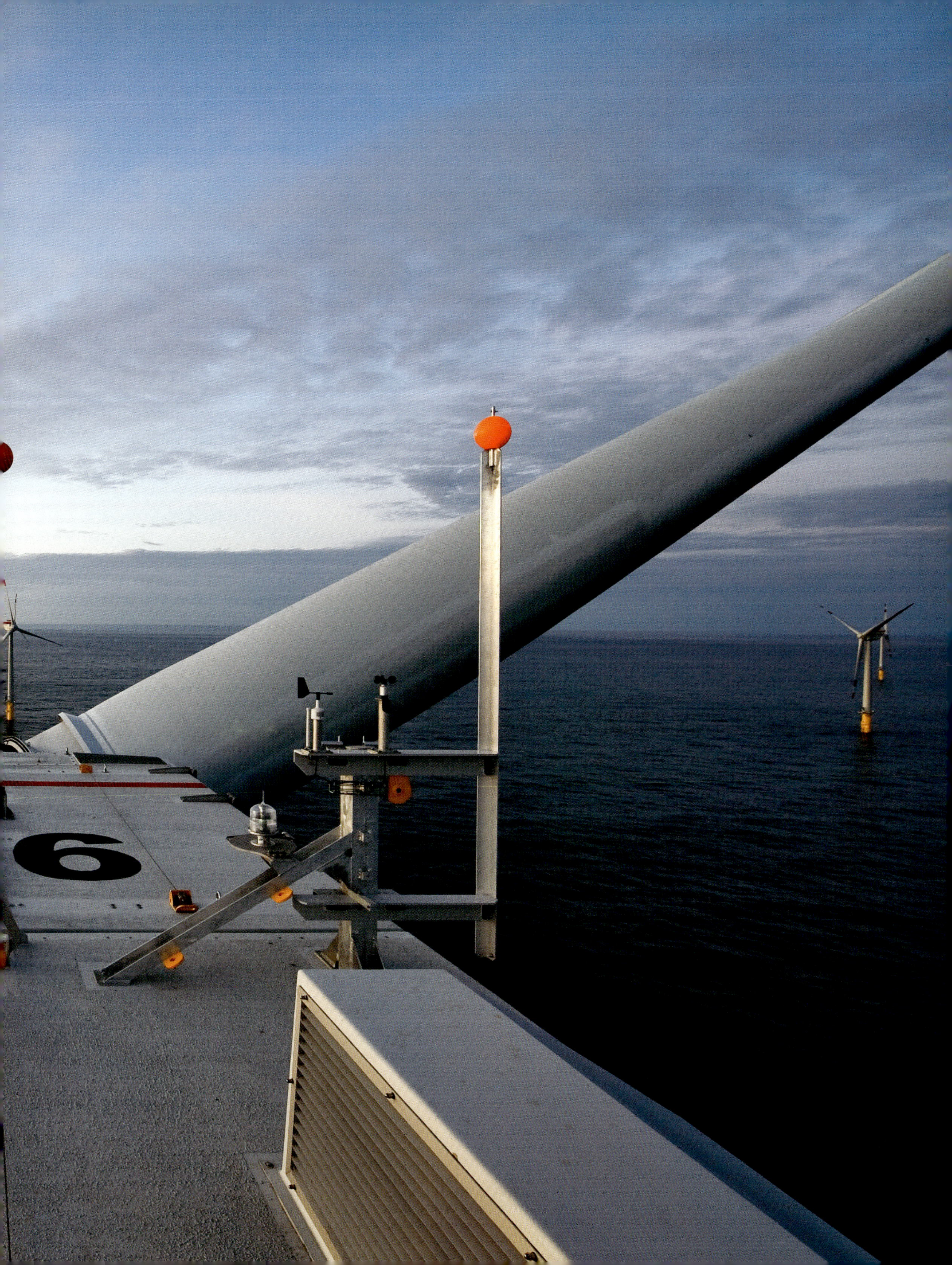
6

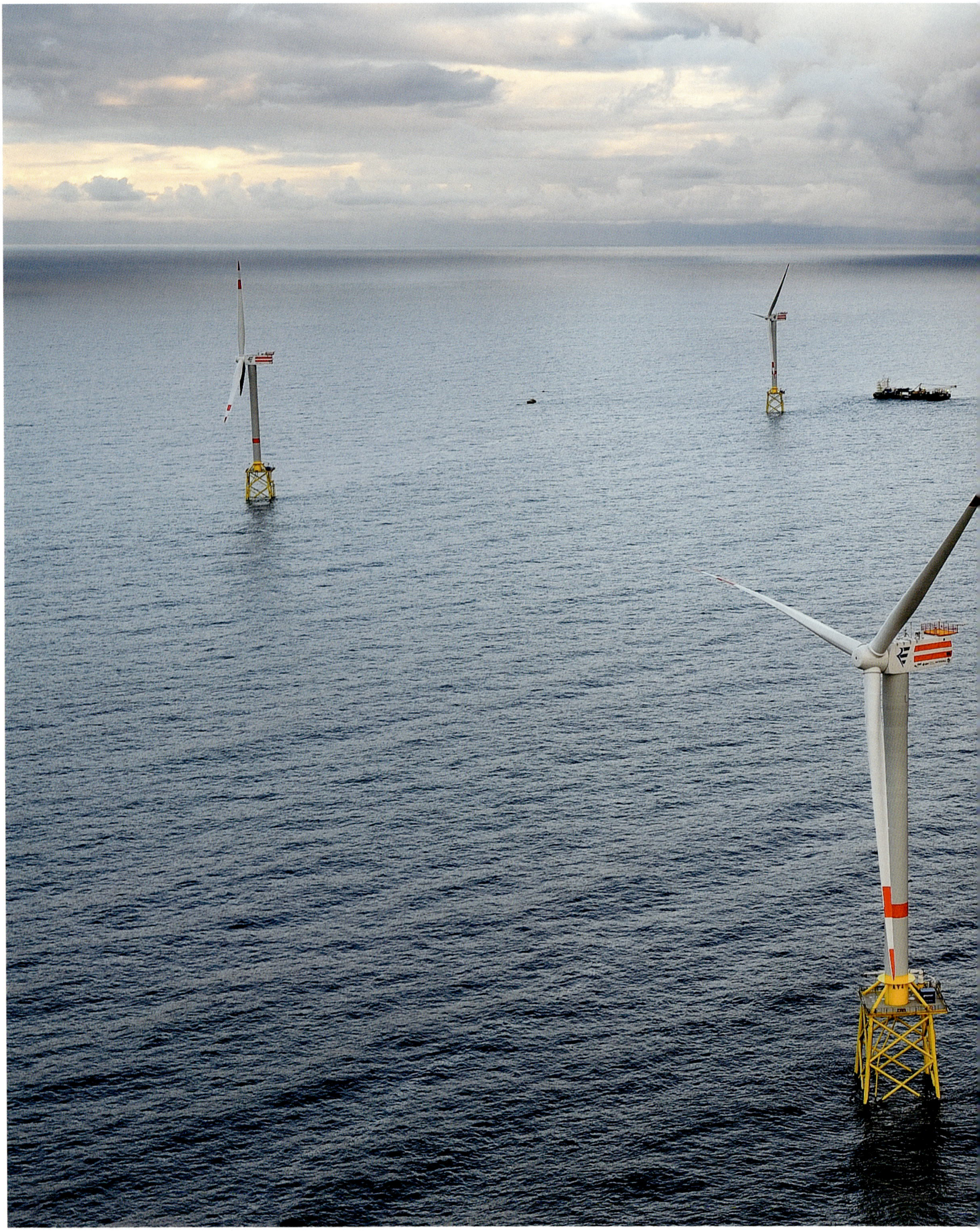

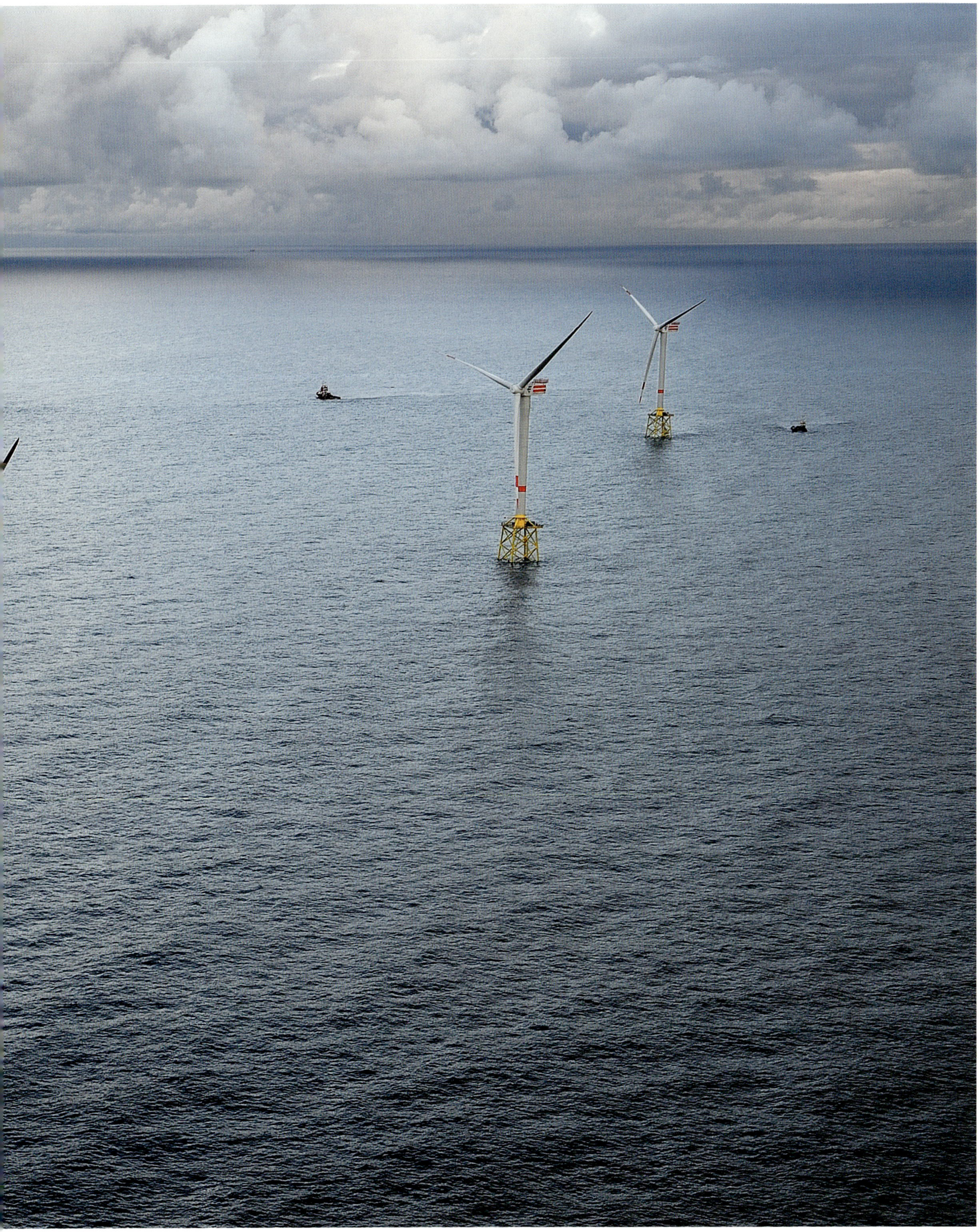

Wichtiger Impuls Key impetus

MATTHIAS SCHUBERT TECHNOLOGIEVORSTAND REPOWER SYSTEMS AG
CHIEF TECHNOLOGY OFFICER, REPOWER SYSTEMS AG

Matthias Schubert

Matthias Schubert ist seit April 2001 Technologievorstand (CTO) der REpower Systems AG. Er hat in Bonn, Berlin und Ann Arbor (Michigan, USA) studiert und schloss sein Studium als Diplomingenieur der Fluiddynamik sowie als Master of Science in Engineering (MSE) für Aerospace Engineering ab. Nach dem Studium arbeitete er unter anderem als Gutachter des Forschungsministeriums an Windenergiesystemen für netzunabhängige Anwendungen. Seit 1991 ist er in verschiedenen Positionen in der Windindustrie tätig. Als Geschäftsführer leitete er die Engineering-Firma pro + pro Energiesysteme in Rendsburg, die bis zur Verschmelzung 2001 mit REpower komplette Windenergiesysteme entwickelt und als Lizenzprodukt vermarktet hat.

Matthias Schubert is Chief Technology Officer (CTO) of REpower Systems AG since April 2001. He studied in Bonn, Berlin and Ann Arbor (Michigan, USA) and finished his studies as a Graduated Engineer in the field of fluid dynamics and as Master of Science in Engineering (MSE) for Aerospace Engineering. After his studies, he worked amongst other jobs as an expert for the Ministry of Research in the field of wind-power systems for grid independent applications. He has been working in the wind industry in different positions since 1991. As Managing Director he led the engineering company pro + pro Energiesysteme in Rendsburg, that developed and licensed complete wind-power systems until its merger with REpower 2001.

Herr Schubert, wie weit reichen die ersten Ideen zur Entwicklung der 5M zurück?

Bei der 5M ist es interessant, dass wir schon 1999, also noch zu Zeiten der Rendsburger pro & pro Energiesysteme GmbH, die später in der REpower Systems AG aufging, untersucht haben, wie eine wirklich große Anlage aussehen sollte. Zu jenem Zeitpunkt war die größte Serienanlage der von uns entwickelte Prototyp der 1,5-Megawatt-Anlage (MD70), die im Kaiser-Wilhelm-Koog stand – nur um hier einmal die Relationen zu verdeutlichen. Damals konkretisierten sich erste Planungen vor der deutschen Küste und es zeichnete sich ab, dass viele Projekte weit draußen in tieferem Wasser entstehen würden. Auf dieser Grundlage haben wir die ersten Überlegungen angestellt, wie denn so ein Offshore-Produkt aussehen könnte und müsste. Uns war eines klar: Groß muss es auf jeden Fall sein, weil nur dann die hohen Kosten für Fundamente und Seekabel bei Anlagen mehr als 35 Kilometer vor der Küste und in mehr als 30 Metern Wassertiefe spezifisch kleiner sind. Aus unserer Initiative heraus entstand später das norddeutsche

Mr. Schubert, how long ago was it that the first ideas emerged to develop the 5M?

What is interesting with the 5M is that we were already investigating what a really large turbine would look like back in 1999. That was still in the days of the Rendsburg pro & pro Energiesysteme GmbH, that later became REpower Systems AG. Just to put things into perspective, at that time the largest turbine in serial production was our prototype of the 1.5-megawatt turbine (MD70) that was erected in Kaiser-Wilhelm-Koog. The first plans for turbines off the German coast were being made at the time and it was becoming obvious that there would be numerous projects out there in deep waters. That was the starting point on which we based our considerations about what such an offshore product would be like – and needs to be like. One thing was obvious to us: it has to be big, as only then can the very high costs for foundations and sea cables be reduced in relative terms; after all, we want turbines that are more than 35 kilometres from the coast and in water deeper than 30 metres to be working profitably! It was our initiative that led to the North German Offshore Consortium,

Offshore-Konsortium, bestehend aus pro & pro, Jacobs und Nordex AG. In dieser Dreierkonstellation haben wir ein Team gebildet, das eine Machbarkeitsstudie für eine 5-Megawatt-Anlage erarbeitete. Erstaunlicherweise weicht dieses erste technische Konzept gar nicht sehr weit von den Grundabmessungen der heutigen 5M ab.

Wie kamen Sie zu den Maßen?
Wir sind damals zu den Lieferanten gegangen und haben sie gefragt, in welchen Größen-

consisting of pro & pro, Jacobs and Nordex AG. Within this group of three we created a team that worked on a feasibility study for a 5-megawatt turbine. Astonishingly, that initial technical concept is not so different to the basic parameters for the current 5M.

How did you arrive at those parameters?
At the time, we went to the suppliers and asked them what sizes they would trust themselves to build. What makes economical and technical sense? That's how we arrived at

Blick in die Fertigungshalle der REpower Systems AG in Bremerhaven.
View of the REpower Systems AG production facility in Bremerhaven.

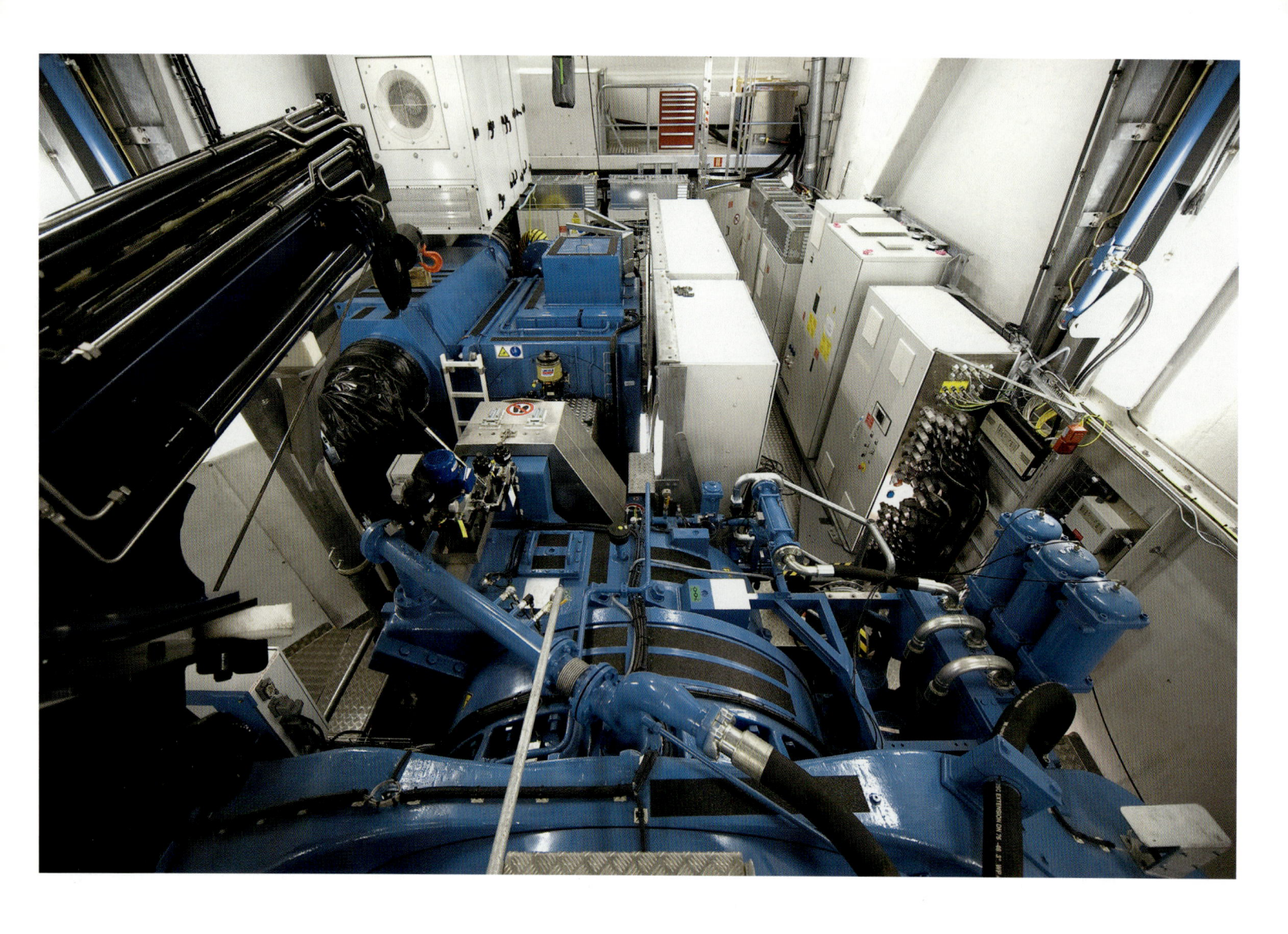

ordnungen sie sich zutrauen würden zu bauen. Was ist ökonomisch und technisch sinnvoll? Auf diesem Weg sind wir zu den Abmessungen gekommen und haben damit gleichzeitig für unsere technischen Ideen einen Rahmen bekommen. Am Ende ging es darum, wie viel Drehmoment das Getriebe überträgt und wie viel Rotorblattlänge wir uns zutrauen.

Ein getriebeloser Antrieb stand nie zur Debatte?
Am Anfang war alles offen. Wir haben uns in den Detailstudien natürlich mit allen möglichen Triebstrangvarianten beschäftigt: Vollumrichter, Synchrongenerator, doppelt gespeistes System, mehrere Generatoren und Direktantrieb. Wir haben uns schließlich aus Gründen der technischen Bewertungen und letztlich auch wegen der Kostenstruktur für das doppelt gespeiste System entschieden, so wie es heute in der 5M zu finden ist. Dabei ist die 5-Megawatt-Anlage keine lineare technische Vergrößerung der 1,5-MW-Turbine.

Ging die Arbeit an der Offshore-Anlage mit der Gründung von REpower nahtlos weiter?
Das Offshore-Anlagenkonzept ist direkt von REpower übernommen worden. Schon auf der allerersten Vorstandssitzung im Jahr 2001, damals noch mit Prof. Dr. Fritz Vahrenholt, stand das Offshore-Thema auf der Tagesordnung. Wir mussten eine Entscheidung darüber fällen, ob wir die Offshore-Entwicklung fortsetzen oder vorrangig unser Produktportfolio in Richtung 3-Megawatt-Turbine ausweiten wollten. Wir haben uns für eine 5-Megawatt-Anlage entschieden. Das war damals eine mutige Entscheidung! Wir wollten mit diesem Produkt in einem neuen Unternehmen ein Alleinstellungsmerkmal im Markt erreichen. So stand schon gegen Ende des Jahres 2002 das Konzept für die 5M mehr oder weniger fest.

War denn die strategische Ausrichtung für die Entwicklung einer Offshore-Maschine ein unternehmerisches Risiko?
Jede Pioniertat ist auch ein Risiko. Für die damals noch kleine REpower Systems AG war es eine zentrale Frage, ob das Offshore-Projekt ein substanzielles Risiko würde. Wir hatten aus der Erfahrung mit der MD70 gelernt, dass wir die those dimensions – and at the same time this gave us a framework for our further technical considerations. At the end of the day it was all about how much torque the gearbox would transmit and what rotor-blade length we imagined would be feasible.

Did you ever consider a direct-drive version?
At the beginning everything was possible. Of course, we looked into all possible types of drive train in the detailed studies: full converter, synchronous generator, double-fed system, multiple generators and direct-drive. At the end of the day we decided, based on the technical assessment – and not least due to cost structures – on the double-fed system, like the one found in the 5M today. Technically speaking, however, the 5-megawatt turbine is not a linear further development of the 1.5-megawatt turbine.

Did the work on the offshore turbine continue seamlessly with the founding of REpower?
The offshore turbine concept was taken over directly by REpower. The subject of 'offshore'

Entwicklung über den Prototypen finanzieren können. Letztendlich rentierte sich nämlich die Entwicklung dieser Baureihe über den Betrieb des Prototyps. Zugleich haben wir das Brot- und Buttergeschäft mit der 1,5- und später der 2-Megawatt-Anlage absolviert, die damals schon gut im Markt etabliert waren. Ab 2002 haben wir die Business Unit Offshore gebildet, um die sich Dr. Martin Skiba bis Mitte 2008 intensiv gekümmert hat. Die Abteilung sollte sicherstellen, dass unsere zukunftsweisende Entwicklung nicht im Tagesgeschäft verloren geht. Es war nicht immer leicht für einen Bereich, der zuerst viel Geld kostete, aber noch nichts einbrachte. Dennoch war die 5M nie ein Unternehmensrisiko. Ganz im Gegenteil, heute sind wir Vorreiter in dieser Technologie und die Entwicklung der 5M hatte und hat weiterhin eine positive Ausstrahlung auf unsere Onshore-Geschäfte.

Was hat die Entwicklung der 5M insgesamt gekostet?

Auf den Cent genau haben wir das nicht berechnet. Es ist ja auch immer die Frage,

was already on the agenda at the very first board meeting in 2001, at the time still with Prof. Dr. Fritz Vahrenholt. We had to make the decision on whether to pursue the development of offshore technologies or concentrate on extending our product portfolio in the direction of 3-mega-watt turbines. We chose the 5-megawatt turbine – and that was a daring decision at the time! We intended to use this product as a differentiating feature on the market for the new company. Thus, at the end of 2002, the concept for the 5M had already been more or less decided on.

Was the strategic orientation to develop offshore machines a business risk?

All pioneering work is a risk. For what was at the time a still-small REpower Systems AG it was pivotal whether the offshore project would turn out to be a substantial risk or not. We had learned from the experience with the MD70 that we could finance the development with prototypes. At the end of the day, the development of this series had been paid off with running the prototype. At the same time

Links: Das Innenleben der 5M.
Left: Inside the 5M nacelle.
Rechts: Einer der letzten Handgriffe beim Aufbau: Der so genannte „Spinner" wird zugeklappt.
Right: The rotor hub is closed and the construction almost finished.

welche laufenden Kosten noch zur Entwicklung zählen und welche nicht. Es gab zudem eine Förderung durch das Land Schleswig-Holstein aus dem Förderprogramm 2000 sowie durch die Europäische Kommission. Die Mittel aus beiden Programmen betrugen zusammen rund drei Millionen Euro.

Zurück zur Technik. Über die Größendimensionen sprachen wir, aber welche Besonderheiten weist Ihre Offshore-Anlage im Detail auf?

Wenn Sie gute Ingenieure an Bord haben, dann kommen sie in der Frage der Dimensionen schnell zu übereinstimmenden Ergebnissen. Das Interessante liegt tatsächlich in der Detailbetrachtung. Wir haben uns im Vorfeld im Markt umgehört und abgefragt, welche Anlage eigentlich von den Kunden gewünscht wird. Für kein anderes Produkt haben wir eine so intensive Marktanalyse betrieben. Aber außer dem allgemein geäußerten Wunsch, dass die Turbine so groß wie möglich sein sollte, erhielten wir sehr unterschiedliche und leider oft nur vage Äußerungen. Wir mussten also unsere eigenen Schlüsse ziehen. Eine wichtige Überlegung beschäftigte uns lange: Wollen wir bei anfallenden Reparaturen die ganze Gondel austauschen oder reparieren wir vor Ort? Wir haben uns am Ende bei der 5M für eine modulare Bauweise entschieden, um etwaige Schäden möglichst vor Ort reparieren zu können. In der Gondel wurde deshalb ein relativ großer, mobiler Kran integriert. Zudem haben wir uns für eine klassische Rotorlagerung entschieden. Die Welle wurde dementsprechend mit zwei Hauptlagern ausgestattet. Damit können wir das Getriebe herausheben, ohne den Rotor ablegen zu müssen. Das ist gerade auf dem Meer ein großer Vorteil, weil man dort nirgendwo irgend etwas ablegen kann. Überhaupt haben wir die Gondel geräumig konzipiert, weil die Monteure auf dem Wasser sonst keinen Platz zum Arbeiten vorfinden. Aus demselben Grund haben wir zwischen Oberkante Triebstrang und Dach viel Raum gelassen: Der Kran muss dort gut manövriert werden können. Unser Ansatz beinhaltet auch, dass die Gondel zur Montage komplett fertig und verdrahtet sein muss, damit nach der Errichtung auf See sofort alles in Betrieb gehen kann.

Aus all diesen Gründen ist die 5M auch ein ziemliches Schwergewicht geworden ...

Zum einem liegt das Gewicht bei der Größe dieser Anlage in der Natur der Sache. Aber Offshore spielt das Gewicht aus unserer Sicht keine so große Rolle. Wir brauchen zudem eine steife Maschinenkonstruktion, um die komplett im Gondelheck montierte Elektronik vor starken Vibrationen durch Wind und Wellen zu schützen.

Herrscht während des Betriebes der 5M Überdruck in der Gondel, damit keine salzhaltige Luft eindringt?

Nein, darauf haben wir verzichtet. Ohnehin wird die Korrosion auf dem Meer überschätzt. Wir haben an küstennahen Standorten, wie beispielsweise bei unseren Projekten an der Küste Australiens, durch die Brandung sogar höhere Salzgehalte als auf der Nordsee.

Hat sich REpower über Offshore-Gründungen schon frühzeitig Gedanken gemacht?

Durchaus. Es war unerlässlich, dass wir hier die nötige Fachkompetenz aufgebaut haben. Während der Entwicklungsarbeit wurde schon bei den ersten Verkaufsgesprächen ersichtlich, dass die Gründungsstruktur sehr teuer wird, wenn man sie falsch konzipiert.

Das war auch für REpower ein völlig neues Betätigungsfeld, oder?

Absolut. Wir haben uns deshalb schon ganz früh und von Anfang an einen Fachmann von der Universität geholt, der diesen Bereich kontinuierlich aufgebaut hat. Inzwischen haben wir die Kompetenz für Offshore-Gründungen. Die Motivation, in diesem neuen Bereich etwas Eigenes aufzubauen, lag aber in erster Linie in dem Bestreben, unsere Kunden erfolgreich zu beraten, weniger in dem Wunsch, selbst zu fertigen und zu liefern. Wie wichtig eigene Kompetenz ist, zeigte sich schon beim ersten Projekt vor der schottischen Küste. Dank unserer Beratung hat die Gründung am Ende nur halb so viel gekostet wie anfänglich veranschlagt. Mit unserem Input wurde das norwegische Ingenieur-Büro OWEC Tower AS beauftragt, das die Jackets auf eine sehr elegante Weise entwickelt hat.

Wollte REpower vor der Premiere auf dem offenen Meer ursprünglich nicht noch mehr Offshore-Anlagen an Land testen?

Das stimmt. Wir hatten anfänglich die Idee, nach dem Prototyp in Brunsbüttel im November 2004 erst noch mehrere 5M an Land aufzustellen, um so viele Erfahrungen wie irgend möglich zu sammeln. Doch dann kam plötzlich das Angebot, im schottischen Offshore-Ölfeld Beatrice zwei Anlagen aufzustellen. Die Chance haben wir natürlich nicht vorbeiziehen lassen und so standen bald die zweite und dritte 5M im Wasser. Wir haben bisher mit kleinen Projekten und einem vernünftigen Risikomanagement die Lernkurve geschickt durchschreiten können: Zuerst we continued our everyday business with the 1.5 and later the 2-megawatt turbines, which had already established themselves on the market at the time. In 2002 we formed the 'Offshore' business unit, which Dr. Martin Skiba managed intensively until the middle of 2008. This unit was intended to ensure that our forward-looking development did not get lost amongst all the day-to-day business. It wasn't always easy for this company area, as it initially cost a lot of money but did not generate any income. Nevertheless, the 5M was never a corporate risk. On the contrary, nowadays we are the forerunners in this technology and the development of the 5M had, and still has, a positive impact on our onshore business.

What did the development of the 5M cost in total?

We haven't worked it out to the penny. And the question is always which overhead costs count as development and which not. And, moreover, we received subsidies from the state of Schleswig-Holstein from the Development Program 2000 as well as from the European Commission. The funds from both programmes all together added up to around three million euros.

Let's get back to the technology: we've talked about dimensions, but what special features does the offshore turbine have in particular?

If you have good engineers involved then you will quickly agree on the question of dimensions. What is interesting in this respect really are the details. We had listened around on the market beforehand and asked what turbine was really required by the clients. Never before, for any other product, had we conducted such an intensive market analysis. However, other than saying that they would like the turbine to be "as large as possible", we received widely varying and frequently vague responses. So we had to draw our own conclusions. There was one important consideration that we had to think a long time about, though: when repairs are required do we want to replace the complete nacelle or do we do the repairs on site? With the 5M we ended up deciding on a modular construction, so that we could repair any damage on site wherever possible. Therefore, there was a relatively large, mobile crane integrated into the nacelle. Moreover, we chose a classic rotor bearing. Accordingly, the shaft was fitted with two main bearings, meaning that we could lift out the gearbox without removing the rotor. This is a great advantage at sea, as you can't put anything

Beatrice mit zwei, dann im nächsten Schritt Thornton Bank mit sechs und alpha ventus wieder mit sechs Anlagen. Als nächstes folgt Ormonde in der irischen See mit 30 Anlagen. Danach trauen wir uns auch an die größeren Projekte heran.

Beatrice war also ein guter Start ins Offshore-Geschäft?

Beatrice war mit zwei Turbinen ein Superglücksfall für uns. Wir konnten dort in einer überschaubaren Dimension die Leistungsfähigkeit der Maschinen im Wasser demonstrieren. So greifen wir seit 2006 auf Erfahrungen im Betrieb zurück, die für uns sehr wertvoll ist. Ohnehin haben wir schon früh versucht zu vermitteln, dass die sehr ambitionierten Pläne der Bundesregierung aus dem Jahr 2002 – rund 3.000 Megawatt bis 2010 – nichts werden würden, wenn wir über keine Test- und Demonstrationsflächen verfügen. Dieses riesige Investment geht doch niemand ein, wenn sofort 80 Anlagen aufgestellt werden müssen. Offshore-Parks wie Horns Rev hätten wir als REpower als Einstiegsprojekte nie gemacht. Trotzdem haben wir es mit unserem norddeutschen Patriotismus etwas bedauert, zuerst nach Schottland gehen zu müssen.

… und dann gleich ins Herz der Ölindustrie!

… das fand ich gar nicht schlecht. Wir haben den Prototypen neben dem Atomkraftwerk Brunsbüttel hingestellt und die zweite und dritte Anlage dann auf das Meer in direkter Nachbarschaft einer Ölplattform. Das finde ich sehr reizvoll. Zudem war beim Beatrice-

157 m Kölner Dom **Cologne Cathedral**
155 m Blattspitze **Blade tip**

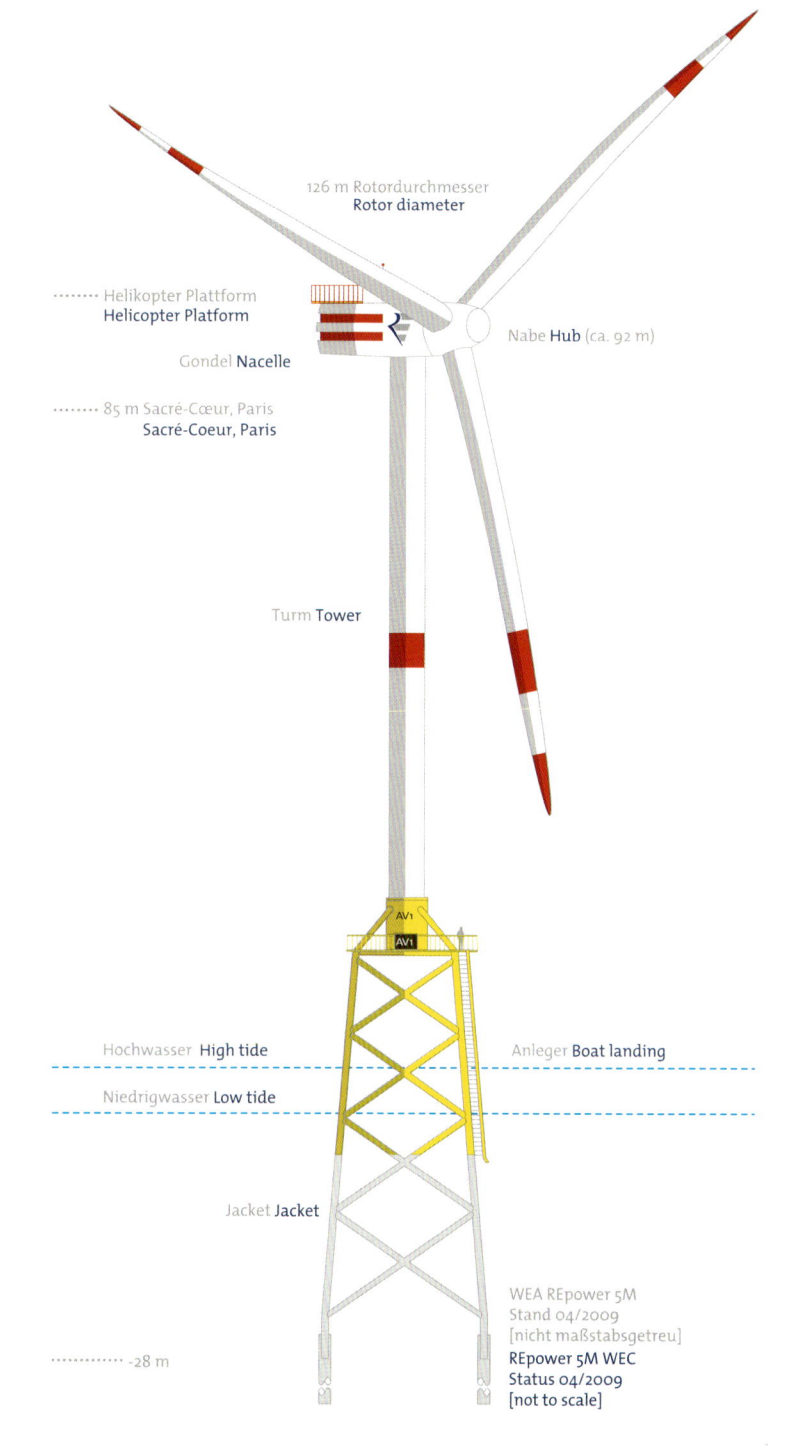

126 m Rotordurchmesser **Rotor diameter**

Helikopter Plattform
Helicopter Platform

Nabe **Hub** (ca. 92 m)

Gondel **Nacelle**

85 m Sacré-Cœur, Paris
Sacré-Coeur, Paris

Turm **Tower**

Hochwasser **High tide**
Anleger **Boat landing**
Niedrigwasser **Low tide**

Jacket **Jacket**

WEA REpower 5M
Stand 04/2009
[nicht maßstabsgetreu]
-28 m
**REpower 5M WEC
Status 04/2009
[not to scale]**

TECHNISCHE DATEN REPOWER 5M
TECHNICAL DATA REPOWER 5M

Gesamthöhe ab Meeresgrund **Overall height above seabed**	185 m
Nennleistung **Rated capacity**	5 MW
Drehzahl **Speed**	6,9 bis 12,1 U/min **5.9 to 14.8 rpm**
Einschaltwindgeschwindigkeit **Cut-in wind speed**	3,5 m/s (Windstärke 3) **3,5 m/s (wind force 3)**
Nennwindgeschwindigkeit **Rated wind speed**	13,0 m/s (Windstärke 6) **13,0 m/s (wind force 6)**
Ausschaltwindgeschwindigkeit **Cut-out wind speed**	30 m/s (Windstärke 10) **30 m/s (wind force 10)**
Blattspitzengeschwindigkeit **Blade tip speed**	80 m/s (288 km/h)
Gondelmasse mit Rotor und Nabe **Nacelle mass with rotor and hub**	410 t
Stahlmasse (Gründung, Turm, Gondel) **Steel mass (foundation, tower, nacelle)**	1.120 t
Stahlmasse der Gründung allein **Steel mass of foundation alone**	500 t

Projekt enorm wichtig, dass wir mit Talisman Energy Inc. und Scottish and Southern Energy (SSE) die passenden Partner hatten. Talisman kennt sich mit dem Offshore-Geschäft hervorragend aus. Dagegen pflegen viele klassische Energieversorger, allein schon von ihrer Unternehmenskultur her, ein anderes Risikomanagement. Entscheidungen über mehrere hunderttausend Euro werden über fünf Hierarchie-Ebenen getroffen. Bei Offshore geht das nicht. Der Projektmanager muss vor Ort schnelle, manchmal sehr teure Entscheidungen treffen, da kann man nicht lange warten. Wie Talisman das Projekt gemanagt hat, war für uns sehr lehrreich.

Für REpower hätte alpha ventus also durchaus zwei Jahre früher kommen können?
Ja, das ist so. Aber ich glaube, nicht nur für uns.

War alpha ventus für Sie ein halber Salto zurück?
Nein, ganz und gar nicht. Sie müssen Lernkurven mehrmals durchschreiten, mit verschiedenen Partnern, in unterschiedlichen Ländern. Von daher ist alpha ventus ein sehr, sehr wichtiges Demonstrationsvorhaben, weil es eben die typischen Rahmenbedingungen aufweist, die wir in deutschen Offshore-Gewässern vorfinden. Aber es bleiben in Deutschland noch viele Fragen offen. Wo sind beispielsweise die Basishäfen? Wo liegen die Engpässe in der Logistik-Kette? Diese Fragen müssen geklärt werden, wenn wir wirklich etwas bewegen wollen. Über diese zentralen Herausforderungen müssen wir in Deutschland noch mal ernsthaft nachdenken. Es gibt Flaschenhälse. Nicht umsonst wurde alpha ventus vom niederländischen Eemshaven aus errichtet.

Welche Bedeutung hat alpha ventus nun für REpower?
Für uns ist es der Startschuss ins deutsche Offshore-Geschäft und somit eine sehr wichtige Referenz für diesen Markt, der ja auch unser Heimatmarkt ist.

Was hat REpower aus alpha ventus gelernt?
Aus unserer Perspektive haben wir am meisten von der Logistik in extremen Wassertiefen lernen können. Zeiteffizienz ist ein äußerst wichtiger Faktor. Wir haben unsere Anlagen im Testfeld von alpha ventus bereits effizienter aufgestellt als beim Thornton Bank Projekt. Schon bei einer etwas schnelleren Logistik kommen unglaublich hohe Summen zusammen, die eingespart werden können. Der nächste Lernprozess liegt nun im Betrieb und in der Wartung. Welche Ansatzpunkte haben wir, die Kostenstruktur zu verbessern? Dabei liegt down anywhere out there. We took a generally spacious approach to the nacelle's design, as the mechanical fitters don't have much space to work at sea. We left a lot of space between the upper edge of the drive train and the roof for that very same reason: it needs to be possible to easily manoeuvre the crane. Our approach also took account of the need to have the nacelle completely ready and wired for installation so that it can go into operation immediately after being erected at sea.

All this means that the 5M has become quite a heavyweight ...
On the one hand, it's obviously going to weigh a bit due to the sheer size of this turbine. However, we consider the weight not to be that important at sea. Furthermore, we require a solid machine construction to protect the electronics, which are assembled completely in the back of the nacelle, from powerful vibrations caused by the wind and waves.

Is there a pressure in the nacelle when the 5M is running so that no salty air can get in?
No, we didn't do that. Corrosion at sea is overestimated anyway. We even get higher amounts of salt in places around the coast than we do on the North Sea, due to spray from the breaking surf – for example, with our projects on the coast of Australia.

Did REpower look into the offshore foundations early on?
Very much so. It was absolutely necessary for us to build up the necessary expertise in this area. Even during the development work, during our initial sales pitches it became obvious that the foundation structure would be very expensive if wrongly designed.

So this was a completely new area even for REpower, wasn't it?
Absolutely. That's why we brought in an expert from the university right from the start, who has been continually developing this area. Nowadays, we have the required know-how for offshore foundations. The motivation to develop something of our own in this new area was first and foremost our efforts to advise our clients successfully, less the desire to manufacture and supply by ourselves. The first project off the coast of Scotland demonstrated just how important possessing your own expertise is. Thanks to our advice the foundations only cost, at the end of it all, half of what was quoted at the start. Our input lead to the Norwegian engineering company OWEC Tower AS being commissioned, who developed the jackets in a very elegant way.

im Bereich Service sicherlich noch die größte Lernkurve vor uns.

Was ist für Sie in Sachen Offshore die größte technische Herausforderung?

Die schiere Größe der Anlagen. Es werden für den Bau Komponenten in Dimensionen gebraucht, die weit über gängige Industriestandards hinausgehen. Wenn man als Hersteller zu etablierten Lieferanten geht, bekommt man diese Maße noch nicht in Serie gefertigt. Das ist die große Herausforderung. Wir müssen die Lieferanten schon im Vorfeld dazu bewegen, diese Komponenten im Industriemaßstab herzustellen. Nehmen Sie zwei Beispiele: Lager und Maschinenträger, auf den ersten Blick einfacher, klassischer Maschinenbau. Im Bereich der 2-Megawatt-Anlagen können diese Komponenten noch von vielen Firmen in Europa gefertigt werden, für die 5-Megawatt-Anlage ist das nicht mehr der Fall. Das kann nur eine Handvoll Unternehmen europaweit. Es ist ausgesprochen wichtig, diesen Lieferanten Marktperspektiven zu vermitteln, damit sie langfristig in eine solche Fertigung einsteigen. Deswegen sind Rahmenlieferträge, wie wir sie beispielsweise mit RWE Innogy getroffen haben, sehr bedeutsam, um den Zulieferern zuverlässige Aussichten für ihre Produktion aufzuzeigen.

Ist Offshore ein Paradigmenwechsel für die Windenergieindustrie?

Offshore ist in der Tat ein vollkommen neues Geschäftsfeld. Mit neuen Kunden, neuen Partnern und neuen Lieferanten. Wer das nicht versteht und akzeptiert, wird scheitern. Manche vollziehen den Paradigmenwechsel mit, andere nicht. Wir müssen ins Seriengeschäft einsteigen. Nehmen wir als Beispiel die Gründungsstrukturen, die sehr teuer bleiben werden, wenn sie auf der Manufakturebene verharren. Deshalb stellen wir in Bremerhaven Experimente an, wie wir unsere Jacket-Struktur fertigungsgünstiger herstellen können. Das Jacket ist ja mehr oder weniger ein Gitterturm; an jedem Verbindungsknoten liegt prinzipiell also eine gleiche Geometrie vor. Wenn man diese Knoten nun per Hand zusammenschweißen muss, ist das sehr aufwändig und teuer. Wir versuchen daher Standardrohre einzusetzen, die durch kreisförmige Schweißnähte automatisiert mit gegossenen Knotenelementen verbunden werden.

Wann geht die 6M erstmals offshore?

Sie wird der direkte Nachfolger der 5M sein. Wir planen einen schrittweisen Übergang von 2012 bis 2014. Die ersten Ergebnisse unserer drei Prototypen onshore in Ellhöft

Didn't REpower initially intend to test more offshore turbines on land before the premiere on the open sea?

That's correct. We initially had the idea, after running the prototype in Brunsbüttel in November 2004, to first set up several 5Ms on land, in order to gather as much experience as possible. Then all of a sudden we had the chance to set up two turbines in the Scottish offshore oil field Beatrice. Of course we didn't want to miss that opportunity and soon the second and third 5M was up and standing in water. We have, up to now, been able to climb our learning curve with small projects and sensible risk management: first Beatrice with the two turbines, then the next step was Thornton Bank with six and alpha ventus again with six. The next to follow is Ormonde in the Irish Sea with 30 turbines. Then we will also dare to take on the larger projects.

Beatrice was a good start into the offshore business, then?

Beatrice was, with the two turbines, a tremendous stroke of luck for us! We were able to demonstrate the performance of the machines on the water within manageable parameters. Since 2006 we have been able to make use of this very valuable experience. Early on we tried to make it clear that the very ambitious plans of the German Federal Government approved in 2002 – of 3,000 megawatts by 2010 – would not be possible anyway if we had no test and demonstration fields. No one is going to make this huge investment if they need to set up 80 turbines right from the outset. As REpower we would never have worked with offshore farms such as Horns Rev as start-up projects. Nevertheless, as North Germans we did slightly regret that we first had to go to Scotland.

... and then straight into the heart of the oil industry ...

... I didn't think that was a bad thing at all. We set up our prototypes next to the Brunsbüttel nuclear power station and the second and third turbine at sea directly neighbouring an oil platform. I regard that as very appealing. Moreover, with the Beatrice project it was hugely important to have the right partners in Talisman Energy Inc. and Scottish and Southern Energy. Talisman had excellent knowledge of the offshore business. As opposed to this, some classic energy providers, simply due to their corporate culture, exercise a different risk management. There are frequently five levels of hierarchy that you have to go through to get decisions made on just a few thousand euros.

You can't do that in the offshore business. The project manager has to make quick, sometimes very expensive decisions on the spot; you have no time to waste. We learned a lot from how Talisman managed the project.

Would it have been better for REpower if alpha ventus had come two years earlier?

Yes, that's right – but not only for us.

Was alpha ventus one step back after two steps forward?

No, not at all. You have to climb your learning curve a number of times, with various different partners, in various different countries. For that reason alpha ventus is a very, very important demonstration, as it illustrates the typical framework conditions that we find in German offshore waters. But there are still several unanswered questions in Germany: for example, which are the best ports to start from? Where are the bottlenecks in the logistics chain? These questions need resolving if we really do want to do great things. We have to take a serious look at these key challenges in Germany once again. There are bottlenecks. There was a reason why alpha ventus was set up from the Dutch port of Eemshaven.

What significance does alpha ventus now have for REpower?

For us it means the starting gun for our entry into the German offshore business and thus a very important reference on this market, which is also our domestic market.

What has REpower learned from alpha ventus?

From our perspective we have been able to learn the most from the logistics required in extreme water depths. Efficient usage of time is an extremely important factor. We were already able to erect our turbines in the alpha ventus test field more efficiently than in the Thornton Bank project. Even slightly quicker logistics can add up to incredibly large savings. The next learning process involves operation and maintenance. What starting points are there to improve cost structures? We certainly have a steep learning curve ahead of us when it comes to the areas of maintenance and operation.

What would you say is the greatest technical challenge in offshore matters?

The sheer size of the turbines. Components are required that have dimensions well over and above common industrial standards. As a manufacturer, if you go to the established suppliers you won't get equipment in these dimensions serially produced yet – that's the great challenge. We have to get the suppliers to make these components in industrial

nahe der dänischen Grenze sind sehr gut. Sie spiegeln das wider, was wir in unserer Entwicklungsabteilung prognostiziert haben. Wir sind deshalb sehr zufrieden.

Einige Experten sprechen schon von Anlagen der 10-Megawatt-Klasse. Planen auch Sie noch größere Offshore-Anlagen?

Wir reden zwar auch über 10-Megawatt Turbinen, obgleich es im Markt vermutlich erst einmal mit sieben Megawatt weitergehen wird. Viel wichtiger ist für mich im Moment aber, wie ich die Industrietauglichkeit der 5M und 6M voranbringe. Ich bin fest davon überzeugt, dass wir in der Lage sein werden, die Kosten nochmals erheblich zu senken. Es geht nicht nur um die Anlage an sich, sondern auch um die Gründung, Logistik und Errichtung auf dem Meer. Wir müssen uns als Hersteller weiter intensiv um diese Dinge kümmern, um nicht von anderen abhängig zu werden. Wir wollen uns in all diesen Fragen weiterhin kräftig einmischen.

Zu welchen Einspeise-Tarifen ist Offshore-Windenergie wirtschaftlich?

Diese Frage lässt sich eindimensional nicht beantworten. In jedem Land herrschen eigene Rahmenbedingungen. In deutschen Offshore-Gewässern wäre ein Betrieb ohne das Infrastrukturplanungsbeschleunigungsgesetz derzeit wirtschaftlich sicher noch nicht darstellbar.

Wie beurteilen Sie den Netzausbau auf See?

Wir Deutschen sind ja in vielen Dingen Planungsweltmeister. Allerdings gibt es für die Netzanbindung noch keinen Masterplan, und wir sind mit der Netzanbindung noch nicht sehr weit vorangekommen. Darüber wundere ich mich sehr. So ist auch weiterhin nicht eindeutig klar, wie wir den Strom von den besagten 20 Gigawatt, die in der Nord- und Ostsee geplant sind, an Land bekommen. Die Situation ist auch insofern erstaunlich, als doch jeder weiß, wie lange es dauert, bis ein Projekt dieser Größenordnung realisiert wird. Wir brauchen heute große zusätzliche Investitionen, um die Offshore-Windenergie von morgen ins Netz einzuspeisen. Dies würde auch die Finanzierung erleichtern. Ob die Banken tatsächlich ins Offshore-Windgeschäft einsteigen, hängt sicher auch davon ab, ob wir beweisen können, dass die Windenergie auf See genauso profitabel sein kann wie an Land.

Wie viele Offshore-Anlagen von REpower stehen bis 2020 im Meer?

(Überlegt etwas länger) Die 1.000. Offshore-Anlage müssten wir dann installiert haben.

dimensions beforehand. Let's look at two examples: bearings and mainframe, which at first glance are simple, classic machine components. In the 2-megawatt turbine area there are several companies in Europe that can manufacture them; this is no longer the case for the 5-megawatt turbine. There are only a handful of companies in the whole of Europe who can do it. It is extremely important to explain to these suppliers what the market perspectives are so they can enter into this type of production in the long term. That's why large framework contracts, like the ones signed by us with RWE Innogy, are very significant – to demonstrate reliable perspectives to the suppliers for their production.

Does offshore represent a paradigm shift for the wind energy industry?

Offshore really is a completely new business sector, with new clients, new partners and new suppliers. If you do not understand and accept this you will fail. Some can cope with this paradigm shift, others not. We have to get into serial production. Let's take the example of foundation structures, which will remain very expensive if we stay on the manufacturing level. That's why we are conducting experiments in Bremerhaven to find out how we can make our jacket structure cheaper to produce. The jacket is more or less a lattice tower and in principle there is the same geometry at all the connection points. If you have to weld these nodes by hand then that's a lot of work to do and it's expensive. We're therefore looking into using standard pipes that can then be connected to the cast node elements in an automated way, using circular weld joints.

When will the first 6M go offshore?

That will be the direct successor to the 5M. We're planning a stepwise transition from 2012 to 2014. The first results from our three prototypes onshore in Ellhöft near the Danish border are very good and they reflect what our Development Department predicted. We are therefore very happy!

Some experts are already talking about turbines of the 10-megawatt class. Are you also planning larger offshore turbines?

We are, in fact, also talking about 10-megawatt turbines – even though the market will presumably move on initially with 7 megawatts. What is more important to me at the moment is how I improve the industrial feasibility of the 5Ms and 6Ms. I am convinced that we will be able to further reduce the costs considerably. The issue is not only the turbine itself, but the foundation, logistics and erection at sea. As a manufacturer we have to do more to improve these things, so as not to be dependent on others. We want to get thoroughly involved in all these aspects.

At what feed-in tariffs does offshore wind power become economical?

That can't be answered in a one-dimensional way. There are framework conditions that differ from country to country. In German offshore waters, operation would certainly not be economically viable at the moment without the German Act on Accelerated Infrastructure Planning.

What's your opinion on the development of the grid network at sea?

In many ways we Germans are world champions at planning things ... but as yet there is no master plan for grid connections. We have not got very far with this topic – and I am very surprised. It is still not absolutely clear how we will bring the electricity from the aforementioned 20-gigawatt installations planned for the North and Baltic Sea ashore. This is astounding, seeing as everyone knows how long it takes to realize a project of these dimensions. We need large additional investments today to feed tomorrow's offshore wind energy into the grid. This would also make the financing easier. Whether the banks really do get into the offshore wind energy business will certainly depend also on whether we can prove that wind energy at sea can be just as profitable as it is on land.

How many offshore turbines from REpower will there be standing in the sea by 2020?

(After a while of thinking) We should have installed our 1,000th offshore turbine by then.

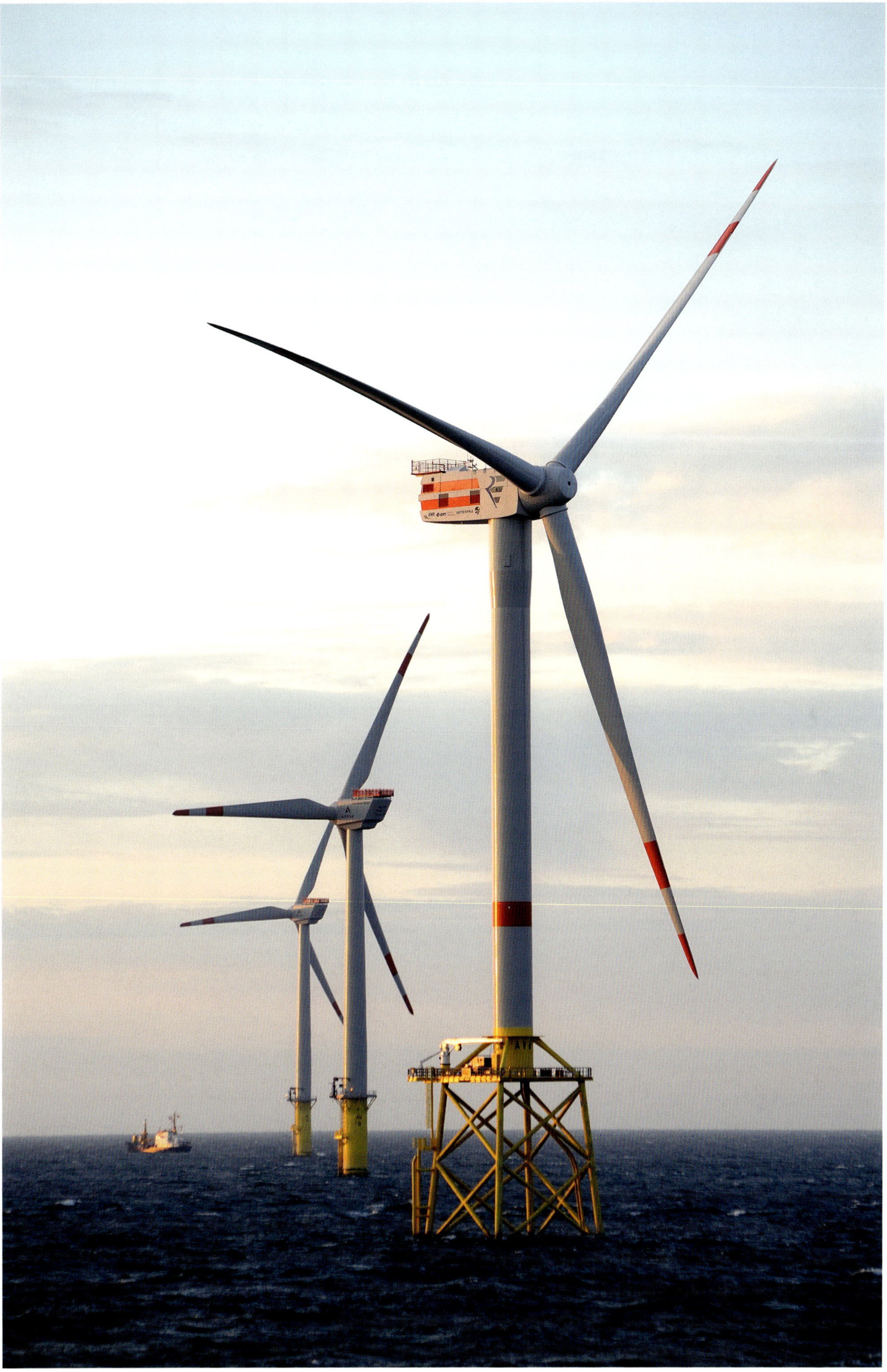

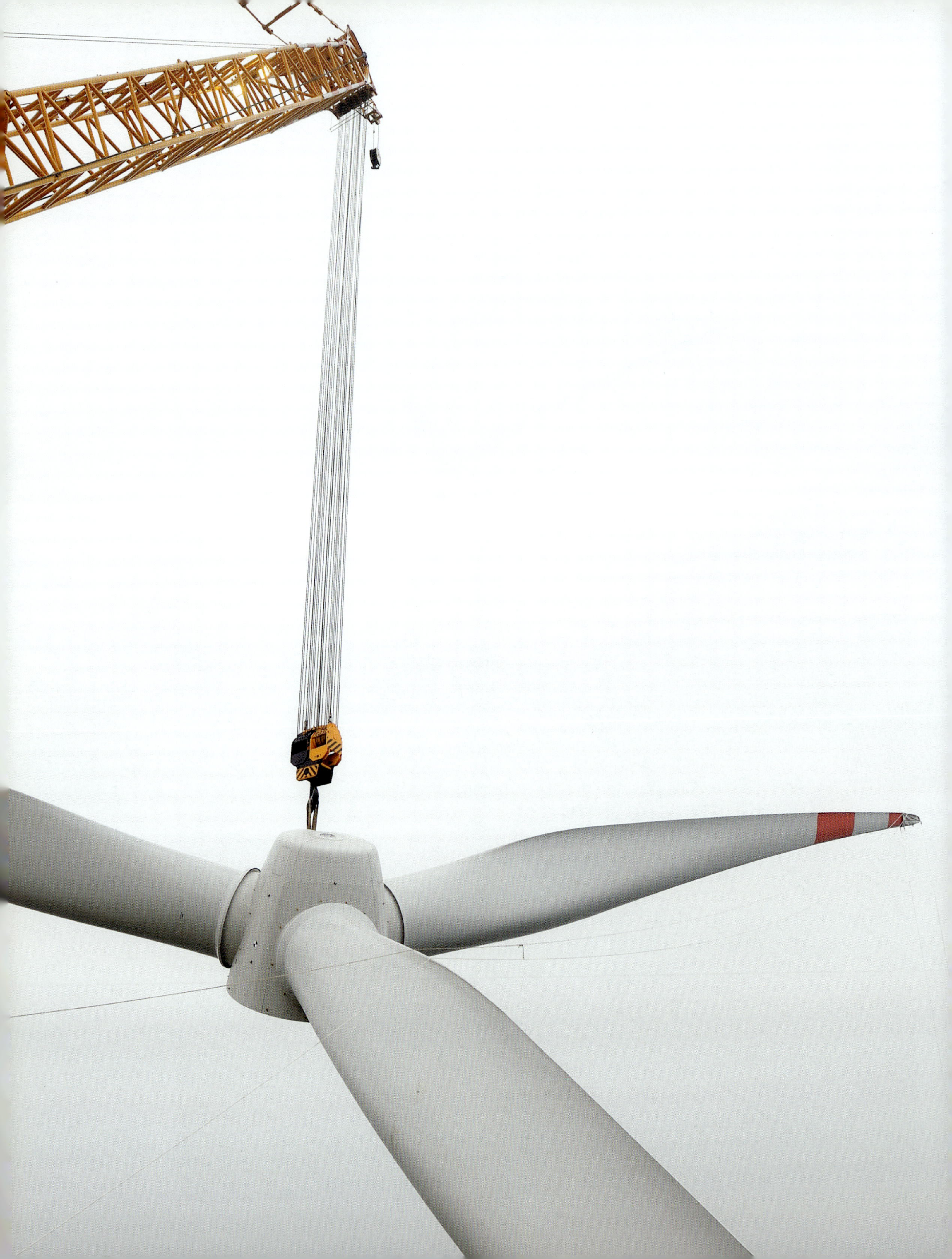

Die Zukunft hat bereits begonnen
The future has already begun

Die Welt blickte im Dezember 2009 gebannt nach Kopenhagen. Der Weltklimagipfel sollte die Wende in der globalen Klima- und Energiepolitik einläuten. Das Ergebnis allerdings enttäuschte: Die Vorstellungen der Regierungschefs aus fast 200 Staaten lagen zu weit auseinander. Immerhin einigte man sich im Grundsatz auf ein verbindliches Minimalziel. Der Ausstoß von Klimagasen soll so weit reduziert werden, dass sich die Erde nicht um mehr als zwei Grad Celsius bis zum Jahre 2050 erwärmt.

Schon heute ist der einsetzende Klimawandel in vielen Regionen der Welt sichtbar und verursacht große Schäden. Dennoch: Es ist jetzt nicht die Zeit, den Kopf in den Sand zu stecken – auch wenn es (noch) kein Nachfolgeabkommen zum Kyoto-Protokoll gibt. Ganz im Gegenteil, denn durch das CO_2-Geschacher in Kopenhagen ist einmal mehr deutlich geworden, dass ein grundsätzliches Umdenken dringender denn je notwendig ist, um auch zukünftigen Generationen Lebens- oder besser gesagt Überlebensperspektiven bieten zu können. Dieses Umdenken erfordert einen Umbau der modernen Gesellschaften, der in alle Bereiche hineinreicht: Mobilität, Transport, private Haushalte, Industrie und nicht zuletzt in die Energiewirtschaft selbst. Dekarbonisierung lautet eines der Schlüsselwörter. Der Terminus meint nichts anderes als die Abkehr von der auf Erdöl, Erdgas und Kohle basierten Wirtschaftsweise. Selbst die größten Skeptiker bestreiten nicht mehr, dass die Kehrtwende nur mit Hilfe der erneuerbaren Energien möglich sein wird. Die fossile wie auch die atomare Energieerzeugung werden Schritt für Schritt abgelöst werden müssen, damit die Welt aus der CO_2-Falle herauskommt. Zudem treiben die schwindenden Vorräte an Kohle, Erdöl, Erdgas und Uran die Energiekosten in die Höhe. Nur die Länder, die rechtzeitig in erneuerbare Alternativen investieren, können aus dieser Preisspirale aussteigen, energiepolitische Unabhängigkeit erreichen und langfristig Versorgungssicherheit gewährleisten.

In dem Umbau-Szenario ist die Windenergie bisher die treibende Kraft. Innerhalb von nur zwei Jahrzehnten hat sie sich von einer Nische zu einer beachtlichen Industrie entwickelt, die weltweit mehrere hunderttausend Menschen beschäftigt. Windenergie ist in Deutschland, Dänemark, Spanien, China und den USA, um nur einige Länder zu nennen, inzwischen eine feste, nicht mehr wegzudenkende Größe in der Stromerzeugung. Jahr für Jahr bricht der Ausbau der Windenergie neue Rekorde. Diese Anstrengungen werden aber noch nicht genügen, will man den Windanteil an der Gesamtstromerzeugung wesentlich ausbauen. Dabei sind sich alle Experten darin einig, dass eine Steigerung nicht allein an Land zu erzielen sein wird. Insbesondere im dicht besiedelten Europa stehen an Land nur begrenzt Flächen zur Verfügung. Außerdem stößt das Wachstum beim Natur- und Landschaftsschutz an seine Grenzen.

In December 2009 the world watched events in Copenhagen, spellbound. The UN Climate Summit was supposed to be the turning point for global climate and energy policy. However, the results were disappointing: the leaders of almost 200 countries in attendance were too far apart in their positions. Yet at least there was basic agreement on a minimal goal – to reduce greenhouse gas emissions in an attempt to stop the planet warming by more than two degrees Celsius by 2050.

The first signs of a changing climate are already evident in many parts of the world, and climate change is already causing much damage. However, this is not the time to stick one's head in the sand and hope it goes away, even if there is not (yet) a successor agreement to the Kyoto Protocol. Quite the contrary: the exhaustive negotiations in Copenhagen once again showed clearly that a fundamental turnaround in outlook is needed more urgently than ever, if future generations are to have a chance of an acceptable quality of life, or even survival. To be effective, a restructuring of modern society is needed across all areas – mobility, transportation, private households, industry, and of course the energy industry in particular. Decarbonisation is one of the key words, meaning a shift away from an economy based on oil, gas and coal. Even the most sceptical no longer dispute that this will be possible only with the use of renewable energies. Fossil fuel and nuclear power will have to be replaced step by step if the world is to escape from the CO_2 trap. Furthermore, dwindling reserves of coal, petroleum, natural gas and uranium are driving up energy prices. Only countries that invest early on in renewable energies will be able to escape this price spiral, become energy-independent and ensure their own long-term energy security.

Wind-energy has thus far been the driving force in this scenario. In just two decades it has grown from a niche market to a major industry that employs several hundred thousand people worldwide. Wind energy is an established and accepted factor in electricity generation in Germany, Denmark, Spain, China and the US, to name just a few countries. The expansion of wind-energy capacity breaks new records year after year. But these efforts by themselves will not be enough to substantially boost wind's share in overall electrical generation. All the experts agree that such an expansion will not be possible on land alone. Especially in densely populated Europe, there is simply not enough space available.

Repowering, that means the replacement of older turbines with larger and more modern ones, will certainly increase in the future, and priority areas for wind energy use will be expanded, but this expansion cannot go beyond a certain limit. Therefore, along with growth in onshore wind energy, the development of offshore capacity must be pursued. The sea offers plenty of space for the clean energy of the future. A con-

Repowering, also das Ersetzen alter Windenergieanlagen durch größere Turbinen, wird in Zukunft sicher zunehmen und die Vorrangflächen für Windenergie werden noch ausgeweitet werden, doch der Ausbau kann über ein bestimmtes Niveau nicht hinausgehen. Parallel zum Windenergieausbau an Land muss die Richtung konsequent „offshore" heißen: Das Meer bietet Freiraum für eine saubere Energie der Zukunft. Mit einem weiterhin forcierten Ausbau der Offshore-Windenergie kann es gelingen, im Maßstab von konventionellen Großkraftwerken die Stromversorgung der Zukunft nachhaltig zu gestalten.

Offshore-Offensive – Ausbau ohne Grenzen?

Eine ganze Dekade dauerte es in Deutschland, bis mit dem Testfeld alpha ventus der erste große Schritt ins Offshore-Zeitalter unternommen wurde. Langwierige politische Diskussionen wurden geführt und so manchem Pionier ging finanziell die Puste aus, bevor der Startschuss endlich fiel. Derweil liefen die europäischen Nachbarn dem Windweltmeister Deutschland in Sachen Offshore-Windenergie den Rang ab. Schaut man aber genau hin, wird deutlich, dass es für den Verzug durchaus triftige Gründe gab. Sprecher von Naturschutz, Tourismus, der Fischerei, der Marine, der Schifffahrt und der Segler brachten ihre berechtigten Bedenken vor und auch aus den Reihen der Energiewirtschaft selbst wurden Einwände laut. Die Debatten verzögerten den

tinued push to expand offshore wind energy capacity can succeed in creating a future source of sustainable electricity generation, on the scale of conventional power plants.

The offshore push – an unlimited expansion?

It took an entire decade for Germany to take its first major step into the offshore age with the realisation of the alpha ventus test field. Lengthy political discussions caused some of the pioneering developers to run out of funds before they could even get started. Meanwhile, European neighbours forged ahead, leaving Germany the leading wind-energy country, behind. But a closer look reveals that there were some good reasons behind the delays. Advocates of nature protection, tourism, fisheries, the Navy and shipping interests were able to make their concerns heard, and the energy industry also expressed its own reservations. The debate caused repeated delays of German offshore projects, while inadequate economic framework conditions, as well as unresolved issues with grid connections hindered all progress. But this long process has brought some benefits, too. Today's offshore wind turbines have much higher rated capacities than a few years ago, and the Infrastructure Planning Acceleration Law passed by the German Bundestag in 2006 has made grid connection easier. In addition, as of 2009 a planning ordinance for the German Exclusive Economic Zone

Beginn der deutschen Offshore-Projekte immer wieder, zusätzlich erschweren die damals unzureichenden ökonomischen Rahmenbedingungen und die ungeklärten Fragen zur Netzanbindung jeden Projektfortschritt. Immerhin hat die lange Wartezeit einige Vorteile mit sich gebracht. Die Hersteller von Windenergieanlagen bauen inzwischen erheblich leistungsstärkere Windturbinen und die Netzanbindung ist durch das Infrastrukturplanungsbeschleunigungsgesetz verbessert worden. Zudem steht seit 2009 mit einer Verordnung zur Raumordnung in der Ausschließlichen Wirtschaftszone (AWZ) erstmals ein Katalog zur Verfügung, der ein nachhaltiges Handeln auf dem Meer vorschreibt. Wildwuchs vor den Küsten soll es nicht geben. Diese grundsätzliche Klärung ist enorm wichtig, um den Konflikt zwischen Meeresraum (Natur) und Offshore-Windenergie schon im frühen Stadium zu vermeiden. Wie an Land sind auch auf hoher See Schutzgebiete eingerichtet worden. Deshalb liegen die deutschen Offshore-Projekte so weit draußen auf dem Meer, in ausreichender Distanz zum Nationalpark Wattenmeer – der Kinderstube der Nordsee und seit 2009 UNESCO-Weltnaturerbe. Der Schutz der Meeresökologie gehört zu den großen Herausforderungen bei der Entwicklung der Offshore-Windenergie in Deutschland; aus diesem Grund nimmt die ökologische Begleitforschung im Testfeld alpha ventus einen hohen Stellenwert ein. Deutschland steht aber mit seinen Offshore-Plänen in der Nord- und Ostsee bei Weitem nicht alleine da: Fast alle Anrainerstaaten wollen

In schwindelerregender Höhe wird der Rotorstern ans Maschinenhaus angedockt. Präzisionsarbeit, bei der vom erfahrenen Aufbauteam höchste Konzentration abverlangt wird.
The rotor star is docked to the nacelle at breathtaking heights. Precision and maximum concentration are required from the experienced construction team.

in den nächsten Jahren offshore gehen. Die European Wind Energy Association (EWEA) prognostiziert sogar, dass bis 2030 in europäischen Meeren rund 150 Gigawatt installiert sein werden. Dies sind bei heutiger Leistung rund 30.000 Windenergieanlagen. Ein Blick auf die jüngste Geschichte und zugleich auf das gegenwärtig Machbare kann den Entwicklungshorizont abstecken: „Ich gehe davon aus, dass die Offshore-Windenergie ein Wachstum erleben wird, das sich mit der Entwicklung an Land in den letzten 20 Jahren vergleichen lässt", prognostiziert Andreas Wagner, Geschäftsführer der Stiftung Offshore-Windenergie. Noch 1995 waren in der gesamten EU lediglich 2.500 Megawatt Windenergieleistung installiert, ungefähr so viel wie die europäische Offshore-Leistung zu Beginn 2010. Die Gründe für die neue Dynamik beim Ausbau von Offshore-Windenergieanlagen liegen auf der Hand: Die Windenergie ist heute in der Lage, im großen Stil erneuerbaren Strom wirtschaftlich zu erzeugen.

Europäische Perspektiven

Die Bundesregierung unterstützt seit Längerem den Ausbau der Offshore-Windenergie. In der deutschen AWZ sollen bis zum Jahr 2030 bis zu 25.000 Megawatt installiert sein und so viel Strom liefern wie keine andere erneuerbare Energiequelle in Deutschland. Nach der „Leitstudie 2050" des Bundesumweltministeriums von 2008 könnten die erneuerbaren Energien schon im Jahr 2030 den deutschen Strombedarf zu 50 Prozent decken. Ein knappes Drittel dieser Strommenge soll allein von Offshore-Windparks erzeugt werden.

Unterdessen schlafen die übrigen Anrainerstaaten von Nord- und Ostsee nicht. Vor allem die britische Regierung hat ehrgeizige Ziele definiert, setzt auf die Nordsee als das kommende Powerhouse Europas. Gemessen an der auf See installierten Leistung ist Großbritannien schon heute führend. Bis Ende 2009 waren rund um die Britischen Inseln insgesamt knapp 600 Megawatt am Netz. Die erste Ausschreibungsrunde Englands ist fast abgeschlossen, eine zweite befindet sich in der Umsetzung und die Ergebnisse der dritten wurden Anfang 2010 bekanntgegeben. Schottland hat eine eigene Ausschreibungsrunde gestartet, sodass sich die Leistung der geplanten britischen Offshore-Windparks auf 40 Gigawatt aufsummiert – deutlich mehr als in Deutschland.

Netzwerke im Meer

Unabhängig davon, was die Zukunft tatsächlich bringt, müssen die Windparks, die in den nächsten Jahrzehnten in Nord- und Ostsee errichtet werden, nach und nach zu einem großen Verbundsystem zusammenwachsen, denn weder Angebot noch Nachfrage nach elektrischer Energie sind konstant. Es wird notwendig sein, regionale Schwankungen der Stromeinspeisung durch einen überregionalen Stromaustausch auszugleichen, um den Strom möglichst bedarfsgerecht und wirtschaftlich anbieten zu können. Die Offshore-Windparks der Zukunft werden also nicht nur jeweils mit ihrem nächsten Einspeisepunkt an der Küste, sondern auch untereinander verbunden sein, sodass ein europäisches Netz („Supergrid") entsteht. Eine Vorreiterrolle könnte das Projekt Kriegers Flak in der Ostsee einnehmen, wo drei Netzbetreiber aus Dänemark, Schweden und Deutschland schon bald ein gemeinsames Meeresverbundnetz errichten wollen. Langfristig wird der Stromaustausch durch Seekabelverbindungen zwischen Deutschland, Skandinavien, Großbritannien, Frankreich, Belgien und den

(EEZ) provided the first official catalogue of measures for sustainable economic activity at sea. This means that chaotic developments off the coasts of Germany will be avoided. This basic tool is of enormous importance for preventing conflicts between the needs of the maritime environment and offshore wind energy at an early stage. Just as on land, nature protection zones have been set up at sea, which is why the German offshore projects are located so far from shore, at a safe distance from the Wadden Sea National Park, the 'nursery' of the North Sea which became a UNESCO World Natural Heritage area in 2009. Protection of the maritime environment is one of the major challenges in the development of offshore wind energy in Germany, and ecological research is a high priority at the alpha ventus test field.

But Germany is not alone in its plans for offshore wind energy in the North and Baltic Seas. Almost all European countries with a coastline plan to go offshore in the next few years. The European Wind Energy Association (EWEA) predicts that up to 150 gigawatts could be installed in European waters by 2030. At today's output levels, that would translate into 30,000 wind turbines. A look at recent history and at what is currently feasible gives an idea of the prospects: "I predict that the growth rates in offshore wind energy will be comparable to the development on land during the last 20 years," says Andreas Wagner, Managing Director of the German Offshore Wind Energy Foundation. In 1995 there were only 2,500 megawatts of wind energy capacity installed across the entire EU. In early 2010, more than 75,000 megawatts have been installed across the EU, of which about 2,000 megawatts offshore. The reasons for the new dynamism in offshore wind expansion are not hard to find: today, the wind industry is in a position to generate renewable energy economically and on a large scale.

European outlook

The German government has been supporting the expansion of offshore wind energy for some time now. Official plans call for up to 25,000 megawatts to be installed in the German EEZ by 2030, delivering more power than any other renewable energy source in the country. According to the 'Lead Study 2050' commissioned by the German Environmental Ministry in 2008, renewable energy could cover 50 percent of Germany's electricity requirements as early as 2030. Just under a third of this is to be generated by offshore wind farms alone.

Of course, other countries around the North and Baltic Sea have not been sleeping. The British government in particular has set itself ambitious goals and is betting on the North Sea as the future powerhouse of Europe. Measured in capacity currently installed at sea, Great Britain has become the European leader. By the end of 2009 there were already just under 600 megawatts of generation capacity off the British Isles. The first Round of British tenders has been almost fully realised, a second one is being implemented, and the results of Round 3 with a total offshore potential of 25 gigawatts were announced in early 2010.

Offshore grids

Whatever the future holds, the wind farms that are to be set up in the North and Baltic Seas in the next few decades will need to grow into one large, networked power transmission system - because neither supply nor demand for electricity are constant. It will therefore be necessary to balance regional power feed-in fluctuations via a cross-regional

Niederlanden überall möglich sein. Eine entsprechende Initiative der Nordseeanrainerstaaten wurde Ende 2009 auf den Weg gebracht. Am Ende könnten dann britische Windparks Strom nach Deutschland liefern, wenn der Wind vor der deutschen Küste abflaut – und umgekehrt. Außerdem muss die Stromerzeugung auf dem Meer mit der an Land abgestimmt werden. Wenn etwa über der Nordsee ein Sturm aufzieht, der alle Windparks in den folgenden zehn oder 20 Stunden mit Nennleistung laufen lässt, müssen die konventionellen Kraftwerke heruntergeregelt werden oder darüber hinaus neue Speicherkapazitäten, wie etwa die norwegischen Wasserreservoirs, ins Stromnetz mit einbezogen werden, damit kein Stromüberschuss entsteht. Dazu muss man das Wettergeschehen mindestens zwölf, möglichst 24 Stunden im Voraus kennen. Die Wettervorhersage durch Prognosesysteme gewinnt also weiter an Bedeutung. Windenergieforscher setzten diese Systeme schon seit einigen Jahren in Zusammenarbeit mit den Übertragungsnetzbetreibern ein. Die Prognose betrifft zwar bisher nur die Stromeinspeisung der deutschen Onshore-Windparks, doch sind die bisherigen Erfahrungen so gut, dass man die Prognosesysteme nun auf die Offshore-Windparks ausdehnen will. Neben den ausgeklügelten Methoden der Windvorhersagen und dem physischen Ausbau der Netze verspricht für die Abnehmerseite beispielsweise die Elektromobilität neue Perspektiven für eine technisch machbare wie intelligente Netzintegration: Große Flotten von Elektroautos könnten mit ihren Batterien in Zukunft einen Teil des gewonnenen Stroms vom Meer speichern.

Sollen bis 2030 allein in der deutschen Nordsee tatsächlich 25.000 Megawatt installiert werden, müssen bis dahin noch gewaltige Anstrengungen unternommen werden. Schon heute sind neue Logistikkonzepte für den Aufbau, Betrieb und die Wartung solcher Anlagen gefordert. Es entstehen derzeit entlang der Küsten schon zusätzliche Fertigungskapazitäten für den Bau von Gründungen und Windenergieanlagen. Die Automatisierung der Produktion wird voranschreiten und eine Standardturbine wird in einigen Jahren wahrscheinlich schon zehn Megawatt oder noch mehr Leistung aufweisen. Die Windenergie bleibt somit ein wichtiger Jobmotor in Deutschland und in ganz Europa. Die EWEA rechnet damit, dass 2030 europaweit etwa 375.000 Menschen in der Windenergiebranche arbeiten werden, davon allein 215.000 Beschäftigte im Offshore-Bereich.

Der Windpark alpha ventus ist nicht nur für die deutsche Offshore-Industrie ein wichtiger Meilenstein, sondern für ganz Europa, weil dieser Pionierwindpark den Beweis liefert, dass Projekte weit draußen auf dem Meer in tiefen Gewässern keine ferne Vision mehr sind, sondern technisch wie ökonomisch erfolgreich realisierbar.

Die Zukunft hat schon begonnen. Sowohl für die Windenergie als auch für die Energiewirtschaft bricht eine neue Ära an. „Der Aufbau der Windenergie seit den siebziger Jahren war schon ziemlich aufregend, aber die nächsten drei Jahrzehnte werden es kaum weniger werden", blickt Jos Beurskens, niederländischer Windpionier der ersten Stunde und Ehrendoktor der Universität Oldenburg, sicherlich stellvertretend für eine ganze Branche, gespannt in die Zukunft. Die Chancen auf dem Meer sind groß, die Herausforderungen wohl noch größer.

power exchange, to offer a power supply that is economical and meets demand. Offshore wind farms of the future will not just be connected to their nearest feed-in point ashore, but will also be interconnected with each other to create a pan-European 'supergrid'. The Kriegers Flak project could play a pioneering role in the Baltic Sea, where three system operators from Denmark, Sweden and Germany intend to establish an interconnected joint offshore grid. Power-supply exchange via submarine cables between Germany, Scandinavia, Great Britain, France, Belgium and the Netherlands will be possible just about everywhere in the North Sea in the long run. An initiative by these North Sea-neighbouring countries was launched in late 2009. Finally, wind farms off the UK will supply their electric power to Germany when there is a lull in the wind off the German coast, and vice-versa. Furthermore, the power produced at sea must be balanced with that generated on land. If a storm over the North Sea makes all wind farms run at rated capacity for ten or twenty hours, conventional power plants will need to be throttled back. Alternatively, new additional storage capacities such as Norwegian hydropower reservoirs will have to be integrated in order to avoid excess power generation. To do this well, it is necessary to know meteorological conditions at least twelve or even 24 hours in advance. This means that accurate wind-forecasting systems will become even more important. Wind-energy researchers have already deployed these systems for a couple of years in collaboration with transmission system operators. To date, forecasting has only concerned the feed-in of power produced by the German onshore wind farms. However, the experience gained thus far has been so positive that it is planned to extend the forecasting systems to offshore wind farms. In addition to sophisticated weather forecasting techniques and physical grid expansion, electric cars and e-mobility systems offer promising new possibilities on the demand side for smart grid integration, already technically feasible today. In future, large fleets of electric cars may be able to store a part of the electricity generated at sea in their batteries.

If 25,000 megawatts are indeed to be installed in the German North Sea alone by 2030, tremendous efforts will need to be made. New logistics concepts are already required for setting up, operating and maintaining these turbines. Additional manufacturing capacity is currently being built for the construction of foundations and wind turbines along the coast. Production automation will make progress, and a standard turbine could have a capacity of ten megawatts or more in a few years' time. Wind energy will remain an important driver of job growth in Germany and throughout Europe. The EWEA assumes that by 2030 some 375,000 people will be working in the wind-energy industry Europe-wide, of which 215,000 alone will be employed in the offshore sector. The alpha ventus test field is a major milestone – not just for the German offshore industry but for the whole of Europe, because this pioneering wind farm proves that projects in deep waters far out at sea are no longer just a distant vision.

The future has already begun. A new era is dawning for wind power as well as for the energy industry. "Building wind-power systems from scratch back in the 'seventies was already exciting, but this will be even more true over the next three decades," says Jos Beurskens, Dutch wind pioneer of the early days and honorary Doctor at Oldenburg University. Just like the rest of the industry, he is very positive about future prospects. Yet while the opportunities out at sea are big, the challenges ahead may be even bigger.

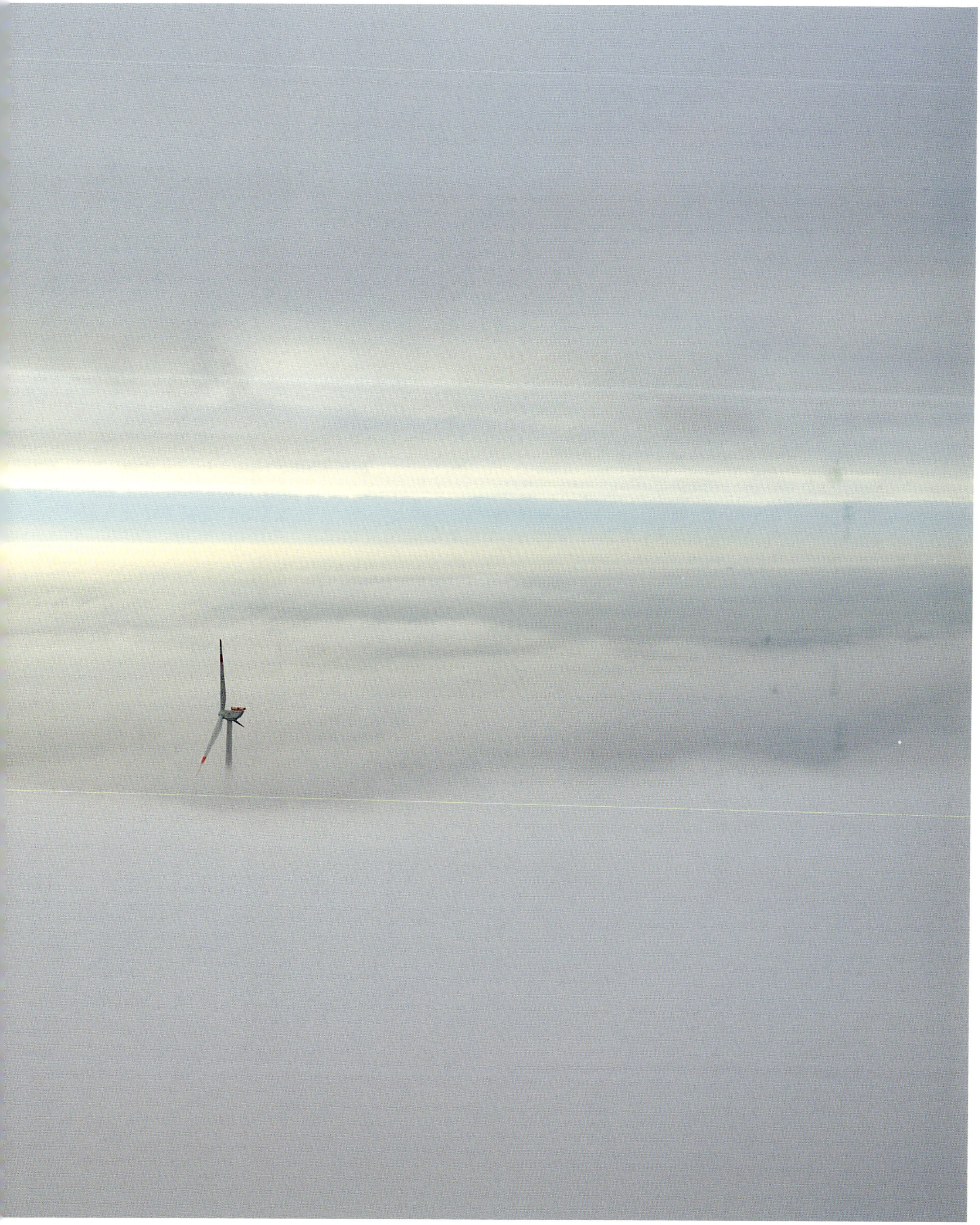

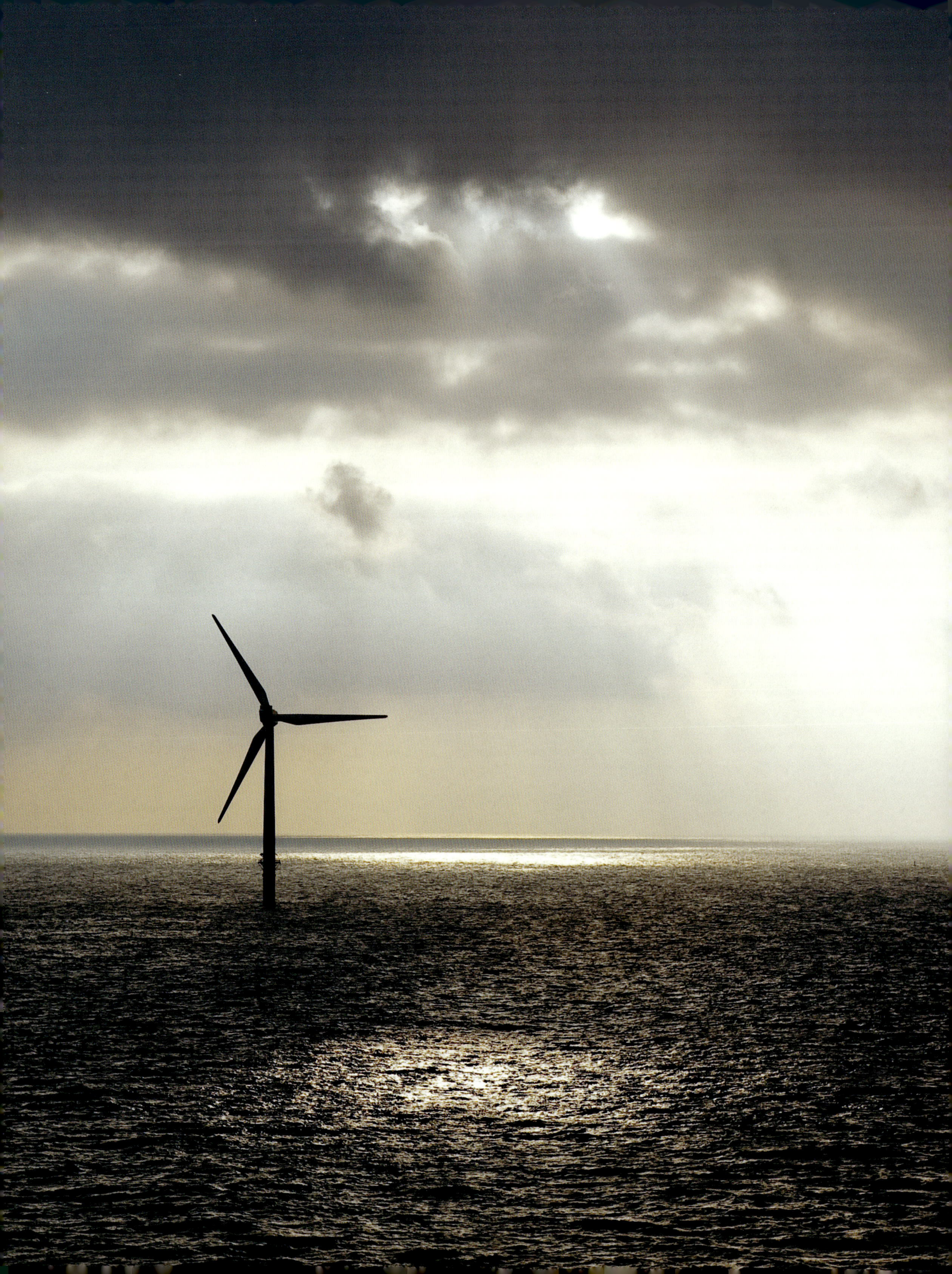

Anhang Appendix

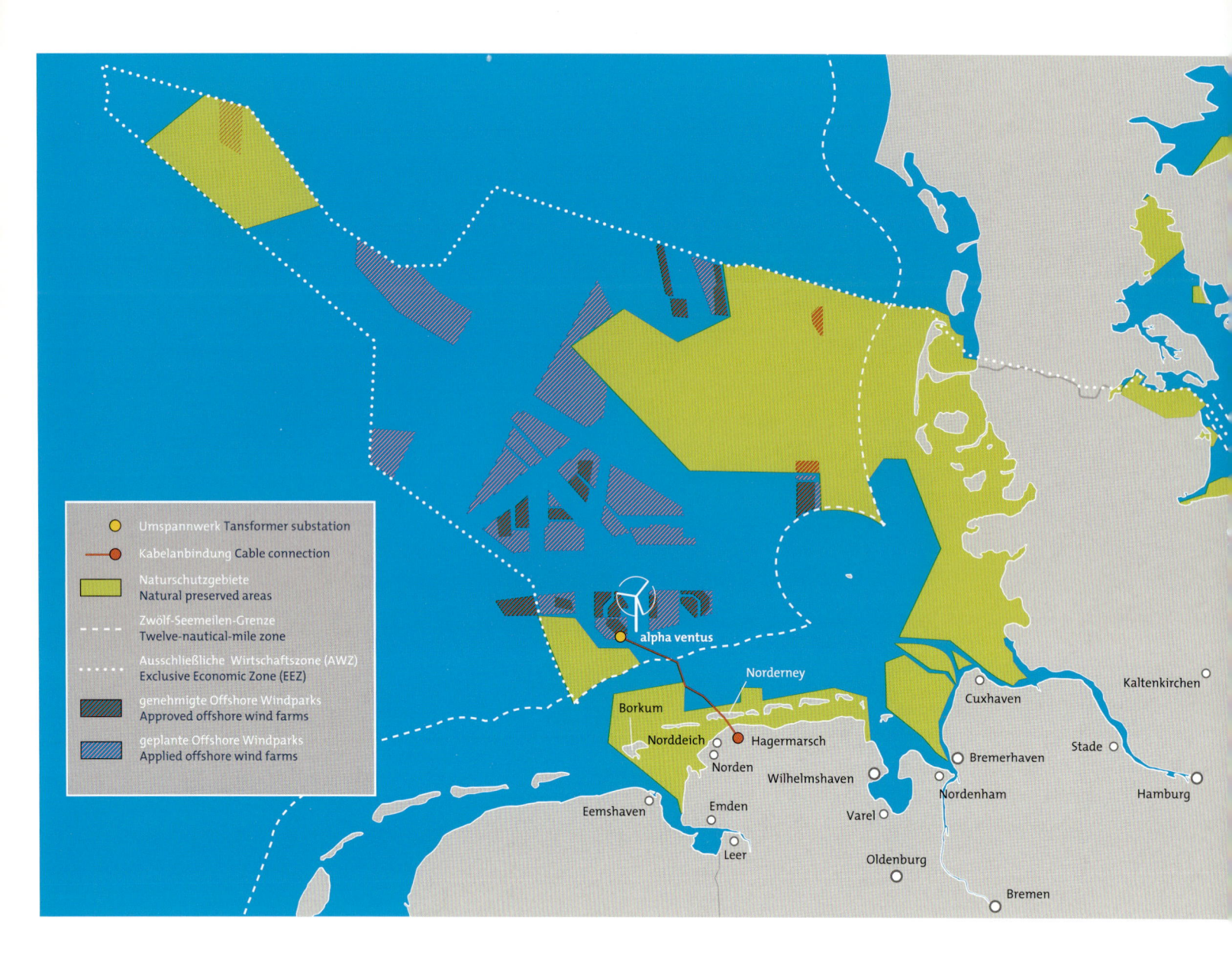

Legend (map):
- Umspannwerk Tansformer substation
- Kabelanbindung Cable connection
- Naturschutzgebiete / Natural preserved areas
- Zwölf-Seemeilen-Grenze / Twelve-nautical-mile zone
- Ausschließliche Wirtschaftszone (AWZ) / Exclusive Economic Zone (EEZ)
- genehmigte Offshore Windparks / Approved offshore wind farms
- geplante Offshore Windparks / Applied offshore wind farms

Betreiber & Initiatoren & Genehmigungs-behörde alpha ventus **Operators & Initiators & Approval Authority for alpha ventus**

BERLIN
Bundesministerium für Umwelt, Naturschutz und Reaktorsicherheit (BMU)
Federal Ministry for Environment, Nature Conservation and Reactor Safety (BMU))

HAMBURG
Bundesamt für Seeschifffahrt und Hydrographie (BSH)
Federal Maritime and Hydrographic Agency (BSH)
Vattenfall AG, Europe Windkraft GmbH

MÜNCHEN
E.ON Climate & Renewables GmbH

NORDEN
Betriebsleitstelle alpha ventus
alpha ventus control centre

NORDDEICH
Servicehafen alpha ventus Service port

OLDENBURG
EWE AG

VAREL
Stiftung Offshore-Windenergie
German Offshore Wind Energy Foundation

An Herstellung, Bau und Logistik beteiligte Unternehmen
Companies involved in manufacturing, installation and logistics

BAYREUTH
transpower übertragungs GmbH

BERGEN Norwegen Norway
NorWind Generalunternehmer für Konstruktion, Bau und Errichtung Jackets für 5M
General contractor for REpower 5M jacket design, construction and installation
ASA Kabelleger Barge cable installer

BREMEN
AMBAU GmbH Fertigung der Türme für 5M und M5000
5M and M5000 tower manufacturing

BREMERHAVEN
AREVA Multibrid GmbH Fertigung Gondel M5000
M5000 nacelle manufacturing
REPOWER Systems AG Fertigung Gondel und Nabe 5M
5M nacelle and hub manufacturing
WeserWind GmbH Arbeitsgemeinschaft Umspannwerk
Transformer station consortium

Burntisland Schottland Scotland
Burntisland Fabrication Ltd Jackets-Fertigung
Jacket manufacturing

CUXHAVEN
DEWI-OCC Testfeld für Offshore-Prototypen
Test field for offshore-prototypes

DRESDEN
AREVA Energietechnik GmbH Umspannwerk (30/110 kV)
Transformer station (30/110 kV)

DUBAI (VAR)
NICO Middle East Ltdo Kabelleger Team Oman
Cable-laying ship

HAGERMARSCH
Umspannwerk ins 110 kV-Netz
Substation onshore

HAMBURG
Hochtief Construction AG Hubinsel Odin
Odin jack-up barge
Arbeitsgemeinschaft Umspannwerk
Transformer station consortium

KALTENKIRCHEN
Menck GmbH Rammarbeiten Tripod
Ramming works for tripod

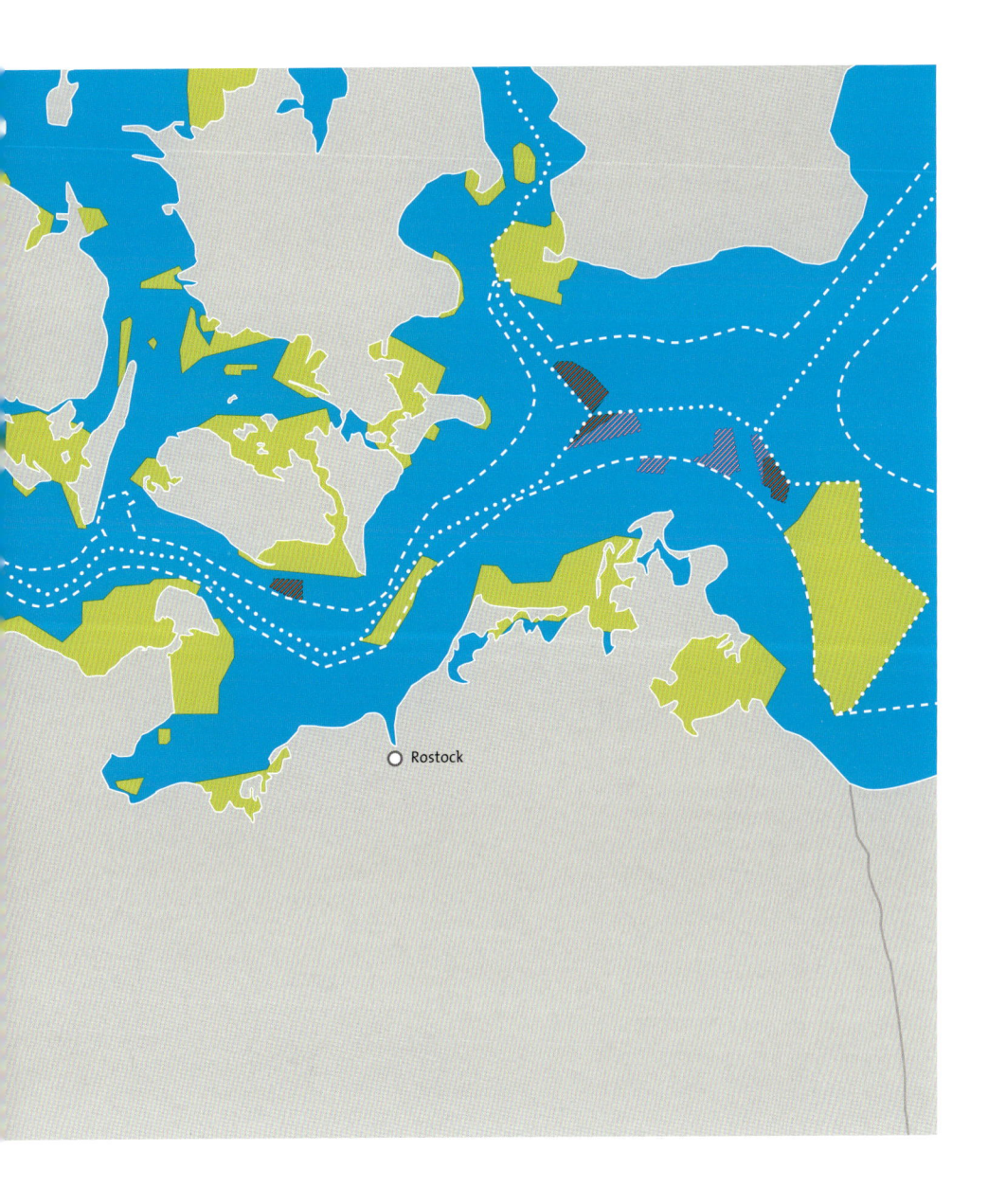

LEER
Offshore Wind Technologie GmbH (OWT)
Engineering für Gründung und Turmhülle M5000
Engineering of M5000 foundation structure
and tower cladding
Reederei Briese Schubverband Mega Motti
Mega Motti pusher barge

LEIDEN Niederlande Netherlands
Heerema Marine Contractors
Hochsee-Arbeitsschiff Thialf
Thialf heavy-lift ocean vessel

LUNDERSKOV Dänemark Denmark
LM Glasfiber Group Rotorblätter für 5M
5M rotor blades

MANNHEIM
Bilfinger Berger AG Arbeitsgemeinschaft Umspannwerk
Transformer station consortium

METHIL Schottland Scotland
Burntisland Fabrication Ltd
Fertigung Jackets für REpower 5M
Jacket manufacturing for REpower 5M

MONTROSE Schottland Scotland
ICH Sasteel Bau der Templates fürs Jackets
Template manufacturing for jackets

NORDENHAM
Norddeutsche Seekabelwerke (NSW)
Kabelleger Stemat 82 für Innerparkverkabelung
Stemat 82 cable laying barge for infield cabling

ROERMOND Niederlande Netherlands
Sif Group BV Röhrenelemente für Tripods
Tubular elements for tripods

ROSTOCK
EEW Maschinenbau GmbH Piles für Jackets
Piles for jackets

ROTTERDAM Niederlande Netherlands
Smit Heavy Lift Schwimmkran Taklift 4
Taklift 4 floating crane

SLIEDRECHT Niederlande Netherlands
Jack-Up-Barges BV
Hubplattform JB 114 und Hubplattform JB 115
JB 114 and JB 115 jack-up platforms

STADE
PN Rotor GmbH Fertigung Rotorblätter AREVA Multibrid
Rotor blade manufacturing AREVA Multibrid

VERDAL Norwegen Norway
Aker Solutions Aufbau Tripod für M5000
Tripod construction for M5000

WILHELMSHAVEN
WeserWind GmbH Fertigung Jacket Umspannwerk
Transformer station jacket assembly

ZWIJNDRECHT Belgien Belgium
GeoSea BV Rammarbeiten Jackets, Hubinsel Buzzard
Ramming works for jackets, Buzzard jack-up platform

CHRONOLOGIE
CHRONOLOGY

1998

Die aerodyn Energiesysteme GmbH präsentiert auf der Hannover Messe erstmals das technische Grundkonzept der Multibrid-Anlage mit fünf Megawatt Leistung.

Aerodyn Energiesysteme GmbH presents for the first time at the Hanover Fair the basic technical concept for the Multibrid turbine with a rated output of five megawatts.

1999

Ingenieure der Rendsburger pro & pro Energiesysteme, die später in der REpower Systems AG aufgeht, stellen erste Überlegungen zu einer Offshore-Multimegawatt-Anlage an.

Engineers at the Rendsburg pro & pro Energiesysteme, later to become REpower Systems AG, consider an offshore multi-megawatt turbine for the first time.

September Die Prokon Nord Energiesysteme GmbH beantragt beim Bundesamt für Seeschifffahrt und Hydrographie (BSH) die Baugenehmigung für den Offshore-Windpark Borkum West.

September Prokon Nord Energiesysteme GmbH applies to the German Federal Maritime and Hydrographic Agency (Bundesamt für Seeschifffahrt und Hydrographie, (BSH) for a construction permit for the Borkum West offshore wind farm.

2000

Ende des Jahres gründet die Pfleiderer AG die Multibrid Entwicklungsgesellschaft mbH und schließt mit aerodyn einen Patent-Lizenzvertrag ab.

Towards the end of the year Pfleiderer AG founds the Multibrid Entwicklungsgesellschaft mbH and signs a patent license agreement with aerodyn.

Dezember Das BMWi (Bundesministerium für Wirtschaft und Technologie) beauftragt den Projektträger Jülich (PtJ), den Bau eines Offshore-Testfeldes zu prüfen. Dafür werden Hersteller, Institute, Zertifizierer und VDMA aufgerufen, Stellung-nahmen abzugeben.

December 2000 The BMWi (Federal Ministry of Economics and Technology) commissions the project management and executing organization Projektträger Jülich (PtJ) to investigate the construction of an offshore test field. Manufacturers, industry, certifiers and VDMA (German Engineering Federation) are all called upon to make a statement.

2001

Februar Das BMWi, das Bundesministerium für Umwelt, Naturschutz und Reaktorsicherheit (BMU) und der Verband Deutscher Maschinen- und Anlagenbau e.V. (VDMA) stimmen zu, dass Mittel aus dem Verkauf der UMTS-Frequenzen für den Bau eines Offshore-Testfeldes und die Errichtung von Forschungsplattformen verwendet werden sollen.

February The BMWi, the German Federal Ministry for the Environment, Nature Conservation and Nuclear Safety (Bundesministerium für Umwelt, Naturschutz und Reaktorsicherheit, BMU) and the German Engineering Federation (VDMA) agree that funds from the sale of UMTS wireless frequencies should be used for the erection of an offshore test field and research platforms.

April Der Vorstand der REpower Systems AG entscheidet sich für die Weiterentwicklung und den Bau einer Offshore-Anlage mit fünf Megawatt Leistung.

April The Board of REpower Systems AG decides to further develop and construct an offshore turbine with a rated output of five megawatts.

Frühjahr Es zeichnet sich ab, dass die Mittel für die Förderung eines Offshore-Testfeldes und den Bau von Forschungsplattformen nicht ausreichen werden. Das BMU übernimmt die ökologische Begleitforschung für die Offshore-Windenergie. Zunächst gibt es auf der Ebene der Ministerien Überlegungen, das Seekabel für den Anschluss eines Testfeldes zu fördern, doch wird dieser Gedanke wieder verworfen. Das BMWi konzentriert sich fortan auf den Bau von Forschungsplattformen.

Spring It becomes clear that the funds for promoting an offshore test field and the construction of research platforms are insufficient. The BMU takes on the accompanying ecological research for offshore wind power. Initial considerations are made at ministerial level about subsidizing the submarine cable for connecting up a test field; however this idea is later rejected. The BMWi now decides to concentrate on the construction of research platforms.

Juli Die Germanischer Lloyd WindEnergie GmbH wird beauftragt, den Bau von Forschungsplattformen voranzutreiben. Anschließend erfolgt die Standortbestimmung für die Forschungsplattformen in Nord- und Ostsee (FINO). Die FINO 1 soll am Standort Borkum West errichtet werden.

July Hamburg-based Germanischer Lloyd WindEnergie GmbH is commissioned with the job of pushing forward the construction of research platforms. Locations are subsequently defined for the research platforms in the North and Baltic Seas (Forschungsplattformen in Nord- und Ostsee, FINO). FINO 1 is to be erected in Borkum West.

November Die Prokon Nord erhält für Borkum West als erstes Offshore-Projekt eine Baugenehmigung von der zuständigen Genehmigungsbehörde BSH.

November Prokon Nord is granted construction approval for Borkum West by the responsible authority (BSH). This is the first consented offshore project.

2002

Februar Die Bundesregierung proklamiert ihr „Strategiepapier zur Nutzung der Windenergie auf See". Geplant sind 500 Megawatt bis 2006 sowie 2.000 bis 3.000 Megawatt bis 2010. Als langfristiges Ziel (bis 2030) sollen bis zu 25.000 Megawatt installierte Leistung erreicht werden.

February The German Federal Government announces its 'Strategy paper for utilizing wind power at sea'. 500 megawatts are planned by 2006 and 2,000 to 3,000 megawatts by 2010. The long-term goal (by 2030) is to achieve 25,000 megawatts of installed capacity.

Juni Nach europaweiter Ausschreibung wird der Bauvertrag für FINO 1 unterzeichnet. Der Auftrag wird an die Arbeitsgemeinschaft der F + Z Baugesellschaft mbH, Hamburg, und die Bugsier Reederei- und Bergungsgesellschaft mbH & Co, Bremerhaven, vergeben. Die Germanischer Lloyd WindEnergie GmbH (GL-Wind) koordiniert Bau, Aufstellung und Inbetriebnahme.

June After a European-wide invitation to tender, the construction contract for FINO 1 is signed. The task goes to the consortium of F + Z Baugesellschaft mbH, Hamburg, and Bugsier Reederei- und Bergungsgesellschaft mbH & Co, Bremerhaven. Germanischer Lloyd WindEnergie GmbH (GL Wind) coordinates construction, erection and commissioning.

Dezember Das BMU übernimmt die Verantwortung für die Forschung der erneuerbaren Energien und damit auch für die Forschungsplattformen.

December The BMU takes over responsibility for researching renewable energies and therefore also for the research platforms.

2003

FINO 1 wird installiert. Die Messungen auf der FINO starten.

FINO 1 is erected. Measurements start on this research platform.

Dezember Die Prokon Nord Energiesysteme GmbH übernimmt von der Pfleiderer AG die Multibrid-Entwicklungsgesellschaft mbH.

December Prokon Nord Energiesysteme GmbH takes over Multibrid Entwicklungsgesellschaft mbH from Pfleiderer AG.

2004

Oktober Der Aufbau des Prototyps der REpower 5M in Brunsbüttel ist abgeschlossen, am 16. November wird sie an das Stromnetz angeschlossen.

Die Enercon GmbH schließt die Errichtung einer E-112 ab, die in unmittelbarer Deichnähe in der Ems steht. Sie ist die erste Nearshore-Anlage Deutschlands.

October The erection of the prototype of the REpower 5M in Brunsbüttel is completed; on 16th November it is connected up to the power grid.

Enercon GmbH completes the erection of an E-112, standing in direct proximity to the embankments of the River Ems. It is Germany's first near-shore wind turbine.

Dezember Der Prototyp der Multibrid M5000 geht in Bremerhaven in Betrieb.

December The prototype of the Multibrid M5000 goes into operation in Bremerhaven.

2005

Januar Die 4. Nationale Maritime Konferenz des Bundeskanzlers findet in Bremen statt. Erstmals setzen Landespolitiker, Verbände, Institutionen und Hersteller von Windenergieanlagen einen Workshop Offshore-Windenergie durch. Teilnehmer des Workshops richten an die Politik den Wunsch, ein Testfeld für die Multimegawatt-Turbinen zu errichten.

January The 4th National Maritime Conference of the German Federal Chancellor takes place in Bremen. For the first time, state politicians, organizations, institutions and manufacturers of wind turbines set up a workshop for offshore wind power. Participants in the workshop express their desire to the politicians to set up a test field for multi-megawatt turbines.

Juni/Juli Die „Stiftung der deutschen Wirtschaft für die Nutzung und Erforschung der Windenergie auf See", kurz Stiftung Offshore-Windenergie, wird gegründet. Sie stellt einen Förderantrag an das BMU, um die Genehmigungsrechte an einem deutschen Offshore-Testfeld zu erwerben.

June/July The German Industry Foundation for the Use and Exploration of Wind Energy at Sea (Stiftung der deutschen Wirtschaft für die Nutzung und Erforschung der Windenergie auf See), shortened to the 'Offshore Wind Energy Foundation', is formed. It makes an application to the BMU for support in purchasing the license rights to a German offshore test field.

August Der Förderbescheid über fünf Millionen Euro geht an die Stiftung Offshore-Windenergie.

August A grant of 5 million euros to the Offshore Wind Energy Foundation is approved.

September Die Stiftung Offshore-Windenergie erwirbt von der Prokon Nord Energiesysteme GmbH die Rechte des Offshore-Projektes Borkum West für fünf Millionen Euro.

September The Offshore Wind Energy Foundation buys the utilization rights to the Borkum West offshore project from Prokon Nord Energiesysteme GmbH for five million euros.

2006

April Energiegipfel im Kanzleramt. Die Energieversorger E.ON, EWE und Vattenfall sagen Kanzlerin Merkel zu, ein deutsches Offshore-Testfeld zu errichten und zu betreiben.

April Energy summit in the German Chancellery. The energy suppliers E.ON, EWE and Vattenfall agree to Chancellor Merkel's proposal to set up and run a German offshore test field.

Mai BMU-Strategiegespräch zur Windenergieforschung in Bad Zwischenahn. Diskussion mit Herstellern und Instituten über Forschungsvorhaben und -ziele im Testfeld.

Das BMU teilt mit, dass für die geplante Forschung im Offshore-Testfeld 50 Millionen Euro zur Verfügung gestellt werden.

Acht führende Windenergieforschungs-Institute unter Federführung des Kasseler Instituts für Solare Energieversorgungstechnik (ISET), das im Januar 2009 mit dem neu gegründeten Fraunhofer-Institut für Windenergie und Energiesystemtechnik (IWES) verschmolz, unterbreiten Vorschläge zu Forschungsprojekten.

May BMU strategy talks on wind-energy research in Bad Zwischenahn. Discussions are held with manufacturers and institutes regarding research projects and goals for the test field.

The BMU announces that 50 million euros are being made available for the planned research in the offshore test field.

Eight leading wind energy research institutes make proposals for research projects – coordinated by the Kassel Institute for Solar Energy Supply Technology (Institut für Solare Energieversorgungstechnik, ISET), which merged in January 2009 with the newly-founded Fraunhofer Institute for Wind Energy and Energy System Technology (Fraunhofer-Institut für Windenergie und Energiesystemtechnik, IWES).

Juli EWE, E.ON und Vattenfall gründen die Deutsche Offshore- Testfeld und Infrastruktur GmbH, kurz DOTI.

July EWE, E.ON and Vattenfall establish the German Offshore Test Field and Infrastructure (Deutsche Offshore- Testfeld und Infrastruktur) GmbH, abbreviated to DOTI.

August Die erste 5M der REpower Systems AG wird auf dem Meer errichtet. Sie steht nahe dem Offshore-Ölfeld Beatrice vor der schottischen Ostküste auf einem Jacket-Fundament in 44 Metern Wassertiefe.

August For the first time a 5M from REpower Systems AG is erected at sea. It is located near the offshore oil field Beatrice off the east coast of Scotland, standing on a jacket foundation in a depth of water of 44 meters.

September Das BMU veröffentlicht Fördermaßnahmen im Bereich Windenergie mit Forschungsschwerpunkten im Testfeld. Vorausgegangen war eine intensive Diskussion über Inhalt und Wichtigkeit verschiedener Forschungsprojekte.

September The BMU publishes support measures for the wind-energy sector, with emphasis on research in the test field. Preceding this had been an intensive discussion about the content and importance of various research projects.

Herbst Unter Federführung der Stiftung Offshore-Windenergie gelingt es, die Kabelanbindung zu klären. Es wird eine Netzanschlussgesellschaft GbR gegründet, in der acht potenzielle Windparkprojektierer vertreten sind, die sich auf eine gemeinsame Kabeltrasse über Norderney einigen. Diese Trasse wird von den Auflagen des Nationalpark Wattenmeers befreit.

Autumn Lead-managed by the Offshore Wind Energy Foundation, intensive discussions lead to agreement on the issue of power-cable connections. The Netzanschlussgesellschaft (grid connection company) GbR is founded, in which the eight potential wind-farm project organizers are represented and who then agree on a common cable route through the island of Norderney. This cable route is exempted from the regulations covering the Wadden Sea National Park.

Dezember Der Pachtvertrag zwischen der Stiftung Offshore-Windenergie und der DOTI wird unterschrieben. Die DOTI verpflichtet sich, die Forschung im Testfeld aktiv zu unterstützen.

DOTI-Ausschreibung für zwölf Testfeld-Anlagen.

Das Infrastrukturplanungsbeschleunigungsgesetz tritt in Kraft. Es verpflichtet den Netzbetreiber E.ON Netz GmbH zur Finanzierung und zum Bau des Kabelanschlusses.

December A lease agreement is signed between the Offshore Wind Energy Foundation and DOTI. DOTI is obliged to support the research in the test field actively.

DOTI issues a Request for Tenders for twelve test-field turbines.

The German Act on Accelerated Infrastructure Planning (Infrastruktur-Planungsbeschleunigungsgesetz) comes into force. It obliges the grid operator E.ON Netz GmbH to finance and to build the cable connections.

2007

Januar Das BMU wählt geplante Forschungsvorhaben aus. Die DOTI stimmt mit den beteiligten Forschungsinstituten ISET, DEWI, BSH und PTJ die inhaltliche Koordination ab.

Das Deutsche Windenergie-Institut (DEWI) erfasst die technischen Anforderungen der Einzelvorhaben für ein zentrales und mit der DOTI abgestimmtes Messungskonzept.

Auf Norderney beginnen die Bauarbeiten für das so genannte Leerrohrbauwerk über Norderney, durch das später die Kabel für alpha ventus gezogen werden, um den Windpark mit dem Einspeisepunkt an Land zu verbinden.

January The BMU selects planned research projects. DOTI coordinates the contents with the research institutes involved: ISET, DEWI, BSH and PTJ.

The German Wind Energy Institute (Deutsche Windenergie-Institut, DEWI) defines the technical requirements for the individual projects for a central measurement concept, coordinated with the DOTI.

Construction work commences on Norderney for the so-called 'empty conduit', through which the cable is later to be run that will connect the wind-farm with the onshore feed-in point.

Februar Die Nordex AG vollendet den Aufbau der N90 mit einer Leistung von 2,5 Megawatt 500 Meter vor der Kaimauer des Rostocker Ölhafens im Breitling, einem boddenartigen Gewässer, das in die Ostsee mündet. Sie geht als erste deutsche Offshore-Anlage in die Annalen ein.

DOTI-Ausschreibung für Gründungen.

February Nordex AG completes the construction and installation of the N90 wind-energy generator, with a nominal output of 2.5 megawatts, 500 metres in front of the quay wall of the Rostock oil port in Breitling, a shallow, brackish body of water that opens into the Baltic Sea. This goes down in the books as the first German offshore wind turbine.

DOTI issues a Request for Tenders for foundations.

September Die AREVA erwirbt von der Prokon Nord Energiesysteme GmbH 51 Prozent der Multibrid GmbH.

September

AREVA purchases 51 percent of Multibrid GmbH from Prokon Nord Energiesysteme GmbH.

2008

14. April Die Bauarbeiten für das Umspannwerk Hagermarsch an Land beginnen. Hier wird der auf See produzierte Strom künftig ins 110-kV-Netz eingespeist.

14th April Construction work starts on the onshore transformer station in Hagermarsch. This is where the power produced at sea will be fed into the 110 kV grid in future.

8. Mai Das BMU bewilligt größtenteils die Forschungsprojekte im Testfeld. Die BMU-Forschungsinitiative nimmt unter dem Namen RAVE (Research at alpha ventus) bei einer Auftaktveranstaltung in der Berliner Landesvertretung Niedersachsens ihre Arbeit auf.

8th May BMU approves most of the research projects in the test field. The BMU research initiative starts work under the name RAVE (research at alpha ventus) at an opening ceremony in the offices of the Lower Saxony state delegation in Berlin.

Juni Der Deutsche Bundestag verabschiedet die EEG-Novelle (Erneuerbare-Energien-Gesetz) mit verbesserter Einspeisevergütung für Offshore-Windenergie.

June The German Bundestag (lower house of the Federal Parliament) passes the EEG (renewable energies law) amendment, allotting improved remuneration for offshore wind energy

Das erste Kabel für den Anschluss des Windparks wird in das im Frühjahr fertiggestellte Leerrohrbauwerk auf Norderney eingezogen.

The first cable is inserted through the empty conduit completed in spring on Norderney to connect up the wind farm.

Mai bis August Das 4,5 Kilometer lange Landkabel von Hilgenriedersiel zum Umspannwerk Hagermarsch wird verlegt.

May to August The 4.5 kilometre-long land cable is laid from Hilgenriedersiel to the transformer station in Hagermarsch.

5. September Die ersten Meter des Kabelabschnittes durch den Nationalpark Niedersächsisches Wattenmeer sind verlegt. Rund zwei Wochen werden für die knapp fünf Kilometer im Watt benötigt.

5th September The first metres of cable section are laid through the Lower Saxony Wadden Sea National Park. Around two weeks are required to lay almost five kilometres of cable through the mudflats.

19. September Die Bauarbeiten auf See beginnen. Erster Rammschlag für das Fundament des Umspannwerks.

19th September Construction work begins at sea. The first blow to drive the foundation piles of the transformer station is struck.

27. September Die rund 55 Kilometer Seekabel auf offener See sind bis auf die letzten 1.000 Meter vor dem Umspannwerk verlegt.

27th September Around 55 kilometres of submarine cable are laid from the open sea right up to the last 1,000 metres from the transformer station.

28. September Das Offshore-Umspannwerk wird fertiggestellt. Es ist das erste Bauwerk des zukünftigen Windparks alpha ventus. Die Bauarbeiten werden anschließend wegen schlechter Witterung unterbrochen. Auch das Umspannwerk in Hagermarsch ist inzwischen fertiggestellt.

28th September The offshore transformer station is completed. This is the first structure completed for the future alpha ventus wind farm. The remaining construction work is subsequently interrupted due to bad weather. The transformer station at Hagermarsch is also now completed.

28. Oktober Umweltminister Sigmar Gabriel nimmt die BARD 5.0 als erste deutsche Offshore-Anlage in der Nordsee offiziell in Betrieb. Die fünf Megawatt große Test- und Demonstrationsanlage der Firma BARD Engineering GmbH steht in der Außenjade vor Hooksiel auf einem markanten Tripile-Fundament.

28th November Germany's Federal Minister of the Environment, Sigmar Gabriel, officially commissions BARD 5.0 as the first German offshore turbine in the North Sea. The five-megawatt test and demonstration turbine from the company BARD Engineering GmbH stands in the estuary of the River Jade off Hooksiel, on a striking tri-pile foundation.

2009

1. Januar EEG-Novelle tritt in Kraft.

1st January The EEG amendment comes into force.

23. April Die Bauarbeiten werden nach der Winterpause wieder aufgenommen.

23rd April Construction work is recommenced after the winter break.

5. Mai Die Zuschaltung der 110-kV-Netzanbindung für den Windpark wird gemeldet – Seekabel und Offshore-Umspannwerk sind betriebsbereit.

5th May It is reported that the 110 kV grid connection for the wind farm has been switched on. The submarine cable and offshore transformer station are ready for operation.

1. Juni Die sechs Tripod-Fundamente sind fest im Meeresgrund verankert.

1st June The six tripod foundations are firmly anchored onto the seabed.

15. Juli Die erste deutsche Offshore Windenergieanlage (AREVA Multibrid M5000) in der AWZ ist errichtet.

15th July The first German offshore wind turbine in the EEZ – an AREVA Multibrid M5000 – is erected.

12. August Der erste Strom fließt vom Testfeld alpha ventus ans Festland.

12th August The first power flows to the mainland from the test field alpha ventus.

9. September Das Hochsee-Arbeitsschiff Thialf, der leistungsfähigste Schwimmkran der Welt, beginnt mit der Errichtung der sechs Jacket-Fundamente für die REpower-Anlagen. Die Arbeiten sind nach wenigen Tagen abgeschlossen.

9th September The high-seas work-ship 'Thialf', the most powerful floating crane in the world, starts erecting the six jacket foundations for the REpower turbines. The work is completed within just a few days.

Herbst 2009 Die sechs REpower-Anlagen werden aufgebaut.

Autumn The six REpower turbines are assembled and installed on the open sea at the alpha ventus site.

16. November Die sechste 5M von REpower ist errichtet. Damit ist der Windpark alpha ventus mit zwölf Windenergieanlagen komplett.

16th November The sixth 5M from REpower is erected. The alpha ventus wind farm, with its twelve turbines, has now been completed.

GLOSSAR

A

Arbeitsschiff Ein Schiffstyp, der für Arbeiten auf dem Wasser oder vom Wasser aus konstruiert ist. Beispiele: *Hubinsel, *Kabelleger, *Schwimmkran.

AWZ (Ausschließliche Wirtschaftszone) Küstengewässer, das jenseits der Zwölf-Seemeilen-Zone liegt und durch die jeweiligen Seegebiete der Nachbarländer begrenzt wird. Für Baugenehmigungen innerhalb der AWZ ist in Deutschland das *BSH zuständig.

B

Beaufort-Skala Zwölfstufige Skala, die zur Abschätzung der Windstärke und zur Klassifizierung der Windgeschwindigkeit dient. Sie ist nach dem britischen Admiral Francis Beaufort benannt. Offshore-*Windenergieanlagen können ab Windstärke 3 (schwache Brise, 4,0 bis 5,5 Meter/Sekunde) Strom erzeugen. Bei Windstärke 6 (starker Wind, 11,5 bis 14,0 Meter/Sekunde) erreichen sie ihre Nennleistung. Je nach Anlagentyp schalten sie sich bei 25 Meter/Sekunde (Windstärke 10, schwerer Sturm) oder 30 Meter/Sekunde (Windstärke 11, orkanartiger Sturm) automatisch ab.

Benthos Gesamtheit der festsitzenden und frei beweglichen Tier- und Pflanzenwelt am Meeresboden (z.B. Schnecken, Muscheln, Würmer und Krebse).

BMU Bundesministerium für Umwelt, Naturschutz und Reaktorsicherheit in Berlin. www.bmu.de

BSH Bundesamt für Seeschifffahrt und Hydrographie in Hamburg. Zuständig unter anderem für die Genehmigung von Offshore-Windparks in der *AWZ. www.bsh.de

D

DEWI (Deutsches Windenergie-Institut in Wilhelmshaven) Die Forschungseinrichtung ist unter anderem für die Messungen der Windgeschwindigkeit sowohl auf der Forschungsplattform FINO 1 als auch im Testfeld von alpha ventus im Rahmen der *RAVE-Forschung verantwortlich. www.dewi.de

DOTI (Deutsche Offshore-Testfeld- und Infrastruktur- GmbH & Co. KG) Um ihre Aktivitäten sinnvoll zu bündeln, gründeten die drei Energieversorger E.ON, EWE und Vattenfall im Juli 2006 die DOTI als gemeinsames Unternehmen.

E

EEG (Erneuerbare-Energien-Gesetz) Es regelt seit 2000 in Deutschland die Einspeisung von Strom aus erneuerbaren Energiequellen in das öffentliche Netz. Für die Einspeisung von Strom aus Offshore-Windparks gilt: Vergütet werden in den ersten zwölf Betriebsjahren 13 Cent pro Kilowattstunde. Bei Inbetriebnahme bis zum 31.12.2015 erhöht sich diese Vergütung auf 15 Cent pro Kilowattstunde. Die Vergütung wird nach zwölf Betriebsjahren auf 3,5 Cent pro Kilowattstunde abgesenkt. Die hohe Anfangsvergütung wird jedoch länger als zwölf Jahre gezahlt, wenn der Windpark mehr als zwölf Seemeilen vor der Küste liegt und in mehr als 20 Metern Wassertiefe errichtet wurde.

Einspeisepunkt Einspeisepunkt ist die Landstation onshore, in der der auf See erzeugte Windstrom ins Stromnetz eingespeist wird.

F

FFH-Gebiet (Flora-Fauna-Habitat-Schutzgebiet) Ein nach der FFH-Richtlinie der EU ausgewiesenes Gebiet zum Schutz naturnaher Flora (Pflanzen), Fauna (Wildtiere) und Habitate (Lebensräume). Dazu kommen die gleich gestellten Vogelschutzgebiete. Ziel ist es, diese Gebiete in ganz Europa miteinander zu vernetzen (Projekt Natura 2000). Die Gebiete werden von den Bundesländern vorgeschlagen und von der EU-Kommission nach Prüfung registriert. Ende 2008 waren in der EU 22.945 Gebiete mit 661.503 km² Landfläche (13,3 % der Landfläche der EU) und 92.893 km² Meeresfläche als Gebiete von europaweiter Bedeutung ausgewiesen; davon in Deutschland 4.675 Gebiete mit 54.343 km² Landfläche (9,9 % der Landfläche) und 19.134 km² Meeresfläche. Dazu gehört auch fast das gesamte Wattenmeer vor der deutschen Nordseeküste.

FINO Kurzbezeichnung für Forschungsplattform in Nord- und Ostsee. Errichtet wurden bisher drei Plattformen: FINO 1 am Rande des Testfeldes alpha ventus, FINO 2 in der Ostsee, etwa 30 Kilometer nördlich der Insel Rügen, FINO 3 in der Nordsee, etwa 80 Kilometer westlich der Insel Sylt. Die wichtigste Aufgabe dieser Forschungsplattformen ist die Messung der Windgeschwindigkeit und Windrichtung in verschiedenen Höhen, außerdem die Erfassung des gesamten Weltergeschehens sowie Daten der Ozeanographie und Ökologie. www.fino-offshore.de

Fraunhofer IWES (Fraunhofer-Institut für Windenergie und Energiesystemtechnik) Es entstand im Januar 2009 aus dem Zusammenschluss vom Institut für Solare Energieversorgungstechnik (ISET) in Kassel und dem Fraunhofer Center für Windenergie und Meerestechnik (Fraunhofer CWMT) in Bremerhaven. Das Fraunhofer IWES hat je einen Standort in Bremerhaven und Kassel. www.iwes.fraunhofer.de

G

Gondel Alternative Bezeichnung für *Maschinenhaus.

Gründungsstruktur Fundament einer Offshore-*Windenergieanlage. Es kann aus Stahl oder Beton bestehen. Im Testfeld alpha ventus kommen zwei verschiedene stählerne Gründungsstrukturen zum Einsatz: Eine Dreibein-Struktur (Tripod) und eine Gittermast-Struktur (Jacket). Die einfachste Gründungsstruktur besteht aus einem Stahlrohr, das in den Meeresboden gerammt wird (Monopile). Es ist jedoch nur für geringe Wassertiefen geeignet und kam deshalb für das Testfeld nicht in Frage.

H

HGÜ (Hochspannungs-Gleichstrom-Übertragung) eine elektrische Energieübertragung mit Gleichspannungen von 100.000 bis 1.000.000 Volt. Der von den Stromerzeugern (z.B. *Windenergieanlagen) gelieferte Drehstrom wird zunächst gleichgerichtet und am Ende der Übertragungsstrecke wieder in Drehstrom umgeformt. Die HGÜ eignet sich zur Überbrückung größerer Entfernungen und größerer Leistungen. Während beim Testfeld alpha ventus eine Drehstromübertragung genügt, werden in den kommenden Jahren die Offshore-Windparks, die weit von der Küste entfernt liegen, durch HGÜ-Leitungen mit den Einspeisepunkten an Land verbunden sein.

HSE Health, Safety and Environment (Gesundheit, Sicherheit und Umwelt; auch Environment, Health & Safety, EH&S genannt), ein in vielen großen Unternehmen bestehendes Managementsystem für Umwelt- und Arbeitsschutz.

Hubinsel Wasserfahrzeug in Gestalt eines Pontons (engl.: barge), der an jeder der vier Ecken ein absenkbares Bein hat. Mit den vier Beinen kann er sich auf dem Meeresboden sicher abstützen (engl.: jack-up). Dadurch entsteht eine Plattform (Hubplattform), die ein vom Seegang unbeeinflusstes Arbeiten auf dem Meer ermöglicht. Hubinseln, die mit einem oder mehreren Kränen ausgerüstet sind, zählen zur Klasse der *Arbeitsschiffe. Hubinseln ohne eigenen Antrieb werden von Schleppern gezogen.

Hubplattform Siehe *Hubinsel.

I

Infrastrukturplanungsbeschleunigungsgesetz Gesetz zur Beschleunigung von Planungsverfahren für große Infrastrukturvorhaben. Es trat am 17. Dezember 2006 in Kraft und verpflichtet unter anderem die Übertragungsnetzbetreiber, für die Netzanschlüsse der Offshore-Windparks in ihrer Regelzone zu sorgen.

Innerparkverkabelung Elektrische Verbindung der *Windenergieanlagen eines Windparks. Im Testfeld alpha ventus wurden die Leitungen von jeweils sechs Windenergieanlagen in einem Ring zusammengefasst und als Seekabel zum Offshore-Umspannwerk geführt.

ISET (Institut für Solare Energieversorgungstechnik in Kassel) Es fusionierte im Januar 2009 mit dem Fraunhofer Center für Windenergie und Meerestechnik (Fraunhofer CWMT), Bremerhaven, zum *Fraunhofer IWES, und hat die Aufgabe, das *RAVE-Programm zu koordinieren.

IWES Siehe *Fraunhofer IWES.

J

Jacket *Gründungsstruktur von *Windenergieanlagen.

Jack-up-Barge, Jack-up-Plattform Siehe *Hubinsel.

K

Kabelleger *Arbeitsschiff, das zur Verlegung von Seekabeln dient.

L

LIDAR (Light Detecting And Ranging) Messung der Windgeschwindigkeit mit einem Laserstrahl. Gemessen wird die Rückstreuung des gebündelten Laserlichtes durch die in der Luft stets vorhandenen Staubpartikel und Aerosole. Das Verfahren hat eine Reichweite von mehreren hundert Metern.

M

Maschinenhaus Teil der *Windenergieanlage, in der die mechanische Energie in elektrische umgewandelt wird. Im Maschinenhaus befinden sich das Getriebe und der Generator. In einigen Offshore-Windenergieanlagen werden auch Umrichter und Transformator im Maschinenhaus untergebracht.

Monopile Eine von mehreren möglichen *Gründungsstrukturen von *Windenergieanlagen.

N

Nabe Teil einer *Windenergieanlage. Die Nabe sitzt auf der Hauptwelle, an ihr sind die drei Rotorblätter befestigt.

Nabenhöhe Abstand des Mittelpunkts der *Nabe einer *Windenergieanlage vom Boden bzw. Meeresspiegel.

Nationale Maritime Konferenz Eine regelmäßige Veranstaltung des Bundesministeriums für Wirtschaft und Technologie zu Fragen der maritimen Wirtschaft (Schifffahrt, Schiffbau, Offshore-Technologien usw.). In den Jahren 2000 bis 2009 fanden sechs dieser Konferenzen statt. Die Offshore-Windenergie wurde erstmals im Jahr 2005 in einem eigenen Workshop behandelt.

Nationalpark Wattenmeer Großräumige Naturlandschaft vor der deutschen Nordseeküste, geprägt durch das bei Ebbe trockenfallende Watt. Wegen vieler nur hier vorkommender Tier- und Pflanzenarten steht das Wattenmeer unter strengem Naturschutz und unterliegt weitgehenden Nutzungsverboten. Rechtlich besteht diese Landschaft aus drei Nationalparks: dem Schleswig-Holsteinischen Wattenmeer, dem Niedersächsischen Wattenmeer und dem Hamburgischen Wattenmeer. Sie sind von der UNESCO seit 2009 als Weltnaturerbe anerkannt.
www.wattenmeer-nationalpark.de

Nearshore-Windpark Windpark, der im Meer errichtet wurde, aber weniger als einen Kilometer Abstand von der Küstenlinie hat.

O

Offshore-Windpark Windpark, der im Meer errichtet wurde.

Ökologische Begleitforschung Untersuchungen mit dem Ziel, das Wissen über die bau- und betriebsbedingten Auswirkungen der Offshore-Windparks auf die Meeresumwelt zu verbessern und den Ausbau der klimafreundlichen Offshore-Windenergie naturverträglich zu gestalten.

Onshore-Windpark Windpark auf dem Festland.

P

Pile Pfahlrohr, das einen Durchmesser von etwa einem Meter hat und in den Meeresboden getrieben wird, um Gründungsstrukturen sicher zu verankern. Die Piles werden durch Hülsen (engl.: pile sleeves) geschoben, die mit den Fußpunkten der Gründungsstruktur verschweißt sind.

R

Raumordnung Fachübergreifende, übergeordnete Planung, die über das Gebiet der kleinsten Verwaltungseinheit (Gemeinde) hinausgeht. Aufgabe und Leitvorstellung ist eine nachhaltige Raumentwicklung, die die sozialen und wirtschaftlichen Ansprüche an den Raum mit seinen ökologischen Funktionen in Einklang bringt und zu einer dauerhaften großräumigen Ordnung führt.

RAVE Research at Alpha Ventus (Forschung bei alpha ventus). Ein Programm, das die gesamte begleitende Forschung im Testfeld alpha ventus zusammenfasst. RAVE wird durch das Bundesumweltministerium (BMU) mit insgesamt 50 Mio. Euro finanziert. Die gesamte Forschungstätigkeit ist in 15 einzelne Projekte aufgeteilt.

Rotorstern Teil der *Windenergieanlage, der aus den drei Rotorblättern und der *Nabe besteht. Kurzbezeichnung: Rotor.

S

Schweinswal Meeressäuger, gehört zur Familie der Zahnwale. Er kommt an den mitteleuropäischen Küsten, aber auch im Unterlauf einiger Flüsse vor und wird etwa zwei Meter lang.

Schwimmkran Ein mobiler, auf Gewässern schwimmender Kran, der zur Klasse der *Arbeitsschiffe gehört. Er wird in der Regel zum Heben und Umsetzen besonders schwerer oder umfangreicher Objekte eingesetzt.

Seeanlagenverordnung Verordnung über die Errichtung und den Betrieb von Anlagen im Bereich der *AWZ. Errichtung und Betrieb müssen vom *BSH genehmigt werden. Dabei sind die Ziele der *Raumordnung zu beachten.

Service-Schiff Schiff für den Transport von Servicepersonal, Werkzeug und kleinen Ersatzteilen.

T

Template Schablone, die auf dem Meeresboden abgelegt wird und die Position der *Piles fixiert, bevor diese in den Meeresboden getrieben werden.

Tripod Eine von mehreren möglichen *Gründungsstrukturen von *Windenergieanlagen.

U

Umspannwerk Anlage zur Änderung der Netzspannung mittels Transformatoren. Das Umspannwerk besteht aus einer Schaltanlage, den Transformatoren und einer Schaltwarte mit den Mess- und Schutzgeräten.

UVP (Umweltverträglichkeitsprüfung.)Verfahren, in dem Projekte, die negative Auswirkungen auf die Umwelt erwarten lassen, überprüft werden. Das Ergebnis der UVP ist bei der Entscheidung über die Zulässigkeit des Projektes zu berücksichtigen.

V

Verkehrstrennungsgebiet Gebiet mit getrennten Schifffahrtswegen für unterschiedliche Richtungen. Sie dienen vorrangig dazu, auf stark befahrenen Schifffahrtswegen den Schiffsverkehr zu kanalisieren, um die Gefahr von Kollisionen zu verringern. Verkehrstrennungsgebiete sind ähnlich wie Autobahnen aufgebaut und bestehen aus je einer Zone für jede Fahrtrichtung sowie einer Trennzone in der Mitte, deren Befahrung verboten ist. Das Testfeld alpha ventus liegt zwischen zwei Verkehrstrennungsgebieten.

W

WEA Siehe Windenergieanlage.

Windenergieanlage (WEA), auch Windkraftanlage Windkraftmaschine, die die kinetische Energie des Windes in elektrische Energie umwandelt. Eine Windenergieanlage besteht im Wesentlichen aus dem Turm, dem *Maschinenhaus und dem *Rotorstern. Im Meer aufgestellte Anlagen benötigen eine spezielle *Gründungsstruktur.

Windstärke Siehe *Beaufort-Skala.

Z

Zwölf-Seemeilen-Zone Küstengewässer, das zum Hoheitsgebiet eines Küstenstaates gehört und sich zwölf Seemeilen (22,2 Kilometer) seewärts erstreckt. Für Baugenehmigungen innerhalb der Zwölf-Seemeilen-Zone sind in Deutschland die jeweiligen Landesbehörden zuständig.

LEISTUNGS- UND ARBEITSANGABEN

Leistung
1 Megawatt = 1.000 Kilowatt
1 Gigawatt = 1.000 Megawatt = 1.000.000 Kilowatt
1 Terawatt = 1.000 Gigawatt = 1.000.000 Megawatt = 1.000.000.000 Kilowatt
Zum Vergleich: Ein Hochgeschwindigkeitszug der Baureihe ICE 3 leistet 8 Megawatt. Ein großes Kernkraftwerk (z.B. Grohnde) leistet 1.300 Megawatt.

Arbeit (Energie)
1 Gigawattstunde = 1.000 Megawattstunden = 1.000.000 Kilowattstunden
1 Terawattstunde = 1.000 Gigawattstunden = 1.000.000.000 Kilowattstunden
Zum Vergleich: Eine Gigawattstunde entspricht dem durchschnittlichen Verbrauch von etwa 250 Vierpersonenhaushalten. Der jährliche Nettostromverbrauch Deutschlands liegt bei etwa 540 Terawattstunden.

GLOSSARY

A

Accompanying ecological research Analyses and measures aiming to improve knowledge of the constructional and operational impact of offshore wind farms on the marine environment. They also aim to develop climate and ecosystem-friendly offshore wind power.

B

Beaufort Scale A 12-stage scale to estimate the wind force and classify wind speeds. It is named after the British admiral Francis Beaufort. Offshore *wind-energy converters can produce electricity from Wind Force 3 (gentle breeze, 4.0 to 5.5 metres/second). They reach their rated power at wind force 6 (strong breeze, 11.5 to 14.0 metres/second). Depending on turbine type, they cut off automatically at 25 metres/second (Wind Force 10, storm) or 30 metres/second (Wind Force 11, violent storm).

Benthos The entire group of small, seabed-dwelling immobile and mobile flora and fauna (including snails, mussels, worms and crabs).

BMU The German Federal Ministry for the Environment, Nature Conservation and Nuclear Safety, based in Berlin: www.bmu.de

BSH The German Federal Maritime and Hydrographic Agency (FMHA) located in Hamburg. The BSH decides on the approval of offshore wind farms in the *EEZ. www.bsh.de

C

Cable-laying ship *Work-ship used for laying submarine cables.

Connection point Connection point is an onshore sub-station where the wind power produced at sea is fed into the power grid.

D

DEWI The German Wind Energy Institute in Wilhelmshaven. Some of this research facility's responsibilities are to measure wind velocities at the FINO 1 research platform and to coordinate upcoming research projects as part of *RAVE. www.dewi.de

DOTI German Offshore Test Field and Infrastructure GmbH & Co.KG. In July 2006, the three energy utilities E.ON, EWE and Vattenfall established DOTI as a joint venture in order to pool their activities effectively.

E

EEG Renewable Energy Act – REA. It has governed the feeding-in of electricity produced from renewable energy into the public grid since 2000. The following applies to the feed-in of power generated in offshore wind farms: 13 eurocents/kWh are paid within the first twelve years of operation. The tariff rises to 15 cents per kilowatt hour if the project will be operational by December 31, 2015. It is reduced to 3.5 cents per kilowatt hour after 12 years of operation. However, the high initial tariff is paid for longer than twelve years if the wind farm is located more than twelve nautical miles off the coast and is set up in water depths of over 20 metres.

EEZ Exclusive Economic Zone. Coastal waters that lie beyond the 12-nautical-mile zone and are limited by the territorial waters of the neighbouring countries. In Germany the Federal Maritime and Hydrographic Agency (BSH) is responsible for issuing construction permits within the EEZ.

EIA Environmental impact assessment. A procedure for examining projects whose impacts are likely to be detrimental to the environment. The EIA's report must be considered in project licence decisions.

F

FFH area Flora-Fauna-Habitat protection area. An area designated according to the EU's FFH directive for the protection of natural flora, fauna and habitats. Bird sanctuaries of equal status are also included. The objective is to link these areas together across Europe (Natura 2000 project). The areas are proposed by the German federal states and registered after analysis by the EU Commission. In late 2008, 22,945 regions throughout the EU with a combined land sur-face area of 661,503 km^2 (13.3 % of EU land area) along with maritime territory of 92,893 km^2 were designated as areas of Europe-wide interest. Some 4,675 areas with a land surface of 54,343 km^2 (9.9 % of land surface) and maritime territory of 19,134 km were in Germany. This includes almost the entire Wadden Sea off the German North Sea coast.

FINO Abbreviation of Forschungsplattform in Nord- and Ostsee (Research Platform on North and Baltic Seas). To date three platforms have been set up: FINO 1 at the rim of the alpha ventus test field, FINO 2 in the Baltic Sea, about 30 kilometres north of the island of Rügen and FINO 3 in the North Sea, about 80 kilometres west of the island of Sylt. The chief task of these research platforms is measuring the wind velocity and wind direction at various heights. Furthermore, they collect all the meteorological information, such as oceanographic and ecologic data. www.fino-offshore.de

Floating crane A mobile crane floating on waters which belongs to the *work-ship class. It is normally used for lifting and moving especially heavy or large objects.

Foundation structure Foundation of an offshore *wind-energy converter. It may consist of steel or concrete. In the alpha ventus test field, two different steel foundation structures are used. A three-legged structure (tripod) and a lattice structure (jacket). The simplest foundation structure consists of a steel tube which is driven into the seabed (monopile). This, however, is only suitable for low water depths and therefore was not an option for the alpha ventus test field.

Fraunhofer IWES The Fraunhofer Institute for Wind Energy and Energy System Technology. In January 2009 the Institute was formed after the amalgamation of the Institute for Solar Energy Supply Technology (ISET) in Kassel and the Fraunhofer Center for Wind Energy and Maritime Technology (Fraunhofer CWMT) in Bremerhaven. The Fraunhofer IWES is located both in Bremerhaven and Kassel. www.iwes.fraunhofer.de

H

HSE Health, Safety and Environment (also called Environment, Health & Safety, EH&S). The collective name given to a variety of environmental and work safety management systems applied by many major companies.

Hub Component of a *wind-energy converter (wind turbine). The hub is mounted on the end of the main drive shaft, to which the three rotor blades are attached.

Hub height Distance of the wind turbine hub's centre point to the ground, or mean sea level.

HVDC High-voltage, direct-current transmission. Electrical energy transmission with direct current voltages in the range from 100,000 to 1,000,000 volts. The three-phase AC current supplied by electricity generators (such as wind turbines) is first rectified to DC and then re-inverted to three-phase AC current at the end of the transmission line. HVDC is suitable for power transmission over longer distances and to transfer higher power capacities. A three-phase AC line is sufficient for the alpha ventus test field. However, offshore wind farms that are further than 100 kilometres off the coast will be connected by HVDC lines with connection points onshore in the years to come.

I

Infield cabling Electrical interconnection of *wind-energy converters within a wind farm. The power cables from six wind turbines each will be formed into a ring and then routed as a submarine cable to the offshore transformer station in the alpha ventus test field.

Infrastructure Planning Acceleration Act German law to accelerate planning procedures for large-scale infrastructure projects. It came into force on December 17, 2006 and obliges transmission grid operators to equip offshore wind farms with connections to the grid in their balancing zone.

ISET Institute for Solar Energy Supply Technology in Kassel. By joining forces with the Fraunhofer Center for Wind Energy and Maritime Technology (Fraunhofer CWMT), Bremerhaven, in January 2009 it formed the *Fraunhofer IWES. Its brief is to coordinate the *RAVE programme.

IWES See *Fraunhofer IWES.

J

Jacket *Foundation structure of an offshore *wind-energy converter.

Jack-up platform Seagoing craft in the form of a pontoon, with legs that can be lowered at each of the four corners to support it securely on the sea floor. The platform is jacked up to permit working at sea even when the sea is rough. Jack-up platforms which are equipped with one or several cranes belong to the *work-ship class. Jack-up platforms with no drive of their own are towed by tugs.

L

LIDAR Light Detecting And Ranging. Measuring the wind speed using a laser beam. Backscattering of the bundled laser light is measured by the ever-present dust particles and aerosols. The method has a range of several hundred metres.

M

Marine Facilities Ordinance An ordinance regulating the installation and operation of facilities in the area of the *EEZ. Installation and operation must be approved by the *BSH. Attention has to be paid to the *regional planning objectives.

Monopile One of several possible *foundation structures of offshore *wind-energy converters.

N

Nacelle Component of the *wind-energy converter where mechanical is converted into electrical energy. It accommodates drive train and generator. In some offshore wind turbines, converters and transformers are also integrated into the nacelle.

National Maritime Conference A regular event hosted by the German Federal Ministry for Economy and Technology on maritime economic issues (shipping, shipbuilding, offshore technology, etc.). Six of these conferences took place between 2000 to 2009. In 2005, a workshop was devoted solely to offshore wind power for the first time.

Near-shore wind farm A wind farm set up at sea but less than one kilometre offshore.

O

Offshore wind farm Wind farm set up on the open sea.

Onshore wind farm Wind farm on land.

OWEC Offshore *wind-energy converter

P

Pile Pile tube, about one metre in diameter, that is driven into the seabed to securely anchor *foundation structures. The piles are pushed through pile sleeves which are welded to the foundation structure's base points.

Porpoise Marine mammal that belongs to the toothed whale family. It is found on central and southern European coasts, but also in the lower reaches of some rivers. It can grow to about two metres long.

R

RAVE Research at Alpha Ventus. A programme integrating the accompanying research at the alpha ventus test field. RAVE is financed by the German Federal Environment Ministry (BMU) with a total of 50 million euros. All the research activities are divided up into 15 individual projects.

Regional planning Multidisciplinary, top-level planning that extends beyond the area of land of the smallest territorial division (municipality) in Germany. Its responsibility and mission is to provide sustainable spatial development and to align social and economic requirements of spatial development with ecological aspects, in order to apply them long term to large surface areas.

Rotor star Component of the *wind-energy converter consisting of the three rotor blades and the *hub. Or in short: rotor.

S

Service ship Vessel for transporting service personnel, tools and smaller spare parts.

T

Template A template which is laid on the seabed and determines the exact position of the *piles, before these are driven into the seabed.

Traffic Separation Scheme – TSS Area with separate shipping lanes for different directions. They primarily serve to channel shipping traffic on busy shipping lanes to reduce the risk of collisions. Traffic separation schemes are arranged similarly to motorways. They consist of one zone for each traffic direction as well as a separation zone in the middle where sailing is forbidden. The alpha ventus test field is located between two Traffic Separation Schemes.

Transformer substation Facility for changing the supply voltage using transformers. The transformer substation consists of a switchgear unit, transformers and a control centre with the measurement and safety equipment.

Tripod One of several possible *foundation structures of offshore *wind-energy converters.

Twelve-nautical-mile zone Coastal waters that are the sovereign territory of a coastal state and extend twelve nautical miles (22.2 kilometres) into the sea. In Germany the state authorities concerned are responsible for issuing project licences within the twelve-nautical-mile zone.

W

Wadden Sea National Park An extensive nature conservation area off the German North Sea Coast, characterized by mudflats that surface at low tide. The Wadden Sea is subject to strict nature conservation regulations and tight restrictions as far as its usage is concerned. Legally this area consists of three national parks: the Schleswig-Holstein Wadden Sea National Park, the Lower Saxony Wadden Sea National Park and the Hamburg Wadden Sea National Park. Since 2009, UNESCO has recognized these as World Natural Heritage sites.
www.wattenmeer-nationalpark.de

WEC See *wind-energy converters.

Wind energy converter (WEC), also wind turbine generator (WTG) A power generator which converts the kinetic energy from wind into electric energy. A wind-energy converter essentially consists of a tower, *machine housing and *rotor star. Wind turbines installed at sea require a specific *foundation structure.

Wind Force See *Beaufort Scale

Workship A type of ship that is designed for work on, or from water; work-ships include *jack-up barges, *cable-laying ships and *floating cranes, amongst other types.

POWER AND WORK UNIT INDICATORS

Capacity
1 megawatt = 1,000 kilowatts
1 gigawatt = 1,000 megawatts = 1,000,000 kilowatts
1 terawatt = 1,000 gigawatts = 1,000,000 megawatts = 1,000,000,000 kilowatts

By comparison, an ICE Type 3 high-speed train has a rated output of 8 megawatts, while a large nuclear power station (such as Grohnde in northern Germany) has a capacity of 1,300 megawatts.

Power
1 gigawatt hour = 1,000 megawatt hours = 1,000,000 kilowatt hours
1 terawatt hour = 1,000 gigawatt hours = 1,000,000,000 kilowatt hours

By comparison, one gigawatt hour corresponds to the average annual consumption of around 250 four-person households. Germany's annual net power consumption totals approximately 540 terawatt hours.

BILDNACHWEIS
PHOTO CREDITS

Matthias Ibeler

© DOTI/Ibeler: Titelbild
© DOTI/Ibeler: S.11, 13, 35, 49, 71, 74, 75, 79, 86 o., 102, 120/121, 122/123, 130, 133, 134, 135, 136, 137, 138, 140, 141, 143, 144, 145 u., 146/147, 148/149 152/153, 163, 164, 166, 167, 170/171
© WeserWind/Ibeler: S.66, 68, 69, 82, 83, 84, 85, 109 u.l.

Jan Oelker

© Areva Multibrid/Jan Oelker: S.8, 10, 12, 15, 17, 18, 19, 21, 22/23, 24/25 26/27, 28/29, 32, 44/45, 48 o., 57, 58/59, 61, 63, 65, 91 u., 107, 110 u., 111
© Offshore-Stiftung/Repower/Jan Oelker: S.36, 105 o., 105 u.l., 142, 145 o., 150/151, 157
© Offshore-Stiftung/Multibrid/Jan Oelker: S.72, 86 u., 88, 91 o., 110 o., 124/125, 126/127, 128/129
© Offshore-Stiftung/Jan Oelker: S.73, 172
© Repower/Jan Oelker: S.40/41, 99 o., 155
© ProkonNord/Jan Oelker: S.53
© Jan Oelker/Agentur Focus: S.87, 95, 96/97, 99 u.

Detlef Gehring

© Offshore-Stiftung/Multibrid/Gehring: S.31
© Offshore-Stiftung/REpower/Gehring: S.105 r.
© Offshore-Stiftung/Gehring: S.109 o. und u.r., 156
© Offshore-Stiftung/transpower/Gehring: S.112, 114, 115, 116, 117

Weitere

AREVA Multibrid/Heike Winkler: S.30
Karin Desmarowitz (Porträt Christian Dahlke): S.48
Ralf Grömminger, S.154
Industrie- und Handelskammer zu Schwerin (Porträt Jörgen Thiele): S.48
Privat: S.7, 60
Sebastian Fuhrmann: S.93